indonesia

1993

Archipel
No. 57 (April)

© 1994, Cornell Southeast Asia Program

Guest Editors:

Denys Lombard, James Siegel

Editor: Audrey Kahin
Contributing Editors: Benedict Anderson, Takashi Shiraishi
Associate Editors: Donna Amoroso, Roberta Ludgate, Dolina Millar

Editorial Advisory Board

Milton L. Barnett	George McT. Kahin	John U. Wolff
Martin F. Hatch	Stanley J. O'Connor	O. W. Wolters
	James T. Siegel	

Submissions: Submit manuscripts in a typewritten or computer-keyed, *double-spaced* format with footnotes and other stylistic conventions in accordance with *The Chicago Manual of Style*, 13th ed. Double space footnotes and group them at the end of the article. Include a short statement of your institutional affiliation and status to be used in the "List of Contributors" if the article is published.

Address: Please address all correspondence and manuscripts to *Indonesia*, Cornell Modern Indonesia Project, 640 Stewart Avenue, Ithaca, NY 14850.

Computer submissions: Submissions on disk facilitate and accelerate the publication process. The editors will request disk copies and FAX, telex, and telephone numbers when your manuscript is accepted for publication.

Reprints: Contributors will receive ten complimentary reprints of their articles and one complimentary copy of the issues in which their articles appear. They may order additional reprints at cost *at the time the manuscript is accepted for publication*.

Abstracts: Abstracts of articles published in *Indonesia* appear in *Excerpta Indonesica*, which is published semiannually by the Centre for Documentation on Modern Indonesia, Royal Institute of Linguistics and Anthropology, Leiden.

Subscription rates: US $20.00 per year or $10.50 per issue. For mailings outside the United States, add US $5.00 per year postage. Order from Southeast Asia Program Publications, East Hill Plaza, Ithaca, NY 14850.

ISBN 0-87727-857-1

Cover design by Kaja Maria McGowan.

Contents

Introduction *Denys Lombard*	1
The Beamwork Illustrated at Prambanan *Jacques Dumarçay*	5
The Political Iconology of the Indonesian Postage Stamp (1950–1970) *Jacques Leclerc*	15
Ki Ageng Suryomentaraman, Javanese Prince and Philosopher (1892–1962) *Marcel Bonneff*	49
State, City, Commerce: The Case of Bima *Henri Chambert-Loir*	71
Banten in 1678 *Claude Guillot*	89
Islam and Chineseness *Denys Lombard and Claudine Salmon*	115
Religion, Tradition, and the Dynamics of Islamization in South Sulawesi *Christian Pelras*	133
Collective Memory and Nomadism: Ethno-Historical Investigations in Borneo *Bernard Sellato*	155
The Second Life of Bung Karno: Analysis of the Myth (1978–1981) *Pierre Labrousse*	175
The New Order and Islam, or the Imbroglio of Faith and Politics *François Raillon*	197

Abbreviations

BEFEO	*Bulletin de l'Ecole Française d'Extrême Orient*
BKI	*Bijdragen tot de Taal-, Land- en Volkenkunde van Nederlandsch-Indie*
JMBRAS	*Journal of the Malayan Branch of the Royal Asiatic Society*
JSBRAS	*Journal of the Singapore Branch of the Royal Asiatic Society*
JSEAS	*Journal of Southeast Asian Studies*
KITLV	*Koninkljik Instituut voor Taal, Land- en Volkenkunde*
TAG	*Tijdschrift van het Koninklijk Nederlandsch Aardrijkskundige Genootschap*
TBB	*Tijdschrift voor het Binnenlandsch Bestuur*
TBG	*Tijdschrift voor Indische Taal-, Land- en Volkenkunde*
VBG	*Verhandelingen van het Bataviaasch Genootschap*

INTRODUCTION

Denys Lombard

The initiative undertaken by the advisory board of *Indonesia*, at Jim Siegel's suggestion, to devote its first issue of 1994 to a selection of articles drawn from the *Archipel* journal is certainly praiseworthy. At any rate, all students of the archipelago will be grateful for such an initiative....

Started in Jakarta in the spring of 1971, six years after *Indonesia*, by a small group of French Indonesianists (who since then have been working mostly in Paris) the journal *Archipel* has regularly been publishing two issues each year, and has reached its 47th issue. In it one finds a resolve to be interdisciplinary, as well as an ear for the most diverse "research echoes." Nonetheless, if any good French Indonesianist knows that he must "practice" *Indonesia*, conversely it seems that *Archipel* still is casting a somewhat odd shadow in America. At best, it is only accepted in small doses....

A given vision of Southeastern Asia actually leads one to think that only the Netherlands was able to develop a knowledge of their Indies; just as the English did of theirs (or again the French of Indochina). This approach, induced by the colonial partitioning which slowly took place after the Congress of Vienna (1815), does not take account of the fact that the Indies were actually accessible to any navigator from Europe, and that there exist often considerable sources written in languages other than those of the "colonizer," be it Portuguese, German, or French. The first Frenchmen who sailed toward the Archipelago in order to buy pepper reached Tiku, on the western coast of Sumatra in 1529 (that is to say, 67 years before de Houtman reached Banten), and they have left us an exquisite account from that first expedition.[1] Other travels followed, individual or collective ones, which have offered us a whole series of equally valuable eyewitness accounts.[2]

As for scientific "Indology," it was equally precocious in France. If China had attracted missionaries' attention since the 17th century, and that of the "philosophes" since the start

---

[1] Published by Ch. Scheffer. *Discours de la navigation de Jean et Raoul Parmentier* (Paris, 1883; reprint, Amsterdam: Philo Press, 1971).

[2] See D. Lombard, "Voyageurs français dans l'Archipel insulindien, XVIIe, XVIIIe, et XIXe s." in *Archipel* 1 (1971): 141–68.

of the 18th, the "Malay tongue" was considered important enough to be included among the program of the Ecole des Langues Orientales Vivantes ever since its foundation in Paris in 1796. The Chair actually remained empty until 1840, the date of Edouard Dulaurier's nomination,[3] but ever since then instruction has been actively maintained up to present times, thanks to a succession of distinguished orientalists, such as l'Abbé Favre, author of the first large Malay-French Dictionary (1876), of Antoine Cabaton, the author of a dictionary of the Cham language, and also of Pierre Labrousse, author of the recent General Indonesian-French Dictionary (1984), who collaborated in this collection. As for the Ecole Française d'Extrême Orient (EFEO), founded in Saigon in 1898, though of course it was mainly interested in Vietnamese and Khmer cultures, it nevertheless sent missions to Java (including that of Paul Mus, who published in 1935 his own two large volumes on Borobudur), and it also opened in Jakarta, in 1955, a permanent position, which the epigraphist Louis-Charles Damais filled until 1966.

Moreover, there is a third register also explaining the deep and ancient interest of the French regarding the Indies, and that's the one ruled by the imaginary. From very early on, the exotic novel genre had transported all over Europe—and in France particularly—an entire set of oriental and far eastern cliches, and it just so happens that since the start of the 19th century, the "Malay pirate" appears throughout a whole range of "seafaring novels" as one of the mythical figures haunting perilous Asia.[4] The visit to Paris by the painter Raden Saleh in 1848 made many people curious, and a short while later, the Netherlands-Indies pavilions at the great universal or colonial *Expositions* (1878, 1889, 1931) drew crowds thanks to their strange objects and their ballet corps. During the 1889 fair, the *gamelan* music accompanying the Javanese female dancers made a strong impression on Debussy, and a wallpaper was produced on which the aforementioned dancers were represented right next to the Eiffel Tower (which had been inaugurated that very same year).

There is, therefore, nothing surprising in the fact that a small group of Frenchmen, brought by chance to live and to meet in Indonesia, should have thought at the beginning of the 1970s of starting a journal which would reflect their common interest, and which would be, at first, printed in Bandung. Since then, the group has grown and the contributions have become diverse, especially since, upon returning to Paris, the journal's three founders, P. Labrousse, D. Lombard, and Ch. Pelras have been teaching (at the Ecole des Langues Orientales, INALCO, and at the Ecole des Hautes Etudes en Sciences Sociales, EHESS), and have been leading research teams.

From among the rather considerable amount of writings thus produced during the past twenty-three years, ten articles have been selected here, unavoidably in an arbitrary way, but chosen mostly in function of the diversity they might evoke.

The first three articles illustrate, punctually, the *diversity of documents* that are possible. **Jacques Dumarçay** (EFEO), an expert architect who spent most of his career in Angkor (and who is now there again to resume interrupted work) was working in Java during the whole time Cambodia remained "closed." He notably participated in the works of restoration in Borobudur and at the Candi Sewu, and he tells us here, on the basis of a few bas-reliefs of

---

[3] See Ed. Dulaurier, *Mémoire, lettres et rapports relatifs au cours de langue malaye et javanaise fait à la Bibliothèque royale pendant les années 1840–41, 1841–42 et à deux voyages littéraires entrepris en Angleterre* (Paris: Benjamin Duprat, 1843).

[4] See D. Lombard, "Aux origines du thème du 'pirate malais'" in *Rêver l'Asie, Exotisme et littérature coloniale aux Indes, en Indochine et en Insulinde,* ed. D. Lombard, C. Champion and H. Chambert-Loir (Paris: EHESS, 1983), pp. 153–66.

the Prambanan, about the history of carpentry in Java. **Jacques Leclerc**, a researcher at the Centre National de la Recherche Scientifique (CNRS), has devoted himself to the history of the Sukarno epoch; he takes here as an iconological corpus the set of postage stamps issued during that period, and uses it to analyze its underlying political discourse. **Marcel Bonneff**, a Javanologist, has lived for a long time in Yogyakarta (as a teacher in Gajah Mada), then in Jakarta (where he currently represents the EFEO). His text, which reconstructs the history of a rather non-conformist Javanese prince from the turn of the century, is included here to exemplify the virtues of biographical studies. Prosopography, which is used systematically in European (and Chinese) studies deserves to be utilized all the more in Indonesia.

The following three articles are properly "historical." Basing themselves on the study of both texts and sites, they aim to reestablish the ancient importance of *routes* and *networks*, all too often obscured by too static a view of "ethnicities." **Henri Chambert-Loir** (EFEO) has been interested above all in Malay manuscripts—as much in their philological and literary aspects as in their historical. The Western sources and the archeological evidence allow him in the main to reconstitute here the role of the Bima sultanate, which until the 19th century was an important relay station on the routes of greater eastern Indonesia. **Claude Guillot** taught in Yogya for a long time, before also joining the CNRS. As a historian he first devoted himself to the history of Christianity in Java, then to the history of the Banten sultanate, which he studies through the European accounts, and by way of digs conducted in collaboration with the Indonesian Archeological Service. He presents to us here a detailed description of the city of Banten, a short time before its fall; it was then a great international crossroads and "the most important urban center of the Archipelago." **Claudine Salmon** (CNRS) and **Denys Lombard** (EHESS/EFEO), both Indonesianists and Sinologists, have notably studied the history of Indonesia's Chinese communities, and they have published a monograph on Chinese temples in Jakarta that takes into account the wealth of epigraphic texts. They reconsider here the ancient relations existing between Chinese and Islamic cultures, which leads them somewhat to modify the point of view according to which all Chinese people of the South China Seas constitute no more than a "foreign body" (an error willingly made by political scientists . . .).

The next two articles obviously are the accomplishment of "ethnologists" used to working "on location," in regions wherein one could assume the past to be less promising than in Java; but as a matter of fact, just as in the three preceding ones, they take into account the entire historical past, and they could stand for that kind of *historical anthropology* through which the *Archipel* group could also define itself. **Christian Pelras** (CNRS), who went on long missions to the Archipelago, notably in Sulawesi and on the Malay Peninsula, has published varied studies of the Bugis; here, he expounds his point of view on the delicate question of the "Islamization" of the southern Celebes. Before joining the CNRS also as an ethnologist, **Bernard Sellato** spent long months in Borneo as a geologist; from his prior training he has retained a deep sense of "strata," and he examines here societies from the center of Kalimantan, not as an aggregate of "ethnic groups," but as the product of a historical process just as complex and exciting as in the case of Javanese, Normans, or Texans.

The last two articles bear on what is called by convention the "contemporary period," that is to say on the "New Order," but both scholars, as much as possible, attempt to take into account the full *weight of the past*. **Pierre Labrousse** (INALCO), already mentioned, is mostly known for his lexicography studies, but he has also given *Archipel* relevant analyses of the present, and he is preparing an extensive study of the "looks" the French have cast upon Indonesia over time. He is studying here the process of rehabilitation the memory of

Sukarno has undergone, in particular between 1978 and 1981. **François Raillon** (CNRS) was first interested in the student movements following 1965; he has since been regularly observing the evolution of the Indonesian political conjuncture, and deals here with the delicate relations that have always existed between the authorities and Muslim milieus.

Is there, finally, some specificity which would allow us to tie together all these articles extracted from *Archipel*? Doubtless, it is not up to the archipelagist himself to pronounce on this matter, but up to the reader, when he has finished decrypting these ten "looks" which have been deliberately chosen to be different.

From a personal point of view, there seems to exist among all these texts a family resemblance, and here are, for the taking, a couple of rather simple formulas: a) "Everything is a source" (the bas-reliefs of Prambanan to the same extent as the postage stamps from the Sukarno period . . .); and b) "The present cannot be explained without the past," which is another way of referring to the Braudelian "longue durée," as well as to the "historical anthropology" practiced at the École des Hautes Études en Sciences Sociales.

The times are ripe for the expansion of "cross-studies." About ten years ago, a selection of thirteen articles also drawn from *Archipel* were put into Indonesian, and printed in Indonesia by the publishing house Sinar Harapan.[5] More recently, Cornell University's Southeast Asia Program took the initiative in producing in English a selection of Japanese studies on the Archipelago.

"To each one's own Indonesia" (or Japan, or United States, or France . . .). These translating projects which grant a privilege to the "perspective" rather than to the object itself, are extremely precious inasmuch as they aim at unmasking the a priori, and introduce that "triangulation" which alone will enable an exact mapping of the field.

One might perhaps attain some day a true "trigonometrical anthropology," with more freedom from these constraining "cultural gravitational forces" which are still affecting the field. At any rate, the present translation goes in that direction, and those who made it possible must be thanked for it one more time.

Translated by Victor Aboulaffia

---

[5] *Citra Masyarakat Indonesia* (Jakarta: Sinar Harapan, 1983), 281 pp.

The Beamwork Illustrated at Prambanan

Jacques Dumarçay

The balustrades surrounding the terraces on which are built the three main shrines of Prambanan in Central Java are decorated on the inner side with reliefs illustrating Indian epics. The scenes showing the different episodes often include some architectural details. The sculptors, to produce these views, used several representational techniques. The simplest is an orthogonal projection of a building (Figure 1) which is often combined with a perspective effect obtained by reducing a facade. Aerial perspective is also used (Figure 2), and also a method deriving from this: an almost axonometrical view upwards (Figure 3), in contrast to the aerial view, which looks down. None of these devices is followed rigorously and a concern for accurate representation does not prevail to the same degree in all three shrines. Details of buildings are completely absent in the southern shrine, numerous but unvaried in the central shrine, and few but carefully illustrated in the northern shrine.

The three buildings which we shall try to reconstitute are, for this reason, on the inner side of the balustrade of the northern shrine. Two are near the northeast corner, and the third on the western facade. The first construction is entirely without partitions and is raised on piles; it consists of a main building with an adjacent lean-to. The sculptor has used aerial perspective for the roof of the lean-to, but for the main building has employed an orthogonal projection with a face folded on the same plan.

On the inside, the two floors shown in aerial perspective (Figure 2). The pillars are illustrated in orthogonal projection but the sculptor has utilized the possibilities which the third dimension gave to indicate different planes. Thus, the rabetting in the pillars to take the beams for the floor is shown as slightly projecting. The details of the beamwork appear above all in the folding of the gable of the main building, but to produce the external shape we have also used the side illustrated in orthogonal projection. It can be noted here that on the two sides is a roof with two projections like those carved in the round on the stone models found in the Jakarta and Trowulan museums.

---

* This article first appeared in French in *Archipel* 7 (1974): 139–50.

6   *Jacques Dumarçay*

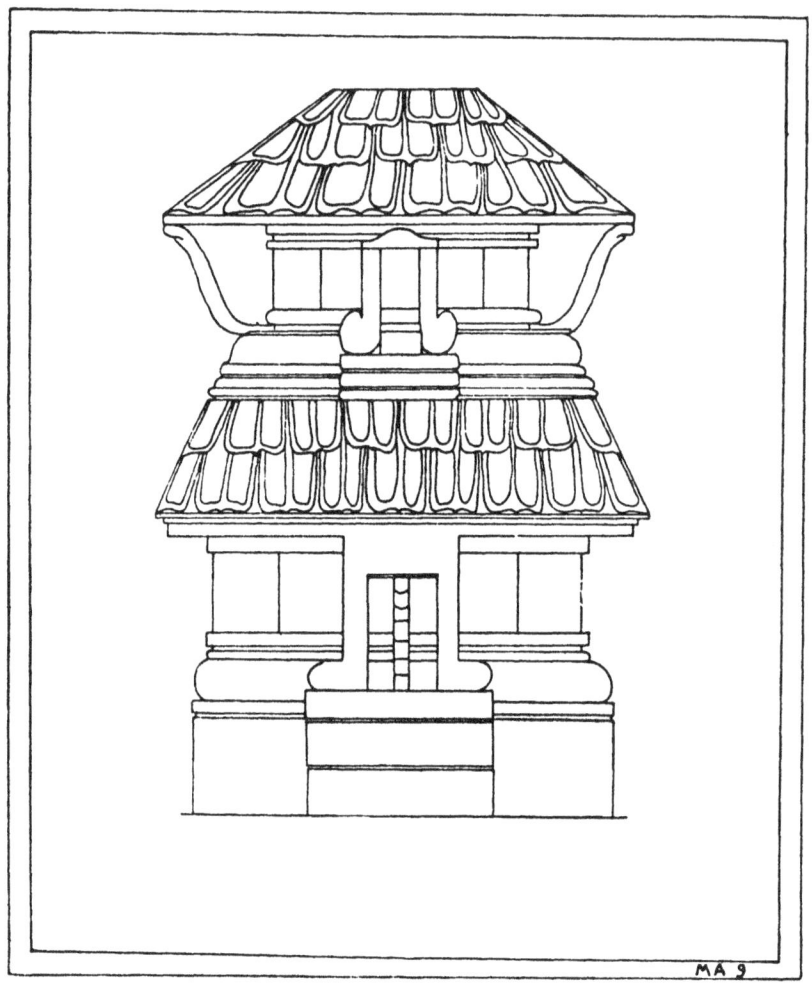

Figure 1. Prambanan Temple, north balustrade, west side, central panel (MA9).

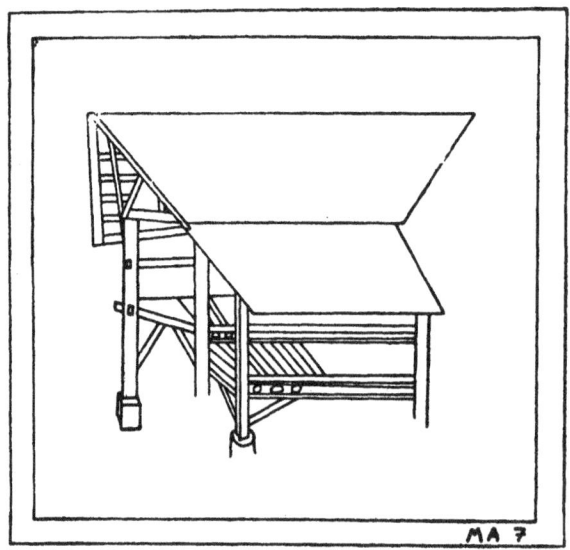

Figure 2. Prambanan Temple, north balustrade, north side, west panel (MA7).

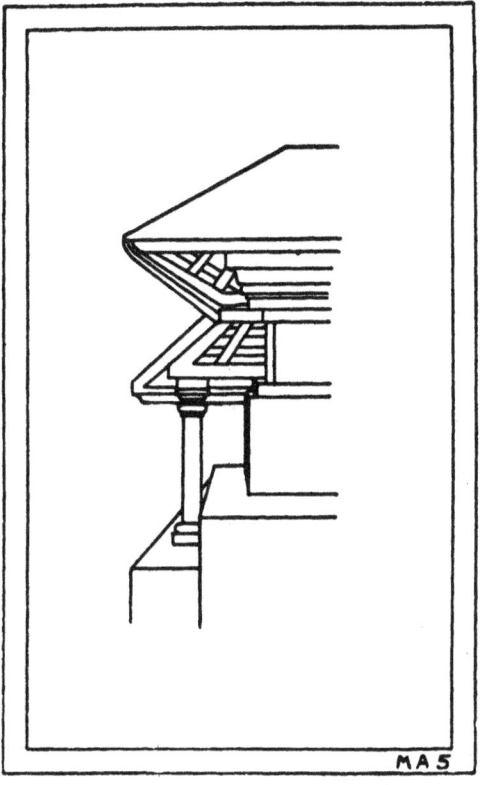

Figure 3. Prambanan Temple, north balustrade, north side, west panel (MA5).

The ridge-pole is supported by a sloping bracket at each end of the building and taking support from the tie-beam of the gable. These two brackets are of considerable technical interest. The ridge-pole was not only held in place but also in tension, which would have done away with every king-post and give a large internal volume.

Yet in our reconstitution (Figure 4) we have shown a king-post in dotted lines. It seems likely that for a building of some size, to avoid bending under the weight of the roof, a simple king-post placed on a tie-beam was essential. Moreover, even to this day, the carpenters of Central Java support the ridge-pole.

This type of tensioned beam existed before the construction of Prambanan. It is shown in Borobudur (north side, west wing lower level of the first gallery). The beamwork is completed by rafters fixed to the top of the ridge-pole and at the base on the stringer. Laths are placed on the rafters at widely spaced intervals, to hold the roof material which is not shown. The stringer is doubled longitudinally. This stiffening is still used now even though, as the gables are no longer sloping, it is possible to place a tie to the ridge-pole, as is often done in Cambodia in similar cases. The beams supporting the floor are inserted in the pillars and held in position by pegs going right through the butt-end. These beams have their strain reduced by the struts which rest on the pillars. The floors appear to be formed from pointed billets between two beams the whole length of the building. The floor of the lean-to is at a lower level than the main building.

The second construction selected for detailed study is in stone (Figure 3), built on a very high and solid base; on the longitudinal side, facing the viewer, the building is extended with a lean-to roof resting on columns. The roof of the main building has four sides. An orthogonal representation of this type of roof is the most common, leaving no indication of the structure, but here, the sculptor has managed to show us the underside of the roof, and the following reconstitution is possible.

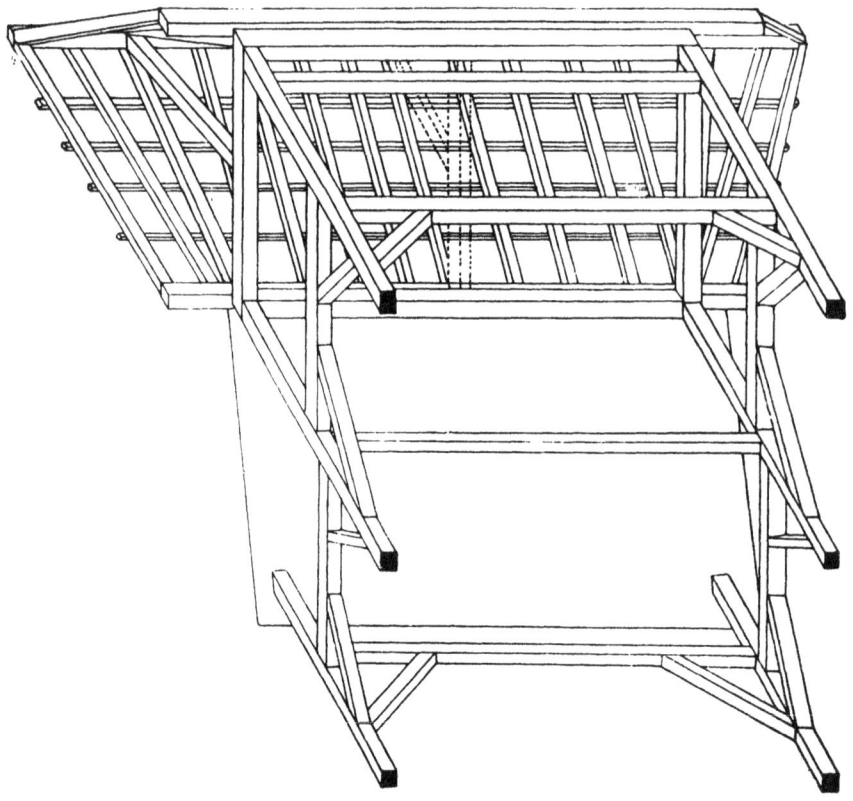

Figure 4. Reconstituted beamwork of the building shown in Prambanan Temple, north balustrade, west side, central panel: see figure 2 (MA8).

We think (Figure 5) that a radiating beamwork is indicated, the rafters of which would be inserted at the top into the ridge pole, then over the masonry into a stringer and ending at their base in a wall plate located slightly behind the guttering edge of the roof. The materials used to cover the roof are not shown, but some birds are shown pecking at its surface, so it is possibly thatch. In this type of beamwork, still very common in Java and Bali, it was not necessary to insert intermediary trusses because the ridge-pole was compressed throughout by the rafters inserted in the stringer whereas, in the previous example, the roof-line was in tension by brackets leaning outwards and allowing the rafters to be free on the wall plate on the projecting part of the building.

In the two examples described, the materials used in the roof covering are not shown. This is generally true in Prambanan, except for two very similar buildings: one on the west balustrade of the southern shrine, the other on the west balustrade of the northern shrine. We shall describe the latter. It has two storeys though perhaps it is only the outer building of a much more important construction outlined in the rear of the relief. The ground floor is built on a level base, crossed by a stairway leading to a door whose movement is shown. The door is surrounded by a carving interrupting the ogee moulding on which the windows rest. The whole is surrounded by a cornice which is partially broken by the door frame. Above the markedly projecting cornice resting directly on the doorway are shown two rows

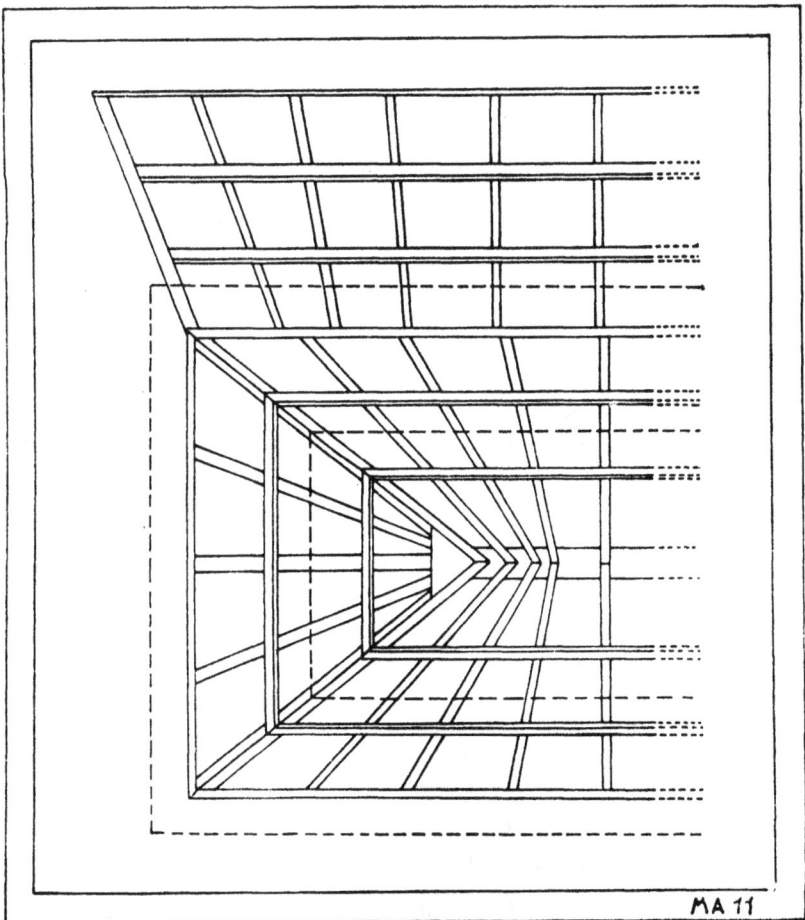

Figure 5. Reconstituted beamwork of the building shown in Prambanan Temple, north balustrade, north side, west panel : see figure 3 (MA11).

of broad flat tiles. We believe that these were made of terracotta, with a raised central point, the sides and the center slightly depressed to allow for a rapid run-off of rainwater. The upper row of tiles is inserted beneath a small projecting string-course forming the ridge tiling. Above this the outline of the base is carved, broken by a stairway leading to a doorway. In consequence, this represents, as with many temple constructions, a false storey corresponding to no internal volume.

This last structure is covered with a four-sided roofing extending well beyond the structure. Some braces were doubtless placed only at the corners to maintain the greatest overhang. The roofing consists of three rows of tiles similar to the ground floor; there is no carved ridge tiling. This illustration is of the greatest importance, showing that, besides the stone shrines, wooden shrines existed with a similar disposition: a ground floor upholding one or two false storeys corresponding to no internal volume. As for the beamwork, this building shows us that lath work was used to place the tiles. It is likely that the beamwork is also radiating here, as in the previous example, but instead of a few parallel beams to the wall to hold in place the thatch or broad wooden wedges, it was necessary to fix laths on the rafters for each row of tiles.

The location of the different types of roof frames illustrated in the shrines is detailed in the following summary description of all the architectural representations on the monument, beginning on the axial east doorway and keeping the structure on the right, the reliefs being consequently on the left. In all cases, the buildings are shown in orthogonal projection, except where indicated.

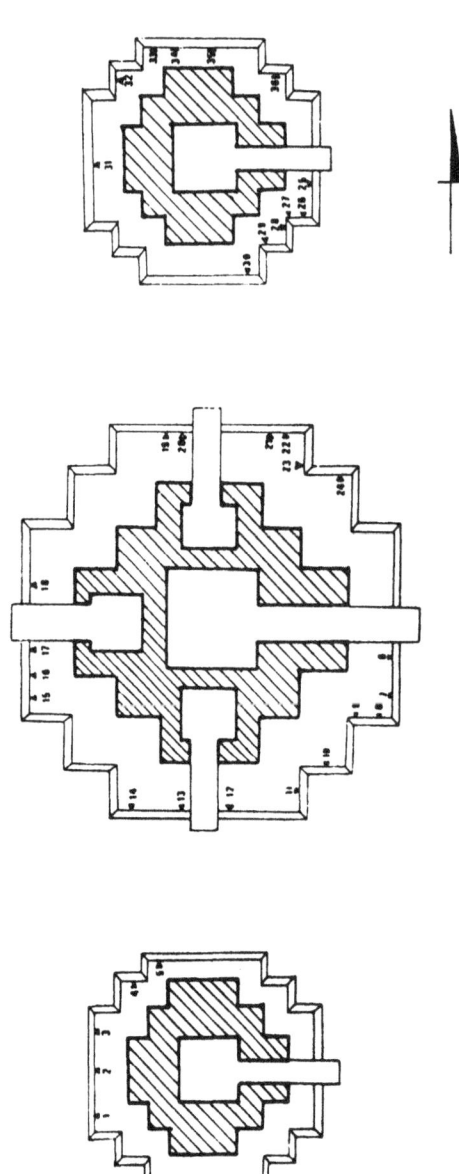

Figure 6. Location of all the buildings illustrated on the bas-reliefs at Prambanan.

A. The South Temple (Candi Brahma)

1. On the west side, central panel, unfortunately flaking away, is a building, whose tiles are shown as in Figure 1.

2. Also on the west side, a building with lean-tos, having a two-sided roof and projections, the sloping bracket is accurately shown, as well as the perpendicular beams.

3. The same side is a two-storeyed building with a reduced facade and a two-sided roof, and under the tie-beam of the gable represented on the reduced facade is a small lean-to roof which links the two high longitudinal stringers. On this building the lower stringer goes all round and is possible that between the two stringers spaces were provided for aeriation. (See Plate 1.)

4. On the north side is a small shelter on piles with a two-sided roof doubtless without any projection.

5. On the north side is a small shelter very similar to the previous one, shown on stone in very poor condition.

B. The Central Temple (Candi Siva)

6. On the east side, southern section, is a building with a four-sided roof.

7. On the same panel is a boor with an indication shown in perspective of one of the door-leaves.

8–14. On the south side, eastern section, are shown six buildings with four-sided roofs. This is doubtless the same construction serving as a backdrop for different scenes.

15. On the west side, southern section, is a building with a reduced facade showing a gable. This construction has two floors, the upper one appearing to be quite low; it may be that because of the tension in the ridge there were no fixed intermediaries, allowing the whole space to be filled.

16. On the same panel is a building with a four-sided roof.

17. Still on the same panel is a building with a two-sided roof without a reduced facade clearly showing the extent of the lateral projections.

18. On the west side, northern section, is a building shown in aerial perspective, the wallings of which could be removed by raising them.

19. On the north side, western section, is a building having a four-sided roof.

20. Also on the north side, western section, is a building with a two-sided roof and a reduced front showing the beams perpendicular to the brackets, as is normal, but here the sculptor has respected the proportions of the cut of the wood; the lower beams are shorter than the upper ones.

21. On the north side, eastern section, is a building with a two-sided roof and a reduced front.

22. On the same panel is a two-storeyed building with a surrounding lean-to roof above the ground floor and a four-sided roof on the upper floor set back from the lean-to roof of the ground floor.

Plate 1

23. On the east side, northern section, is a building shown in aerial perspective, the partitions of which can open.

24. On the east side, northern section, is shown a two-storeyed building on piles with a reduced facade and a surrounding lean-to roof on the ground floor; the roof of the upper floor has two sides and a stretched ridge; the slope of the visible brackets is parallel to that of the projection and the extension of the perpendicular beams is regular. (See Plate 2.)

Plate 2

C. The North Temple (Candi Visnu)

25. On the east side, southern section, is a building with a four-sided roof.

26. On the south side, eastern section, is a building shown in orthogonal projection but with elements of aerial perspective, having a two-sided roof and partitions which can be raised longitudinally; they are made of wickerwork.

27. On the same panel, is shown a building with a four-sided roof.

28. On the east side, on the first step south, is a small building shown in aerial perspective whose four pillars are illustrated.

29. On the south side, on the eastern panel, is a building with a four-sided roof.

30. On the south side, in the central panel is a building with a two-sided roof, with one of the gables reduced. (See Plate 3.)

31. On the west side, the central panel is illustrated in Figure 1.

32. On the west side, on the northern panel, a building is outlined.

33. On the north side, on the western panel, a building is illustrated in Figure 2.

34. On the same panel, another building appears, illustrated in Figure 3.

35. On the north side, on the eastern panel, is a building with a four-sided roof.

36. On the same panel is shown a small pavilion on piles, in aerial perspective.

14 *Jacques Dumarçay*

Plate 3

In addition to the elements described above, modern beamwork has kept numerous traditional cuts. Among those noted near Prambanan are timber frames with two projections which are rare and in all cases without sloping brackets. In contrast, many four-sided roofs can be seen very similar to those illustrated in the reliefs, notably in the village of Tengal Bendo, where the roof frame has a double stringer, the radiating rafters resting on the ridge, itself upheld by a king-post. In the *kraton* or palaces of Yogyakarta and Solo, there are many oblong timber frames. Above an entrance of the Yogyakarta *kraton* can be seen a radiating beamwork without a ceiling and without a king-post, which is very close to many of the models of Prambanan. Finally, if all the roofs with a ridge in tension have disappeared in Java, they still exist in Sumatra, notably among the Batak, and in the huge Toraja houses in Sulawesi.

Translated by Michael Smithies

THE POLITICAL ICONOLOGY OF THE INDONESIAN POSTAGE STAMP
(1950–1970)*

Jacques Leclerc

1 Working hypotheses

1.1 The starting point of our investigation is the fact that the issuing of postage stamps is at once the issuing of images and of images controlled by the State through the intermediary of special commissions of the postal service. At the same time, it must be kept in mind that the iconic function of the stamp is, *in principle,* subordinate to the fiscal function, which privileges face value, that is the amount of the tax which, when affixed to the piece of mail, can be collected.

The image and the franking value can also be presented as an illustration reduced to the figure(s) expressing this value: such is the case of the Indonesian "post paid" (*bajar porto*) stamps. But even in this extreme case, the colors of the stamp and the design of the figures add an aesthetic level to the fiscal information.

At the other end of the scale, certain issues are less concerned with the necessities of franking than with the potential philatelic market: moreover, the face value of the stamp is often *defaced* by a surtax, the resulting sum being, in fact, the sales price of a certain type of picture. Even though collectors are not motivated primarily by the elegance of the image, stamps for collectors often fall back on internationally established iconography, something I would call the "scenic" stamp: flowers, butterflies, birds, landscapes, various oddities, and particularly touristic sites. The Indonesian postal service addressed stamp collectors as early as 1949 with its first-day cancellations; first-day covers appeared in 1954 and, in 1961, first-day sheets, featuring, significantly enough, a set of ten stamps promoting tourism.

---

* The French version of this article appeared in *Archipel* 6 (1973): 145–83. The author would like to express his gratitude to the Fondation Nationale des Sciences Politiques and to the Centre d'Etudes et de Recherches Internationales for funding the translation of this article, as well to the translator, Nora Scott, who has done more than simply translate.

That scenic stamps often bear a surtax is justified by the fact that they are issued for the benefit of what are called charitable or "social" concerns. But behind such a justification, which in fact takes refuge behind the image from the social reality it claims to be easing by the surtax, lies nothing but the fashionable superficiality typical, in the Western World at least, of charity drives. Of the eleven sets issued between 1960 and 1970 to celebrate *Hari Sosial*, the annual "Social Works Day," only two (1960 and 1967) referred to social themes; the others featured, in order: fruit, orchids, butterflies, birds, flowers again, reptiles, more fruit, sea shells, insects; "Social Works Day" seems to have been more the occasion than the reason for their issue.

In view of the difference in levels of iconic signification from one set to the next, we wondered if it might not be possible, by examining a sequence covering a relatively long span of time (20 years), to single out a number of elements and tendencies constituting what might be called "an official mental picture."

1.2 Our starting point is 1950 (constitutionally speaking: August 15, 1950, two days before the fifth anniversary of the proclamation of Indonesian independence), when Indonesia inaugurated its history as one republic, indivisible, liberated from foreign occupation (which had lasted well beyond the proclamation of independence into the early days of 1950). The edification of a unified State as well as the generalization of national feeling demanded an intense ideological activity on the part of State authorities; they needed to define their cultural specificity and provide the country with socio-historical references that would enable others to identify it. These could be embodied or reactivated in the collective consciousness by such events as commemorations and national holidays, the outline and signals of a differentiated practice of economic and political development.

The broad lines of this practice can be condensed into a form of official ideology, by which I mean an ideology officially described and taught as such, which was to emerge, effectively and with more or less force, at the end of the 1950s. The diffusion of this ideology, in the general course of the circulation of ideas, led to systematic State intervention. Are these potential elements of an "official mental picture" which, for example, finds its public formulations in the early 1960s under the name of *indoktrinasi*? For which commemorations and for which memories are Indonesian stamps in reality the channel or the locus? Of what chronicle, of what history—past, future, or only dreamed—were they, on their level, to be the "picture strip," to borrow a term from the movie world? To what *image* of Indonesia did they contribute?

2 Sources

2.1 In our search for answers we used the following:

2.1.1 Catalogues:

Katalogus dari Perangko Perangko Republik Indonesia, Surabaja, Popular, 1967 (stamps issued from December 1948 to May 1966);

Catalogus van de Postzegels der Republik Indonesia, Amsterdam, Zonnebloem, 1972 (stamps from 1943 to December 1970).

These catalogues contain reproductions (nearly complete in the Popular catalogue, larger gaps in the Zonnebloem), authors (with a number of discrepancies between the two sources), date of issue and (in the Popular catalogue only) date of withdrawal, perforation, and where the images were printed.

2.1.2 A collection containing approximately 90 percent of the stamps studied.

2.2 This material allows only an initial approach to the problems mentioned, however, in that the images are described, but not the conditions surrounding their selection.

2.2.1 The conditions preceding the issue are: the political, fiscal, aesthetic, and technical justifications for producing the stamp, no doubt formulated in the discussions of the committee entrusted with the program of releases, the minutes of which can theoretically be found in the archives of the postal service headquarters in Bandung (not forgetting the interventions and general guidelines of the Union Postale Universelle—we have been unable to ascertain whether the headquarters in Bern keeps a record of these). These justifications articulate the design/format/color/face value/print run complex, each component of which modulates the signification of the stamp and the way it is perceived by the user.

2.2.2 Following the issue, the terms are: the conditions of diffusion, supported by sociological statistics on the users: which stamps have the largest diffusion? which are most used? by whom? who writes (and receives) letters? and consequently *sees* the stamps? who collects them? etc.

2.3 It is for lack of such important details—the author would be grateful for any help in gathering such details—that the present investigation is entitled "iconology" and not "ideology" of the Indonesian postage stamp.

3 Displaying the Image

3.1 Aside from the *bajar porto* stamps and those restricted to parts of Indonesia endowed with a special political or fiscal status (Riau: stamps that circulate throughout the rest of Indonesia, but with a "Riau" surtax; Irian Barat: from 1963–1968, ordinary stamps endorsed "Irian Barat" and a special face value; from 1968–1970, separate stamps), 382 images were issued, between August 17, 1950 and December 31, 1970, which, counting the various face values of a single image, came to 617 different stamps or an annual average on the order of 20 images/30 stamps, attained in 1960. (See fig. 1, A. The solid lines represent the total number of images issued each year, the broken lines represent the face values).

3.2 The graph shows an overall rise in the number of stamps issued, increasing regularly from 1952 to 1958, irregularly from 1959 to 1970, peaking between 1961 and 1967, with the high in 1962.

3.2.1 This trend cannot be fully explained by the development of the postal service, the growing volume of mail, the diversification of postal rates, and their modification in respect of currency changes. A limited number of designs, even as few as one, given a broad enough range of face values and a high enough run, would be enough to satisfy such needs: that was, in fact, the case in 1951 with the issue of the sets that were gradually to replace those in circulation before the proclamation of the Unitary Republic, on August 15, 1950, a reality subsequently reiterated on the stamps by the imprint REPUBLIK INDONESIA, which appeared for the first time since 1947: a total of 40 face values for five images.

3.2.2 But the constitutional reference to the Unitary State implied in the words *Republik Indonesia* reinforced in the largest set (15 face values) by the image, directly inherited from Dutch usage, of the head of State, in this case President Sukarno, gives the revenue band the weight of a political statement.

3.2.3 This is confirmed by the fact that part of the Sukarno set would be printed as the inaugural run of the Kebayoran printing house, the first Indonesian printing works for stamps. This printing was purely symbolic on several levels, however, since the printing house would not be in full operation and able to cover Indonesia's needs in stamps until 1956–57; the rest of the 1951 Sukarno set had to be printed in Haarlem, in the former "mother" country.

3.3 The variety of Indonesian stamps is explained rather by the variety of functions they fulfill and the need to renew them, something certainly not peculiar to Indonesia: that the philatelic practice of "first-day cancellations" was introduced in 1949, on the occasion of the 75th anniversary of the Union Postale Universelle, with a commemorative stamp is a measure of its international character.

It is the growing capacity of Indonesia's stamp industry to respond to these manifold extant functions that explains the increase in the number of issues themselves. This capacity is confirmed not only by the opening of the Kebayoran printing house, but by the fact that, as early as 1950, Indonesian stamps were designed by national artists, maquettistes, and engravers, working on commission or full time, whom the postal service of Indonesia, unlike so many other newly decolonized countries that ordered their stamps from specialized international agencies or from the ex-colonial power, was able to recruit.

3.4 Figure 1 E shows this recruitment, as well as the periods of activity of the nine artists most frequently used:

1	Amat bin Djupri
2	Junalies
3	K. Risman Suplanto
4–7	(in alphabetical order) Kartono J., Mahriajub, S. Sumarsono/ Suwarsono,[1] Suroso
8	Sudirno
9	Suripto

3.5 The role of the maquettiste seemed destined to grow apace, if the tendency visible in the graphs beginning in 1967 to start attributing a single face value per image was maintained: for example, since 1969, the standard set used for ordinary franking was a set of 10 different vignettes illustrating the goals of the five-year development plan, which replaced a set, issued two and a half years earlier, of 16 stamps each showing a different traditional musical instrument. This type of standard set took the place of those comprising a large range of face values for a single image (President Sukarno, whence the obviously political rather than technical reason behind their withdrawal), clearly indicated by graphs A and B (1951, 1965, 1966).

3.6 It is difficult to measure the precise impact of each artist or team of artists on the program and the aesthetics of stamp production; all that can be shown are trends.

3.6.1 A gradual shift may be observed away from the descriptive, easily read subject picture toward geometric stylization, symbolic representations, and what might be called heraldic attempts at *coats of arms* (returning to what we said in 1.1 concerning the naturalist decor of surtax stamps: nature is the coat of arms of the social sphere), at *signs* (in correlation with international poster and billboard art), that is, at an *apparently* arbitrary system of figuration representing the programmed occasion of the stamp's issue (a sign which is sometimes imposed by the worldwide character of the occasion: a "day" designated by the

---

[1] The catalogues we consulted mention *S. Sumarsono*, from September 1961 to December 1965, and then, from December 1966, *Suwarsono*. The possible disappearance of Sumarsono in 1966, a deadly year if ever there was, is less unlikely than the coincidence of the consecutive names.

Figure 1

A Number of stamps issued annually: total number of different images and face values. (1) In the absence of adequate information, we attributed to 1951 the 15 small Sukarno figures, some of which did not appear until 1953.

B-E Search for areas of dominant significations. Graph B shows the wide discrepancy, in 1966, between the number of images issued (solid line) and the face values in the Sukarno set—issued in 1964 to replace the 1951 set—following the devaluation of the rupiah: to the 10 stamps issued in 1964 were added 6 more, overprinted 65, in new currency, then 20 in 1966, and one in 1967, before Sukarno's ouster in the same year made it necessary to withdraw the entire set; furthermore, in 1965 the same image was issued, overprinted conefo (Conference of the New Emerging Forces, being planned at the time), making a total of 52 different values for the same stamp design. Graph E: The short vertical lines of graph E show—in numbers of images, not values—the stamps that represent a postal event, including themselves (e.g. the stamp honoring the Centenary of the Indonesian postage stamp, see pl. I).

For the artists' names, see 3.4. For analysis of the graphs, see 3.1, 3.2, 3.7.1.

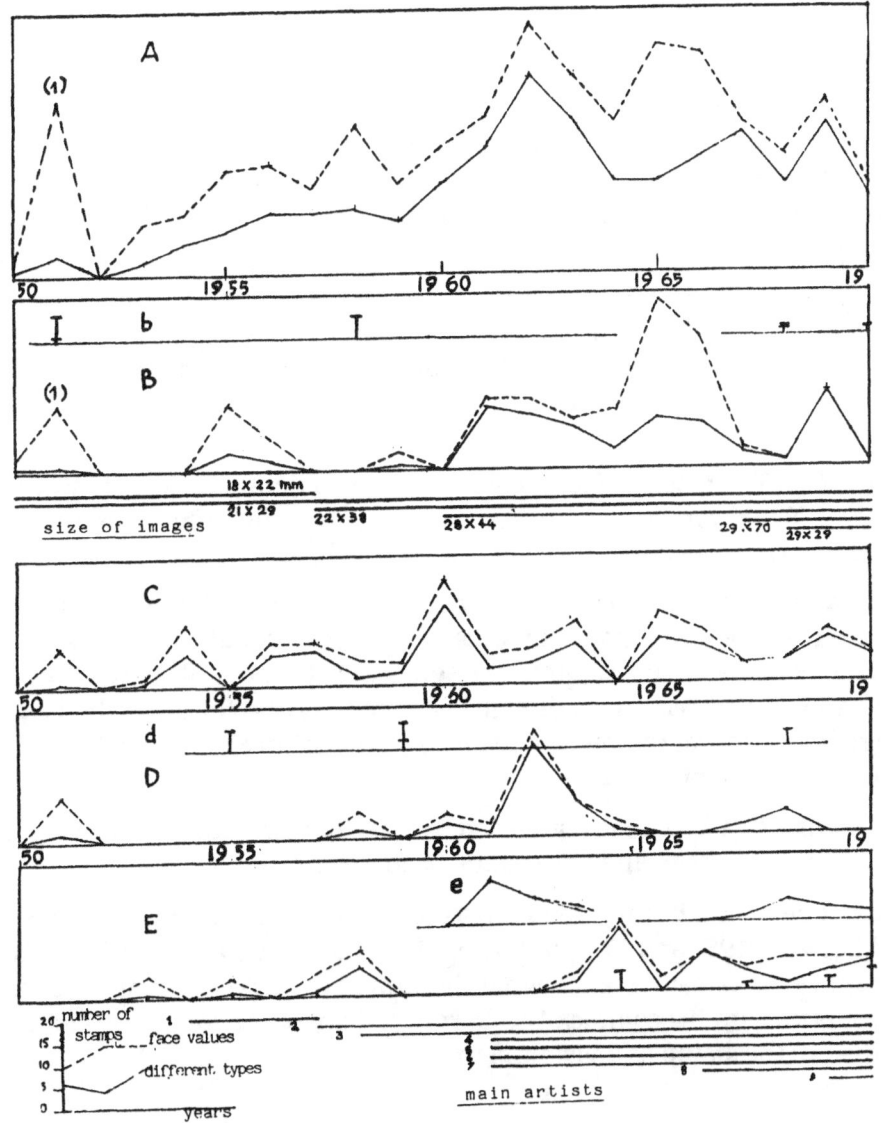

UN or by one of its agencies, UNESCO, WHO, FAO, and signified by an internationally fixed and diffused image which is also internationally decodable).

3.6.2 The period from 1954 to 1958, for example, was characterized by sets of "typical scenes" on surtax stamps devoted to social concerns (1954: children; 1956: the blind; 1957: the physically handicapped; 1958: orphans), a genre in which Amat bin Djupri excelled, unlike the rather poor "stylizations" he would deliver when the commission had to do with a commemoration (1955: 10th anniversary of "Heroes' Day"; 1956: "Cooperation Day"), a genre in which Junalies, recruited in 1957, felt more at ease.

After 1957–58, "typical scenes" were relegated to the "post card" stamp and sets of picturesque scenes promoting tourism. Arbitrary signs, symbols, objects, and landscapes eliminated the "slice of life."

3.6.3 But more revealing than this evolution are the crises that punctuate it. One at least, in 1967–68, is reflected in the violent dramatization of the figure/color/format complex.

Violent subjects: in October 1967, two stamps were issued of "wild animals fighting," by the painter Raden Saleh Sarif Bustaman (1813–1880) without any particular reason for honoring him, no anniversary being near; in December 1967, the annual "Social Works Day" set forsook the usual flowers and butterflies for catastrophes: a flood, landslide, conflagration, volcanic eruption; violence was evoked as well with the issuing, on August 17, 1967, the national holiday, of three scenes showing the maquette of the colossal monument raised around the well at Lubang Buaya, into which, on October 1, 1965, the bodies of the officers executed by the Untung group were thrown and which had become the site of a pilgrimage, thus determining the origin, center, and sanctuary of the new power, the founding sacrifice.

Hypertrophy and sophistication of new formats (cf. fig.1B chronology of formats): one 29 x 70 mm image (July 1967: International Tourism Year; June 1968: Scout Camp), that tears into 3 separate stamps corresponding to a 21 x 29 mm format, even though the three form a continuous picture (March 1968: Borobudur). The same process of splitting was subsequently used in the 29 x 44 mm format already in circulation for some time (October 1968: Mexico City Olympic Games).

Use of loud colors: The mixing of loud colors, previously not practiced, is sometimes linked to the 29 x 70 mm format; it takes over such thematically different issues as those devoted to tourism (1967, 1968) or "Aviation Day" (April, 1967).

3.6.4 Whereas any one of these elements is not significant in itself, the emphatic treatment of typical scenes (even reproductions of works of a painter or sculptor, that is of a monument outside the postal service), acquires as a series the value of testimony, the transfer, through the sharpening of certain iconic signs of a national and/or individual trauma, an unplayed tragedy, an unprogrammed occasion, even if the break, the will to instigate a figurative revival was intentional.

By 1969 the crisis had apparently subsided, the use of many colors was relegated to the annual set promoting tourism, and once again armories prevailed.

3.7 The catalogue makes it simple enough to construct graph A, with all the types and values issued between 1950 and 1970, but using it to construct graphs, each of which brings together homogeneous semantic sets, so that the sum of these partial graphs tends to reproduce A, confronts us with the complexity and multiplicity of the conscious and unconscious means embodied in the stamp as a visible sign.

3.7.1 Although there was some initial arbitrariness in the classification, which we hope to reduce later in this article, we have, within the general field of a dominant meaning whose function is political (by political we mean anything that implies a short-term relation to the governing of people), narrowed the possibilities down to four preferential areas, shown respectively in graphs B/b, C, D/d, E/e:

- B Commemoration of struggles for independence, institutions, portraits of the head of State, development plans, the Bandung Conference and Afro-Asian solidarity (in *b*: international integration institutionalized by the UN), roughly speaking what is announced by the Indonesian concepts : *kebangsaan, kedaulatan rakyat,* and *perikemanusiaan* (see 4.1.4).

- C Social solidarity, safety, and justice (with the exception of development plans), which cover images concerning food, housing, health, education, better working conditions, including images commemorating International theme days (declared by the FAO, WHO, UNESCO, ILO): graph C is punctuated by special *Bentjana Alam* (natural disaster) surtax issues: 1953, flooding in Aceh; 1954, eruption of Mount Merapi; 1961, various disasters; 1963, eruption of Gunung Agung; 1966, Solo River flood; and from 1960, the annual commemoration of *Hari Sosial* (it does not appear on the graph for 1964 because it was celebrated late, in 1965); in 1967, the two themes coincided: the *Hari Sosial* set was devoted to *Bentjana Alam* (see above 3.6.3).

- D Sporting events: every three years, from 1958 to 1967, there was an issue celebrating the world championship Thomas Cup for badminton (*bulutangkis*), held during that period by Indonesia, but the outstanding feature is the ballooning of the number of values issued in 1962–63 (32 out of a total 66 values for the entire graph), which bears witness to a quantitative and perhaps even qualitative change in the functions connected until then with such events and their commemoration by stamps (we have plotted on the graph all types of stamps marked "ASIAN GAMES IV DJAKARTA 1962" and "GAMES OF THE NEW EMERGING FORCES DJAKARTA NOVEMBER 10–22 1963," even if the image did not show a sport, players, or the playing field); *d* shows the fairly related field of scouting.

- E Communications, transportation, and meeting places (other than those dealt with previously, political halls, sports stadia…) post office, bank, international expositions (including those promoting tourism, which have been grouped together on graph e). The postal service makes generous use of these stamps to diffuse the image it wants to give of itself: graph E shows nothing but the post, in fact, until the end of 1957; moreover, the first public building shown on an Indonesian stamp was, in January 1953, the main post office in Bandung, and the first head, other than that of the President of the Republic, was, in September 1955 for the 10th anniversary of the Indonesian postal service, that of its first director: narcissism of the center and the head which encloses and freezes into a State within a State a service whose *raison d'être* is the creation of links between people and the circulation of information, openness and exchange, and therefore mobility. It was not really until 1964 that a set of 12 figures by Suroso merged the postal service with the other means of transportation, which he showed *being operated*, that is, by postal employees (mail carriers, switchboard operators, teletypists) *working* in the midst of a complex of vehicles, both traditional and new, air mail, sea mail (also commemorated by special issues in 1958, 1964, 1966, 1967, 1969, but perhaps less as *means* of transportation than as *signs* of prestige and modernity) restored here to their original calling as a *public service*, an

22   *Jacques Leclerc*

authoritative instrument for measuring, appropriating, and unifying the national space.

3.7.2 Here we can state conclusively that the four areas—no stamp having been included in more than one graph—work together and that this very fact points to one of the dimensions of the mental picture under investigation.

4   Institutional Coats of Arms

4.1   The choice of August 17 as the issue date for new stamps is an affirmation on the part of the postal service of the political significance of stamps as commemorating the act that legally founded the Indonesian State, the proclamation of independence on August 17, 1945.

4.1.1   The catalogue of these stamps is as follows (see fig. 2)

Figure 2

Year	Commemoration *indicated* on stamp	Description of figure
1950	5th anniversary of Independence	arms of the Republic
1955	10th anniversary	grouping of 3 classic figures from August 17, 1945: Sukarno, Hatta on his left reading the Proclamation, Sukarno and Hatta at first raising of the flag; reproduction of manuscript of the Proclamation
1959	"Restoration of the 1945 constitution" (KEMBALI KE UUD 1945)	text in Sukarno's handwriting
1960		set of 8 stamps showing *hasil bumi* (fruits of the land), from the smallest to the largest face value: oil palm, sugar cane, coffee bush, tobacco, tea bushes, coconut palm, hevea, rice
1961		first set of *pahlawan* (national heroes)
1965	1945-1965	5 stamps featuring the *Panca Sila* (5 principles) set out by Sukarno on June 1, 1945, represented by their symbol on the arms of Indonesia (cf. stamp issued August 17, 1950)
1967	MONUMEN PAHLAWAN REVOLUSI LUBANG BUAJA, 1 OKT. 1965	presentation in 3 stamps of the maquette of the monument to those who died on Oct. 1, 1965 (see above 3.6.3)
1969	PELITA (*Pembangunan Lima Tahun*): 5-year development	a set of 10 figures illustrating the goals of the five-year development plan just adopted
1970	a quarter century of Independence	an obelisk-shaped design

4.1.2 Only three of these issues actually claim to commemorate the event—in 1950, 1955, and 1970. The evolution of their iconography, from the 1955 reproduction of photographs of the August 1945 ceremonies to the symbolic obelisk on the 1970 stamp, (see pl. VI) seems to confirm the transition, already mentioned, from description to abstraction.

The function of the other issues is, then, to integrate directly into the memory of independence, as consubstantial elements, figures which no longer project the moment of the Proclamation but now proclaim the conditions, either institutional (1959, 1965, 1967) or economic (1960, 1969), for achieving and preserving the declared independence.

4.1.3 An important anniversary, the *dwiwindu* (twice eight years), of the Proclamation was celebrated, but the commemorative set anticipated the date and appeared on July 6, 1961 (see pl. VII, lower right). The image is made up of two elements: on the left, a stylized drawing of modern buildings and factory smoke stacks, which can be identified from other figurative contexts (set XI, Conference of the Colombo Plan Countries, 1959; Census, 1961; Regional Family Planning Conference, 1969 . . .) as a sign of production and economic development; on the right, a group of three silhouettes differentiated only by their headgear (a *pici*, a conical hat, and a hard hat), carrying a beam on their shoulders, symbol of the team work, *gotong-royong* that, since his 1926 article, "Nationalisme, Islamisme dan Marxisme," on the three ideological components of the Indonesian national movement, Sukarno never tired of invoking. The "all together, heave-ho!" "*ho-lopis-kuntul-baris,*" of the June 1, 1945 speech, and the call for *tritunggal*, for the convergence of these three tendencies to shoulder Indonesia's burden, punctuated the speech, which in its ternary title, "Revolusi Sosialisme Pimpinan" (RESOPIM), commemorates this *dwiwindu*.

4.1.4 It was to mark the 20th anniversary of the June 1, 1945 speech, the one which formulated the *Panca Sila*, the five principles of national unity, *alat pemersatu ... bukan alat pemetjahbelah*, "instrument of unity, not division," as its author recalled in RESOPIM, August 17, 1961—and which would subsequently be condensed into *gotong-royong*—that five stamps were issued on August 17, 1965 (and not June 1). The sharply differentiated face values of these stamps place the principles described in a hierarchical order :

Figure 3

Face value (tax + surtax, in rupiah)	Principle (as featured on the stamps)
10 + 5	KEADILAN SOSIAL social justice
20 + 10	PERIKEMANUSIAAN humanitarianism
25 + 10	KEBANGSAAN national unity
40 + 15	KEDAULATAN RAKJAT sovereignty of the people
50 + 15	KETUHANAN JANG MAHA ESA belief in one God

This vertical listing of the *Panca Sila*, God first and social justice last (the order of the other principles is not rigid, and *Perikemanusiaan* can just as well be exchanged with *Kedaulatan Rakjat*), represented, from the outset, a challenge to the horizontal conception preferred particularly by the Communists and Sukarno, and which a few months later was officially to prevail.

4.1.5 Thus the axis of the obelisk (1970) rises in the space symbolically delineated by the arms of the nation (1950): it recapitulates twenty-five years of history. All that went before—the "heroes" portraits (in 1961) are concerned with history itself, the history that grounded the 17th of August and which is punctuated by its annual commemoration—can be read in two trajectories: that of the institutional legitimacy of political power and that of its confirmation by economic growth, which are linked by the images of the nation, the constitutional source of power, at work, the economic justification of the political order that designs the basic axis.

If, in 1961, the issue was to establish a link between the proclamation of independence and those who prepared it, the commemoration of the proclamation being divided between two dates, July 6 and August 17, in order that it might be understood on the two levels of meaning attributed to it, in 1959 and 1967 the issue was to integrate institutional discontinuities into the anniversary of the Republic, that is, into the historical continuity of the country, and to present them as a return to the origins, a return to August 17. That was the slogan that justified the abrogation, on July 5, 1959, of the provisional constitution of August 15, 1950: KEMBALI KE UUD 1945, "restoration of the 1945 constitution," and it was also the slogan that appeared on the stamp issued August 17, 1959, because the July 5th slogan could not symbolically take effect on any day other than August 17, this particular August 17, 1959, which was also the day Sukarno pronounced his Political Manifesto, the founding text of "Guided Democracy." The same preoccupation with legitimation was evident in the homage paid to those who died on October 1, 1965 with stamps issued on August 17, 1967, as General Suharto had just been declared President of the Republic of Indonesia, replacing the ousted Sukarno, and was the one now speaking for the State.

4.2 In its heraldic pictogram form (*padi-kapas*, an ear of rice, a branch of cotton, metaphor for the slogan *sandang-pangan* [food and clothing] used as the basic reference for "standard of living,") *keadilan sosial* "social justice" is relegated, in the 1965 set, to the lower ranks of the five principles. Nevertheless, it is the only one that circulates so visibly outside the coat of arms of the State, entering into the composition of other armories (the Military Academy, 1968; the Railroad, 1968; Justice, 1970; the Post Office, 1970) or into occasional insignia (10th anniversary of the Bandung Conference, 1965). All are external emblems that the stamp merely diffuses, but they also comprise an isolable unit of specific iconic utterances symbolizing projects of a social (*Hari Kooperasi*, 1957; *Hari Sosial*, 1960) or an economic nature (for instance, the 11th Conference of Colombo Plan Countries and the Regional Family Planning Conference already mentioned, in which, in contrast to images of industry and transportation, these are more closely identified with agriculture alone, and in which, among the industrial images, the construction trades now add to the basic requirement of food and clothing expressed by *padi-kapas*, that of housing). But it appeared first and foremost in 1951, as the only picture frame out of a set of nine values, the first of this importance after the restoration of the Unitary Republic, a historic priority, then, and one capable of bringing the economic and social spheres together in the armories of institutions and programs (pl. VII).

5 Identifying the Space

5.1 The Asian Games, under the aegis of the International Olympic Committee, were held for the first time in 1951, in New Delhi. For the occasion, Indonesia's postal service issued a small single-colored stamp, in five face values, bearing a map of South and Southeast Asia; the Olympic torch marked New Delhi, and Indonesia was designated by the Borobudur *stupa*, the entire design being overprinted with the five Olympic rings.

The Fourth Asian Games were held in Jakarta and began, in the huge sporting complex that had just been completed, on August 24, 1962. Exactly five months before, on March 24, the first set of stamps announcing the Games appeared. Their format (28 x 44 mm) was recent and at that time used almost exclusively for ceremonial occasions: it was inaugurated in February 1961, featuring President Sukarno holding a hoe, to celebrate the launching of a new national development plan; it was not seen again until January 1962, bearing six figures from the *Ramayana* in front of Siva's temple in Prambanan, then in February with the maquette of the Mosque of Independence in Jakarta, the construction of which had just begun. The March 1962 release, with a salvo of four stamps of different values but all carrying the single figure of an archer, a Javanese sculpture from the classical period, encompasses the gaze in the great tradition of royal culture,[2] which brings together worship and the State into great festive gatherings and, from the outset, diffuses one possible meaning of the approaching Games.

5.2 In one of his books on Romanesque art in west-central France, René Crozet, comparing the frescoes of churches between the rivers Loire and Cher, makes a passing contrast between the "large symbolic figures" of the first and the "narrative style" of the others.[3] In the same manner, we might contrast the two sporting events reproduced on and by the 1958 stamps: the Thomas Cup, that the Indonesian Men's Badminton team won for the first time at the Triennial Championships held that year in Singapore (in 1961 they were held in Jakarta, in one of the first-completed buildings of the architectural complex built for the Fourth Asian Games: the stamp issued for this occasion featured not only the cup, but where it was won), and the first (and only) Tour de Java.

5.2.1 *Karunia Tuhan Jang Maha Esa*
Berkat Doa Restu Seluruh Bangsa

This formula of thanksgiving ("Thanks be to God and to the prayers of the whole nation"), inscribed on the 1964 stamp, presenting the Thomas Cup beribboned in the colors of Indonesia, confirms the competition as both liturgy and ordeal; the stamp is an *ex-voto* of the winning team, itself the image of and model for the "whole nation." When the stamp came out, like the final sky rocket of a fireworks display, it had been three months since the athletes who had won the Thomas Cup for the third time in a row had been officially received by the head of State and paraded triumphantly, like astronauts in other countries, through the streets of Jakarta lined with giant murals in preparation for the nineteenth anniversary of the *Panca Sila*.[4]

---

[2] I give the term "great tradition" the same general meaning as Robert Redfield in his *Peasant Society and Culture* (Chicago, 1956), ch. 3.

[3] René Crozet, *L'Art roman en France, bassin de la Loire et Ouest* (Paris, 1961), p. 22.

[4] See *Indonesia*, vol iv, pp. 117–23, chapter "World Champions Three Times Over" (*Indonesia* was published yearly, in English, as an international platform for the Indonesian Ministry of Foreign Affairs):

"[. . .] To the Republic of Indonesia, sports are a useful vehicle for building a nation out of a people oppressed for centuries.

In 1967 Indonesia became world champion for the fourth (and last) time in a row: while one of the stamps issued marks, with a drawing of the four cups, the rhythm and continuity of the victories, the other indicates the scope: the trophy is shown against a globe of the world—the sign of temporal but also royal power.

5.2.2 Because it was run from August 17 to 30, the 1958 Tour de Java was an extension of the National Independence celebrations; and it was even more of a celebration of national unity that year inasmuch as, in February, a rebel government had been proclaimed in Padang, backed by peripheral guerrillas in Sulawesi and Maluku.

And yet the maquettiste K.R. Suplanto (author of the Thomas Cup sets of 1958, 1961, and 1964) chose to devote the entire rectangle of the stamp to a map of Indonesia, and, using the French version, Tour de Java I 1958, superimposed a speeding racer, his bicycle astride the island of Java, which seems to be drawn on the plane the man is crossing (cf. pl. III).

This graphic solution begs the political question of Java's relationship to Indonesia—is it syntagmatic (Java as part of Indonesia and proposed as such) or paradigmatic (the part, Java, as a metaphor for the whole, Indonesia)—for it cannot in fact respond to the ambiguous meaning of a circuit.

Ambiguity both technical and political, then.

The Archipelago of a thousand islands is not a good candidate for a bicycle circuit, for the narrative continuity of a race. Moreover, as a survey of the domain, a tour of the possessions, which redistributes along the route the excitement elsewhere concentrated in stadiums, the Tour also traces the outline imposed by the course of the race, showing up the weaknesses and deficiencies, the clearings and routes to be opened if the whole Archipelago is to be encompassed: Java alone appears to be served. As the stamp shows, what is drawn as Indonesia, is restricted to what is called Java.

But to call Java by name in this way, whatever may be the meanings with which the sign Java is and will be invested, because at the same time attempts at establishing centrifugal poles—or even counter-centers—are going on in the periphery, is to formulate a doubly false statement which excludes the unstable periphery from the domain and recognizes its secession: it is a technical dodge which runs the risk of formulating a political defeat, whereas there is need both to display and to assert the totality and the center, the totality in its center.

5.2.3 The "sports" stamps for 1958 placed two things on trial, then: the Cup and the Tour, the first for the way it ended, the second for the way it was run; each had its own function, which, for the first, was to unveil the name, and the second, to unveil that which was

---

"Train for health, and the disciplines learnt will do much to withstand debilitating disease. Train in teams, and the team spirit will help contribute towards national unity. Train to struggle for victory and to take defeat as a call to further effort, and the sporting spirit will help the nation build resolution and resistance [...]"
On the same page (p. 118), is the photo of a mural devoted to badminton and the Thomas Cup with the caption:
"So important are sports considered for nation building and character building that a place was given to sports on the Panca Sila poster painted to honor the nineteenth anniversary of the birth of the philosophical basis of the State."
The publication's main byword, and consequently one of Indonesia's official slogans in 1964, was: "nation building and character building to consolidate independence" (p. 27).

Indonesian Postage Stamp 27

Plate I. Centenary of postage stamps in Indonesia, 1964 (maquette: Kartono).

A set of seven stamps evokes Indonesia's history, by means of the names of the successive States which named its territory: *Ned. Indië*; Japanese characters; *Repoeblik Indonesia*, in the Dutch spelling still in use during the "Physical Revolution"; *Indonesia*, as it was after the *Renville* agreements; *Republik Indonesia Serikat*, which came out of the Round-Table conference; and finally *Republik Indonesia*, the de-Netherlandization of the spelling of the primordial institution. The head of the Chief of State, symbol and upholder of the Constitution, on the last stamp, reinforces the identification of the stamp, on the occasion of this commemoration, with the State seal (which may also explain the frequent use of coats of arms as a motif: the transparent stamp gives way to the institution). The taxonomic role of the Constitution, as Kartono perceives it in his short history of the Indonesian postage stamp, as a witness to institutions, legitimates from within, as it were, the corpus used in this article: the stamps carrying the caption *Republik Indonesia*.

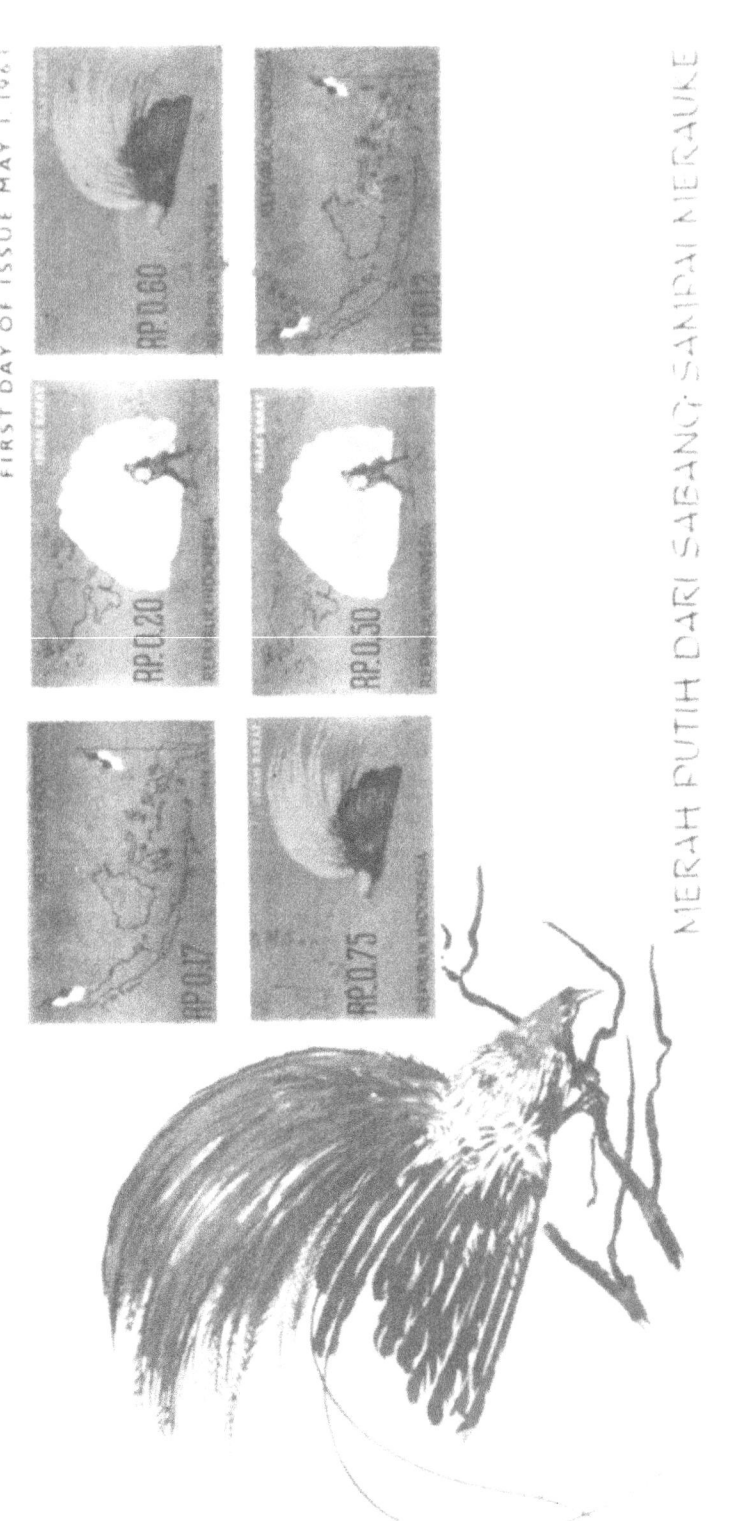

Plate II. First-day cover: on the occasion of Irian Barat's affiliation to the Indonesian Republic and the unification of Indonesia, from Sabang to Merauke, on May 1, 1963 (maquettes: Suroso).

The linguistic message on the envelope, "Merah Putih dari Sabang sampai Merauke," corresponds to the .12 and .17 rupiah stamps: the map of Indonesia with the red (*merah*) and white (*putih*) national flag at both the northwest (Sabang) and southeast (Merauke) ends. Irian, on the .60 and .75 rupiah stamps is designated by its map overprinted with a possibly totemic bird, the bird of paradise, the feathers of which were one of the forms of tribute most demanded from the peoples of Irian by the petty maritime rulers of the Moluccas; and its name (*Cendrawasih*) was taken by the newly established military command and by the University of the now Indonesian province, Irian Barat. History is actively present only on the .20 and .50 rupiah stamps, in the *center* of the system, thus both fiscally and ideologically joining the two ends: the Indonesian paratrooper *coming to the region*, giving the center back its periphery, a center therefore legitimated by its capacity for military intervention.

named. Identified in this way, the trials were not only concomitant, they were first and foremost complementary.

The outcome, that is the attribution of the prize, and its attribution to Indonesia, was attested by the issue of the stamp (had Indonesia not won, there would have been no stamp: it is not the playing that counts here, it is the winning); and by the ribbons in Indonesia's national colors that decorated the Cup at the award ceremonies, and which the stamp reproduces, thus confirming the holder's name. On the 1958 stamp, which kicked off the set, an Indonesian flag flies in the background and a bilingual inscription DJUARA DUNIA BULUTANGKIS / BADMINTON WORLD CHAMPION underscores the proclamation.

Whether it be flags, sashes, or ribbons, the Indonesian national colors figure so rarely on stamps that their presence has a discriminatory value. Outside the context of the Thomas Cup, they appear only twice: once in 1963 on one of the stamps saluting Irian Barat's incorporation into Indonesia (see pl. II), and again in 1965, in the *Panca Sila* set, on the *Kebangsaan* stamp; both times they have a direct, figurative relation with the establishment of national identity through territorial integrity, the extension of Indonesian power to the whole territory of the former Dutch Indies.

The beribboned cup, object and sign of victory belonging to the winner alone, functions on its own level as an insignia and an attribute of Indonesian power.

Figure 4. The search for identity. Flag and national territory in their respective contexts (for the reproduction of the stamps mentioned, see pl. III).

The diagram is constructed around a double set of entries (the key-words: flag and national territory) while retaining significant secondary entries (as tools for covering the territory). Each stamp is designated by a rectangle indicating the object of the commemoration (these are all commemorative stamps) and the date of issue.

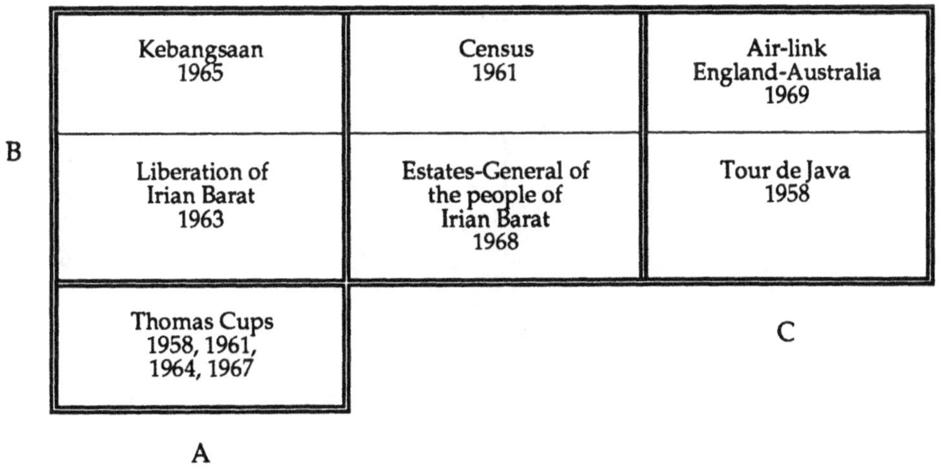

B	Kebangsaan 1965	Census 1961	Air-link England-Australia 1969
	Liberation of Irian Barat 1963	Estates-General of the people of Irian Barat 1968	Tour de Java 1958
	Thomas Cups 1958, 1961, 1964, 1967		C
	A		

Key: A Presence of Indonesian flag (ribbon, sash, etc.)
      B Map of Indonesia on part of all of the stamp
      C Presence of a means of transportation

NB: The stamp issued in Irian Barat in 1968, which figures here, was not circulated in the rest of Indonesia; it is therefore not included in the graphs of figure 1. Note the cluster constructed around the key-word Irian Barat and the possible semantic link between *Kebangsaan* and Population census, which by the *name* and the space occupied guarantee the force of *numbers*. It should also be noted that the limited field analyzed here is just one of the many intersections of the several groups indicated by figure 1 as a working hypothesis ("politics," "social work," "sports," "communication").

30 Jacques Leclerc

Plate III. Flag and national territory (cf. figs 4 and 5)

For technical reasons, we have also reproduced the stamps which repeat or in some way carry on the biplane/Borobudur theme (cf. 5.3.2), by using, as a symbol for Indonesia, *Garuda*, Vishnu's eagle, which stands for both speed (*Postkilat*: express; *kilat*: lightning) and development (the Indonesian pavilion at the Osaka exposition). *Garuda* is also the name of Indonesia's national air transport company and a basic component of the State arms, as they figure, for instance, on the stamp issued August 17, 1950 (cf. 4.1.1).

Indonesian Postage Stamp 31

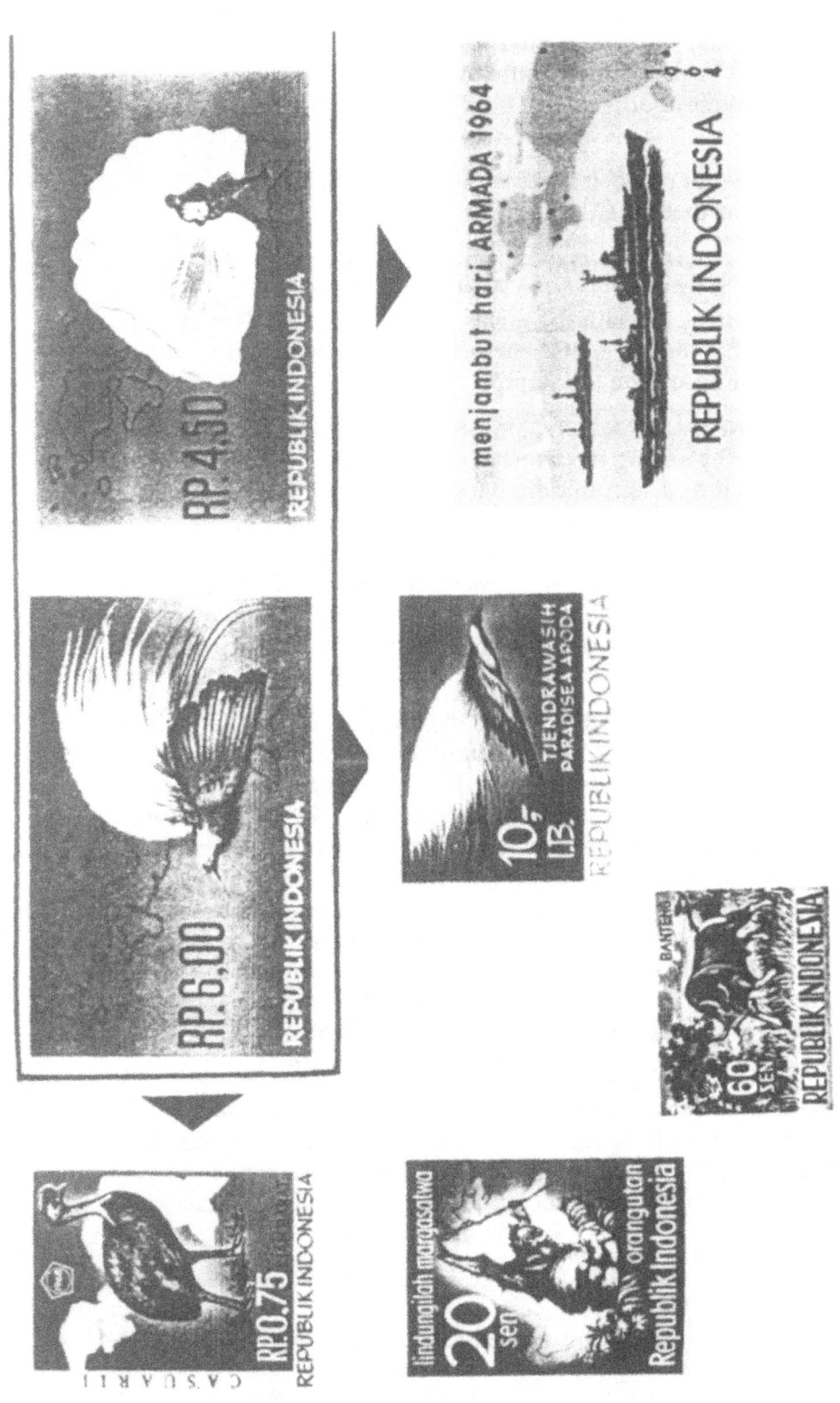

Plate IV. Bird and Paratrooper in the 1963 "Irian" set.

Plate III sought out the isolated elements—map of Indonesia, national flag—that had been grouped on one of the stamps shown on plate II. Here we take a closer look at the field and the formal components of the two other stamps in the set. If the paratrooper gives rise to the 1964 stamp that associates the navy (*Hari Armada*: Fleet Day) with him, in the struggle to recover Irian, the territory/"totemic" bird system featured on the last stamp fits into a circuit of symbolization–desymbolization—announced here first of all by two stamps that appeared only on Irian: the one isolates the bird; the other takes over the map as the geographic and non-historical location of another bird (the cassowary: the complete set presents, against a background map, four different plants and four animals); the animals pictured against their background map bring us back to a set, *Lindungilah Margasatwa* (Protect Wildlife), issued in 1958 (cf. fig 10), which, if the geographic indication is removed, brings us back to the 1956 *Khewan* (Wild animal) set, into which the above-mentioned isolated bird of paradise, also fits. From the *Khewan* set we have chosen the *banteng* to illustrate the desymbolization of an animal highly charged with national symbolism (shown holding the Indonesian flag on the first stamp of *Repoeblik Indonesia* in 1945; the head of the *banteng* on Indonesia's coat of arms, and thereby on the stamps patterned on it, indicates the *Sila Kedaulatan Rakyat* (sovereignty of the people).

32   *Jacques Leclerc*

The 1963 and 1965 configurations[5] combine the colors of the map of Indonesia with the name of the territory it names: flags raised at Sabang and Merauke in 1963, a sash delineating the space already indicated, in 1958, with respect to the Tour de Java, a trial run that turns into a perpetual-motion circuit broken only by human time, the course and the wheel, a course which imposes upon the image another actor, the cyclist, the worker, the man (fig.4).

What counts, then, is not a winner or a cup, it is the race and those who run it, who identify it, giving its land in the name that the Cup has pronounced.

5.3   Is the 1969 stamp, with its map of Indonesia overprinted with the biplane in which Rose and Smith made their 1919 flight from England to Australia, a double of the Tour de Java? But, for these aviators, the territory beneath them was the Dutch East Indies, and it was their eyes—and theirs alone—that measured its spaces, and it was their flight that went down in history, and their story that figures on the stamp.

5.3.1   The inscription 50 TAHUN PENERBANGAN PERTAMA INGGRIS INDONESIA AUSTRALIA 1919–1969 emphasizes INDONESIA by setting the word in a larger type size than the rest, thereby creating a redundancy with the background map (see pl. III). But Indonesia's role in the event was limited to providing a fleeting stopover (like colonization, the English plane stopped only to refuel), a result not of its history but of its geographical location; the landfall is purely an object, and doubly so, since it is Indonesia only for the author of the stamp and his contemporaries. The stamp issues an invitation to a retrospective celebration; this is the Visitation, the allegory of Indonesia touched by the grace of Aviation, the intoxication of a desire and the revelation of a promise.

While the Tour de Java circumscribed a dwelling place, the England–Australia flight indicated a passage, a channel. Antithesis: the bicycle was a point on the circuit that was Indonesia, Indonesia was a point on the route of the plane; from the discovery of the national space to the discovery of the wide world, if the traveler was from here. The Jatiluhur relay station, too, was a point in space, inaugurated the same day as the issue of its commemorative stamp, on September 29, 1969: President Suharto opened the satellite communications station (cf. fig. 5) by calling Indonesia's ambassadors in Washington, London, and Tokyo— America, Europe, and Asia—the entire world, but not just any place there,[6] this was the triangulation of financial capitals for which Indonesia represented a well-placed investment. Representing a transition, perhaps, from politics to economics, the PELITA set (PELITA means lamp, but is also the acronym for *Pembangunan Lima Tahun* —the five-year development plan just launched), issued on August 17, 1969, defines the coordinates.

5.3.2   But two stamps are devoted to the 50th anniversary of the England–Australia flight. On the second, the biplane is passing over Borobudur, which is pictured as being identical with Indonesia, an identification already established (see 5.1) on the 1951 stamps announcing the first Asian Games, if not an arbitrary choice, at least a product of chance. Borobudur,

---

[5] In the sense of a montage of figures in one technically and culturally defined place, in this case the stamp (cf. Pierre Francastel, *La figure et le lieu* [Paris, 1967], p. 347).

[6] *Indonesia Magazine*, a show-case semi-official bilingual publication aimed at a foreign audience, devoted pages 2 and 3 to pictures of the station's parabolic antenna and the President on the telephone; the second issue (1970) showed a picture of the antenna with the following caption: *Antene stasiun satelit bumi di Jatiluhur. Proyek komunikasi yang dapat menghubungkan Indonesia dengan Washington, London dan Tokyo melalui satelit Intelstat III telah diresmikan pemakaiannya oleh Presiden Suharto pada 29 September tahun yang lalu* (p. 28).

Figure 5. Space, image and relational function. Confrontation of stamps signalling mobility and immobility. The prestige of power and the power of prestige (the dates are issue dates).

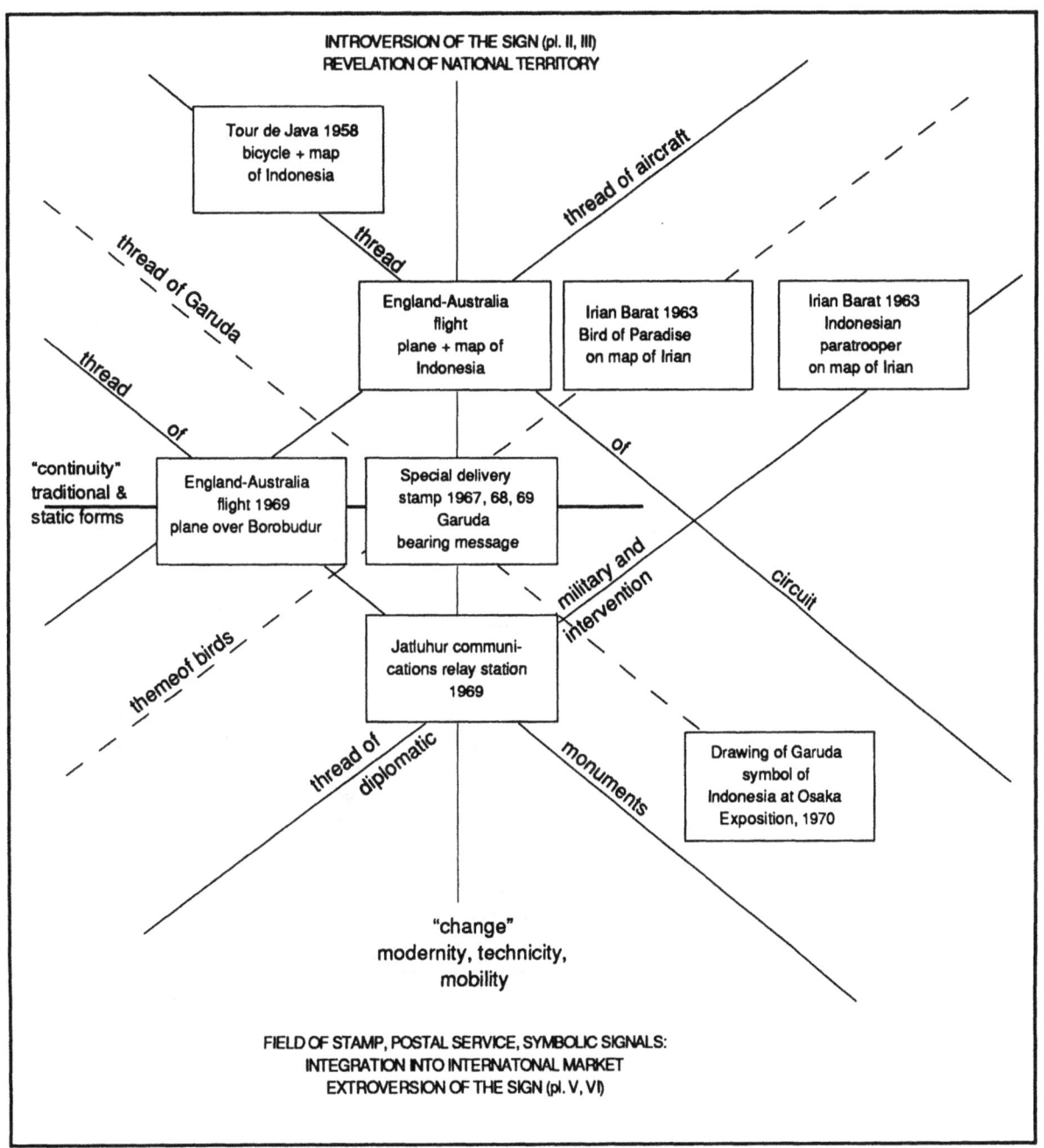

Figure 6. National, political, and technical identity, after the stamp "50th Anniversary of the England-Australia air-link," showing the biplane flying over Borobudur (maquette: Suwarsono, 1969; see pl. III)

"Enclosed in being, one must always issue forth. Hardly has one come forth from being, than it is time to return. And so, within being, all is a circuit, all is circuitous, full circle, locution, circumlocution, stays, delays; all is a refrain of couplets without end." (Gaston Bachelard, *La Poétique de l'espace* [Paris, 1957], p. 193).

INSIDE	OUTSIDE
historical time	dilution of the territory
circle of the political space	periphery
dynastic culture	trajectory
the mountain	the cloud

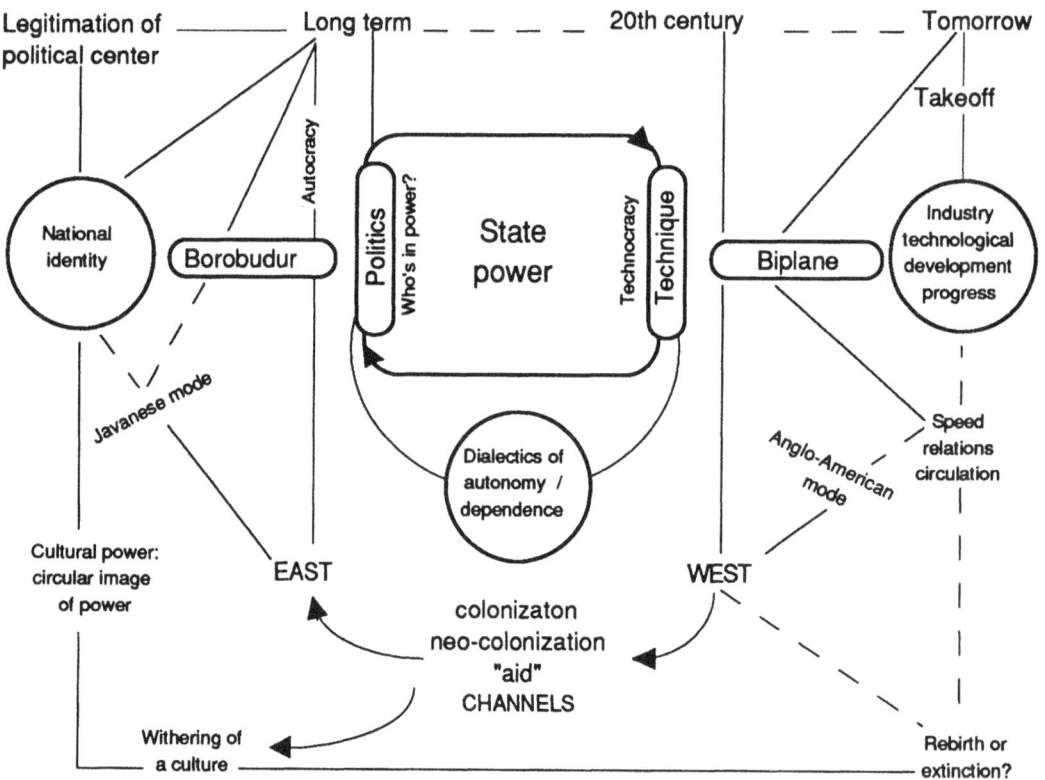

which identifies Indonesia by its central monument[7] and its relationships with ancestors and dynasty gods, opposes the verticality of one tradition, singled out because of its architectural visibility, with the "biplane," sign of the relation with others in the horizontality of contemporary life. But also the vertical plane in which is inscribed the curve of the takeoff, the line of development traced by its own product, the "figure of an arrow" working, as Bachelard says,[8] "in harmony with the imagination of dynamicity,"[9] put into accord with the finite ground which the shores of memory mark off with the surveyor's measure.

Is there no escaping Borobudur?

The rock rooted to the ground, clinging to the earth like a child to the breast, like a breast to the mother, the sacred weight of rural sedentary habits, a concentric blueprint organizing and closing forever the space and its history, the hieroglyph of power. To the Westerner who has exhumed it from its millenial ruins, Borobudur is a mirror into which the Occident looks and recognizes its own Orient, seizes its soaring reflection, the desirable object of a dream-Occident, mechanical and fluid: a transfer of Othernesses.

But what was the circuit constructed by this external gaze? Inner space, ceremony, and ritual, as an alienated spectacle, was soon no more than a commodity on which the plane unleashed its antique dealers.[10] Singled out in this way, for the unique Other, as venal

---

[7] The identification of Borobudur with Indonesia, which calls up the Java/Indonesia relation on the 1958 Tour de Java stamp, is not self-evident: it implies choosing among the *pusaka*, the inheritance in which law is grounded, the choice that asserts or confirms (this is not the place to discuss the matter) the preeminence of the Javanese states over the other historical states of the Archipelago as builders *of its* unity, and singles out the Hindu-Buddhist culture as being most representative of the country (whence certain centrifugal reactions, in activist Muslim circles, against a certain political élite's "modjopaïtisme," which they denounce as an archaic relic of the dominating bureaucracy of these former states (cf. Kahar Muzakar's article cited by H. Feith and L. Castles in *Indonesian Political Thinking, 1945–1965* [Ithaca, 1970], p. 330). None of the stamps issued between 1945 and 1950, during the "Physical Revolution," a period of intense national demands, carries a picture of Borobudur, the symbolism of which appears to be more a function of the interest on the part of representatives of Western culture operating in Indonesia, that is, introducing de facto international recognition of the country. Curiously enough, the exhibition, "Indonesian Art," organized by the Amsterdam Museum of the Tropics, then the Museum of the Indies, at the Chicago Institute of Art in the spring of 1949, presents, out of a catalogue of 686 items, 218 objects from Sumatra-Nias and only 213 from Java-Bali (and 73 from Irian Barat, which no one at the time dreamed of excluding from Indonesia: the police had just carried out their second operation, and the Netherlands were no doubt still on the defensive), while nearly all later catalogues and art books concentrate on Java-Bali (we know that the Round-Table agreements, signed in the last days of 1949, reduced the Republic of Indonesia to precisely the region of Borobudur, in other words, roughly the eastern half of Java and the area west of Sumatra); not only works entitled "Ancient Indonesian Art"—those by Bernet Kempers (Amsterdam, 1959) or the one by J. Fontein, R. Soekmono, S. Suleiman (New York, 1971), which carries the subtitle "of the Central and Eastern Javanese Periods"—but also those taking in the whole formal and temporal scope of Indonesian art—F. Wagner, *L'Art d'un archipel* (Paris, 1961), 40 photos for Java-Bali, 23 for the rest of the archipelago; C. Holt, *Art in Indonesia* (Ithaca, 1967), out of 150 illustrations, only 25 outside Java-Bali; only the recent work by Tibor Bodrogi, perhaps both because it was commissioned by UNESCO and because it was written by a specialist on Oceania, devotes only 77, out of 188, illustrations to Java-Bali (*L'Art de l'Indonésie*, [Budapest, 1972]).

[8] *La Poétique de l'espace* (Paris, 1957), p. 212.

[9] The signal of the arrow appeared twice on stamps in 1970, "The Year of Productivity," and figures again in the shape of upward curving half-circles on one stamp in the PELITA series already mentioned; it also informs the "obelisk" signs (cf. pl. VII); the "thread of the airplane" mentioned in figure 5, for which the arrow is one possible metaphor, occurs frequently, especially in 1958 and 1967 (Aviation Days); cf. fig. 1, graph E/e and its explanation.

[10] "Visit the Orient Year" (1961 set, including a view of Borobudur).

Figure 7. National holidays and commemorative issues (cf. 4.1.1)

Four commemorations are considered here, the most important being that of the Proclamation of Independence, August 17, then *Hari Pahlawan*, November 10 (1961 and 1962: *Pahlawan Kemerdekaan* stamps; 1963: the GANEFO set; 1966: the dead of October 1, 1965), October 5, "Army Day," which in 1961 and 1962 is marked by stamps in the *Pahlawan Kemerdekaan* set, and in 1964 by a set in honor of the war fleet (cf. pl. IV); May 20, the anniversary of the foundation of the *Budi Utomo* movement which does not appear until 1962, for the presentation of the National Monument. The use of stamps for commemoration is remarkably regular from 1959 to 1967, which roughly corresponds to the period of Guided Democracy.

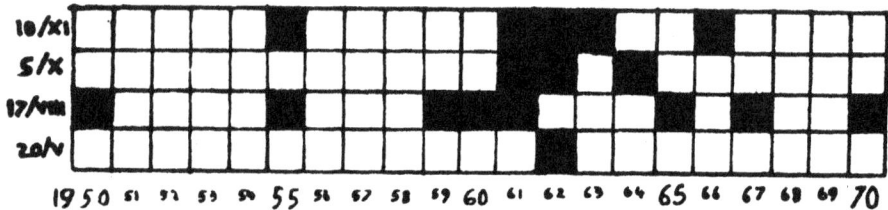

curiosity, long inaudible at this price, Borobudur died a shoddy death, unless it died simply from being reborn, from returning, with no power, to a land with no means.[11]

5.3.3 From piecing together the terms of the dilemma, no more could be learned about relationships than from such titles as *Tradition and Modernity* or *Continuity and Change*, Anglo-American sociological treatises on transition. Contradiction or filiation, confrontation or coexistence, domination or cooperation, internal or external factors, all combinations are (apparently) allowed.

Correlations there have been between within and without, center and fringe, point and expanse, planet and satellite, immobility and movement, stagnation and development, the lasting and the passing, continuity and break, but for all that, the image has not indicated any choice among these impassive terms of a debate which, already in the 1930s, divided the *Pudjangga Baru* contributors over the question of Indonesian culture: a correlation founded on a figurative reduction of history to objects of worship, monument-moments in a civilization that brought them forth, convergences of both a host of types of knowledge and of techniques, crystallization of the meticulous work of thousands of engineers and laborers, would-be instruments of domination and prestige of the caste or class that lays hold of them for its own glory when it incorporates this into the history of a flight, a flight above history, simply dissimulating behind the unformulated invasive thrust of desire the only question, the twofold question: who is at the controls, and where is he heading?

5.4 The 1962 Asian Games precipitated the largest issue of stamps of the 1950s and 1960s, in terms of the variety of images diffused, twenty-one in all: the run up, publicity drives, one of the public works that accompany, underwrite, and qualify the organization of Olympic encounters, some of which are featured on the stamps themselves.

5.4.1 In a certain sense, the Indonesian stamp missed out on Bandung. The greatest international event in the 20th century history of the Archipelago produced, in 1955, four values for one small stamp, whose discretion, moreover, corresponded with that of the other

---

[11] The "Save Borobudur Monument" set (1968) in connection with the restoration campaign launched by UNESCO. The linguistic message on this set of stamps is in English only.

stamps issued at the time. In 1962, the Games, as an international manifestation on the scale of the Asian Continent, demanded—this was a new international recognition of Indonesia, where they were to be held—that, in return, Indonesia confirm its legitimacy. This was not a mere Badminton World Championship, hosted by Jakarta, as the previous year; this was a gigantic system of *qualification*, of which the selection of Indonesia as host was only the first stage. The Games, a civic celebration, a placement examination, were continued in the very welcome extended: stamps were one of the most flexible and colorful instruments. And in fact the progress of the Games through qualification and elimination, made them symbolically more significant than the Bandung Conference, for the functional reality of the Games and their organization, like that of all ceremonies, is purely symbolic.

As what was important in the philatelic celebration of the Badminton Championships was Indonesia's victory; what was important in 1962 was Indonesia's qualifying as the very locus of the championship of championships: the nation proved itself to itself by proving itself, by carrying out its function of host, to all the other nations. On every level the championship, a tournament system, a system of binary oppositions finally established Indonesia as a discrete whole that could be seen and identified, taking an active and willing hand in its own identification and, in so doing, fashioning its own identity.

5.4.2 That is a very different qualification from the also internationally acknowledged one illustrated by Borobudur: the history that produced Borobudur also gave the archer his place of honor among the first stamps introducing the Games (see above 5.1), but this piece of history needs to be recaptured; of this recapture, the Games were a sign grounded in experience. As an international competition, they were an abridged version of the nation's history, a metaphor of survival and the struggle for life, the inexorable parade of challenges continuously to be accepted in order first to assert and then to fortify the nation's attitude toward challenge, as the principle of sovereignty, the act that names Indonesia the subject of its history, a history of effort, presence, and communication.

5.4.3 But exactly what kind of communication and, in the end, what kind of sovereignty? It was not Indonesia that did the choosing, it was the International Olympic Committee that decided the teams Indonesia was to host. Were Indonesia to refuse to receive the bad sports, Israel or Taiwan, the IOC would immediately withdraw its accreditation. Whence came the defiant GANEFO (Games of the New Emerging Forces): Indonesia decreed who and when. Who? The criterion was not gymnastic activity but political solidarity, without which the sports were mere amusement and Bandung a dead letter: bring together birds of a feather, as it were, so that the competition might be truly peaceful and the challenge of the Games a new type of communication. When? The 10th of November "Heroes' Day" (see explanation pl. VIII), celebrating the pioneers of Independence. Because the games were a fight, there was no question of fighting indiscriminately friends and enemies; and if fighting was a game, then let friends play together to fight the enemy, by isolating him. The November 10, 1963 issue of a set of eight stamps devoted to the GANEFO, seems modest enough: the Asian Games had given rise to 24. But it was no doubt of no use once more to describe the various sports on the program, for that was not the meaning of the event: the parading of the GANEFO banners, a show of group exercises (no struggle but the discipline of one movement, performed in unison), and the symbols: the official badge and the motto launched by Sukarno, *Ever onward, no retreat*, and the Olympic flame, which is not the exclusive property of the IOC, which takes its place beside the flame of the National Monument (pl. VI), axis and growth of Indonesia—civic education covers physical education, rejecting the purely technical and technocratic conception of the heirs of English leisure.

Plate V. Recipient, welcome, gathering: games and urbanism; importance of the hotel, the official guest room of a State that can choose its friends and issue invitations—sign of sovereignty (cf. 5.1, 5.4, 6).

Plate VI. The beacon and the center: the National Monument, obelisk and flame, like a figure of *paku alam*, *paku buana* ("nail of the universe," royal titles in Central Java); the open arms, sign of freedom and welcome (*selamat datang*), which parallels the obelisk; the Jatiluhur antenna, a kind of synthesis of the cloverleaf as a traffic regulator, of the stadium as a parabolic form, of the minaret and the obelisk (pointing skyward), open like the arms of the statue, oversignified by its technological prestige (but eccentric—we are 100 km from Jakarta—and having the inverse function, cf. 5.3.1).

40 *Jacques Leclerc*

When, in 1968, the Indonesian postal service first mentioned the Olympic Games, then being held far from Indonesia in Mexico, it was done by the graphic decomposition of a movement (weight lifting, a basketball player shooting a basket, a sail boat leaving the starting line), the space of a movement encompassed in the space of a stamp. The world was at last called by its name, but it was a mere student drawing.

6 Inscribing the Center (see pl. V and VI)

6.1 The building, organization chart/maquette of the city/society, by its manifestly visible physical solidity, settles down complete with privilege in the desire of the power for idealization/ monumentalization, political stability and historical memory, and the permanence of its identity/identification.

6.2 Jakarta's public works projects, samples of which were featured mainly in the sets issued for the Asian Games and GANEFO: cloverleaf, stadium, conference hall, press center, hotel, all organize a passageway, a space for receiving, gathering, informing, marked out by statues, obelisks, spouting fountains. The outline of the center.

6.3 Public buildings, which does not mean administration buildings.

As far as the administration is concerned, little more had appeared on stamps, from 1953, than the post's own issuing center, the Bandung headquarters of Post and Telecommunications; and what was first featured of the Bank of Indonesia's headquarters in Jakarta, in 1963, were the fountains. The public authorities and administrations are designated by the mark of their authenticity: not their headquarters, but their official seals. The face of the administration is its coat of arms; big buildings are something else again.

6.4 Take, for instance, the case of hotels. The maquette of the *Hotel Indonesia* (Jakarta) appeared in the "Asian Games" set; in 1965, a set entitled "Hotels" featured two maquettes: *Samudra Beach Hotel* (*Pelabuhan Ratu*) and *Ambarrukmo Palace Hotel* (Yogyakarta); half the stamp is occupied by the head of Sukarno. In 1969, the set devoted to "Tourism," issued yearly since 1967, shows various features of Bali; in this case, half of each stamp is taken up by a map of the island on the southeast point of which is located its emblem, a copy of that of the *Hotel Indonesia*,[12] the international hotel that had just been completed. The configuration, as well as the iconic context of each of these sets—1962, 1965, 1969—obliterates any semantic convergence there may have been, but traces an itinerary of meaning.

The only link, in the list of hotels published on stamps, between the *Samudra Beach Hotel*, on the southwest coast of Java, practically equidistant from Jakarta and Bandung—the capital and its twin—and the *Ambarrukmo Hotel* in Yogyakarta—capital of the anti-Dutch resistance movement—is the existence of a legend, a myth relating the founding and the transmission of power, the legend of the Queen of the South (*Roro Kidul*), to whom the beach belongs (*Pelabuhan Ratu*, the Queen's port), the regular renewal of the alliance[13] which

---

[12] This emblem was featured on a stamp issued in 1972 for the tenth anniversary of the *Hotel Indonesia*. There is a semantic identity between the Balinese hotel shown in 1969 and the Jakarta hotel as perceived in 1972.

[13] On the ritual of alliance at the court of Pakubuwono, another of Mataram's heirs, in Surakarta, see K.G.P.H. Hadiwidjojo, "Danse sacrée à Surakarta," *Archipel*, n° 3, p. 117. The 1965 stamps fall outside the myth: two are greenish in color, whereas green, the color of the sea, is unfavorable for alliances. Or, in view of the issue date figuring in big numbers on the stamp, December 1965, might it not also be a way of asserting that, however dramatic the events rocking the country may be, Sukarno is still the founder and architect of the nation's stability. Or even to remind Sultan Hamengkubuwono of Yogyakarta, Sukarno's most constant and serious political enemy, that then, as always, the appanage of Yogyakarta is part of the Indonesian Republic and not the contrary.

Plate VII. Blazoning and un-blazoning: *padi-kapas* and building (cf. 4.2)

The trend toward the use of coats of arms appears as a figurative practice, the instituted or, better, institutional vocation of which is the assertion and recognition of identity (cf. "Signes de reconnaissance," Pierre Francastel's preface to the catalogue of the exhibit *Emblèmes, totems, blasons* (Musée Guimet, Paris, 1964) and Georges Mounin's criticism in "Le Blason," *Introduction à la Sémiologie* (Paris, 1970). The stamp reveals this vocation either by repeating an external, already established coat of arms (cf. pl. I) or by organizing itself as an insignia by regrouping elements that are identifiable as possible armorial features. The *padi-kapas* combination seems to be one of the first constant, isolable discrete units of a nascent heraldic code. But context can also disfigure the emblem and give it a new meaning. Here another configuration, *dwiwindu kemerdekaan* (cf. 4.1.3) has been added to the examples using *padi-kapas*.

42 *Jacques Leclerc*

Plate VIII. Reproduction of the *Pahlawan Kemerdekaan* brochure cover.

This is a 36-page brochure measuring 24 x 34 cm, written by Nasrun A.S. and D.P. Sati Alim, illustrated by I.T.Man, Ismail Usman and Agus Gardjito, at the request of the Ministry of Information. The preface is dated *Djakarta, 10 Nopember 1953*, establishing the publication as a contribution to the celebration of Heroes' Day (*Hari Pahlawan*), which commemorates every November 10 the resistance, in October-November 1945, of the population of Surabaya, to the British occupation of the city. Using a simple narrative underpinned by large illustrated blocks, the authors evoke the struggle of 17 figures against the Dutch occupation: each character, in alphabetical order, is given two pages. The cover, reproduced here, presents a group portrait (see key below):

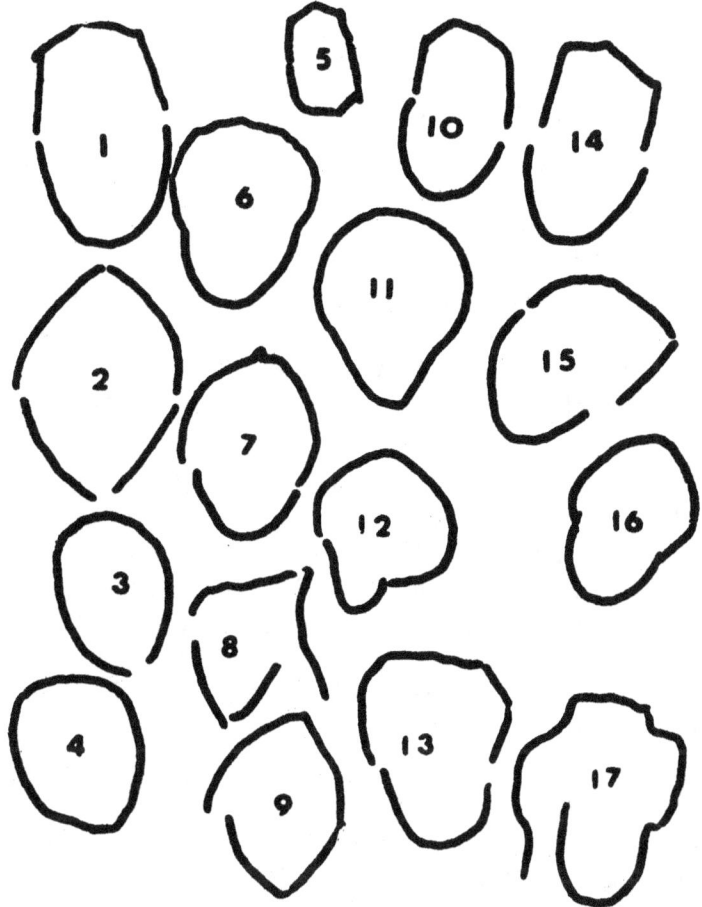

1. M.H. Thamrin; 2. Tjipto Mangunkusumo; 3. G.S.S.J. Ratulangie; 4. R.A. Kartini; 5. Sudirman; 6. Pattimura; 7. Wahidin Sudirohusodo; 8. Sultan Hasanuddin; 9. H.O.S. Tjokroaminoto; 10. W.R. Supratman; 11. K.H. Ahmad Dahlan; 12. Imam Bondjol; 13. Pangeran Hidajat; 14. Setiabudhi (E. Douwes Dekker); 15. Pangeran Diponegoro; 16. R. Sutomo; 17. Thji' di Tiro.

The brochure directly influenced the program of the set also entitled *Pahlawan Kemerdekaan*, which appeared in 1961 and 1962. Of 12 stamps issued in 1961, 8 featured figures commemorated in 1953, *using identical portraits*; the other 4 are in memory of, on the one hand, political figures who died *after* 1953—Abdul Muis, Surjopranoto, and Ki Hadjar Dewantoro (who all died in 1959); on the other, Teuku Umar, a late 19th-century war leader from Aceh. As for the 8 stamps issued in 1962, 5 of the names illustrated had also appeared in 1953, but only Setaiabudhi's portrait is taken from the same source; the portraits of Agus Salim (died 1954), Samanhudi (died 1956), and Singamangaradja (19th century) have been added. Perhaps the four public figures featured in 1953 and dropped from the release program (Hidajat, Supratman, Tjipto, Wahidin) were reserved for a later issue that did not come about (cf. 12 stamps in 1961 and only 8 in 1962). As far as Tjipto is concerned, see 7.3.

legitimates the Javanese Mataram dynasty, whose princely families in Yogyakarta are among the heirs. Sukarno's presence is meant, then, to attach to the person of the head of State the legitimating network that the capacity for founding the signal that reveals it centralizes, in the last instance, in Jakarta. The aim, then, is to inscribe the center, its genealogy and its space, the sovereign and his sovereignty.

Nothing remains of the problematic of the State by the time the "Tourism" sets are issued: tourism as a technique for financing without political intent, without political pedagogy, using the symbolic arrangement of the territory.

6.5 The arms are outstretched; the hands open; the chains that had bound the hands and feet, broken: TUGU SELAMAT DATANG and TUGU IRIAN BARAT echo each other, welcoming those who free themselves, and welcoming those who come, when it is to help us in our struggle for national unification. The couple from the Selamat Datang group of the 1962 Monuments set is greeting the newly arrived guests and, as masters of the house, showing them around the recent improvements in their domain. But, every bit as much as the city, the couple closes the space of time that the archer, like his arrow, had sent flying over the centuries, closing an era of dispossession and renewing the ties between history and the world.

6.6 In the wake of the ongoing public works program in Jakarta, meeting places and signals of dynamism suddenly appear in the space of the stamp, and the Asian Games and GANEFO themselves convoke them, outside and inside, concentration and expression, and the National Monument diffuses their dialectic. A pictoral sign of this relationship, the stamp is inserted into the horizontal thread of the postal network that was to cover the open, many-faceted country, scaling down the center and its monumental axis, the signals that crisscross the cardinal space of the new-world capital, a round trip from the symbolic to the non-symbolic, a representative system.

The mosque, stadium, and hotel, all center monuments, organize the function of a capital, which is not the sovereign's place of residence but the place from which sovereignty is exercised, the measure of the domain and the gathered nation, fragmentation of the palace, ultimate subversion of Borobudur, the public locus of the demonstrations, meetings, and deliberations, the people's ticket to history because it is there that it can be seen, there that others come to see it, and there that the people can receive. A call to rise up, in the civic center, where the festival of nations unfolds.

7 Inventing Time (see pl.VIII)

7.1 It was for *dwiwindu kemerdekaan* (see above 4.1.3) that the first portion (4 figures) of a set devoted to "Heroes of National Independence": *Pahlawan Kemerdekaan Nasional)* was published; the second installment was issued the following October 5 (Army Day, one of the major national holidays); the third was issued November 10, *Hari Pahlawan*; the fourth, October 5, 1962; the fifth followed on November 10; making, for 1961–62, a collection of twenty public figures. The set was then suspended for what were most likely political reasons; in 1969 it seemed to reappear in a new form (different format, different maquettiste, same face value for all stamps, no connection with national holidays), but this issue of six figures was short lived.

7.2 Until then there had been few heads: two in all, the chief of State and, for the tenth anniversary of the postal service, its first director. But in 1953, we can see the beginnings of a filiation; *satriya*, the nobleman, the knight, figured on a set of standard values issued in January, and ten years after the battle of Surabaya, a homage to those who died, a cenotaph inscribed with HARI PAHLAWAN 10 NOP. 1955. History was no longer anonymous, but these were special selections.[14]

7.3 Two groups of fighters can be read from these issues: on the one hand, those who struggled against colonial expansion from the 17th to the beginning of the 20th century and, on the other, the public figures who, for one reason or another, took part in the national liberation movement proper, after the beginning of the century (see fig. 8–9). If we compare the names on the 1961–62 stamps with those found in various popularized texts or summaries of Indonesian history, we might well wonder if we are not dealing with a closed list, set in its finitude to balance the regions with a view to highlighting the role played by all the peoples of Indonesia, each in its own time, in building the nation.[15]

Of the 13 public figures of the second group featured in 1961–62, 10 are from Java (1 *Indo*, 1 Jakartanese, 8 Javanese *stricto sensu*), 2 from Sumatra (Minangkabau), 1 from Sulawesi (Minahasa); 6 can be said to represent the Muslim branch of the national movement (5 for Sarekat Islam, 1 for Muhammadyah), 5 illustrate other national movement tendencies: Setiabudhi (the name later taken by E. Douwes Dekker) and Ki Hadjar Dewantoro (formerly Suwardi Suryaningrat) for the Indian National Party—but Ki Hadjar is better known as the founder of the school system Taman Siswa; Sutomo, Ratulangie, and Thamrin, for the initially regional associations which after 1935 became the Party of Greater Indonesia (Parindra). In a class apart are Kartini, as lone woman of the set and *the* tutelary figure of Indonesia's feminist movement, and Sudirman, organizer of the Indonesian army, who carries on the tradition of featuring war leaders—picked up once again in the 1969 set with the head of General Gatot Subroto. This selection leaves out figures from the lower classes (e.g. Samin), admitting only representatives of the aristocratic levels of colonial society, heirs to the former principalities or former states, traditional or religious leaders, traditional local dignitaries turned senior civil servants, guardians of an ancestral legitimacy that must be maintained or recovered, representatives of the durability of the Indonesian State through all the vicissitudes of history. That is probably why no leader of any insurrection, such as the national uprising of 1926–27—because such movements demand a new State, a State for the people and not for former princes or new dignitaries—is found in this State Gallery, nor any of those who, even though historically linked with the demands of the dispossessed elites, looked favorably on popular demonstrations: Tjipto Mangunkusumo, for instance, is not among the figures, even if he is generally recognized as one of the fathers of the national movement, of the National Party, inseparable from Setiabudhi and Ki Hadjar:[16] an absence

---

[14] It would be interesting to compare this selection with the nomenclature of the streets of Jakarta since 1950: the central figures of political time as they stand in the central figure of political space, i.e. the *center* as it is drawn by the governing circles of Indonesia.

[15] The leaflet *Indonesia*, distributed in 1971 by the Indonesian Embassy in France, reads: "Among the Indonesian patriots who opposed and fought the Dutch, we can mention: Thomas Matulessy (Pattimura, Moluccan uprising 1916–18), Pangeran Diponegoro (Java War 1825–30), Tjik di Tiro, Teuku Umar (Aceh War 1873–1903), Tuanku Imam Bondjol (Padri War in West Sumatra 1830–37), Si Singamangaradja (Batak War 1907.)" All these characters were featured on stamps and all were listed—with one or two exceptions—in other widely distributed brochures (see pl. VIII). This political concern with regional balance does not exclude denouncing either Javanese domination (it was claimed, for example by Kahar Muzakar, see above note 7, that the choice deliberately passed over important figures of other islands) or the use of these figures to denature the true meaning of their fight, which was not a fight for Indonesia (the thesis of advocates of the Republic of the South Moluccas, for example; cf. J.A.Manusama, *The South Moluccas, Rebellious Province or Occupied State* [Leiden, 1960]).

[16] Adopting Sukarno's thesis on the *tritunggal* constituting Indonesian unity, Ruslan Abdulgani, as early as 1952 (see *Basic Information on Indonesia* [Jakarta: Ministry of Information, 1953], the same year, then, as the brochure shown in pl.VIII) and, once again, Sajuti Melik in 1963 (see *Indonesian Political Thinking*, p. 372), indicate Tjipto as

Figure 8. *Pahlawan Kemerdekaan*, 1961-62 (cf. pl. VIII and ch. 7)

	Face value	Public figures featured			
		Name	Official dates of birth and death	Ethnic group	Political group
1961-62 maquettes by Much.Gozjali	0.20 0.25 0.30 0.40 0.50 0.60 0.75 1.00 1.25 1.50 2.00 2.50 3.00 4.00 4.50 5.00 6.00 7.50 10.00 15.00	Abdul Muis *Hasanuddin* Surjopranoto *T.Tjhik di Tiro* *T.Umar* Samanhudi *Pattimura* Kartini A.Dahlan *Imam Bondjol* *Singaman-garadja* M.H.Thamrin Dewantoro Gen.Sudirman G.S.S.J. Ratulangie *Diponegoro* Setiabudhi Tjokroaminoto Agus Salim Sutomo	1886-1959 1631-1669 1872-1959 1831-1891 1840-1899 1868-1956 1782-1817 1879-1904 1868-1923 1772-1864 1846-1907 1894-1941 1889-1959 1912-1950 1891-1949 1785-1855 1879-1950 1883-1934 1884-1954 1888-1938	Minang Bugis Java Aceh Aceh Java Maluku Java Java Minang Batak Jakarta Java Java Minahasa Java Indo Java Minang Java	S.I. S.I. S.D.I. Muhamma- diyah Kaum Betawi, Parindra Ind. Partij Persatuan Minahasa, Parindra Ind. Partij S.I. S.I. Parindra
1969 maquettes by Suroso and Sudirno	15.00 15.00 15.00 15.00 15.00	*Tjut Nja' Din* *Tjut Nja' Meuthia* Dewi Sartika Gen. Gatot Subroto St. Sjahrir F.L.Tobing	1848-1908 1870-1910 1884-1947 1909-1962 1909-1966 1899-1962	Aceh Aceh Sunda Java Minang Batak	 P.S.I.

Note: S.D.I.: Sarekat Dagang Islam; S.I.: Sarekat Islam; P.S.I.: Partai Sosialis Indonesia; Ind. Partij: Indische Partij (but Dewantoro and Setiabudhi are names taken after the party's dissolution by the people represented, which means that party affiliation is not a determining criterion in this case).

In italics: the names of war leaders, indicated by a circle on the map in figure 9.

The distribution of face values on the 1961-62 stamps does not seem to indicate any ideological choice: there does seem to have been a problem, however, since the stamps of the 1969 set (like those of the 1966 "Victims of October 1, 1965," issued in 1966) all have the same face value. It may also be considered that the choice of the three men featured in 1969 is tied to their birthdays.

---

personifying the *Nasional* branch, alongside the *Islam* (H.O.S. Tjokroaminoto) and *Komunis* (Semaun) branches: of the three, only Tjokroaminoto, in the 1961 and 1962 sets, is given his painting.

Figure 9. The "Heroes of independence" selected for 1961, 1962, and 1969
(geographic origin and typology by sex and main activity)

Key
- • 1961 issue
- × 1962 issue
- + 1969 issue
- O a circle over the issue code: war leader (colonial era)
- ▫ woman

We see that out of 26 public figures mentioned, 10 come from Sumatra, 12 from Java (a 13th sign, on Java, indicates the Eurasian E. Douwes Dekker, alias Setiabudhi Danudirdjo) and that, of the 13 from outside Java, 8 represent the princes' resistance to colonial penetration, whereas the national liberation movement leaders are concentrated on Java.

Fig.10. Curiosities, tourism, and taking possession of the space

Key

Sets with a background map showing the subject's place of origin
- ⊞ wild animals, 1958
- ▲ musical instruments, 1967
- Ø tourism on Bali, 1969

Sets with no background map
- H major hotels, 1962, 1965 (cf. pl.V)
- × The Year of the Orient, 1961
- • 12th Conference of the Pacific Area Travel Association, 1963
- ⊙ tourism, set issued yearly from 1967

Already in 1938, one of the creators and masters of Indonesian painting, Sudjojono, urged his colleagues to wake up to the fact that Indonesia had more to offer than just landscapes; there were events, even though, we would add, a landscape may be an event, as the Impressionists proved. Now what characterizes the event in this case is that it has become nothing more than a landscape, a monument, that is, a memory, diluted in the stereotyping of voyage and cruise, for which the bloody history of peoples is only an exotic breeze. And yet, such cries as "Save Borobudur" and "Lindungilah Margasatwa" sometimes recall that this landscape, too, is history and may die.

Because the "Tourism" set mentions places, festivals, products, a specified environment, it also fulfills the function of teaching about the territory, sometimes using a map for more detail; this territory can be compared with the version provided by the *Pahlawan* set (fig.9). Madura has been credited with one 1961 stamp (Year of the Orient) marked "Bull Race," bearing no place name; the location of the other subjects mentioned here—monuments, sites, dances, objects—is either printed on the stamp or is obvious. Those stamps valid only on Irian are not indicated (cf. pl. VI).

perhaps due to the interruption of the set, or, more likely, to Tjipto's interest in Saminism and communism (he was arrested following the 1926–27 uprisings), and to his hostility to fascism and the Japanese.

This lesson taught by a history that extends from princely resistance to prefectural government can be found again in the 1969 set, with one new development: half of the figures are women (cf. fig. 9), an advance that can be linked, with respect to the preoccupations of those responsible for the release programs, to the issue some weeks later of a small figure in honor of "Women's Emancipation" (*Kebangkitan wanita*); and while one of these women, Dewi Sartika, was the founder of the first schools for girls in Indonesia (in Bandung), the men, S. Sjahrir (whose appearance is a sign of his political rehabilitation after the repression he underwent under Guided Democracy) or F.L.Tobing, were administrators whose audience vanished as soon as they left the halls of power. If the ethnic range of the six figures for 1969 is remarkably broad—Acehnese (Tjut Nja' Din, represented for Aceh, together with Tjut Nja' Meuthia, was the wife of T. Umar; cf. pl. VIII), Batak, Minangkabau, Sundanese, Javanese—the political range had not changed: there were the civilian governor (Tobing), the military governor (Gatot), the head of the government (Sjahrir); it was a question of formulating neither political ideas nor activities, but the machinery of the State.

7.4 It was the State that designated territorial alliances, legitimation by history defined by the succession of ancestors: the quest for one's name. The postal service inaugurated the process when it presented, in 1953, its headquarters, and in 1955, its founder, an umbilical collusion between space and time; in 1966–67, Sukarno's end was inscribed in two sets, one of which spelled out the ten soldiers killed in the Untung coup; the other of which published the maquette of the monument raised on the spot where the bodies had been found, the center of a new pilgrimage that instituted a new regime.

8   The Flow of the Meaning

8.1 The stamp—tax and relationship figure—outlines a flow space, within which a circulation takes place, that is at the same time an area within which meaning is diffused: between 1958 and 1963, in the main, it exhibited proof of the convergence of a name, a territory, a kinship, duration and legitimacy of a State.

8.2 The stamp built a capital, the fusion of the center and the space, of the name and the named, of the inside and the outside. The capital organized the environment and summoned it, faces from the past, statues of the future, the making of motion and progress. If crowds came, they were regaled with celebrations that called the country by its name and engraved it in the memory of its own and other peoples. Indonesia came to the capital to see itself, to look at itself, to hear itself, in other words to come together, to make acquaintance, and to unite: to recognize each other as brothers living in the same house.

8.3 A people needs education over and above all other rights, and the State alone has a voice, with which it identifies the nation and provides it with a body.

8.4 But the civic center soon gave way to the business center and the deposed monument became a site with no memory, good for providing the commerce of the named with universals. The symbol was subverted. Bali had won.

Translated by Nora Scott

KI AGENG SURYOMENTARAMAN, JAVANESE PRINCE AND PHILOSOPHER (1892–1962)[*]

Marcel Bonneff

The Javanese love of religious and philosophical contemplation is clearly seen in the many groups, associations, and movements whose common goal is the realization of a certain spiritual fulfilment. A summary generalization, however, runs the risk of distorting "Javanese spirituality." The vast "corpus" of ideas and doctrines must be considered in all its diversity.[1] This article sets out to study the philosophy—the so-called "science of the psyche"—of the "dissident" Prince K.A.Suryomentaraman (KAS) and to show that, although such thoughts are original, when set in their social context, they can be seen to be the expression of a certain mentality.

Suryomentaram's Legacy

One of KAS's close friends relates how he had pointed out to KAS the value of having his writings translated into Indonesian, or indeed into a foreign language, so that his philosophy might enjoy the recognition it deserved. This conversation took place shortly before KAS's death, while he was in hospital in Yogyakarta. The Javanese philosopher reacted forcefully. Were there not already enough people seeking popular acclaim? In their efforts to commend him, were not those around him merely seeking to boost their own self esteem and reputation? Such a reply demonstrates KAS's faithful adherence to the simple, disinterested style of leadership he had fashioned more than thirty years earlier.[2]

It is now fifteen years since his death; there are still many people alive who knew him, many who continue to think of themselves as the *Pelajar Kawruh Jiwa*,[3] "disciples" of this

---

[*] The French version of this article appeared in *Archipel* 16 (1978): 175–203.

[1] In this field, *Archipel* (No. 4, 1972) has already published, a study of the Pangestu Movement by J. Indrakusuma.

[2] S. Wirjosoedojo, "Sapa Kang ngedegaké PETA?" *Mekar Sari* 19,17 (November 1, 1975): 13–14.

[3] For dialectal words and quotations the current forms of both the Indonesian and Javanese languages have been used. In Javanese the double orthographical signs *dh* and *th* have been used to denote retroflexes. Proper names and book titles have, however, been cited as found; nonetheless, the current practice of writing the names of

"science of the psyche," as KAS never tired of defining it, conference after conference. Such definitions have been recorded in short articles, still sometimes to be found on the bookshelves of private homes and in second-hand book collections. Recently the Idayu Foundation undertook the publication of these articles in Indonesian, so that vast numbers of readers (and in particular non-Javanese speakers) might have access to ideas which the editor compares to those of Socrates, Zarathoustra, and Krishnamurti. To recognize the "international dimension" of such praise is not, however, to conceal the fact that this publication (whose editor is very closely linked to government circles) probably owes its origins, at least in part, to the official intention to reveal a vision of existence which is heavily imbued with "Javanism."

The elder son of the philosopher, Dr. Grangsang Suryomentaram, who continues to head the Kawruh Jiwa Movement (or Kawruh Beja, the "Science of Happiness"), is for these two reasons the one best able to keep alive his father's memory. Recently, several articles written by himself or his late father's friends have been published by the press about KAS's life and work. However, in these articles, KAS's warning about the danger of "hagiography" does not seem to have been fully understood.[4] In addition to recalling his philosophical ideas, these articles assign an important place to KAS's role as a nationalist, clearly demonstrated by his participation in Paguyuban Selasa Kliwon—a patriotic cause which inspired the educational movement Taman Siswa—as well as his widely believed role as creator of the PETA and the lectures extolling nationalism he delivered after Independence. This renewed interest in a person who lived through contemporary history without ever appearing at the forefront of the political stage seems, nevertheless, to indicate that he exercised a considerable moral influence.[5]

The Prince's Disillusion

In trying to piece together KAS's biography and clarify his role, one is dependent on very limited and unconfirmed sources, insofar as the story of his life sometimes appears to be told for allegorical purposes.[6]

Born on May 20, 1892 in the *Kraton* of Yogyakarta, he was the 55th of Sultan Hamengku Buwono VII's 79 children. His mother, B.R.A. Retnomandoyo, a second ranked wife (*garwa ampéyan*) was the daughter of the *patih* Danurejo VI. Having completed his primary education at the Srimenganti Palace School, he went on to prepare for the Klein Ambtenaar (junior civil servant) examination, which enabled him to take up an administrative position at the

---

certain well-known persons according to the rules of *ejaan baru* has been followed: Suryomentaram (Soerjomentaram) is a case in point.

[4] Reference to articles will be made as and when they occur. A complete reference of KAS's works can be found at the end of the article.

[5] For example B.R.O'G. Anderson in his otherwise very detailed study of the political events of the period 1945–1946, which took place for the most part at Yogyakarta, makes no mention of Suryomentaram (*Java in a Time of Revolution: Occupation and Resistance* [Ithaca, Cornell University Press, 1972]).

[6] In particular, use has been made of Dr. Grangsang Suryomentaraman's articles which appeared in the Jakarta newspaper *Berita Buana*: "Riwayat singkat Ki Ageng Suryomentaraman" (July 24 and 25, 1975), and "Rahasia di balik pembentukan Tentara Pembela Tanah Air (PETA)" (July 19, 1975), Ki Atmosutidjo's work, *Gandulan kanggé kontja-kontja peladjar Kawruh-djiwa* and Kjai Pronowidigdo's article entitled "Riwajatipun Kawruh Djiwa," published in *Buku Peringatan* . . . (cf. bibliography). There is also a biography of KAS by Ki Djojodinomo, but this source has not been used.

M. Agus Suwito and Dr. Grangsang kindly allowed use to be made of a number of documents and the author would like to thank Dr. Grangsang and Ki Haditomo for the information they related to him (interviews May 1975).

Yogya Residence; he appears to have held this position, for which he needed a knowledge of Dutch, for just two years. He also learned Arabic—in the course of his religious studies?—and later English, and is said to have made up for his lack of formal education by prodigious reading.

At the age of 18 he became a Prince, exchanging his title and name (Bendoro Raden Mas Kudiarmaji) for that of Bendara Pangéran Harya Suryomentaram.

Little else is known about his early life. He himself was to relate how he was struck by the back-breaking work done by the field laborers he glimpsed through the train window one day on the way to a wedding ceremony at the court of Surakarta: whilst others were suffering extreme hardship, he and others like him, were getting ready to partake of the splendors reserved for those of noble birth. But, as his closest friend, Prawirowiworo, was later to remark, were those peasants any unhappier than the Prince himself, who could feel rather more sorry for himself than for them, since they at least were satisfied with their lot? Prawirowiworo (who died in 1960) was the Prince's confidant, the oldest and closest of his friends. The two men were cousins; but as Prawirowiworo's rank was much lower, he was employed as a servant at the Sultan's Palace.

On the one hand, there was the Prince, showered with honors and riches, on the other, the *abdi dalem* whose very small salary barely enabled him to discharge his duties. Both men, however, were dissatisfied: neither had ever "known Man" ("*saprana-sapréné aku kok durung tau kepethuk wong*"); the Prince knew only his masters and their tempers. The sheltered life he had led was the main reason for Suryomentaram's feeling of dissatisfaction. As a result he absented himself more and more often from the *kraton* to go to meditate in various places believed to be propitious (the Goa Langse or Goa Cermin caves, the beach at Parangtritis, and certain *kramat* tombs). Prawiro, whose duties were now less onerous, began also to travel about. They told each other of their respective experiences. Sometimes they shut themselves away to pray. At other times they went to talk to spiritual leaders and were keen to learn about things of a religious or mystical nature.

The Prince's entourage became worried: believing material possessions to be an obstacle to happiness, he began to give away his personal property. So it was that one of the wealthiest princes in Yogya gave his car to his driver, his horses to his groom.... Then one day he fled the *kraton*; dressed as a merchant and using the name Notodongso, he traveled about the Cilacap region selling batik. His father, the Sultan, sent men to look for him. They found him at Kroya digging a well and brought him back to the *kraton*.

These events took place while the Prince was in his twenties and before 1920, the year when an official letter was sent by the Resident Jonquière to the Governor General, together with a translation of a letter from Suryomentaram in which he asked to renounce his title of Prince. He had asked his father's permission which was refused, as was his request to be allowed to make a pilgrimage to Mecca.[7] But that year, his biographers tell us, Suryomentaram was in a state of utter confusion: in just a few months he had seen his grandfather, the *patih* Danurejo, relieved of his office and his mother divorced by Hamengku Buwono VII; finally and most importantly his wife had died, just after giving birth to their son.

---

[7] The document is dated August 21 and KAS's letter August 14, 1921 (*Mailrapport* No. 948 Geheim/*1920*; verbaal dated 6-1-21, No. 81). In his letter the Resident stresses that he tried himself to dissuade the Prince. The author is indebted to Mr. Kenji Tsuchiya for making this document available to him. This document is also relevant to Mr. Tsuchiya's own research into the history of the Taman Siswa Movement; see his article: "The Taman Siswa Movement. Its Early Eight Years and Javanese Background," *JSEAS* 6, 2 (1975):164–77.

In 1921 the Sultan abdicated and his successor, Hamengku Buwono VIII, agreed to allow Suryomentaram to leave. The Prince refused to accept the allowance proposed by the Dutch and instead made do with the small annuity paid to him by the sovereign. Having disposed of the last of his possessions, he settled down in the village of Bringin, near Salatiga, where he bought some land. Henceforth, he was to lead the life of a *petani*, like those he had originally seen laboring in their rice fields. In 1925 he remarried. His reputation grew. Ki Gedhe (or Ageng) Bringin[8] was certainly an eccentric personality. Some people believed him to be a *dhukun* and came to seek his advise. He had long since given up his royal robes in favor of the black shorts and leather belt worn by the peasants; he went about barefooted, of course, but around his neck he wore a length of batik cloth dyed with the *parang rusak barong* motif, which was then still worn only by the sovereign. Such a gesture is indicative of a certain dissatisfaction; some years earlier in the same spirit Suwardi Suryaningrat had had his servants wear a similar kind of *kain* when they went into town.[9] Suryomentaram was again to be considered a figure of curiosity because of his clothes and strange behavior at his father's funeral (1931); at Imogiri, where the ceremony took place, his former family and friends thought him mad; they moved away from him; Suryomentaram frightened them.

One day, dressed as ever in shorts and with bare feet, as he was about to board a bus, he was taken for a porter: a traveler gave him his suitcase, which he took and carefully stowed away . . . thus foregoing his journey for fear of embarrassing the honest traveler. Such was Suryomentaram; or at least such were the stories told about him,[10] a man more attentive to others than himself, or rather so mindful of himself that he could see his own embarrassment in another's unease.

In fact Ki Ageng had never given up his quest for "Man." One night in 1927 he wakened his wife saying "I have found what I was looking for . . . it's Suryomentaram who is discontented; he's the disillusioned *pangéran*, the dissatisfied merchant, the disappointed peasant; he's the source of disappointments (*tukang ora puas*). He has been unmasked (*konangan*). Henceforth I will always be able to find the man who bears the name of Suryomentaram." If Dr. Grangsang is to be believed, this was more or less what Ki Ageng said to his wife lying beside him. KAS had discovered the source of his problems: the confusion between the active-self and the passive-self; it is the passive-self one must at all costs learn to recognize and cultivate in oneself so as to avoid the trials of everyday contingencies and achieve "lasting happiness." "What I have been searching for, and have failed to find, is the concept of man (*gagasan wong*) who in fact exists only in my imagination."[11] The "Science of Happiness" (Kawruh Beja) was born. KAS was to convert his companions, of whom Ki Prawiro was the first, and then win over an ever-increasing number of followers.

It is relevant now to consider those aspects of KAS's career more immediately concerned with politics. To do so, however, it is necessary to return to the years 1921–22. At that time he was the leader of the Paguyuban Selasa Kliwon, which took its name from the day on which meetings were held; this group is well known as the originator of the Taman Siswa

---

[8] Suryomentaram means "Sun (*surya*) of Mataram." *Ki* is a term of address used by working class people when addressing elderly men renowned for their wisdom. (*Nyi* is used for women; as with *kiyai* and *Nyai*, although these two words have Islamic conotations). Gedhé—or Ageng—means "Great." Several people (real or legendary) in Javanese history have had such a title: Ki Ageng Séla, Ki Ageng Pamanahan, etc.

[9] Cf. Pranata, *Ki Hadjar Dewantara perintis perdjuangan kemerdekaan Indonesia* (Jakarta: Balai Pustaka, 1959), p 36.

[10] Interview with Ki Haditomo.

[11] Cf. articles by Grangsang S. and Ki Atmosutidjo.

Movement.¹² There were nine *priyayi*, among whom mention should be made of Suwardi (Ki Hajar Dewantoro), the faithful Prawirowiworo, B.R.M. Subono (KAS's youngest brother), and Pronowidigdo. Some of them, such as the future Ki Hajar, or in fact Pronowidigdo,¹³ had the opportunity on many occasions to air their nationalist convictions (through their participation, amongst other things, in the Budi Utomo). The group (*Paguyuban*) was run along the lines of a "*kebatinan* society,"¹⁴ but the business at hand was clearly defined: deliberation on the means of winning independence. In 1922 the group disbanded after reaching agreement that liberation was to be achieved through the development of the general level of education and the national consciousness of the Indonesian people. The educational initiative was of prime importance. Ki Hajar Dewantoro was to be responsible for young Indonesians, and here he is well known for organizing their formal education (opening the first Taman Siswa school on July 3, 1922). KAS was himself to be in charge of "adult instruction."

Some years later, in 1930, KAS was amongst the founders of the Pakempalan Kawula Ngajogjakarto whose president was Prince Suryodiningrat. This too was a movement whose humanitarian and social initiatives were of greater importance than its political objectives. The committee, made up of Prince Suryodiningrat and the enlightened *priyayi*, with the agreement of His Majesty Hamengku Buwono VIII, fixed on the objective of improving the general living standards of the sultanate's peasants: until the outbreak of war in the Pacific, the PKN—and similar organizations which arose out of it, and which likewise advocated autonomy and democratization for the administrations of the "principalities"—took several very popular initiatives which attracted large numbers of penniless farmers to its ranks:¹⁵ these included the setting up of agricultural cooperatives and *lurik* factories, propositions to revise the taxation system, elimination of illiteracy etc. In 1931 it joined forces with organizations (PPPPA and PPII) which were protesting against the practice of buying and selling women and children and, in 1932, with groups such as the Budi Utomo, Taman Siswa, and even Muhammadiyah, to protest against the Wilde Scholen Ordonnantie.¹⁶ At a meeting in

---

¹² On this point, see in particular: Suratman, "Masalah kelahiran Taman Siswa," *Pusara* 25, 1–2 (1964); and Kenji Tsuchija, "The Taman Siswa Movement," pp. 166–67.

¹³ Ki Pronowidigdo (Prono) died recently in Yogyakarta aged 96 (see *Mekar Sari*, May 1, 1976). A trained teacher and committed nationalist, he was among the earliest members of the Budi Utomo and was their spokesman in Yogya around 1920. He was closely associated with both KAS's and Ki Hajar Dewantoro's undertakings; he is thought to have been a founding member of Taman Siswa; until his death he was a respected and valued counselor. It should be noted that Ki Prawirowiworo was also a member of the first Taman Siswa Committee.

¹⁴ *Kebatinan* can be translated as "spiritual life." Many societies and groups are known to exist in Java whose members consider a knowledge of the "inner self" the fundamental element in the search for the Absolute. In general, the theoretical philosophy borrows a number of principles from Indian religious and/or Muslim mysticism, which are often expressed in esoteric terms. The "practical" aspect places great importance on meditation and certain contemplative exercises, indeed asceticism. But the concept of *kebatinan* (or *Kejawèn* as the Javanese would say) may in fact encompass very diverse approaches, some of which claim to be "scientific." A common denominator might be, as will be seen later, the principal concept of psychological wholeness.

¹⁵ In 1938 the PKN numbered 253,218 members (of whom 30,471 were women), almost all of whom were peasants (90 percent). The other organizations were the Pakempalan Kawula Surakarta (set up in 1932), the P.K. Mangkunegaran (1933), and the P.K. Pakualaman; see *Ensiklopedi Indonesia*, pp. 926–27.

¹⁶ A colonial decree which strengthened control over "local" schools and limited their numbers. For the PKN's activities, see the book published to celebrate the organization's eighth anniversary (*satu windu*): *Boekoe pengetan windon Pakempalan Kawoela Ngayogyakarta (PKN), 1930–1938*, ed. PKN (1939), 103 pp. During the Japanese occupation and after Independence, the organization's founder, Prince Suryodiningrat, appears to have followed a rather more spiritualist course; he was considered an inspired *guru kebatinan* and the meetings he organized were eagerly attended by a large number of "followers." However, the PKN was again to become a political force in 1951, as the Gerinda party, whose members, according to Selosoemardjan, still viewed (in 1955) the

1932 Ki Hajar put forth his ideas on education and Ki Ageng explained the principles of the "Science of Happiness," putting particular stress on the fact that all men are involved in the same search for psychological well being and that the effect of such an experience was to put everyone on an equal footing.

When the Japanese entered the war, KAS was a member of a group of 13 nationalists (Manggala 13)[17] who were planning the course of action to be followed in the event that fighting broke out on Indonesian soil between the Dutch and the "liberators of Asia." But when Java fell to the Japanese, the invaders encountered no opposition. The occupying force soon began to take an interest in KAS's activities (the Dutch had also had suspicions about him). Amongst those officers who came to call on him, a certain Asano (a member of the Secret Service) remarked that Suryomentaram gave the impression of being grateful to the army which had freed the Indonesian people from the yoke of colonialism and that, subject to receiving appropriate training, he and his friends would be prepared to fight alongside the Japanese. The former Prince defined what he called "Jimat Perang" (literally "a fetish for war"), as that absence of fear in the face of death which is the source of military courage. He was invited to speak on Jakarta radio and authorized to hold meetings to spread this idea. In the capital in 1943, thanks to the intervention of Mr. Sudjono, he met the group of four nationalists whom the Japanese trusted (Empat Serangkai: Sukarno, Hatta, K.H. Mas Mansur, and K.H. Dewantoro). On this occasion he appears to have convinced Sukarno to adopt the idea of Jimat Perang as his own; the nationalist leader was to refer to it on many occasions.

The Japanese, however, remained skeptical as to the possibility of forming an Indonesian militia; hence the categoric refusal given by the military governor of Yogya, Colonel Yamanuchi, to KAS's request to set up such a force. This being the case, Asano proposed laying the matter before the Emperor himself. KAS assembled eight of his companions to draw up a kind of petition which each of them signed in his own blood. To the surprise of the occupying authorities, Tokyo gave its approval. Ki Ageng would himself have begun to sign on volunteers, but the military government quickly took over the recruitment and training of this army known as the PETA (Pembela Tanah Air: Defenders of the Fatherland).

This version of the PETA's origins (an organization which was to play an important part in the attainment of Independence and whose officers were to form the backbone of the new Indonesian Army) has recently been disclosed by Dr. Grangsang.[18] It is partially substantiated by statements made by Ki Prono and Ki Asrar Wiryowinoto, two of the petition's signatories.[19] But, even if the conception of Jimat Perang was in fact inspired by KAS, many doubts remain about subsequent events and the role of the petition; in any event this is the conclusion reached by S. Wirjosoedojo—another of KAS's old friends—who disputed this version of events and who was unable to obtain M. Hatta's confirmation that the meeting

---

party's role as "following the ways of mysticism, namely, the unity of man and God, materialized in this world by the unity of subject and King and practiced in the Gerinda by the unity of party member and party president." (*Social Changes in JogJakarta* [Ithaca: Cornell University Press, 1962], pp. 188–89).

[17] The *manggala* is the invocation at the beginning of a poem. The word also has the connotation of "avant-garde." Amongst this group's 13 members, it is interesting to note again the presence of Ki Hajar, Ki Prono, and Suryodiningrat, together with that of Radjiman Wediyodiningrat, Sutopo Wonoboyo (one of the founders of Taman Siswa), etc. (*Berita Buana*, July 25, 1975).

[18] *Berita Buana*, July 19, 1975.

[19] "Sapa kang ngedegaké PETA?" *Mekar Sari* 19,15 (October 1, 1975).

between KAS and the group of four[20] did, in fact, take place. Such an account is also puzzling in view of all that has already been written about the matter either by historians or other direct witnesses, and in particular by Gatot Mangkupradja, who is usually credited with having initiated this organization.[21] The matter remains open to debate.

However, despite the fact that KAS's son's version of the events may be disputed, it is quite interesting for the light it sheds on Ki Ageng as an active participant in the struggle for Independence and thus an ardent nationalist. Of this there can be no doubt, his readiness to take up arms during the period 1947–1949 at the head of a Pasukan Rakyat Jelata detachment to confront the Dutch Army near Yogya being well known.

With the restoration of peace, he left his farm at Bringin, which had been devasted in the fighting, and went to live in Yogya, where he devoted himself to his philosophical teachings until his death at the age of 70. In his telegram of condolences, President Sukarno paid tribute to him on behalf of the nation.[22]

KAS's Philosophy

Like his life, KAS's writings are characterized by the idea of a search for a certain "happiness," or more particularly a psychological state of mind which resembles a kind of "spiritual detachment." At first commonly known as Kawruh Beja, this philosophy was later more often called Kawruh Jiwa ("Science of the soul / of the psyche" or Self-knowledge). The change of terminology, which aimed rather to focus attention on the means of achieving such knowledge, undoubtedly corresponded to its founder's deepening reflection.[23]

The basis of the "Science of Happiness," indeed its principal axiom, is the recognition of human existence as an interchange of joys (*bungah*) and sorrows (*susah*). The feelings of happiness (*raos beja*) and unhappiness (*raos cilaka*) which such states of mind produce are what differentiates man from other animals. Although man is subject to the same vital needs as other animal species—assuring his survival (*pangupa-jiwa*) and that of his race (*lestantuning jenis*)—he is different from them because he is aware that he has these needs (*raos gesang*: awareness of life). Thus, for man, satisfying or failing to satisfy basic needs is linked to the concepts of happiness and unhappiness. Moreover, once his primary needs are met, man becomes aware of secondary needs which are the figment of his imagination. KAS cites as an example of a man's imaginary needs the idea which persuades him to prefer tea to coffee or beer, when any kind of liquid (water) would quench his thirst, a primary need felt equally by everyone. Thus man becomes the victim of his supposed needs which result in his desires (*karep*) exerting such a powerful influence on his life that he confuses desire with true human existence: "Man equals longing" (*Karep punika tiyang*); "Whilst still in his

---

[20] Wirjosoedojo, "Sapa kang ngedegaké PETA?" *Mekar Sari* 19, 17 (November 1, 1975).

[21] See in particular: Nugroho Notosusanto, *The Peta-Army in Indonesia, 1943–1945* (Dept of Defence and Security, Centre for the Armed Forces History, 1971), 23 pp.; and Raden Gatot Mangkupradja, "The Peta and My Relations with the Japanese: A Correction of Soekarno's Autobiography," *Indonesia* 5 (April 1968). It is interesting to note that Gatot (who died in 1968) claims also to have sent a request signed in his own blood.

[22] See Kus Sudyarsana, "Kawruh Bedja," *Mekar Sari* 6, 3 (April 1, 1962). KAS was buried beside his mother in the cemetery with the other Nitinegara descendants (Trah Nitinegaran), at Kanggotan (about 7 kms. south of Yogya, near the ancient city of Kerto, once Sultan Agung's capital).

[23] The writings which most particularly deal with the exposition of the general principles are as follows: *Wedjangan Kawruh Bedja Sawetah* (adapted into Indonesian under the title: *Wejangan pokok Ilmu Bahagia*), *Ngèlmi-Kawruh-Pitedah sedjatining gesang wedjangan KAS* (by M.Soedi), *Pilsapat Raos Gesang* (adapted into Indonesian as: *Filsafat Rasa Hidup*); *Tandesan: Wedjangan Kawruh Bedja sawetah*.

mother's womb, the desire to be born is already present" (*Nalika wonten wetenganing biyung sampun wonten karep lahir*); desire is everlasting, eternal (*karep punika langgeng*), and since at times it generates happiness and at times unhappiness, these two feelings are as ever-present in man as his desire; they are man's eternity (man is eternal because his desire knows no beginning or end).[24]

Some sort of law seems to govern the life of this longing: though a need may be satisfied, it may still give rise to new demands which may well grow more urgent (*mulur*), whereas an unsatisfied need is ever present, but may take the form of a less vital demand which grows less urgent (*mungkret*). Desire is influential in three clearly defined areas, "wealth" (*sémat* in the general sense of "material goods"), public recognition (*drajat*; one's place in the social hierarchy), and magic powers (*kramat*). The knowledge that one cannot be happy for more than three consecutive days renders the search for such things futile. KAS's other main postulate was as follows: "There is nothing on earth worth so much that it should be sought after or shunned at all costs."[25] All his writing is characterized by examples which underline this principle; a single illustration will suffice: a man had a child who was getting married and he wanted to offer his guests the best possible hospitality by organizing a *wayang kulit* for them; however, he did not have enough money and wondered anxiously how he might borrow some. If he could not manage to borrow any he would find himself in an embarrassing situation and feel ashamed (*wirang*). But this would not last long; once the ceremony was over, how relieved he would feel not to be in debt![26]

The desire for *sémat-drajat-kramat* means that each one of us is guided only by his own self-interests and, by giving free rein to one's egoism, one does just as one pleases (*sawenang-wenang*); thus it is not only a source of personal anxiety (*sumelang*) and regret (*getun*), but also a cause of social competition and inequality. Those who have not are jealous (*mèri*) of those who have, whilst those who have, fearful of losing their possessions, take comfort in their sense of personal worth (*pambegan*) and despise those less fortunate.[27]

KAS describes "*kramadangsa*" as that part of us which drives us to seek our own well being without due consideration for others and often to their detriment ("*mila kramadangsa punika mesthi pados sakéca pribadi lan mboten parduli tangga inggih punika ingkang murugaken sewenang-wenang*").[28] It is this same *kramadangsa* which makes us believe in the reality of our desires, which prevents us from seeing the world as it really is rather than the image which we have of it. It buries deep in one's consciousness one's true Self, independent of all contingencies. In short, the "contingent-self" is balanced by the "essential-self" (*Aku*). As a result of man's awareness of his existence and his predisposition for reflection and for furthering his knowledge, he is able to lower the veil (*aling-aling*) which conceals his inner being and so realize true self-awareness (*raos aku*).

We have seen how KAS one day succeeded in discovering his true self, a discovery which led him to declare: "*Suryomentaram dudu aku*" (Suryomentaram is not my self). To illustrate the effect of this "finding of his new Self," he liked to recall an incident which

---

[24] Cf. in particular *Wedjangan*, pp 22–24.

[25] "*Salumahing bumi sakurebing langit, punika boten wonten barang ingkang pantes dipun aya-aya dipun padosi utawi dipun ceri-ceri dipun tampik*" (as for example: *Tandesan*, p. 20).

[26] *Wedjangan*, pp. 3–4.

[27] On the question of social relationships see in particular: *Pilsapat Raos Gesang; Aku iki wong apa?; Ukuran kaping sakawan* (adapted into Indonesian as: *Ukuran keempat*).

[28] *Mawas diri*, p. 23.

marked his life: one day on the way to Parangtritis he was held up by the flooded Opak River. No boatman wanted to risk the crossing. KAS decided to swim across to the other side. But the torrent swept him away. As he was drowning, it became clear to him that his haste to make the crossing come what may, suggested a desire on his part to end his life (he had just lost his first wife). Suryomentaram's passionate nature, which was disappearing under the water, had nothing in common with the "serene-self" which was floating on the surface.[29] "This is not me" (*dudu aku*).

One must learn from experience (*piageming gesang*) to contrast moments of joy with moments of sorrow, to sharpen one's *rasa*. It is a matter of time and practice (*latihan*). The approach KAS suggests is none other than "introspection" (*Pengawikan pribadi* or *mawas diri*).[30] This approach is a highly individual one, but where one may nevertheless depend on the help of others: to secure such help one has only to talk about oneself, to ask for the judgement of one's fellow student-companions, go back with them "from the effects to the causes." The feeling of happiness suggested is in no way the antithesis of unhappiness, rather it is the tranquillity (*tentrem*) and liberation (*mardika*) which ensues from such a standpoint in the face of one's existence. One should aim to find "self-awareness" not "happiness," which is but the result of it. Since it comes from one's innermost being (*aku*), this happiness is as lasting as one's self-awareness. Fortified by this wisdom, one's only possible course of action is to appear "resolute" (*tatag*), that is to assume one's destiny independently of circumstances ("no matter where, no matter when, no matter how"). To break free from the "diabolic" cycle of fear for the future–regret for the past,[31] to put an end to the interchange of happiness–unhappiness, one must act according to the principle of the six "*sa*": *sabutuhé, saperluné, sacukupé, sabeneré, samesthiné, sakepenaké* (in accord once with one's needs, with one's circumstances, with moderation and fairness, and in an appropriate and easy manner). If Suryomentaram preferred coffee rather than tea to quench his thirst, his "ego" (*aku*) would just have to make do with a glass of water!

Personal stability is the prime requirement for social harmony. In fact, it is man's desires which persuade him to force his will on others or else to see himself as the victim of inequalities; one of KAS's favorite examples is taken from a family context: very often people are content just to pretend to love their children; their so-called love comes partly from the assurance of having descendants and partly from the fact that the parent can count on his child's help in the difficult days of his old age; he can also transfer to him all his hopes for success.[32] If, for example, the child repeats a class, his parents are furious. The arguments they put forward are many, but the underlying reason for their anger is none other than their fear of seeing their hopes dashed. Thus parents should be aware of the true nature of their feelings and, consequently, understand that the source of their anger lies in themselves, in their own egotism, but that the child is stimulated by completely different motives. Then, their criticisms of him will be made not in anger, but in a peaceful atmosphere (*raos damé*) and account will be taken of all the reasons for which the child might be motivated not to work. This is real love; it is seen clearly when one puts aside one's own interests. It ensures harmony and highlights resemblances between parents and children

---

[29] *Ganḍulan*, pp. 10–11.

[30] The book titles are self-explanatory: *Piageming gesang* [The Test of Existence]; *Pangawikan pribadi* [Self-awareness]; *Mawas diri* [literally: Being mindful of One's self].

[31] "*Luwar saking naraka sumelang lan manjing swarga tatag*" (leaving the hell of regret-fear and entering the heaven of determination); *Wedjangan*, p. 30.

[32] "... *gegayuhanipun inggih punika tandon pensiun lan garan moncèr*," in *Buku Peringatan* ... (the article: "*Wudjuding Kawruh Djiwa*").

(*raos sami*); in fact, disregarding individual instances, men, rich or poor, king or coolie, live through the ups and downs of life in the same way; everyone is equal from a psychological point of view. To know oneself one must know others, feel what they feel (*ngraosaken raosing tiyang sanès*). This social sensibility is what KAS termed the "fourth dimension" (*Ukuran kaping IV*). In the same way that one thinks "*dudu aku*" (this is not me) when one catches sight of oneself in all one's selfishness, so the fourth dimension is what prompts one to say "*dudu kowé*" (this is not you) when one sees what others have done. Love and mutual respect would be characteristic of a society in which the fourth dimension prevailed.[33]

Not content merely to define the general principles outlined here, KAS also held many meetings to look at specific ways in which his philosophy could be put into practice. The situations in which an individual may find himself vary throughout life (*lelampahing gesang*)[34] and he has various fields of interest, each one of which requires an appropriate response. In the order in which the author gives them, these centers of interest are: material possessions, public recognition, power, the family, group life, the nation, knowledge, "spiritualism" (*kebatinan*), and aptitudes (*kesagedan*; or "awareness of one's possibilities").[35] There are, furthermore, difficult periods dotted throughout the course of one's life: the awakening of feelings of love at adolescence, one's choice of spouse, certain situations related to married life, the education of children, one's approaching death.[36] At each instance it is vital for man to be aware of his needs and to know what is hindering the development of his personality. Sexual desire, for example, should be accepted as the consequence of a vital need; it finds total fulfilment in marriage which is an appropriate context for procreation. Respect for one's partner, that is acceptance of his or her differences, should be the basis of married love (KAS insisted amongst other things on monogamy as well as parental love).[37]

KAS gives careful consideration to those situations which are among the most testing one faces in life (*pengalaman pait getir*): the death of parents or their divorce when one is young; the death of a brother, sister, or friend; illness; an unhappy love affair; an arranged marriage; poverty; the loss of social prestige, etc. He shows how a lesson may be learned from each occasion which will help us to maintain or re-establish our psychological equilibrium.[38]

Worrying about things of a metaphysical nature is a result of one's ignorance of man's true nature. Man's soul is as one with his desire, which has no beginning or end: it occupies a human form for a time, then disappears once again into the universe (*Alam Agung*). Why then worry about death? By looking closely at his desire, man will have been able to make the best of his life, because of his ability to distance himself from what is going on. It then matters little if he is reincarnated as a wild pig (*cèlèng*); such a creature's fate is different, but neither better nor worse than man's. Thus, it is absurd to seek to attain perfection (*kasempurnan*) in this life in the hope of a better life in the hereafter. Such a life does not exist; it does so only in our imagination, in answer to our unsatisfied desires which lead us to hope for eternal happiness. KAS, therefore, argued against the superstitions and religious beliefs such hope engenders ("superstition is a way of seeing relationships between causes and

---

[33] Cf. *Ukuran kaping sakawan*.

[34] On this subject see in particular: *Aku iki wong apa?*

[35] Cf. *Mawas diri*, pp. 33–54.

[36] Cf. *Piageming gesang*.

[37] On conjugal love and marriage, see *Kawruh Laki-rabi*; on children's education: *Kawruh pamomong*.

[38] *Piageming gesang*.

effects which do not exist").[39] He thought the *guru kebatinan*'s teachings "bizarre" (*aneh*), denounced the trust certain people put in the *dhukun*, and rejected the practices of fasting, sexual abstinence, etc. as unnatural.[40]

Another important aspect of KAS's teachings deals with the life of the Indonesian nation. His readiness to work alongside the nationalists for whom independence was contingent upon intellectual progress has already been recounted; likewise his active support of the "enlightened" artistocrats who sought the emancipation of the sultanate's peasantry, and finally of the rebels when the country's fate depended on the use of force. His political beliefs always reflected one of his major concerns: respect for others as a measure of one's own self-respect. To explain the colonial reality, he had only to put his conception of individual existence on a national footing. If Indonesians had been able to suffer the yoke of colonialism for so many years, it was not because of any violent domination (*angkara-murka*) on the part of the Dutch, still less because it was their destiny (*sampun pinasthi*); it was simply because, divided as they were, they had no national identity. What is a nation? How should the lives of men who share a common interest be organized? What is the role of such a group's culture? Is the group's cohesion determined by the degree to which its social functions complement each other? KAS's replies leave no room for doubt as to the need for a national recognition of individual responsibility in community affairs, a perception which can be summed up by the expression: *aku duwé nagara*, "I have a country of my own."[41]

In the troubled world of the early 1950s, Indonesia's unity had to be particularly strong in order to avoid the trap of alternating between capitalism and communism, a trap laid by the two rival world powers for the newly independent countries. Keeping faith with the tenets of his philosophy, KAS explained to his listeners that states which feared the outbreak of a third world war, just as much as those which sought such an occurrence, believed they could deny the reality of their own problems by making them appear dependent on things outside their control.[42]

In the Pancasila, Indonesia has a collection of principles capable of giving rise to a new mental attitude and consequently of supporting national unity. The most important of the five principles is "popular sovereignty" (*panguwasa rakyat*) which KAS interpreted as the recognition of the individual's right to be free, or the triumph of a social spirit over those instinctive forces which lie dormant in each one of us ("the animal [cow]which is in man"). From this point all the finest sentiments (*raos luhur*) embodied in the Pancasila are accessible to him: humanitarian sentiments, a spirit of nationalism, and a sense of justice. Finally, it should be noted that Belief in God appears in KAS's writing as a result of the four other principles, as the highest refinement of the social spirit; as far as this author knows, this is the sole reference to God throughout the whole of the philosopher's works.[43]

The "Patriarch" and his Followers

With obvious "pedagogical" concern, KAS reflected at length on the approach a person studying the "Science of the psyche" should take.[44] First of all he must realize that this

---

[39] "*Guyon tuhon punika nyambet-nyambetaken sebab lan kedadosan ingkang mboten sambet,*" Wedjangan, p. 27.

[40] *Hal Kesempurnaan*.

[41] *Pembangunan djiwa warga negara*.

[42] *Perang dunia kaping III*.

[43] *Raos Pantja Sila*.

[44] For the most part these procedures are explained in *Tandesan*.

science is very simple in its principles, but also very difficult when it comes to putting it into practice.

Simple was indeed the way he described his thinking. It is a discourse steeped in imagery, where every idea is illustrated by examples drawn from everyday life, which runs the risk, at times, of seeming (to us) somewhat trivial. "A person who wants to ensure the continuation of his lineage must first have in-laws and then a child, which is not the case for bovines who do not have in-laws."[45] Constant recourse to allegory fits perfectly well with the idea that one's own experience is the primary source of the awakening of one's consciousnesse.

The elements of each different proposition are carefully defined and analyzed one by one. The rationale proceeds through a series of antitheses, according to a dialectic designed to arouse in the listener or reader the sense of harmony the dissertation is advocating.

Few foreign words or "Indonesianisms" are to be found. Although KAS invented his own particular terminology (*Kramadangsa, ukuran kaping sakawan, raos sawenang-wenang*, etc), in general he used a simple vocabulary, eschewing all literary devices. If his syntax is not always rigorous, this is above all due to the fact that his lectures were originally delivered orally, as well as, in part, to a predilection for paradoxical phrases.

In short, the stylistic techniques marry well with the author's intentions. They reflect his didactic attitude and attest to a determination to rationalize, which is in marked contrast to the gibberish found in many of the *kebatinan* doctrines; they also underline the respect Ki Ageng felt for his public. In fact, the philosopher addressed them in *krama*, whilst carefully avoiding the use of any honorific terms (*krama inggil*), overlaid with feudalistic connotations. On the contrary, the use of *ngoko* in short conversations or incidental comments brings the lecture to life and introduces just at the right moment a hint of familiarity, which suited the relaxed atmosphere of the meetings at which he spoke.

For Javanese people the tone of the discourse and the choice of words—particularly in regard to the emotional effect of their sounds—are extremely important. Thus, in his preface to the Indonesian translation, Ki Oto Suastika takes a number of precautions: "The difficulties encountered in translating this work, stem from the many terms of phrase and constructions of the spoken Javanese language which involve the concept of 'sensitivity' (*rasa*)."[46] As for Ki Sangoebrangta (Ki Pronowidigdo), one of the first to spread KAS's teachings (or rather his "advice," that is *wejangan*), he explained in a foreword to *Poesara* readers, that he had retained the use of the Javanese language for fear of betraying the spirit of the advice "as it related to the understanding of sensitivity and temperament" and went so far as to make excuses for having to use Latin letters (rather than Javanese characters).[47]

For the Kawruh Jiwa student (*pelajar*), Ki Ageng's teachings, whether spoken or written, were but a first step. Understanding the advice as it related to real life situations would only come after the general principles had been mastered and, above all, after sufficient thought had been given to the process of learning the principles. A student had to "understand how he understands" (*ngertos caraning ngertos*) in order to get to the very heart of things (*nandhes*), that is to arrive at a "firm" understanding (*kekah pangertosipun*). It mattered little that the recommendations were arranged in a pedagogical order, for they were but food for

---

[45] *Raos Pantja Sila*, p. 5.

[46] Cf. *Filsafat rasa hidup*, p. 7.

[47] Ki Sangoebrangta, "Pendidikan oentoek ketentraman doenia, wedjangan Toeankoe Pangéran Soerjamataram (Kiai Ageng Beringin)," *Poesara* 1,10 (January 1932).

thought. What was important was that the followers of the "science" should debate the ideas contained in the collection. The most experienced were to offer guidance to the novices at "meetings" (so called when even just two people met together) known as *Junggring Salaka*.[48] In fact the period of learning was life-long: each new "misfortune" (*raos cilaka*) demanded to be considered in its own light and thus was it possible for one's feeling of self to be refined. It would, moreover, be wrong to think of Kawruh Jiwa as a doctrinaire approach or a Holy Word. Of fundamental importance was the purity of the learner's intentions and, even more so, of the teacher's. KAS was opposed to proselytizing zeal; he wanted his counsel to be adapted to suit the learner's needs and mental ability. Knowledge of other philosophical systems or faith in a *Kebatinan* doctrine was a priori a hindrance.

There were two kinds of meetings between *pelajar*: *pasinaon* and *jawah kawruh*. The first of these was devoted to study (*sinau*) and the development of the techniques of self-analysis. When they had reached the stage of feeling familiar with the principles and terminology, students could then move on to the second kind of meeting, "scientific showers" (*papanggihan jawah Kawruh*). These consisted of trying to help those suffering from psychological disorders by carefully analyzing with them the cause of their problems (*ngudhari rerebeb*: explaining the difficulty). For this kind of psycho-therapy (as it might be termed), the fourth dimension, the ability to "feel what others are feeling" was essential.

Generally, apart from these meetings which had direct and practical consequences, a *pelajar* had to be able, by the example he himself set, by his own personal radiance, to exert beneficial influence on his social environment.

Finally, to look at the role of the teaching "auxiliaries" which, in the case of Kawruh Jiwa, are poetry and drama: Ki Ageng himself composed a number of "songs" (*uran-uran*) in the *macapat* meter and some *panembrama* (songs of welcome) designed to help students to memorize the most important pieces of advice;[49] they were read or chanted collectively at meetings. As for drama, in an allegorical play—*Raos Mlenet* ("feeling of constraint")—KAS reiterated the most important of his ideas about marriage: that one should be free to marry the partner of one's choice. In a family there were three protagonists: father, mother, and daughter, whose choice of a future husband for the daughter had brought them into conflict with one another. Each had his own candidate. The young girl threatened to commit suicide if her parents tried to impose their choice (note that the allusion to suicide, an indication of a psychological disorder, was ever present in KAS's works). The conflict was resolved following the intervention of a local Kawruh Jiwa *pelajar* who helped all of them to see that their points of view were governed solely by their lack of understanding of their own motivation and their selfishness.

It has already been noted that KAS found an immediate supporter of his theses in Prawirowiworo. Ki Prono, himself a former member of the Selasa Kliwon group, was also one of the first to lend his support. For Ki Haditomo, one of KAS's disciples, these two personalities, together with Ki Ageng, formed a sort of *tri-tunggal* in which Ki Prono represented the mind (*cipta*), Ki Prawiro the "heart" (*manah*), and Ki Ageng the body (*raga*).[50]

---

[48] In the *wayang*, *Junggringsalaka* was designated as the home of the gods, and, by extension, the meetings held there.

[49] In particular: *Uran-uran Bedja*.

[50] From an interview with Ki Haditomo (May 1975).

One of the first of KAS's public lectures was reproduced and a commentary given by M. Soedi,[51] then translated into Dutch by R. Imam Moehni in a work entitled: *Inwijding tot het eeuwigdurende geluk van B.R.M. Soerjomentaram* [An Introduction to lasting Happiness, by B.R.M.S. . . . ; with a foreword dated March 9, 1930].[52] The translator gives an explanation of the Javanese terms he has retained and, in a long introduction, paraphrases and comments on the statements made by the person he still calls "Prince." It was a similar, though somewhat fuller speech, made at Surakarta in 1931, which was to form the basis of KAS's teachings.[53] It could be said that KAS already had a number of pupils.

1932 onwards saw a succession of Junggring Salaka Agung—a sort of annual conference where delegations from many local *pelajar* organizations met together.[54] Nevertheless KAS and his companions also denied having created a structured organization: local organizations were not formally constituted; followers were not required to pay subscriptions and could withdraw from their study group whenever they wished to do so (it has already been noted that just two people could hold a meeting; it was, moreover, a "non-directive" group, no-one could claim the title of guru for himself, not even Suryomentaram, whose companions merely called him "*bangkokan.*"[55] Nevertheless, such co-ordination as was necessary was provided by regional committees, in collaboration with a central committee (*Panitya Umum*) located in Surakarta.

Little or no organization, therefore, but a movement which, during the 1930s, as one conference followed another, became increasingly important. The earliest conferences seem to have given rise to a number of derisive remarks, soon quashed, however, as each new Junggring Salaka Agung prompted discussions and publications in which the doctrine became more firmly established. The conference at Yogya in 1937 was the last to be held before the war. Was the movement losing momentum? During the Japanese occupation, it is true that the country's situation hardly lent itself to philosophical discussions about personal happiness as envisaged by KAS. As has already been said, KAS, preoccupied by the power struggle with the occupying forces, became caught up in the political scene and advocated a fighting spirit which was soon to manifest itself as resistance to the return of the Dutch. Ki Ageng did not lack for supporters. In 1948, after the events at Madiun, he launched an appeal for union in *Djawah Kawruh*, a periodical he founded, but which was published for only two months. At the beginning of the 1950s, once peace had been re-established, he began once more to travel about the country in order to revive the local

---

[51] Excepting an error on the author's part; M. Soedi, *Ngélmi-Kawruh-Pitedah*. The 6th edition of this work includes a preface dated April 15, 1929. It is difficult to reconstruct the chronology of the earliest publications; it would appear that *Uran-uran Bedja* and *Pangawikan pribadi* (written perhaps by Prawirowiworo) date also from this time.

[52] The author is grateful to Mr. K. Tsuchiya who provided this text.

[53] *Wedjangan*.

[54] The first Junggring Salaka Agung took place at Salatiga; in 1933 it was held at Surakarta, in 1934 at Kudus, in 1935 at Madiun, in 1936 at Wonosobo, and in 1937 at Yogya. After a break of thirteen years the 7th Junggring Salaka Agung was held at Magelang (1953), then at Surabaya in 1954, at Semarang in 1956, at Tulung Agung in 1957, and finally at Purwokerto in 1959. In a commemorative brochure (*Buku Peringatan* published for this last conference (March 21, 22, 23), an article by Kijai Pronowidigdo retraced the movement's history ("*Riwajatipun Kawruh Djiwa*").

[55] This term is used for certain animals which, because of their strength and their age, seem to fulfil the function of "leader" of their fellow creatures. The term could here be translated as "patriarch."

associations. He gave a number of lectures in West Java (Jakarta, Bogor, Cianjur, and Bandung) to launch his movement.[56]

At the 1953 Junggraing Salaka Agung in Magelang, he explained the principle of the 4th dimension, an idea which was circulated in the magazine *Dudu Kowé*, itself another short-lived publication.[57] 1953 also saw the foundation of the publishing house Windu Kentjana at Surakarta, which was to publish or re-publish Ki Ageng's lectures. This, together with the publications put out by the company C.V. Harapan at Magelang, managed by Ki Djasoewadi, ensured that the philosopher's thoughts were widely circulated and that the movement had a regular source of income. It would seem that KAS was himself able to cover his own expenses to some extent thanks to this source of income.[58]

Could the movement be said to have remained totally divorced from political life, as its leaders wished? To judge from a pamphlet circulated by the Panitya K.J. from Klaten, at the time of the 1955 general elections, it would seem not. This pamphlet was in fact a poem sung to the accompaniment of the *gamelan* (*sendhonan*) and was an appeal to the people to come forward and participate in the elections, to "develop the country," and to ensure that the demands of the common people (*wong cilik*) were met.[59] As has already been seen, KAS's lectures at this time had a distinctly nationalistic flavor (*Raos Pantja Sila* was a lecture delivered in 1955).

During the colonial era and the Japanese occupation the K.J. movement came under suspicion on several occasions. Once independence was achieved, *pelajar* were advised to exercise a degree of caution: all books studied, which were KAS's sole responsibility, had to appear upright and honest to possible investigators.[60]

Although Ki Ageng often made frequent attacks on the irrational nature of the *kebatinan* teaching and sought to dissociate himself from it entirely, he could not prevent his movement being considered as an *aliran* (movement) of this kind and himself as a *guru*. Was this an error of judgment observers made or was it rather due to the fact that, seen from the outside and in light of the attitude of certain *pelajar*, the movement could have been said to exhibit all the characteristics of a "mystical sect." In any event this was the category into which it was put by Clifford Geertz, following his own observations and comments made by a K.J. "*guru*" from Pare. Nevertheless, to Geertz the K.J. seemed to originate from a "phenomenological analysis," and he stressed the absence of meditation which is known to be particularly important in mystical teaching.[61] When Ki Ageng died, an article appeared in the periodical *Varia* which spoke of him as a "personality in the *Kebatinan* world" (*tokoh di dalam dunia kebatinan*).[62] In the entry "Surya Mataram, Ki Ageng" in the *Ensiklopedi Umum* (pp. 1270–71), one finds, amongst other information: "Prince Surya Mataram (. . .) had taken

---

[56] In 1952 in Jakarta, he spoke to the Panitya Filsafat dan Kebatinan (Philosophical and Kebatinan Committe), to the Yayasan Hidup Bahagia (Happy Life Foundation) presided over by Mr. Wongsonegoro, and to the Chinese Sam Kauw Hwee and Khong Kauw Hwee Associations.

[57] It seems that the movement also published the periodical *Siaran*.

[58] From an interview with Ki Haditomo.

[59] *Sendonan bab Pemilihan Umum*.

[60] "*Manawi Junggring Salaka kedhatengan wakiling Pamarintah ingkang gadhah tugas naliti pakempalan-pakempalan lan grombolan-grombolan kanca-kanca cekap namung nyaturaken buku-buku Kawruh Jiwa wau . . .*" *Buku Peringatan*.

[61] Clifford Geertz, *The Religion of Java* (2nd ed. Chicago and London: University of Chicago Press, 1976), pp. 344–45.

[62] *Varia* 5, 206 (March 28, 1962). The article, however, is signed by Siauw Tik Kwie, himself a *pelajar* and currently translating texts published by the Idayu Foundation under the name of Ki Oto Suastika.

the name Ki Ageng as a *guru* of the *aliran kebatinan* known as Ilmu Begdja. His followers were spread over a large geographical area, despite a lack of organization and information, as is often the case. His teaching took the form of lectures delivered to a chosen audience in a *"lesehan"* manner (Jav: sitting on the ground). . . ." However in 1953, the K.J. movement was not listed among the *aliran kebatinan* of the Daerah Istimewa Yogyakarta.[63]

The booklet distributed to participants at the last Junggring Salaka Agung, held in 1959 at Purwokerto,[64] contained a number of interesting facts about the conduct of the meeting; it also gave valuable information about the geographical and social origins of the movement's members.

The organization of the conference was the work of a local committee headed by Ki Notoamidjojo. After the evening opening ceremony, at which guests were welcomed, KAS delivered a lecture, and the play (*sandiwara*) *Tjipta Djiwa*, was performed, the conference lasted two days. KAS chaired the debates and replied to comments made by *pelajar* regarding the various speeches (by KAS, Ki Kartosumanto, and Ki Prono). Delegates were asked to tell the meeting of the difficulties encountered and progress made by their groups in their study of the "science," as well as their specific needs.

The publication listed 257 names and addresses of local committee members from some fifty large and medium-size towns in Java. There was a particularly large number of towns from central and eastern Java (which backs up other information given elsewhere about the movement's growth). In Temanggung, Magelang, even Jember, there were many more committees than in other places. As for the western part of the island, Jakarta, Bogor, and Bandung all had their own *panitya*. In addition to Java, the document listed representatives, from Madura and the Lampung area.

Except for Suryomentaram (Ki Ageng) and Prawirowiworo (*Kyahi*) the name *pelajar* was usually preceded by the particle *Ki* for men and *Nyi* for women (as is still the case in the Taman Siswa movement); women made up an extremely small percentage of delegates. Dotted about the list of names were references to the delegates' professions: *pegawai* (employee), *guru sekolah rakyat* (primary school teacher), *kepala desa* (village chief), *mantri pengairan* (irrigation worker), and even *dhalang*. Although certain officials lived in a *kauman*, there were few Muslim names. Chinese names were equally rare; and yet (judging from the advertisements placed for the most part by Chinese enterprises: batik, printing, buses, and grocery wholesalers) the financial contribution from this community toward the brochure's publication must have been substantial. It is worth remarking that there is no name ending in -*ningrat* (an indication of nobility) and, on the whole, the names, like the professions already cited, are typical of the so-called "lower and middle-class *priyayi*."

Moving on from this last congress; KAS had only three more years to live, during which time he was ill for several months. After his death, his companions in Yogya carried on the work, with Ki Atmosutidjo providing moral leadership. Several more publications were circulated.[65]

Today, in the capital of the former sultanate, a K.J. group, led by Ki Haditomo, never fails to meet every thirty-five days, that is every Minggu-Pon, the day the philosopher died. It would seem that his widow, Nyi Suryomentaram, has made a point of carrying on Ki

---

[63] *Republik Indonesia: Daerah Istimewa Jogjakarta* (Jakarta: Kementerian Penerangan, 1953); cf. pp. 675–82.

[64] See note 54.

[65] Ki Atmosutidjo, *Gandulan* . . . ; Ki Djojodinomo, *Ular-ular* . . . ; Ki Suwardi Partosardjono, *Sadjimpit Hatsil* . . . (published by the Panitya Kawruh Jiwa in Magelang which was thus still active in 1970).

Ageng's teaching. It is Grangsang (a son of his first marriage) who is thought of as his spiritual heir and the one who will carry on the movement. Despite his professional responsibilities (he is a Lt.-Colonel in the Navy Medical Corps) which mean that he is often called away, he endeavors, as has been seen, to expound his father's ideas, with the help of Ki Oto Suastika and the Idayu Foundation, amongst others; he is equally committed to rebuilding the movement his father began.

***

In the interest of contemporary history it is to be hoped that new sources or fresh evidence will shed light on Suryomentaram's role in the struggle for independence and the social reforms which accompanied the rise of nationalism, which was at first Javanese then Indonesian. Suryomentaram can be seen as quite typical of those members of the Yogya (or Surakarta) aristocracy who have been described as *"enlightened priyayi,"* for, right from the turn of the century, these were the people who were anxious to play a leading role in promoting a new attitude, better suited to the needs of the times, and in advocating more flexible social structures than the ones which had existed during the colonial era. The attention paid to the peasants, the recognition of the essential role they play in maintaining a harmonious social entity, breathed new life into the old saying *"nagara mawa tata, désa mawa cara"* (organization is the work of the capital, application the work of the village).

But it is perhaps thanks to the least known aspects of KAS's biography, to its semi-legendary nature, that the motives and justification for his actions, in light of the particular demands of a Javanese mentality, may best be understood. Thus it was that Prince Suryamentaram-Siddhārta left his palace to discover human misery; then began the quest of the "renouncer," which was to end in the "Awakening" (even the name of his chosen resting place, Bringin, had an underlying meaning); the Buddha-Suryamentaram showing the "middle way." There was Suryomentaram, very upset, even revolted, by the conditions he found in the *kraton*. His behavior was very similiar to that displayed by the classic rebel, examples of which are dotted throughout Mataram's history. His rebellion (*madeg kraman*) like Diponegoro's,[66] for example, stemmed both from a certain moral deterioration (ineffectiveness) and from dissensions or setbacks within the family, even if, in this case, these did not have any dynastic implications. Evidence of his rebellion could be seen in the way he dressed (remember Prince Diponegoro's *jubah* and turban), the way he took refuge in a spiritual life and liked to frequent those places where a pact with the powers could be sealed. Diponegoro also meditated at Goa Langse and ran along the beach at Parangtritis. Such behavior may be thought of as signs of an "awakening of charisma," inspiring fearfulness. Bringin, like Tegalrejo, was a place to which he could withdraw, which enabled him to escape the court's control, and only later became the place from which a new moral order would proceed.

Times, however, had changed since Diponegoro. The awakening of a national consciousness and the liberation of the people were the goals of the new *jihad*. Education was the means. Suryomentaram's Indonesian editor has good reason to mention Krishnamurti.

---

[66] On the history of Diponegoro and the idea of revolt, cf. the excellent thesis by Peter Carey (the present author has consulted a typed copy) as well as a study by the same author entitled: *The Cultural Ecology of Early Nineteenth Century Java; Pangeran Dipanegara, A Case Study* (Singapore: Institute of Southeast Asian Studies, 1974), 25 pp.

Did KAS have access to his work? It seems so.[67] In any event, the two shared a similar pedagogical outlook. They said to their contemporaries: "Learn to know yourself," "wisdom is mid-way between the two extremes," "you are the other person." Their discourse is timeless, universal.[68] Thus, Suryamentaram was *the guru*; as was Ki Hajar. It was Ki Hajar, however, who had assimilated Western pedagogical theories and who wrote for the intellectuals of his generation, justifying his actions in terms of a conflict of cultures; for him Westernization was problematic; not so for Ki Ageng, who never felt the need to promote his Javanese cultural heritage.

No doubt he was too deeply immersed in it to make conscious use of it. It is not difficult, however, to find in his thinking the principal elements of a system of ethics, popular in 19th century Javanese literature, which reveals its relationship to a very old wisdom. Thus, the concept of an individual's responsibility when faced with the hazards of everyday life is reminiscent of a passage from the famous *Wulang Rêh*, a poem by Paku Buwono IV (1788–1820):

> *Bener luput ala becik lawan begja*
> *Cilaka apan saking*
> *Ing badan priyangga*
> *Dudu saka wong liya*
> *Pramila dèn ngati-ati*
>
> (pupuh VII, durma 3)
>
> Truth or falsehood, goodness or evil, happiness
> Or misfortune, the cause is found
> In each one of us
> And not in another
> So must we be watchful . . .

Similarly "detachment" (*sepi ing pamrih*), humility (*andhap-asor*), and "empathetic" understanding of others (*tepa-selira* = KAS's 4th dimension) are principles with which readers of 19th century moral literature were equally familiar. *Mawas diri, éling lan waspada*, that is, that self-control is the way to ensure impeccable social behavior, was just as true for KAS as for the *pujangga*. The phrase "*sapa temen tinememan*" ("he who is just is justified") from poetic literature expresses the determination which was to be shown in all circumstances (*tatag*, for KAS). Many more references can be made to this literature, which is recognized as nurturing all 20th century *kebatinan* thought.

Why, then, did KAS give the impression of disproving the term, if not the idea? The first reason, as has been seen, stemmed from his wish to dissociate himself from the *guru* whose teachings, shrouded in mystery and magic, fostered self-deception and excited false hopes

---

[67] According to Ki Haditomo (interview).

[68] Many similiar remarks may be found in Krishmamurti's and KAS's writing; for example: "Do not be either attached or detached; just look at the facts, and when you understand the facts, then there is neither pleasure nor pain; there is merely the fact." (*Krishnamurti On Education* [Bombay: Orient Longman, 1974], p. 40).

Krishnamurti was born in 1885. The two men were, therefore, contemporaries. They reveal the same liking for simplicity (which was also seen in Krishnamurti's style of dress) and rationalism.

It is not possible to continue the comparison further here, but it is worth noting that K's call for the development of our sense of the aesthetic does not appear in S's work, neither does the idea that a new culture was needed (ibid., p. 37). Such a rapport, it should also be remembered, is unlikely to have been fortuitous, given the historical links between Java and India and the affinity between the two systems of thought. Moreover, for his part Ki Hajar Dewantoro used Rabindranath Tagore as his "Indian model."

in their followers. It should be remembered, however, that Ki Ageng's "charisma" and aristocratic aura must often have detracted from his proclaimed intentions.[69] The second reason is considerably more fundamental: is it possible to give a definition of *kebatinan* when God is merely incidental, as KAS does? Regarding his apparent lack of interest in religious matters, a satisfactory explanation might be that given by Moh. Said; Ki Ageng wanted to restrict himself to an "existential" philosophy: "personally I think it was because he was well aware of man's limitations in understanding what lay behind the realities of every-day life (the here and now) and not because he rejected a priori the existence of an invisible reality."[70] It could also be said that if God has no part in the philosopher's thinking, it is because He is everywhere in it (amongst other things, in the concept of *Alam Agung*, the Universe).

Is it really God or Man, however, who is most important in Javanese thinking? It is definitely Man. Although spiritualist theories have borrowed from the Hindu-Buddhist religion, from Muslim mysticism or some other theosophy (sometimes even from medical science itself), in the end all these theories originate from a single psychological dictate: the spirit is the victim of a singular confusion, it is subject to a fundamental anxiety which must be quieted before inner harmony and psychological fulfilment can be found (or, if preferred, the state of vacuousness: *sunya*). This is a highly individualistic approach, broken into different stages (as much for the mystics as for KAS), each one of which represents some kind of advance toward the Truth, that is another step forward in one's attempts to find freedom.[71] At the same time this is a sort of "psychological focalization" whose ultimate goal is spiritual peace. The "veil" must be lifted, the screen[72] removed, before truth is known. And truth is just as much Suryamentaram's *Aku* as the divine presence mystics experience.

This perhaps is the perfect picture of tolerance, the celebrated Javanese tolerance, except, in fact, where dogmatic constraints are concerned . . . and intolerance! The "political" implications of such an approach should not be underestimated. Personal fulfilment corresponds *de facto* with social achievement (in the sense of human relationships) and a balance in the relationships between the different social classes whom KAS sought to bring together, as symbolized by the black shorts and royal sarong he wore.

Such an attitude, which is but one of the "Javanese attitude[s] to life,"[73] sometimes also called "priyayism," may be termed "traditional." But the taste for meditation is shared by many people in Java and, in this case, by the modest public who were attracted to KAS. Such an inclination is also highly resistant to change. Even if KAS's thoughts emerged from the mental depths where *kebatinan* took root, he nevertheless sought to purify them, in the strict sense of the word (to be rid of the cloak of superstition and mystic phraseology). To reason is thought of as the essential requirement for achieving psychological fulfilment; just as "modern" was the national significance KAS's thinking claimed to have. Rather than the

---

[69] It might also be helpful to look at the nature of his "revelation," the result of a long search and somewhat reminiscent of the spiritual master's *wahyu*.

[70] Moh. Said Reksohadiprodjo, "Ki Ageng Suryomentaram," *Pusara* 44, 4 (April 1975): 138.

[71] In the Javanese spiritual approach, De Jong distinguishes three essential components: the image of the King (*Raja*), "distancing" (*distansi*), and "representation" (*representasi*); see *Salah satu sikap hidup orang Jawa*, (Yogyakarta: Yayasan Kanisius, 1976), p. 151 (Indonesian adaptation of De Jong's thesis "Een Javaanse Levenshouding," Vrije Universiteit, Amsterdam, 1973). This author sees the concept of emancipation (distancing) as the central one, as least throughout KAS's works.

[72] The idea of the "veil" or screen (*warana, aling-aling*), which conceals true consciousness, is common to all *kebatinan* theories.

[73] To use De Jong's phrase (ibid).

word *"ngèlmu"* (science with esoteric connotations), Ki Ageng preferred *"kawruh"* (science, in the rational sense of the word).

Translated by Susan Crossley

Published lectures given by KAS and books or articles relating to the Kawruh Jiwa.

In this bibliography, which is by no means complete, the books the author was not able to consult are included according to a "list of Kawruh Bedja" books, found at the back of certain publications. The order corresponds to the list's order, except where a date is indicated.

M. Soedi, *Ngélmi-Kawruh-Pitedah Sedjatining Gesang (Wedjangan KAS)*, 1929 (?); Magelang, 1965 (4th ed.), 20 p. stencil.

R. Imam Moehni, *Inwijding tot het eeuwigdurende geluk van B.R.M. Soerjomentaram*, Djokjakarta, 71 p. (foreword written in 1930).

KAS, *Uran-uran Bedja*, (1930?); Surakarta, Windu Kentjana, 1955 (6th ed.), 17 p.

(KAS), *Pangawikan pribadi*, (1930?).

KAS, *Wedjangan Kawruh Bedja sawetah*, 1931 conference at Surakarta; 1957 (7th ed.), 37 p. stencil (Translated into Indonesian by Ki Oto Suastika: *Wejangan pokok Ilmu Bahagia*, Jakarta, Yayasan Idayu, 1975, 33 p.).

Ki Sangoebrangta (Ki Pronowidigdo), "Pendidikan oentoek ketentraman doenia wedjangan Toeanku Pangéran Soerjamataram (Kiai Ageng Beringin)," *Poesara* I, 10 (Jan. 13, 1932), pp. 79-81 (in Javanese).

KAS, *Kawruh pamomong*.

KAS, *Djiwa persatuan*.

KAS, *Djiwa buruh*.

KAS, *Ilmu djiwa*.

KAS, *Seni Suara*, 1951 Conference at Magelang; 1956 (2nd ed.), 10 p (in Indonesian).

KAS, *Perang dunia kaping III*, 1951 Conference at Pati; 1956 (4th ed.), 18 p.

KAS, *Pandangan keadaan dunia*.

KAS, *Pembangunan djiwa warga negara*, 1951 Conference, Surakarta, Windu Kentjana, 1955 (2nd ed.), 28 p. (in Javanese).

KAS, *Aku iki wong apa?*, 1952 Conference at Yogya; 1956 (4th ed.), 30 p.

KAS, *Ukuran kaping sakawan*, 1953 Conference at Magelang; Surakarta, Windu Kentjana, 1953 (1st ed.), 39 p. (Translated into Indonesian by Ki Oto Suastika: *Ukuran Keempat*, Jakarta, Yayasan Idayu, 1974, 32p.).

(KAS), *Sendon Djunggring S.A. VII*, 1953 (at Magelang).

KAS, *Taṇḍesan: Wedjangan Kawruh Bedja sawetah* (djilid I); Surakarta, Windu Kentjana, 1954 (1st ed.), 43 p.

KAS, *Mawas diri*, 1954 Conference at Surabaya; 1956 (1st ed.), 54 p.

KAS, *Kawruh laki-rabi*; Surakarta, Windu Kentjana, 1955 (3rd ed.), 60 p.

KAS, *Piageming gesang*; Surakarta, Windu Kentjana, 1955 (2nd ed.), 22 p. (Translated into Indonesian: *Idjazah hidup*; Jogjakarta, "Soejadi," 12 p., stencil).

KAS, *Raos Pantja-Sila*; Surakarta, W.K., 1955 (3rd ed.), 24 p.

KAS, *Uran-uran raos Pantja Sila*.

KAS, *Tata negara*.

KAS, *Djiwa Ngajogjakarta*.

KAS, *Hal kesempurnaan* (Indonesian text by Ki Pronowidigdo); Magelang, Harapan, 1956, 20 p.

KAS, *Sandiwara Raos Mlenet*; Surakarta, W.K., 1956 (1st ed.), 56 p.

KAS, *Pilsapat raos gesang*, 1956 Conference at Semarang; Magelang, Harapan, 1959 (2nd ed.), 17 p.
(translated into Indonesian:
1) by Kjai Pronowidigdo, *Pilsapat Rasa-hidup*, Jogjakarta, 1957 (1st ed.), 30 p.;
2) by Ki Oto Suastika, *Filsafat rasa hidup*, Jakarta, Yayasan Idayu, 1974, 28 p.).

Buku Peringatan Djunggring Salaka Agung ke XI, tgl.21-22-23 Maret 1959, di Purwokerto, Panitya Dj. S.A. ke XI, Purwokerto.

Ki Djojodinomo, Ular-ular djiwa Bangsa Indonesia, Ngajogjakarta, 18 p.

Ki Atmosutidjo, Gaṇḍulan kanggé kantja-kantja peladjar—Kawruh Djiwa, Jogjakarta, 1962, 18 p. stencil.

Ki Suwardi Partosardjono, Sadjimpit Hatsil Njumerepi gagasan (pasinaon Kawruh-Djiwa babon saking Suwargi Ki Ageng Surjomentaram), Magelang, "P.K.D.," 1970, 31 p. stencil.

Moh. Said Reksohadiprodjo, "Ki Ageng Suryomentaram, 20 Mei 1892–18 Maret 1962," Pusara 44, 4 (April 1975), p.137-39.

STATE, CITY, COMMERCE: THE CASE OF BIMA[*]

Henri Chambert-Loir

On the map of the Lesser Sunda Islands, between Bali and Lombok in the west and Flores, Sumba, and Timor in the east, lies the island of Sumbawa, a compact, homogenous fief of Islam in the midst of a religious mosaic, of which history has not yet finished modifying the pattern. From west to east the island, which forms part of the Nusa Tenggara province, is divided into three *kabupaten* : Sumbawa, Dompu, and Bima. Today the latter contains almost 430,000 inhabitants,[1] of whom probably 70,000 live in the twin agglomerations of Bima and Raba.

The Present Town

The Raba quarter developed at the beginning of this century when the kingdom of Bima was integrated into the Netherlands Indies. It contains the main administrative buildings: the offices of the *bupati*, located in the former house of the Assistant-Resident, the regional parliament (DPRD), and the local headquarters of the various administrative services. The urban center remains that of the former capital of the sultanate, in the vicinity of the bay. In contrast to the governmental pole concentrated in Raba, the agglomeration of Bima contains the main centers of social life, both past and present. The former palace of the Sultans (N° 4 on Fig. 2) is an imposing masonry edifice built at the beginning of this century. Today it is practically deserted and will probably be converted into a museum. West of the palace there is a large rectangular square, to the south of which still stands the small mosque which in the last century the Sultan attended every Friday. The large mosque, which is of recent construction, is situated to the northwest of the palace. The market and the commercial area, which naturally constitute the hub of the most animated activity, are located in the direction of the bay, in the area of Kampung Tanjung and Sarae.

---

[*] The French version of this article appeared in *Archipel* 37 (1989): 83–105.

[1] Figure estimated for 1988 based on the 1980 Census (366,740 inhabitants, annual growth rate of 2.1 percent). The very approximative estimate of the population of Bima and Raba is based on that of the *kecamatan* Rasanae (ca. 100,000 inhabitants in 1988), where at least 11 of the 25 *desa* constituted the urban zone (see *Penduduk Indonesia 1980 menurut Propinsi dan Kabupaten/Kotamadya. Hasil pencacahan lengkap Sensus Penduduk 1980* (Jakarta: Biro Pusat Statistik, 1981), *Peta Index Kecamatan dan Desa/Kelurahan di Propinsi Nusa Tenggara Barat. Hasil pemetaan Sensus Penduduk 1980* (Jakarta: Biro Pusat Statistik, 1982), and *Kabupaten Bima dalam angka, tahun 1981* (Bima: Kantor Statistik, 1982).

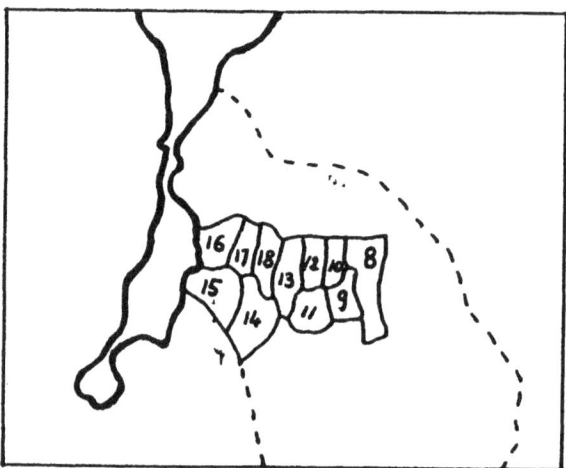

Fig. 1. The agglomeration of Bima and Raba. Map of the 11 urban *kecamatan* according to the official indexation. 8. Raba; 9. Rabangodu; 10. Penaraga; 11. Sadia; 12. Penatoi; 13. Menggonao; 14. Paruga; 15. Tanjung; 16. Melayu; 17. Sarae; 18. Nae (source: *Peta Index 1980*).

Two rivers wind their way through the town. Crossing over the Kali Bageroso, proceeding northwards from the market, one enters the *kelurahan* Melayu, where the three districts frequently mentioned by early travelers are to be found: first there is Kampung Benteng, the eastern part of the former Kampung Walanda where not a trace remains of the former Dutch fort and where the small, poorly maintained Christian cemetery seems to contain only 20th century graves; then comes Kampung Soro or Bugis; and finally Kampung Melayu, which, tradition has it, was given in the 17th century by the second Sultan of Bima (Abdu'l Khair Sirajuddin) to "Malays" entrusted with the propagation and control of Muslim orthodoxy. This part was formerly that of the foreign community: Malays, Bugis, Arabs, Chinese, and Dutch. Now foreigners of pure descent constitute no more than a few dozen families, while the *peranakan* and people of mixed race have been more or less integrated into the Bimanese population. For instance, today the Malays use Bimanese as their mother tongue.

Statistics from 1981 for the whole of the *kecamatan* Rasanae record 98.4 percent Muslims.[2] Nevertheless, the registered places of worship comprise five churches and two Balinese temples, besides 66 mosques, 25 *langgar*, and 11 *mushala*.

A road leaves the town in a southerly direction, running alongside the Bay of Bima; it passes in front of the "heroes' cemetery" (*makam pahlawan*), continues on past the Chinese graveyard, which contains a hundred or so 20th century graves, and the small naval dockyard, before arriving at Palibelo Airport, which was renamed Muhammad Salahuddin, the name of the last Sultan, in 1983. Further on, at the southernmost end of the bay, for centuries saltworks have been producing salt, which today is exported to Java and Flores. The road continues to the west in the direction of Sila, Dompu, and Sumbawa Besar. Two other roads connect Bima with the east (Sape) and with the north (Wera).

The airport links Bima with Denpasar, Sumbawa Besar, and Waingapu. On average there are three small planes a day (1981). There is still a certain amount of activity in the harbor, especially as far as the export of cattle is concerned. However, the commercial wealth of

---

[2] See *Kabupaten Bima 1981*. The remaining 1.6 percent consisted of 906 Christians, 322 Hindus, and 95 Buddhists.

Bima ebbed away a long time ago. The export of foodstuffs has given way to imports; manufactured goods and crafts are of purely local interest and half the budget of the *kabupaten* is provided by subsidies from the province. In 1981, in the whole of the *kabupaten*, there were over 400 motor vehicles registered: 300 commercial vehicles, 96 motor coaches, and 10 private cars. The existence of several hotels may be a sign of a certain amount of activity, but they are rarely used and 79 tourists a year were registered (again in 1981).

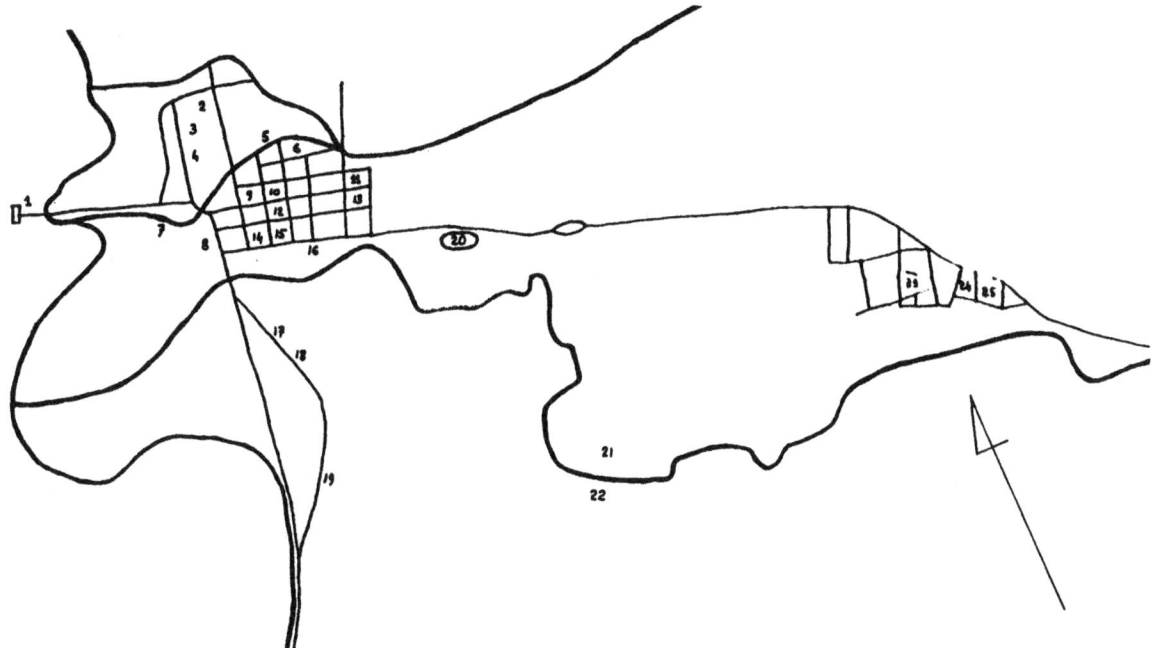

Fig. 2. The agglomeration of Bima and Raba. Schematic plan and toponyms (K. = Kampung). 1. The harbor; 2. K. Melayu; 3. K. Bugis or Soro; 4. K. Benteng; 5. Tolobali; 6. K. Gilipanda; 7. K. Tanjung; 8. K. Sumbawa; 9. K. Sarae; 10. K. Wera; 11. K. Nae; 12. Great mosque; 13. K. Pane; 14. *Alun-alun*; 15. The palace; 16. K. Sigi; 17. K. Dara; 18. Heroes' cemetery (*Makam Pahlawan*); 19. Chinese cemetery; 20. Stade Manggemaci; 21. Dantaraha; 22. K. Sambinae; 23 & 24. Main squares; 25. K. Raba Dompu.

In short, for today's visitors, the town of Bima seems a tranquil and small market town, which is hard to imagine as having once been the capital of a sultanate sufficiently powerful to dominate several of its neighbors as well as a center of commerce, frequented since time immemorial, and the home of an original culture.

The Town in the 19th Century

Travelers who visited Bima in the last century and committed their impressions to paper allow us to form an idea of the town while it was still the capital of an independent sultanate. It was a small town, whose population was estimated at 5,000 by Reinwardt in 1821 and at 7,000 by Braam Morris in 1891.[3] The painting executed by A.J. Bik in 1821 (Fig. 3) shows a village with only a few scattered houses emerging from among the trees.

---

[3] See C.G.C. Reinwardt, *Reis naar het oostelijk gedeelte van den Indischen Archipel in het jaar 1821* (Amsterdam: Muller, 1858), p. 319, and D.F. van Braam Morris, "Nota van toelichting behoorende bij het contract gesloten met het landschap Bima op den 20sten Oct. 1886," *TBG* 34 (1891): 179.

74 *Henri Chambert-Loir*

Fig. 3. The agglomeration and the Bay of Bima in 1821. Engraving by A.J. Bik, published in Reinwardt, *Reis naar het oostelijk gedeelte*. The mosque with the triple roof and the shallows, which made an approach difficult, are clearly visible. The flag in the center probably marks the site of the Dutch fort.

"There are absolutely no stone buildings. All the bricks for the residence of the Sultan and the mosque came from Java," Zollinger noted during his visit in 1847.[4] He added: "The Sultan and the population have not yet summoned up the energy to construct a bridge for pedestrians. When one wishes to visit the Sultan [from the Dutch residency], it is necessary to ford the small river, or have oneself carried across."[5]

The palace itself was a wooden building. The present palace (Bim. Asi Wadu, meaning *istana batu*, "the stone palace") was, it seems, built in the 1920s. Formerly it was a wooden edifice, with an entrance stairway in masonry (see Fig. 4). The previous palace (Asi Bou, *istana baru*, "the new palace"), which was situated to the east of it, was a considerably smaller building and was constructed entirely of wood. It seems to have been started by Sultan Abdul Hamid in 1781.[6] When Rouffaer visited Bima in 1910 this palace, already relegated to second place, was the residence of the crown prince, the Raja Muda.[7] Both these palaces

---

The *Encyclopaedie van Nederlandsch-Indië* (8 vols. [2nd ed. Leiden/The Hague, 1917–1940]), in 1917 cites the figure of 10,000 inhabitants, which was already adjusted to 12,000 in the first supplement (1927).

[4] H. Zollinger, *Verslag van eene reis naar Bima en Soembawa . . . gedurende de maanden Mei tot December 1847. VBG* [Batavia], 23 (1850): 98.

[5] Ibid.

[6] The manuscript journal of Moh. Djafar gives the date of the installation of the Sultan and his consort in the *istana baru* as Safar 19, 1195, i.e. February 14, 1781. (See the manuscript of the Benteng Ujungpandang: Lontara No. 152. Journal in Malay for the years 1775–1790 belonging to Muh. Djafar, Rato Rasanae.) However, the dates in this document must be treated with caution.

[7] J. Noorduyn, *Bima en Sumbawa. Bijdragen tot de geschiedenis van de Sultanaten Bima en Sumbawa door A. Ligtvoet en G.P. Rouffaer* (Holland-USA: Foris, 1987), p. 75

were surrounded either by a wooden fence or by a stone wall.[8] Today all traces of these earlier palaces have disappeared.

The present palace, just as the former wooden one on the site of which it was erected, faces north. However, it is flanked on the eastern and western sides by two large squares. The palisades of the palace open onto the western *alun-alun* by means of a tiered monumental gateway built on an octagonal plan called the *uma lare-lare*. This once served as the entrance for court dignitaries and royal servants, and it was also from this that the Sultan showed himself to the people during the four days of the Maulud festival.[9] At the top of this tower-like construction were hanging "several bells which proclaim the grandeur of the

Fig. 4. The palace of Bima at the beginning of the century. One can make out a row of cannon along the edge of the *alun-alun*, two bells inside the monumental gateway (*uma lare-lare*) and the wooden palace to which has been joined a small masonry building. Collection of the KITLV in Leiden (Afd. DGI, doc. MR. 7411). By kind permission of the KITLV.

---

[8] The journal of Muh. Djafar notes on September 25, 1776: "Today a palisade has been erected around the palace of the sovereign." E. Francis in 1831, and Asselbergs in 1895, speak of a stone wall (E. Francis, *Herinneringen uit den levensloop van een Indisch ambtenaar van 1815 tot 1851* Vol. 1 (Batavia: Van Dorp, 1856), p. 130; A. Asselbergs, "Eene reis naar het eiland Soembawa," *Sint Claverbond* I (1896): 63. Rouffaer, in his turn, describes the high wooden fence, apparently constructed in 1901, surrounding the later palace. (Noorduyn, *Bima en Sumbawa*, p. 71).

[9] See Rouffaer in Noorduyn, *Bima en Sumbawa*, p. 71. There is a photograph of this gateway, dating from the beginning of this century, in Fig. 4, and another, taken in 1976, in H. Chambert-Loir, *Syair Kerajaan Bima* (Jakarta: EFEO, 1982), p. 125.

prince with their metal tongues."[10] In 1910 on the western *alun-alun* stood 13 cannons, including four made of Dutch bronze dating from the 17th and 18th centuries.[11] To the south of the square stands the mosque with its three-storeyed roof which was constructed by Sultan Abdul Hamid in 1780.[12]

The residence of the Chief Minister (*Raja Bicara*) was a large wooden house situated at a place called Nteli (Kampung Nae), northeast of the palace. Zollinger, who was received there in 1847, accords it no more than a contemptuous note which, nevertheless, hints at a certain opulence: "The next day I paid a visit, with the same solemnity, to the *radja bitjara*, or governor. His house, even more than that of the Sultan, is encumbered with all sorts of objects. The interior gallery looks more like a *toko* than a reception hall for foreigners."[13] The ridgepole of this gallery was supported by three moulded pillars supposed to symbolize the three foundations of power: royal administration, Islamic law, and custom.[14]

Close to the shoreline, southwest of Kampung Walanda stood the Dutch fort. "The fort, with its earthern ramparts and ditches, looks fairly dilapidated, which, however, is nothing in comparison to the dwellings and barracks of bamboo it contains," Zollinger notes. It was "armed with eight pieces of artillery, only two of which belong to the Government and are in good condition, the others, the property of the Sultan, being practically unusable."[15] Every traveler noticed the insignificance of this small fort,[16] the garrison of which was also extremely sparse: in 1880 Colfs mentioned a Dutch sergeant, a Dutch corporal, and 15 indigenous fusiliers;[17] fifteen years later Asselbergs mentioned two Germans and a dozen indigenous soldiers.[18]

This fort, as well as the house of the Government representative (*gezagheber*) and those of several resident Dutchmen (*burgers*), was located in the "government territory," very uncomfortably situated in a swampy area on the edge of the bay. Various plans to move them to a more salubrious area came to nothing.[19]

The location of Bima on the inner shore of a wide, deep bay offered ships a secure, sheltered anchorage. The approach was rendered difficult by the presence of a mudbank directly in front of the town itself, which made it impossible to tie up at a wharf and which sometimes had to be crossed on foot. Reinwardt, Zollinger, and Jasper are among those who suffered this experience. "It is a strange phenomenon," writes Reinwardt,[20] "that the water can be so very deep everywhere right to the end of the bay so that one can find absolutely no anchorage at all and that very close to the shore we were still obliged to anchor at a

---

[10] Asselbergs, "Eene reis naar het eiland Soembawa," p. 63.

[11] See Rouffaer in Noorduyn, *Bima en Sumbawa*, pp. 71, 104.

[12] Ibid., p. 87. The journal of Muh. Djafar mentions the stages of construction on December 10, 1778, and January 5 and April 25, 1779. It is the roof of this mosque which one sees on the drawing of A.J. Bik (Fig. 3).

[13] Zollinger, *Verslag van eene reis*, p. 18.

[14] M. Hitchcock, "The Bimanese Kris: Aesthetics and Social Value," *BKI* 143, 1 (1987); 129.

[15] Zollinger, *Verslag van eene reis*, p. 98.

[16] See Rouffaer's remarks: "het kleine onbeduidende fort ... het onnoozele fortje," in Noorduyn, *Bima en Sumbawa*, p. 71.

[17] A. Colfs, *Het journaal van Albert Colfs. Eene bijdrage tot de kennis der Kleine Soenda-Eilanden, door A.G. Vorderman.* (Batavia: Ernst & Co, 1888), p. 45.

[18] Asselbergs, "Eene reis naar het eiland Soembawa," p. 53.

[19] J.E. Jasper, "Het eiland Soembawa en zijn bevolking," *TBB* 34 (1908): 79.

[20] *Reis naar het oostelijk gedeelte*, p. 314.

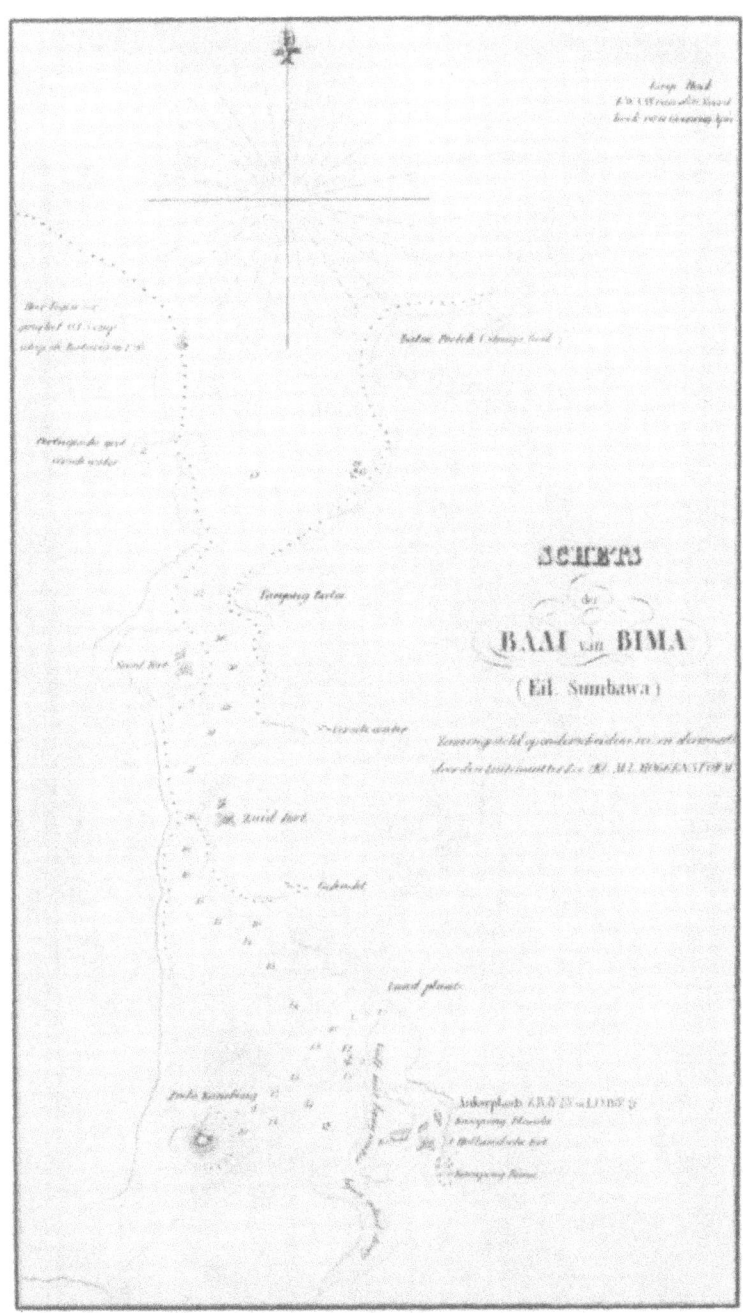

Fig. 5. Map of the Bay of Bima (undated). Marked are the sites of the two small forts and the "Portuguese cave," that is to say the site of Wadu Paa. Collection Algemeen Rijksarchief, The Hague, doc. MIKO 548. By kind permission of the Archives.

Fig. 6. The north coast of Sumbawa (undated). Collection Algemeen Rijksarchief, The Hague, doc. MIKO 65. By kind permission of the Archives.

depth of 13 fathoms. Right in front of the town, at the edge of the bay, one encounters a deep mudbank which, especially at low tide, makes an approach very difficult, even with small craft (...). Therefore I was obliged to have myself carried over the mud, whereas my travelling companions had to resign themselves to crossing the thick mud on foot." Zollinger, who faced the same difficulties, surveyed the unloading of his baggage, which took four days, with alarm. He adds: "Up to the present time the Sultan has promised a hundred times that he would make the landing stage more accessible, which would not incur great difficulties, but he has not done anything about it. The *sappan* wood is loaded half an hour further to the north, where the approach is easier."[21]

When steamships began to call at Bima the Dutch Government installed coal bunkers on the small island of Pulau Kambing which lies in the bay facing the town.[22]

The entrance of the Bay of Bima is easy to locate because of the presence of Mount Soromandi or Vadersmits close to the shore on the western side. The channel rapidly narrows to the point, quoting J.Th. Bik, "where, from on board, one can throw a pebble onto either bank."[23] This was the place where two small forts were constructed on either side of the bay, giving control of the mouth. One was built on a small promontory on the shore to the west of the bay: it was rectangular (ca. 150 x 80 m) with rounded bastions at each of the four corners. Its walls were six feet high. To the south of this fort lay the other one, which was slightly smaller (ca. 95 x 60 m), built on the eastern shore of the bay. Both were armed with cannon.[24] Every traveler noted the military insignificance of these defenses and agreed in commenting that several pieces of artillery would be sufficient to prevent access to the bay. As Noorduyn notes, the construction of these forts must have taken place before the middle of the 17th century.[25]

Even though they are of a late date and are fragmentary, these travelers' notes imbue the capital of the sultanate with the image of an agglomeration of very mediocre importance, at least as regards its size and its buildings: several hundred wooden houses, negligible fortifications, no monument worthy of the name, an open-air local market, a small port with difficult approaches. . . . It is even possible that in volume of commerce and population, at certain times, Bima did not surpass Sape, or even Wera or Kore.

An Urban Society

But Bima was not just an overgrown village which seemed insignificant to the eyes of visitors disembarking from Makassar or Batavia. The urban character of this capital, as indeed it was, does not lie in the number or nature of its buildings: it emerges when one

---

[21] Zollinger, *Verslag van eene reis*, pp. 17, 18.

[22] Jasper, "Het eiland Soembawa," p. 63, and B.F. Matthes ("Eenige opmerkingen omtrent en naar aanleiding van dat gedeelte van Dr. J.J. de Hollander's Handleiding bij de beoefening der Land- en Volkenkunde van Nederlandsch Oost-Indië, het welk handelt over het Gouvernement van Celebes en Onderhoorigheden," BKI 19 [1876]: 91) noted the presence of these fueling stations in the years 1850 and 1860. Today no trace of them remains.

[23] "Aanteekeningen nopens eene reis naar Bima . . . ," TBG 14 (1864): 126.

[24] See the maps in Figs. 5 and 6. The measurements are those given by Rouffaer (Noorduyn, *Bima en Sumbawa*, pp. 102–103), who also provides the plan of the two small forts and a photograph of the southern fort as it was in 1910. The two forts, although now complete ruins, are still visible at the present time, but all the cannon have been transported to Bima. The two forts together are known locally as Asa Kota, literally "the mouth of the town," an expression which the dictionary of A.K. Sahidu defines as "the port, the Bay of Bima."

[25] *Bima en Sumbawa*, pp. 115n., 173.

examines the composition of the population and the nature of its resources, the centralization of the symbols of power, the multiplicity of its external contacts, and its cultural and religious life. The example of Bima is certainly not a unique one of an agglomeration of which the urban character cannot be defined in terms of its physical characteristics (number of inhabitants, importance of buildings, presence of fortifications), but springs from the origin, the divisions, and occupations of the population. When a town is contrasted with a village this is not in terms of size but in the way of life. The ethnic diversity, the presence of a central power and its insignia, the concentration of economic activity and contacts with foreign nations all give rise to special types of apportionment of the area and density of settlement, to social stratification and the administration of individual obligations toward the community as a whole, to the proliferation of service activities, the development of the arts, the integration of foreign influences, and the recourse to the use of a lingua franca; such are the collective traits which define the urban phenomenon.

In this area even more than in others, the documents are incomplete and inconsistent, and one has to resort not only to foreign accounts but also to local sources, and this over a longer period. The origins of the kingdom of Bima stretch back to an unknown epoch. However, the advent of the sultanate dates from the conversion to Islam of the first Sultan, a matter on which Noorduyn has recently shed new light, the fruit of the cross-checking of a number of documents:[26] the Islamization of Bima was the consequence of two military expeditions launched by Makassar in 1618 and 1619, which makes the date of the conversion of Sultan Abdul Kahir as it is given in a Bimanese document, namely February 7, 1621, plausible.

The political and economic situation of the sultanate was modified by contracts signed with Makassar and Bima by the VOC in 1667 and 1669. As a result, its prosperity diminished down the course of the centuries and it was also considerably weakened by the eruption of Mount Tambora in 1815. The absorption of Bima into the territory of the Netherlands Indies in 1905 marked a new phase in its history. In matters which concern the characteristic traits of the town, however, it does not seem that, from the beginning of the 17th century to the beginning of the 20th century, it should be necessary to distinguish different periods according to factual events.

Bimanese society made a categorical distinction between autochtonous people and foreigners. The Bimanese, who were drawn to the capital from all parts of the realm, were divided into two classes: the nobility, among whom the *Ruma* were distinguished from the *Rato*, and the "free men" (*dou mardika*), among whom two terms of address (*uba* and *ama*) effected a subdivision. Slaves fell outside Bimanese society. They came mainly from Manggarai and Sumba.[27]

This hierarchy was superimposed on a horizontal division which unfortunately never attracted the attention of ethnologists; scattered references to it in several sources only give a very imprecise picture: the population was divided into groups (*dari*), which writers generally defined as "guilds" or "corporations," because one of their characteristics was the specified nature of the statutory labor each of them was expected to perform. Zollinger gives the name of 13 of them. Braam Morris and Jasper who copied the same source, probably the report of a local official—and both of whom lament identically about the "confused and more than once contradictory" information provided by the dignitaries of Bima—list

---

[26] Ibid.

[27] From a personal communication from A.M. Daeng Talu, born in 1911, who was the last Tureli Belo.

respectively 43 and 42 of them.[28] Jasper groups these under 13 headings, and this figure is mentioned too in volume 1 of the *Encyclopaedie van Nederlandsch-Indië* in 1917. However, in its first supplement (vol. 5, 1927), this was corrected to 70 on the basis of an unknown source.

On several occasions Zollinger mentions the under-chiefs (*onder-chefs*) but there does not seem to have been any sort of hierarchy in the *dari*, except that each of them was under the authority of a man of note bearing the title of Bumi or Anangguru. Some of them were not assigned to regal corvée, but were in the service of an important personage in order to assist him in his duties: the Dari Sabicara Kae, Luma Rasanae, and Luma Bolo were at the service of the Raja Bicara, the Bumi Luma Rasanae, and the Bumi Luma Bolo respectively. This seems to have involved a strict client system; however, the functions and duties of the *dari* were very complex.

On certain occasions and within certain limitations most of the *dari* were expected to provide precisely defined services for the palace or the State. The nobles of the Dari Ratu provided dancers and pages; members of the Dari Jara Mbojo and Jara Bolo, also aristocrats, formed the palace guard; three other *dari* furnished flautists, another wet nurses. Certain set tasks were assigned to the common people and did not require any real specialization: soldiers in time of war (Dari Suba Nae), the sailors of the Sultan and of the high dignitaries (Dari Pabise), the Sultan's grooms (Dari Jara), the cultivators of the Sultan's ricefields (Dari Tolotui); others required technical specializations and these merit the term guilds: carpenters, sculptors, blacksmiths (Dari Besi), goldsmiths (Dari Mas), fusiliers (Dari Bedi), doctors (Dari Cindawa), and men of religion (Dari Ngaji). Some of the *dari* escaped this classification as they contained persons from the various regions of the kingdom (people from Wera, Sangeang, Sape, or from the area south of the bay), or foreigners (Dari Parisi), or even people from all classes who were exempted from all statutory labor because of their merit (Dari Merdeka).

Membership of a *dari* was hereditary, but it did not actually impose any profession on the people: the Bimanese were free to exercise their talents without regard to the nature of the corvée imposed on their *dari*. In theory each *dari* was endogamous and cases of intermarriage were judged by the chiefs of the *dari* concerned, and involved the transfer of one of the spouses into the *dari* of his or her partner.

Finally this system also had a spatial consequence: first of all because each *dari* had the right to the yield from the harvest of the ricefields assigned to it. Second because each *dari*, or some of them at least, occupied a specific quarter of the town, the goldsmiths for instance lived in an area close to the northern gate in the wall of the palace fortifications.[29]

Therefore this social compartmentalization had manifold consequences: asserting ethnic integrity vis-à-vis the foreigners, concretizing the distinction between aristocrats and the common people, marking geographic origin, dividing the community in endogamous clans, assessing the civic duties, and alloting the social space.

Apart from the Bugis (under the authority of a *matoa*) and the "Malays" (under that of a *penghulu*), both of whom, as we have already seen, had their districts in the northwest part of the town, the foreigners consisted of Chinese, Arabs, and Europeans. These communities, whose history remains obscure, were never numerically important. There is mention of

---

[28] Zollinger, *Verslag van eene reis*, pp. 132–33; Braam Morris, "Nota van toelichting," pp. 200–205; Jasper, "Het eiland Soembawa," pp. 106–108.

[29] Hitchcock, "The Bimanese Kris," p. 129.

several dozen Chinese families in 1900, who also lived close to the shores of the bay. These were merchants and, in 1895, Asselbergs noted that in this rich country it was astonishing not to find rich Chinese, the reason behind this being probably the fact that these merchants were only the representatives of the large trading companies in Makassar.[30] At the end of the last century the Arabs were probably more numerous. Specializing in the export of horses, they also played a religious role and more than one traveler records the ascendency that several Arabs appeared to enjoy at the palace. The European community was always extremely small but its presence went back to the 1680s.[31] According to Zollinger, in 1846, there were 14 Christian families, that is to say 59 people, upon whom 279 servants and slaves were dependent, in Kampung Walanda ("de governments-kampong").[32]

However, the contacts with the Europeans go back to an earlier time. The Dutch, whose first visit to Bima dated from the passage of the fleet of Steven van den Hagen in 1605, immediately found themselves in competition with the Portuguese. The latter regularly took on provisions in Bima; they sometimes built boats there; in 1618 they attempted to convert the king to Catholicism and, even after the contract of 1669 by which the VOC imposed its law on Bima, they occasionally continued to trade there.[33]

Less foreign within the ethnic and geographical framework of the Archipelago, but nevertheless external to the kingdom and people of Bima, were the inhabitants of Java, Bali, Banjar, Makassar, and the Moluccas with whom Bima maintained commercial and political relations. Sparse evidence for these contacts is deposited in the records of the palace of Bima. Several precise examples refer to the reign of Sultan Abdul Hamid (1773–1817): for instance, in May 1779 Javanese from Surabaya gave several *wayang* performances at the palace; between April and July 1787, a troupe, which had come from Batavia under the leadership of a *khalipa*, gave performances of *dabus*, some of which took place in the mosque: "they strike themselves and pierce themselves without being injured by either the iron or the stone."[34] Much later, when Rouffaer visited Bima in 1910, a *komedi stambul* troupe was performing there.[35]

Sultan Abdul Hamid attended the *wayang* and *dabus* performances, just as he used to go along to the scene of popular feasts, notably a kind of wrestling (*begoco*): during a tourna-

---

[30] Asselbergs, "Eene reis naar het eiland Soembawa," p. 59.

[31] The Company considered a permanent settlement at Bima from 1675, but abandoned the idea. *Generale Missiven van Gouverneurs-Generaal en Raden aan Heren XVII der Verenigde Oostindische Compagnie uitg. door W.Ph. Coolhaas*. 8 vols. (The Hague: Nijhoff, 1960–1985), 4: 2–3. There is reference to a Resident of Bima from the year 1689 and the years thereafter (ibid., 5: 395, 455, etc.).

[32] Zollinger, *Verslag van eene reis*, p. 101.

[33] With reference to Portuguese trade with Bima see, for example, Noorduyn, *Bima en Sumbawa*, p. 331: about 1618 the Portuguese visited the north coast of Bima every year, in December or January, in order to load dye wood. The *Dagh Register gehouden int casteel Batavia (1624–1682)* (31 vols., Batavia/The Hague, 1886–1931) [hereafter *Dagh Register*], mentions (on September 21, 1631 and November 21, 1640) ships constructed for the Portuguese in Bima. Noorduyn published unedited documents on the attempted conversion of the King of Bima by the Jesuit Manuel Ferreira. Ibid., pp. 334–38. The complete original (Portuguese) text, accompanied by a summary and notes, of the letter from Father Manuel Barrada S.J. (November 20, 1619) relating the episode, has been published in H. Jacobs, S.J., ed., *The Jesuit Makasar Documents (1615–1682)* (Rome: Jesuit Historical Institute, 1988), pp.17–28. Finally, in 1673, "the King of Bima has conceded to the Portuguese, under the command of one Padre Brave, a whole quarter as their permanent residence, which runs absolutely contrary to the contract, because he tries to have his fortifications reinforced." (*Generale Missiven* 3: 845, letter of January 31, 1673). One may wonder whether this latter episode has any connection with the two forts on the bay, mentioned earlier.

[34] Journal of Muh. Djafar.

[35] Noorduyn, *Bima en Sumbawa*, pp. 76, 79.

ment lasting more than a fortnight in October 1786, he gave a monetary reward to those protagonists who knocked down their opponents.[36]

The Sultan embodied the unity of the realm. The inhabitants of the town, as we have seen, were defined according to the duties which they had to perform for him; and many sites in the town mark either by monuments, toponyms, or simply by tradition, the landmarks of dynastic history, like so many symbols of the continuity of the authority which was centralized there.

To the east of the town, at a place which today is no longer certain, was the lake where the first king of Bima met the celestial nymph who was to give birth to the dynasty.[37] The tomb of the first Sultan is located to the south at Dantaraha (N°25 on Fig.2); those of his three successors lie to the north at Tolobali (N°11), while those of five other Sultans are right in the heart of the town in the courtyard of the mosque situated on the edge of the *alun-alun* (N°13). Also to the south of the town, on the hill of Mbanteli, lies buried the sacred horse: *jara manggila*, which is part of the royal insignia.[38]

The ceremonies attached to the person of the Sultan himself, as well as his entertainment, display a sort of decorum which was the privilege of the court. But the court life largely overflowed the very limited circle of the palace and the high officials; it infused the arteries of the small city with the pomp and luxury which are elements of urban life. The hair of the Sultan was thrown into the sea, having been carried in procession to a musical accompaniment; the end of his religious instruction was the object of a ceremony (*khatam al-Qur'an*); his marriage was an occasion for festivities. Sultan Abdul Hamid liked to disport himself in a boat: in 1775, when he was about 13, he made a trip in his *perahu kora-kora* manned by 74 men; five years later, on several occasions he went out competing with his ministers, with a buffalo and goats or hens as stake.[39] The coronation and the burial of a Sultan were the occasions for much more important ceremonies in which the whole town participated. A poem composed about 1830 by an inhabitant of Bima describes with a great wealth of detail the funeral of Sultan Abdul Hamid and the enthronement of his successor, Sultan Ismail, in 1817. The author stresses, and we have grounds for believing him, the presence of a considerable crowd during these two events.[40]

Within its limits the court of Bima reproduced some of the pomp of more important sultanates. In 1879 the Belgian naturalist, A. Colfs, described as follows the procession entrusted with bearing the letter of the Governor of Makassar to the palace:

> The deputation which arrived to take the letter was composed thus: Right at the very front came a *djouroutoulis* with two men, followed by a drum and a fife; then came twelve court horses mounted by the *adat* (the Sultan's council), which pranced into the courtyard of the *controleur*; here the horses halted and their riders presented their lances

---

[36] Journal of Muh. Djafar.

[37] Cf. H. Chambert-Loir, *Ceritera asal bangsa jin dan segala dewa-dewa* (Bandung: Angkasa-EFEO, 1985), pp. 81–82.

[38] This horse, of which the tradition goes back to Sultan Abu'l Khair Sirajuddin (r. 1640–1682), was led in procession every Friday to be bathed in a river close to this hill. According to the somewhat exotic formula given by Rouffaer (Noorduyn, *Bima en Sumbawa*, p. 102), the Sultan had commanded "that this horse should be mandied in the kali near the kraton every Friday morning" ("dat dit paard elken Vrijdag morgen in de kali bij de kraton zou gemandi'd worden").

[39] These various events are mentioned in the journal of Muh. Djafar.

[40] Cf. Chambert-Loir, *Syair Kerajaan Bima*, stanzas 82–217 and 289–487. A description of a more recent ceremony is found in M. A. Bouman, "Toeharlanti. De Bimaneesche sultansverheffing, "*Koloniaal Tijdschrift* 14, 6 (1925): 710–17.

horizontally with arms extended; then they withdrew; next came a young man wearing a white turban and a long white robe borne by four *coulis* on a sort of stretcher, resembling an armchair without legs, on which he sat with his legs crossed; on his knees he bore a silver salver covered by a kerchief and entered into the house where the *controleur* put the letter on the salver for him. This having been accomplished, it was covered by the kerchief and the two ends of a sort of mantle, which was put on the shoulders of the young man. People say that the yellow letter is considered to be the Governor of *Célèbes* and should the bearer have the misfortune to drop it, he risked being beheaded. The insignia of the Sultan consisting of two red flags waited at the door. These are the same insignia which are thought to be the ancestors of the Sultan. The delivery of the letter was greeted with a salute from 13 cannon fired from the European fort.[41]

Some ceremonies were more imposing than one might imagine. More than one author was astonished by the richness of the costumes of state: for example Asselbergs, who also admired a gun of Turkish origin at the palace: "a weapon entirely encrusted with pure gold and of which I have never seen such a valuable specimen."[42] Among the rare vestiges of the splendors of the palace today one can still admire a collection of weapons including handles of *keris* and sheaths of gold of very great beauty.

One festival with an undeniably popular character, even though it was linked to the palace, was the ceremony of *sirihpuan*, which occurred during the celebration of the birth and death of the Prophet Muhammad (the festival of *Maulud*), which has great significance throughout the whole of the Archipelago. Both Damsté and A. Amin give an account of its origin according to a tradition which still remains alive to this day:[43] the ceremony was introduced by Malay religious teachers in the middle of the 17th century in order to remind the second Sultan of his pious duties. A pavilion with a pyramidal shape (and with a two-tiered roof in the 1928 or 1929 photographs published by Damsté) was constructed from bamboo to represent the cupola which covers the grave of Muhammad at Medina. It was decorated with artificial flowers and contained a copy of the Koran, which the head of the Malay community (the *penghulu*) presented to the Sultan at the end of the ceremony. The *penghulu* and the dancers took their places in this construction which the bearers carried from Kampung Melayu to the palace amid dancing and popular rejoicing. In a comparison (rather overhasty) between this ceremony and the funerary feasts in Bali and Celebes, Damsté concludes that the *sirihpuan* was probably the perpetuance, in Muslim guise, of an autochthonous burial rite. Indeed it was for reasons of orthodoxy, it seems, that the ceremony was to be suppressed at the beginning of the 1950s.

Islam has been an essential component of Bimanese culture since the 17th century, but this is a characteristic which affects the kingdom and even the entire island. It does not seem possible to extract any traits which are specific to the town of Bima, except for a certain concentration of religious education and the gathering of pilgrims at the time of their departure for Mecca. Since the advent of Islamization one new component in this Muslim culture has been the introduction of a literature in Malay. Palace chronicles and literary and historical works were written in Bima; moreover they display evidence of a knowledge of many more original Malay works from the west of the Archipelago. This tradition continued without a break: the chronicles were preserved and recopied; at the time of Sultan Abdul Hamid, in

---

[41] Colfs, *Het Journaal van Albert Colfs*, p. 20

[42] Asselbergs, "Eene reis naar het eiland Soembawa," p. 66.

[43] Ahmad Amin, "Sedjarah Bima. Sedjarah pemerintahan dan serba-serbi kebudajaan Bima" (Bima: Kantor Kebudajaan, 1971, stencil), pp. 53–57, 82–86.

November 1776, "*hikayat* were read" at the palace,[44] and about 1830 a religious scholar, *Khatib* Lukman, wrote a poem about the events which had marked his era.[45]

We shall not linger with this literature, the essential aspects of which have already been discussed elsewhere.[46] It was certainly an appurtenance of the court and of a limited elite, because it is probable that at this period the number of Bimanese who had mastered this degree of Malay would have been negligible. However, the existence of this elite and the creation of a literature in a lingua franca are, in point of fact, two specific features of urban life.

Commerce and State

The adoption of Malay was bound up with the propagation of Islam; these two phenomena are themselves linked to the commercial network in which Bima was a stopping-place, because the town, the main characteristics of which have just been sketched, and the relative luxury which the nobility enjoyed, were based entirely on commerce. As far back as one can delve into history, Bima was a sufficiently prosperous region for the ships which plied the Archipelago to call there to take on provisions.

Before the 17th century there is no detailed information about the exports of Bima. Between 1624 and 1665 the *Dagh Register* records in a repetitive fashion the arrival in Batavia, and occasionally in Ambon, of products purchased in Bima. First and foremost among these was rice, but slaves, brazilwood (Mal. *kayu sapang*; Caesalpinia sappan L., from which a red dye was extracted), wax, sandalwood, tamarind, sulphur, cinnamon, and palm sugar were also included. These registers specifically put Bima in a relationship with Ambon, Banjar, Makassar, Banten, Palembang, and even China.[47] One item for export, which had perhaps been important before the Islamization, was pork: the Dutch purchased this in Bima in 1619, the same year in which the decisive attack from Makassar brought about the conversion of the realm.[48]

Trade with Makassar around 1660, as it was recorded by C. Speelman, apart from brazilwood, which was resold in Macao, involved different Bimanese products: clothes retailed in Manila and Pasir-Kutai, horses re-exported to Macao, buffalo destined for Aceh, and *ganitri/jenitri* nuts (Elaeocarpus ganitrus Roxb.), used as rosary beads, which were also sold in Aceh.[49]

The relative quantities of the various products exported varied from one epoch to the other. The most important items were brazilwood (*sapang*) and wax, the monopoly on which the VOC reserved for itself by the way of contracts, while rice, green soya beans (*kacang hijau*), and onions represented agricultural produce, and horses and buffalo the stockbreeding sector. In the middle of the last century Zollinger added salt, cotton, sugar (both cane and palm), bêche de mer (*tripang*), swallows' nests ("these are the exclusive property of the Sultan . . . [and] are mainly of good, indeed prime, quality"), and goats, as

---

[44] Journal of Muh. Djafar.

[45] Chambert-Loir, *Syair Kerajaan Bima*.

[46] H. Chambert-Loir, "Les sources malaises de l'histoire de Bima," *Archipel* 20 (1980): 269–80.

[47] *Dagh Register*, passim. On March 7, 1627, was noted the arrival in Batavia of several junks from China, one of them bound for Bima.

[48] J. Noorduyn, "Makasar and the Islamization of Bima," *BKI* 143, 2–3 (1987): 312–42.

[49] J. Noorduyn, "De handelsrelaties van het Makassarse rijk volgens de Notitie van Cornelis Speelman uit 1670," *Nederlandse Historische Brommen* 3 (1983): 96–123.

well as heavy textiles, buffalo hides, and the dried meat (*dendeng*) of deer and buffalo, to the former list. Zollinger stresses the "almost incredible number" of horses, trade in which was virtually entirely in the hands of the Arabs. "Someone who has never been to Bima cannot conceive of the number, the strength and the beauty of its horses." Moreover, he also noted the destination of these items; over and above the neighboring states (Dompu, Sumbawa, Makassar, Selayar, and Manggarai), these included Ambon, Timor, Lombok, Bali, Java, and Singapore.[50] These were the same areas which provided Bima with metals, fabrics, dried fish, tobacco, opium (another monopoly of the Sultan), and slaves.

These 17th and 19th century Dutch documents reveal the importance of the trade of Bima, the source of its prosperity, as well as the geographical extent of its outlets. Earlier than this there is the evidence of Tomé Pires, which is of particular interest as it offers a picture of this commercial activity before the intervention of the Europeans. Writing during the second decade of the 16th century Pires also cites among the wealth of Bima: brazilwood, tamarind, horses, slaves, and textiles, to which he adds meat, fish, and gold:

> The island of Bima (. . .) is a large island belonging to a heathen king. It has many *paraos* and many foodstuffs in great plenty; it has meat, fish; it has many tamarinds; it has a great deal of brazil, which they take to Malacca to sell, and they go there from Malacca for it because it sells well in China, and the Bima brazil is very thin. It is worth less in China than that of Siam, because that from Siam is thicker and better. Bima also has a large number of slaves and many horses which they take to Java. This island has trade. They are swarthy people with straight hair. This island has a number of villages, and also many people and many woods. People who are going to Banda and the Moluccas call here, and they buy many cloths here, which sell well in Banda and the Moluccas. This island has some gold. Javanese cashes are current here.[51]

Thus Bima was clearly situated on the route which linked Malacca to the Moluccas. Pires characterizes the indigenous trade in the following fashion: "as they have little capital and the sailors are slaves, they make their journeys long and profitable, because from Malacca they take merchandise to sell in Java, and from Java merchandise to sell in Bima and Sumbawa, and from these islands they take cloth for Banda and the Moluccas, and that which they have kept in reserve from Malacca." [52]

The commercial activity of Bima therefore plainly predated the European sources which described it in some detail. Other evidence proves the existence of a central authority in Bima, and, consequently, the development of the capital even further back in time. First of all there are the archaeological remains[53] which, combined with the mention of Bimanese toponyms in historical Javanese texts, demonstrate the existence of political centers in the eastern part of Sumbawa and the Hindu-Javanese influence exercised there, at the latest in the middle of the 14th century. Van Naerssen has already noted that Bima (Bhima) was mentioned in the *Nagarakertagama* (14.3.4), as are Taliwang, Dompu, Sape, and Sangeang,[54] that the date of the expedition of Majapahit against Dompu was given in the *Pararaton*,

---

[50] Zollinger, *Verslag van eene reis*, pp. 101–109.

[51] Tomé Pires, *The Suma Oriental of Tomé Pires . . . Translated and edited by A. Cortesao* 2 vols. (London: Hakluyt Society, 1944) 1: 203.

[52] Ibid., p. 220.

[53] These remains have been principally described by Rouffaer (cf. F.H. van Naerssen, "Hindoejavaansche overblijfselen op Soembawa," *TAG* [2nd series] 55[1938] and Noorduyn, *Bima en Sumbawa*). Others have been discovered since and have been recorded by the Archaeological Service of Indonesia (*Puslit Arkenas*).

[54] Cf. Th. Pigeaud, *Java in the 14th Century*, 5 vols. (The Hague: Nijhoff, 1960–1963), 3: 17.

namely 1279 S, or AD 1357,[55] and finally that the novel *Rangga Lawe* mentions "the excellent horses acquired at Bhimakore," a name which combines the two toponyms Bima and Kore, as was also the case in Pigafetta.

The second type of evidence relevant to this early period is found in the dynastic myth of Bima, the most complete version of which is found in its Malay edition entitled "History of the Origins of Jinns and *dewa*-s."[56] This "history" begins with the creation by Allah of the first jinn and the first man. The genealogy of the jinns merges into the five Pandawa brothers who reign over the island of Java, while the human line leads to Iskandar Zulkarnain, to whom the Islamization of the countries of the East and the West is attributed. It is from the second of the Pandawas, Bima, that the Bimanese dynasty, which numbered 11 kings before the first Sultan (Abdul Kahir, who reigned at the beginning of the 17th century) issued.

It would be vain to attempt to estimate the antiquity of this dynasty by attributing a hypothetical duration to the reigns of these pre-Muslim rulers. On the other hand, analysis of the myth allows us to determine with some certainty that this is the outcome of a local tradition reshaped at the time of the Hindu realm, before being transformed anew during the process of Islamization. Or, to put it another way, some of the sparse archaeological remains in the vicinity of Bima do indeed tally well with the existence of a Hindu kingdom, of which Bima had also been the capital.

A recent archaeological discovery allows us to push back the first wave of Hinduization to a much earlier date. A rupestral Shivaite site, situated on the western shore of the mouth of the Bay of Bima, known as Wadu Paa (Malay *Batu Pahat*, "chiseled stone"), was noted by the Dutch Resident of Bima in 1862.[57] Subsequently it was studied and described by Rouffaer in 1910.[58] Only about a dozen or so years ago a new site, which perhaps was only part of the previous one, was discovered to the north of it: this contains, amongst other things, a brief inscription in Pallava script and most probably composed in Sanskrit. The brevity and the erosion of this inscription make its palaeographic examination particularly difficult; nonetheless, the most cautious estimate is that it is not later than the 9th century.[59]

It is not possible to assert that either the town or the kingdom of Bima existed at this period, but it is clear that the Bay of Bima was already a place of call on the trade route which brought Hindu merchants from Java to the Moluccas. The site of Wadu Paa is situated on a creek very close to a fresh water source; it was thus an ideal place for a sheltered, easily accessible watering place. Following the example of indigenous merchants, the Europeans made use of it as well: in 1847 (i.e. before the Shivaite cult site had been identified), Zollinger speaks of a "so-called Portuguese cave,"[60] and in 1910 Rouffaer could still make out Dutch graffiti dated 1768 and 1783.[61]

---

[55] Cf. J. Brandes, *Pararaton (Ken Arok), of het boek der koningen van Tumapel en Majapahit* (2nd ed. Batavia/The Hague: VBG 52, 1920), p. 158.

[56] Chambert-Loir, *Ceritera Asal*.

[57] H. Holtz, "Oudheden op Soembawa," *TBG* 11(1862): 157–58.

[58] Rouffaer's notes have been published by Van Naerssen, "Hindoejavaansche overblijfselen," pp. 93–95 and by Noorduyn, *Bima en Sumbawa*, pp. 92–95.

[59] An Indonesian epigrapher first estimated that it could go back to the 6th or 7th century (cf. Chambert-Loir, *Ceritera asal*, p. 91). On the basis of characters similar to certain types from East Java, Prof. de Casparis (personal communication, August 1988) prefers to date the inscription to the 10th–12th centuries.

[60] Zollinger, *Verslag van eene reis*, p. 39.

[61] Noorduyn, *Bima en Sumbawa*, p. 95.

Archaeological excavations would perhaps allow an evaluation of how long the Shivaite site was used. For the time being, we do not know whether it was a religious site from its foundation right up to the era of Islamization. It is even more interesting to see that its status as a privileged, indeed sacred, site has been perpetuated up to our own day and that the site has been somehow incorporated into the urban complex of Bima.

In January 1785, when Sultan Abdul Hamid set sail for Manggarai with 50 ships, he first called at Wadu Paa.[62] And once again, when he set off to Makassar in April 1792, he spent six days at Wadu Paa while "his orchestra played continuously."[63] Up to the present day, as Rouffaer already confirmed in 1910, the site is still covered with recent inscriptions daubed in various languages. The Chinese of Bima, who never had a *klenteng* in the town, go there to celebrate their ceremonies. Bimanese Muslims visit there to make vows and to give thanks when these are realized. Finally, newly built ships from Bima, or those which have returned safe and sound from a long voyage, to Java for example, call at the creek of Wadu Paa to hold a *selamatan* (propitiatory meal or thanksgiving), which is accompanied by the sacrifice of a goat or buffalo.

The perenniality of this religious site is one of the tangible signs of the antiquity and continuity of Bimanese history. An area rich in commercial products, situated on the trade route between the farthest poles of the Indonesian Archipelago, the eastern part of the island of Sumbawa derived its prosperity from commerce. This was probably what favored the concentration of power and gave rise to a Hindu state. It would be useful to study to what extent the flow of commerce was the vehicle for the Javanese, Malay, and Makassarese influences which became the model for Bimanese society in the evolution of a court culture, the manifestations of which are known to us starting from the beginning of the 17th century. Whatever the circumstances, this commercial activity and the centralization which came in its wake, led to the codification of a specifically urban society, which was very original on account of certain aspects of its organization, and at the same time comparable on many points to other towns in the region.

Translated by Rosemary Robson

---

[62] Journal of Muh. Djafar.

[63] Chambert-Loir, *Syair Kerajaan Bima*, pp. 189–90.

BANTEN IN 1678[*]

Claude Guillot

Cities undergo a continual change under the action of men, especially when they grow into successful centers of trade and communication where new ideas flow as well as gold and silver. And the passing of time does not diminish this truth—which explains the precise date given in the title above. Banten in 1678 was no longer the town that the Company of Cornelis de Houtman had discovered eighty years before, as modern Jakarta is no longer the ancient city that it was at the turn of this century. Though it may seem an arbitrary choice, the year 1676 meets four requirements: Banten was still independent; the 1670s definitely were the most prosperous period in the history of this kingdom which was able to adapt itself to a new political and economic situation, with the growing participation of Westerners in the Asian seaborne trade; Sultan Ageng—the old sultan, according to the accurate translation of his contemporaries—had not yet given full authority to his eldest son, who already was his heir and viceroy and would later be known as Sultan Haji, but was still called the young sultan—*sultan anom*—at this time; and this transfer of power would modify even the appearance of the town; furthermore, in 1678, the conflict with Batavia about Cirebon broke out, conflict that would end with the fall of the Javanese kingdom.

Banten on a map looked the ideal port. The city was located on the confluence of two great international seaways, the Malacca and Sunda straits, which were kept under almost total control by Bantenese possessions in the south of Sumatra. It had a large roadstead—18 kms wide and 10 kms deep—with calm waters protected from the open sea by a number of islets and islands. The river that watered this area not only created a natural port, but also offered a convenient way to the plain under cultivation which formed the hinterland.

The river Cibanten, which took its source from the Gunung Karang, about thirty kilometers south of Banten, divided into two arms before reaching the sea. Both mouths formed ports, the "international" port in the west, and the local port, called Karangantu, in the east. The city had developed around them and was thus divided into three main areas: inside the delta, the town itself; in the west, the Chinese district, so large in size that it was often called the Chinese town; and in the east, the great market and the suburbs. For a complete description, one should add the agricultural suburbs in the south, which stretched along the river

---

[*] The French version of this article appeared in *Archipel* 37 (1989): 119–51.

for about ten kilometers to the half-rural, half-urban complex sited on the outskirts of the former capital, Banten Girang (upstream Banten).

Port cities have an ambiguous identity—no one knows whether they belong to the sea which brings them life or to the land of which they are a part. Thus, Banten was described by foreign witnesses as an essentially cosmopolitan trading post, while the Bantenese records depicted it as the capital of a Javanese kingdom where foreigners played but a subordinate part. A description of the city and of each district should help the reader to understand the real nature of Banten behind these two conflicting accounts, and to bring to light the structure of a Javanese port city in the 17th century as well as the mental structures which ruled it.

The Inner City

To describe the principal part of the city is far from easy. A royal city? But the king no longer resided here. A town in itself? But can a port city be deprived of its ports and still keep its identity? However accurate these qualifiers may be, they hardly describe the essential nature of the largest area of the Javanese capital. For a proper description, it seems wiser to start with a physical and unquestionable reality: the town walls. This part of the city was located between two arms of the river forming a delta; a third arm diagonally crossing the delta joined together the first two. Unlike the other Bantenese districts, the inner city was totally surrounded by walls, the importance of which we shall discuss later.

One well knows that urban structures are the product of geographic and economic requirements, as well as the reflection of social and religious concepts. On this last point, it seems that at the beginning, Banten for the most part had taken for itself the concept of space and royalty from which had developed Javanese urbanism, without the influence of emerging and victorious Islam. With respect to this evolution, one notes two significant elements: the center and the orientation.

The Center

In the 17th century, Western travelers all agreed that the town center was the royal square, which they called *paseban* though it had in the Sajarah Banten (SB) the peculiar name of *darparagi*—and which correlated with the well-known *alun-alun* of modern Javanese towns—but this was a mere geographic observation and the foreign visitors did not grasp its cultural meaning. The foundation of the city as related in the SB did not consist, as in the Western tradition, in the delimitation of an urban space—one recalls Romulus's famous furrow, or, closer to Banten in time and space, the Portuguese leather lace in Malacca—but in the designation of an essentially sacred center, where were somehow concentrated the supernatural powers with which the sovereign invested himself. The Bantenese records (pupuh 18 and 19) recount how Hasanudin took possession of the old capital, Banten Girang, in the name of the new faith, Islam, and how his father, Sunan Gunug Jati, ordered him to build the new town at the edge of the sea.

There, Betara Guru Jampang used to meditate on a flat, rectangular stone called *watu gigilang* (the luminous stone), so motionless that birds came and nested in his *ketu* (the religious men's head-dress in pre-Muslim times). After Hasanudin overcame the infidels, Betara Guru Jampang became converted to Islam and disappeared. Sunan Gunung Jati warned his son that in no case should the sacred stone be displaced, this sacrilegious action being susceptible to bringing about the fall of the kingdom. The *watu gigilang* then became the throne of Hasanudin and his successors.

The antiquity of such stones is certified. They are referred to in a mandala in the Rajapatigundala—a Javanese text that could go back to the second half of the 13th century.[1] We see that, much later, these same stones were being used as thrones under the name of *sela gilang* by the sovereigns of Surakarta and Yogyakarta, *sela* being the *kromo* of *watu*. In these late palaces, these stones were often incorporated into the part of the kraton called *pagelaran*. Two elements help to explain their nature as well as their importance. The *sela gilang* of Surakarta was supposed to be the former throne of the last king of Mahapahit; and one very well knows that the court records of Central Java desperately tried to represent the Mataram sovereigns as the legitimate heirs of the kingdom of Majapahit. It seems that the possession of such a stone was enough to justify this legitimacy. As a matter of fact, in 1746, when the capital was officially transferred from Kartasura to Jakarta, a long procession abandoned the former palace, soiled and ransacked by rebel troops, to reach the new royal site which was only a few kilometers further off. A striking fact is that in the description we have of this procession,[2] the only element from the old kraton that the king's people carried off with them was the *bangsal pangrawit*, which was used as a sort of canopy for the *sela gilang*—so that we assume that the sacred stone too was carried away—and that it was following two *waringin* which would be set on the north square of the future palace. The location of this stone inside the palace in Central Javanese principalities did not correlate with the ancient tradition. On the location of Panembahan Senopati's kraton in Kota Gede—the oldest in Mataram—one can still see nowadays, in the shadow of an imposing *waringin* and supposedly set there during the reign of this sovereign, a little edifice sheltering the *sela gilang*, Senopati's throne, which remains the object of a popular cult. It is even said that the angle of this stone could have been broken by the king when he smashed upon it the head of Ki Ageng Mangir, a prince who was opposed to the authority he had just established over this area. According to tradition, this same stone and tree remain where they were in Senopati's time, on the former royal square.[3] From this we infer that at the beginning of the 16th century in Banten, as in Kota Gede at the end of the same century, the *sela gilang* was always set on the royal square.

It seems that this stone was much more significant than the other regalia. On this very *watu gigilang*, Hasanudin took Betara Guru Jampang's place; there, as did the latter, he meditated and then established his throne. All information points to the fact that the stone itself gave him supreme authority over the city, the palace being but a functional building. Are we to believe, as some say,[4] that this stone was a reminiscence of Mount Meru, Shiwa's seat? As Betara Guru is one of Shiwa's appellations this hypothesis may very well be true. One may justly wonder, though, if this unpolished seat did not refer to an older aboriginal past, to the time when the function of these stones was to express the sacred, as they still do in some Indonesian regions. A growing number of megalithic sites discovered during recent decades are obvious proofs that Java had amply participated in this system. Together with this stone, a second element determined the center of the city: a *waringin*, the trunk of which

---

[1] Th. Pigeaud, *Java in the 14th Century*, 4 vols. (The Hague, 1963), 3: 132.

[2] Soepomo Poedjosoedarmo & M.C. Ricklefs, "The Establishment of Surakarta: A Translation from the Babad Giyanti," *Indonesia* 4 (October 1967): 101, 102.

[3] M. Mardjana, *Jogjakarta, Kota Pusaka* (Jakarta, n.d.), pp. 91–93.

[4] T. Behrend, "Kraton and Cosmos in Traditional Java" (M.A. Thesis, University of Wisconsin at Madison, 1983), p. 216.

was surrounded by a barrier from which came its name of *waringin kurung*. It actually seemed to be associated with the *watu gigilang* in the description of the royal complex given by the SB (pupuh 44). One knows the *waringin kurung* which rise nowadays on the squares of Central Java principalties, but these go in pairs, or rather in couples, since one of them is meant to be a male and the other, a female. In their case, again, we assume that this pairing off was the product of a late evolution, as only one *waringin kurung* is to be seen in Banten, and in Mataram tradition recalls but one of them on the *alun-alun* of Kota Gede, set like the Bantenese *waringin kurung* near the *sela gilang*. The fact that new trees were planted when Surakarta was founded show that they did not have a sacred nature in themselves. As a matter of fact, according to the Rajapatigundala,[5] the *waringin* was one of the three species of trees that were likely to be the seat of the sacred spirits *(kayangan)*. Unfortunately, its significance remains obscure. Did it give shelter to the supernatural power of the throne or to the *baureksa*, the local spirit? Seeing it alone on the deserted *alun-alun*, one may wonder if it could not represent the Center Tree[6] which was somehow the axis uniting the chtonian and ouranian worlds. We must note, however, that these two elements remained untouched for a long time, and kept their sacred character despite the vicissitudes of time. At the end of the 18th century, Stavorinius[7] wrote a beautiful description of them, lingering over the majesty of the tree and the coolness of its shadow... and taking the stone for the tomb of an ancient king. But we know that to assimilate some sacred place, a stone all the more, with the tomb of a great figure, is quite usual in Java. Still closer to us, in 1920, a topographer[8] published in a short essay about the vestiges of Banten a picture, which had been taken the year before, of the stone and the tree enclosing it inside its trunk. In this text too he noted the name that was given at this time to the *waringin*: "*purwadinata*," "the ancient king."

In the Dutch First Voyage—a precious testimony—we see that in 1596, the Bantenese did not take this "center" for an empty symbol, since the king, or the regent-governor who at this time acted as a sovereign, used to convene his cabinet outside, on the royal square, under a tree which in all probability was the *waringin*, as appears on a splendid etching inserted in the book. But we will come back to this aspect.

The Orientation

According to the SB, Sunan Gunung Jati, after having chosen a site for the city, told his son where he was to build the market, the royal square, and the palace. These three elements, which appeared as fundamental in a royal city, found themselves in the same order, forming a north-south axis, in Banten as in Majapahit,[9] and in Surabaya at the beginning of the 17th century[10] as in Yogyakarta at the end of the 18th century. Once again, one notes this orientation according to the cardinal points in the layout of the four main streets, which all started from the square, and would have formed a perfect cross throughout the town if the southward street had not shifted from the northward one to bypass the palace. Moreover, until the middle of the 17th century, the walls formed a rather regular rectangle (square?); all sides of this polygon were correlated with a cardinal point, and in each of them a door

---

[5] Pigeaud, *Java in the 14th Century*, 3: 132.

[6] Cf. ibid., 4: 202.

[7] J.S. Stavorinus, *Voyage par le Cap de Bonne-Espérance Batavia, Bantam et au Bengale* ... (Paris, 1798), 1: 54.

[8] G.P. Groenhof, "Enkele Geschiedkundige plaatsen in Bantam, *Jaarverslag van den Topographischen Dienst in Ned. Indie over 1919*, vol. 2 (Batavia, 1920), pl. 4b.

[9] Pigeaud, *Java in the 14th Century*, 5: plan 1.

[10] H.J. de Graaf, *De Regering van Sultan Agung VKI* 23 (The Hague, 1958), p. 14.

was made. The center and cardinal points obviously remained lively concepts under Sultan Ageng, since one finds among his closest counsellors four of the Sultan's brothers whose names respectively were: Pangeran Kidul, Lor, Wetan, and Kulon, which means Prince of the South, the North, the East, and the West.

Can we say, then, that Banten is some sort of mandala, like the Mandalay—the name of which is evocative—that was built in the 19th century by the Burman king Minton? The prophylactic circumambulation executed by the king with the sacred flags—a rite which is still found today in Central Java—is an extra argument supporting this idea. It is probably wiser to note that one could find throughout eastern and southern Asia the same conception of the royal city which integrated into its plan the sacred and the profane, its arrangement reflecting the cosmic order with the king as its center.[11]

Now, after this rather lengthy but necessary survey of the symbolic world, we shall go back to the more solid world of reality.

The Palace

Strangely enough, but few descriptions of the palace are found in the bulk of documentation about Banten that we possess. Van der Chijs[12] quoted a text by Steven Verhalge, dating from the 16th century, which described the square as included in the royal complex and possessing guarded doors and a *pendapa*. With the SB (pupuh 44), one can more precisely imagine the palace before 1651, that is at the end of the reign of Sultan Abulmafakhir, Sultan Ageng's grandfather and predecessor. The *sri manganti* pavilion, where the sovereign's visitors were kept waiting, was built to the south of the square; next to it was found the palace itself, which included a number of yards and pavilions called *madé*, one kampung known under the name of *candi raras*, the treasury, the king's private mosque with its minaret, the famous Ki Jimat cannon, the stables, and guardrooms all over the place. Tavernier,[13] invited by the sovereign in 1648, was received under a *pendapa*, the four pillars of which were 40 feet apart. Very likely, this *pendapa* where the king was sitting "in a manner of armchair made of wood gilded with powdered gold like the frame of our pictures," and which was located on a square where guards and servants were sitting in the shadow of some trees, was the audience hall belonging to the public part of the palace. In short, we are told too little to be able to make a complete description of the place, but we certainly know enough to identify a traditional Javanese palace.

Considering the situation in 1678, one realizes that a significant evolution had taken place in comparison with the previous years. In 1673, a Danish surgeon, whose name was Germanized into Cortemünde, stoppod at Banten and visited the king with the crew of his ship. He enjoyed drawing, and left several sketches to illustrate his travel diary. One of them represents the arrival of the Danish delegation at the court. One recognizes the royal square with, at the bottom, a pavilion which must be *sri manganti*, and behind it, a wall surrounding the palace itself. One catches a glimpse above this wall of two buildings made of durable material, one of which possesses a roof in typical Chinese style. Despite the unlikely smoking chimney surmounting it, this obvious proof of Chinese influence on the palace building is certainly to be taken into consideration. On the one hand, we know that in 1668,

---

[11] Cf. B. Smith and H.B. Reynolds, ed., *The City as a Sacred Center* (Leiden, 1987).

[12] J. van der Chijs, *Oud Bantam, TBG* 26 (1882): 30.

[13] J.B. Tavernier, *Les six voyages de Jean-Baptiste Tabernier*, vol 2 (Paris, 1681), p. 435.

the Sultan had a new dwelling built.[14] Moreover, this sketch we refer to was drawn by Cortemünde himself and not by an engraver working in Europe, as was often the case. One knows, too, that Sultan Ageng had always been very partial to the Chinese,[15] so much so that this favoritism greatly annoyed his son, the young Sultan.[16] Time and again, the old sultan hired two Chinese, the former chabandar Kaytsu and the current one and former customs director, Kiayi Ngabèhi Cakradana, to build edifices in durable material, such as walls, bridges, houses, etc. This Sultan also had a village built near his new residence of Tirtayasa, where the houses were made of bricks, which was quite unusual in Java. More prosaically, these buildings built with durable materials inside the palace not only were safe from the ever present risk of fire but were even more suitable to the new lifestyle of the sovereigns, who lived among foreign curiosities, from Japanese cabinets to European mirrors and clocks. Two years later, in 1680, the young Sultan was to have a new palace built on this very site by the famous Dutch "renegade" Cardeel, this time in the European style and in the shape of a fortress.

Another innovation is that in 1678, Sultan Ageng definitively left the palace, where he hardly resided any more, to settle his court in Tirtayasa. The palace, no longer regal, was currently occupied by his elder son. Here is a further instance of the "instability" of the Javanese courts. In about 150 years, the palace went from Banten Girang to Banten, then from Banten to Tirtayasa. In a more or less similar lapse of time, the Mataram capital rambled from Pajang to Kota Gede, from Karta to Plered, and from Kartasura to Surakarta!

Power itself had evolved with time. One has seen that in 1596, the king used to take decisions among his counsellors on the *darparagi* near the *watu gigilang*. But the political situation had changed a lot since that time, with the settling of Europeans in Banten and above all, with the Dutch presence in Batavia.

Taking into consideration this new deal, Banten benefitted greatly from the new economic networks set up by the Europeans. However, because all of them maintained spies at the court, the great public councils of the government were no longer adequate to the situation. Following his ascension to the throne, Sultan Ageng solved this problem by slowly abandoning the custom of holding these large councils with the dignitaries of the kingdom and made his decisions by himself, relying only on his closest advisors. This was not appreciated either by the dignitaries or the Europeans who accused him of absolutism.[17] At the beginning of 1674 in an attempt to further increase security, he decided to hold these councils at the former court of Banten Girang from then on.[18] Then, he abolished the open air councils which were thereafter held "inside the palace, in a secure place that could only be approached by children between ten and twelve years of age."[19] Finally, after 1678, the councils, now always secret, were held at Tirtayasa where no foreigners lived. Thus, under the pressure of events, a method of ancient governing, somewhat primitive, disappeared, and the royal square lost one of its principal functions.

---

[14] *Dagh Register gehouden int casteel Batavia* . . . (31 vols.; Batavia/The Hague, 1886–1931), 18.10.1688.

[15] India Office Records (IOR), London, E/3/32, 29.12.1671.

[16] *Dagh Register*, 23.1.1674.

[17] IOR, E/3/24, 31.12.1654 and E/3/31, 29.12.1671.

[18] *Dagh Register*, 23.1.1674.

[19] Ibid., 27.8.1675.

It seems that the *watu gigilang* lost its religious and official nature in the minds of the leaders due to political pragmatism and that the stone was no longer more than a symbol and a souvenir of former times.

The description of a Javanese palace would not be complete without its two complements: the animal reserve (*krapyak*) and the water palace (*taman sari*). The latter was first mentioned in the SB (pupuh 44). It can be located in a place known as Pupungkuran near Kenari. It can be identified as the compound known today as Tasikardi. At that time it was called *Kebon alas* (the wild garden) and included a basin with an island at its center which was used, according to SB, to store powder! A structure which is well known elsewhere can be recognized here. During the following reign, another *taman sari* seems to have been constructed by Sultan Ageng, in Banten itself, to the south (?) of the palace. Cortemünde said that the "sultan owns in the part of the city that gives out to the countryside, a beautiful and large garden, richly planted with every fruit imaginable and rare plants" and where he had "just on the side, a bath house."[20] This compound must have disappeared during the construction of the fortress in 1680. In 1706, when passing through Banten, Cornelis De Bruijn was received by the Sultan in his country house at Tasikardi which for three years, he said, served as a water reservoir for the palace,[21] to which it was linked by a stone conduit and a lead pipe that can still be seen today.

Near Kenari, Sultan Abulmafakhir, according to SB (pupuh 44), had an animal reserve built, where deer and male and female water buffalo could be found. No other text dating from the 17th century seems to make allusion to this place. On the other hand, Heydt's map, dating from 1739, indicated a road leading toward the south "in the direction of Grobiak." And Stavorinus called "Grobbezak" a place that clearly corresponded to the *taman sari* of Tasikardi. Van der Chijs, who cited these two sources, admitted not understanding the meaning of these two words that he qualified, correctly, as barbarian.[22] They both must be interpreted as deformations of the same word *krapyak*, which, due to the proximity of the animal reserve at Tasikardi, served probably as a toponym for the entire country estate of the kings of Banten. It must be also mentioned, to be complete, that the toponym of Krapyak can be found at the foot of Gunung Pinang, on the present road that links Serang to Cilegon, at approximately five kilometers to the east of Banten. Unfortunately its ties to the Banten court still remain obscure.

The Royal Square

The royal square, *darparagi*, was located to the north of the palace and extended northward to the river. The trees surrounding the square gave it the pleasant aspect that was noted by Schouten in 1661, as well as Cortemünde in 1673.[23] A certain number of official buildings built along its perimeter helped make it an administrative and political center. It was above all the place where the king appeared to his people, located half-way between the market place, meeting point of the people, and the palace, the sovereign's residence. This had already been noted with the throne that had been installed on the square. The

---

[20] J. P. Cortemünde, *Dagbog fra en Ostiendiefart*, 1672–1675 (Sohistoriske Skriften V, Kronborg, 1953), p. 126.

[21] C. de Bruijn, *Voyages de Corneille Le Bruijn*, vol. 5 (Paris, 1725), p. 53.

[22] van der Chijs, *Oud Banten*, pp. 18–19.

[23] W. Schouten, *Voyage de Gautier Schouten aux Indes Orientales*, vol. 2 (Amsterdam, 1707), p. 302; Cortemünde, *Dagbog*, p. 126.

court of justice, whose supreme judge was the king, held its session also on this square.[24] It was also in front of the palace where the dignitaries had to appear (ng. *séba*; kr. *sowan*), regardless of whether the king appeared or not. Here, after the sounding of gongs or the firing of cannons, the sovereign or one of his representatives announced the important decisions made by the government to the population.[25] The large celebrations given in honor of events relating to the royal family took place there also, such as marriages, circumcisions, etc.[26] The royal palace, for several days, indeed for several weeks, was thus transformed into an immense place of amusement which can be compared to the *sekaten* found today in the principalities of Central Java and of Cirebon. There again the king could be seen when going to the mosque for Friday prayers or to attend the burial of a dignitary in the nearby necropolis.[27] It was here also that the entire population came to pay him homage and offer him presents—obligatory—at the end of the month of fasting.[28] Finally, the king and the dignitaries could also be seen jousting with each other during the Saturday tournaments (*sasapton*), of which the Sultan Ageng was very fond.[29] The SB (pupuh 54) described him in great detail at one of these jousting contests, still young, before his ascension to the throne, and we know that at age 50, he was still participating.[30] The royal animals were displayed on this same square. Occasionally tigers were seen, when one of them had been captured. A German surgeon who lived in Banten from 1682 to 1685, recounted that any tiger caught had to be brought to the palace and merry making was then organized.[31] Scott in 1605 had already described a caged tiger found on the square during the festivities celebrating the circumcision of the king, the future Abulmafakhir.[32] The other royal animal was the elephant. It is known that for all the countries influenced by Indian civilization, this animal represented military power as well as royal grandeur through its strength. It was remarkable that this tradition was followed on Java, where the animal did not exist in the wild. The Negarakertagama (18-1)[33] already mentioned the presence of these animals at the Majapahit court in the 14th century and van Neck, passing through Tuban in 1599, was greatly impressed by those owned by the king of that city. The view of Banten, published by Valentijn, in the first half of the 17th century showed an elephant standing under a shelter on the square of Banten. The SB (pupuh 44) even had a name for it: Rara Kawi. Tavernier[34] had counted sixteen of them inside the palace during the same era, but had added that the king owned an even greater number. Sources no longer mentioned these animals during the reign of Sultan Ageng. Aware that the courts of Central Java maintained the tradition of owning elephants until early in the 20th century, one could think that it had not been abandoned in Banten, even if this sultan was more trusting of modern weapons. In fact, it can be noted that when Cornelis Speelman was nominated to the post of Governor General, in

---

[24] F. Valentijn, "View of Banten," in his *Oud en Nieuw Oost Indiën*, vol.4 (Dordrecht-Amsterdam, 1724–1726), pp. 214–15.

[25] See, for example, *Dagh Register*, 6.5.1672 and 7.2.1678.

[26] Ibid., 1.9.1672, and E. Scott, *The Voyage of Sir Henry Middleton to the Moluccas, 1604–1606* (London, 1943), pp. 152–62.

[27] *Dagh Register*, 10.6.1674.

[28] IOR, G/21/3 III, 13.5.1659

[29] *Dagh Register*, 3.12.1659.

[30] Ibid., 23.1.1674.

[31] *The Barbarous Cruelties and Massacres Committed by the Dutch in the East Indies* (London, 1712), pp. 117–18.

[32] Scott, *The Voyage*, p. 161.

[33] Pigeaud, *Java in the 14th Century*, 3: 23.

[34] Tavernier, *Les six voyages*, 2: 435.

November 1681, which was equal to the crowning of a king, the Banten government sent him an elephant as a present.[35] Several months earlier, in January 1681, the first Siamese ambassadors to the king of France arrived in Banten for a "technical" stop, which stretched into eight months. In the ship were two elephants that the king of Siam wanted to offer to the king of France, Louis XIV.[36]

The mosque was located on the west side of the square. Tradition credited its construction to the son and successor of Hasanudin, Maulana Yusuf, in 966 of the Hegira (AD 1559),[37] a year which would correspond, according to Hoesein Djajadiningrat, with the beginning of Hasanudin's reign. In any case, the mosque that one could see in 1678 could not have dated further back than 1615. In fact, an Englishman, Th. Elkington mentioned that it had collapsed during the night of August 13 to 14, of that year due to lightning.[38] The best description of this mosque at the end of the 17th century is Bogaert's:[39]

> The temple is almost square and built with large beams that are found in abundance on Java. Its roof is in the shape of a tower . . . It has five roofs, one on top of another; the first and largest one covering the body of the temple; the next ones are smaller and smaller so that the last one almost comes to a point. In its center, is raised a high [construction] which forms a real peak.

This descriptioni is echoed by Stavorinus one century later (1769):[40]

> This building, shaped almost in a square, is flanked on two sides by a high wall: The covering rises up like a tower, with five roofs one on top of the other of which the second is smaller than the first, the third smaller than the second, etc. and whose fifth one ends up in a point while the lowest one extends quite a bit beyond the walls of the temple.

This corresponds fairly well to the structure in existence today. All the Western witnesses insisted on the fact that Christians could not enter it. It is possible to imagine that, like today, the compound of the mosque was used for all sorts of popular secular activities as well as religious ceremonies, and that one would come to idle one's time away there under the *serambi* spoken of by Stavorinus. Schouten—for Jepara, it is true—recounted that women came to bathe in the basins of the mosque, and Cortemünde described a group of men playing cards in the interior of the compound.[41]

The Banten minaret, which today is the very symbol of the city, curiously did not seem to attract much attention on the part of Western travelers. This omission and a bad interpretation of the word "tower" induced van der Chijs in his essay, however excellent on the reconstitution of old Banten, to confuse several buildings and to date the minaret from the 18th century, which did not match reality.[42] It is true that Stavorinus was the first to describe it clearly: "there is, near the mosque, a narrow tower but quite high which serves

---

[35] See Archives des Missions Etrangères de Paris (AMEP), Vachet II, 390.

[36] C222, f° 38, 25.1.1681. Archives Nationales, Paris (AN).

[37] Ismail Muhamad, *Banten, Penunjuk jalan dan keterangan bekas kerajaan kesultanan Banten dsb* (Serang, 1956), p. 6.

[38] Purchas, *His Pilgrimes* (London, 1625), 1: 515.

[39] A. Bogaert, *Historische Reizen door d'oostersche Deelen van Asia* (Amsterdam, 1711), p. 134.

[40] Stavorinus, *Voyage par le Cap*, 1: 55.

[41] Schouten, *Voyage de Gautier Schouten*, 1: 64–67; Cortemünde, *Dagbog*, p. 125.

[42] van der Chijs, *Oud Bantam*, pp. 44–45.

the same function as the minarets in Turkey."[43] But older sources are not lacking. Tradition, which is not always right, attributed its construction, around 1620, to an Islamic Mongol (Mandchou?) by the name of Cek Ban Cut.[44] This minaret did not appear on older maps of Banten. However, in the legend of one from 1659,[45] one can read: "their Misquijt or church near which is located a white and straight tower which rises higher than the trees." On the view of Banten in the Bibliothèque Nationale in Paris (Cartes et plans, SH 193/4/1) which dates probably from the beginning of the 1670s, one can clearly see a minaret near the mosque. In 1694, while passing through Banten, Valentijn mentioned a "stone tower seen from far and wide."[46] It is manifestly the same minaret described thereafter by Stavorinus. The minaret, quite uncommon in Java, seems to have been largely adopted in Banten where numerous foreign ulamas had passed through. There was one built before 1650, near the king's mosque inside the palace (SB, pupuh 44). The mosque of Kasunyatan, surely very old and located outside the walls to the south of the city, also had a square-shaped minaret, which brings to mind the more enigmatic one, known as Pacinan-Tinggi that can still be seen in the former Chinese sector. The city's rice warehouse was located to the north of the mosque. One wonders, when one understands the importance and meaning accorded to rice by the Javanese, if construction of the warehouse close to this sacred site, was pure chance. Banten sovereigns have always worried about supplying this city with foodstuffs and were trying, through large irrigation works built throughout the kingdom, to increase cultivatable areas. Even more so because plantations of products for export, pepper, sugar, ginger, etc., thereby had a tendency to reduce food-producing areas. The building of a granary was ordered by Sultan Abulmafakhir, probably at the end of the 1640s (SB, pupuh 56); in 1659, it still had not been finished.[47] It was finished in 1668 because in that year Sultan Ageng had it filled with rice. The Dutch, who reckoned that the quantity stocked corresponded to a year's worth of consumption, wondered if it was not a harbinger of a war with Batavia.[48] One understands these wise precautions taken by the Sultan when one realizes that in 1677, and even at the beginning of 1678,[49] rice had become scarce not only because of wars but also because of disastrous climatic conditions affecting, it seems, a large part of Southeast Asia,[50] and therefore fetched considerable prices. However, it must be noted that this was a rare case, if not the only time when Banten lacked rice.

Near the mosque is the cemetery, known as Sebakingking. In 1678, only two kings were buried there, Hasanudin and his grandson, Maulana Muhamad, killed in the war against Palembang and thus named Seda-ing-rana, "dead far away." The tomb of Maulana Yusuf is located in Pakalangan, to the south of the city, and those of the father and grandfather of Sultan Ageng are in Kenari, near the *taman sari*. Several personalities whom the king wanted to honor, like the former Chinese shabandar Kaytsu,[51] were also buried inside the mosque complex. Nothing here brings to mind the funeral hills like the one of Sultan Agung at Imogiri, and one finds no mention of any cult thus rendered to the tomb of Hasanudin, as is the

---

[43] Stavorinus, *Voyage par le Cap*, 1: 55.

[44] Ismael, *Banten*, p. 6.

[45] J. W. Ijzerman, ed., *Cornelis Buijsero te Bantam, 1616–1618* (The Hague, 1923), XXIII.

[46] Valentijn, *Oud en Nieuw Oost Indiên*, 4: 215.

[47] Ijzerman, *Cornelis Buijsero*, XXIII.

[48] *Dagh Register*, 6.11.1668.

[49] Ibid., 18.3.1678.

[50] Ibid., 24.1.1677.

[51] Ibid., 10.6.1674.

case today. This does not mean, however, that tomb cults were unknown in Banten. To the west of the harbor and on top of a sugar loaf hill, the tomb of a friend of Hasanudin, Kiayi Santri, the object of an ancient cult and visited by Stavorinus in 1769, can be found. And the *kramat* tombs were, it seems, numerous in Banten in the 17th century. Tavernier spoke mockingly of these tombs and of their *juru kunci*: "often, there was a beggar dressed as a Dervich, he builds a hut near the tomb which he is supposed to keep clean and on which he throws flowers. Every time some homage is paid, some ornament is added because the more beautiful a tomb is, the more devotion and saintliness there are and that much more in alms."[52] But the great sacred place remained the tomb of Sunan Gunung Jati at Cirebon where the Banten dignitaries made pilgrimages on several different occasions.

Finally, near the mosque were dwellings for the religious leaders[53] in particular for the Cadi, who had the title of Kiayi Fekih (ar. fiqh). This person played an important role because, in some ways, he was the minister of justice,[54] as was explained in the text, doubtlessly a later one: "The high priest, Khay Fokkée Natja Moedin was named by the king as *fiscaal*, that is judge of disputes arising among the Bantenese."[55]

The map of 1659 showed that to the south of the square, the king's palace was surrounded by the dwellings of his closest advisors, particularly those of his two principal ministers, the Mangkubumi and the Kiayi Arya, thus forming a real administrative compound where all sorts of clerks, writers, interpreters, etc. worked. But in that year, 1678, when the Sultan left for Tirtayasa, these notables dismantled their residences, probably pavilions, and had them moved near the new court.[56] Not far from the palace was the arsenal, closely guarded, where cannons, firearms, and blade weapons were kept in sufficient quantity to equip the army.[57] It was topped with a great drum *(bedug)* eight feet high "whose sound could be heard as far as several leagues into the mountains."[58] Schouten—and then, Hesse who was clearly influenced by his text—described this arsenal as a "tower."[59] Cortemünde on the other hand, simply mentioned a "house for munitions." Unlike van der Chijs, we must consider the word "tower" in its broadest sense, of a building higher than the others. That was the reason mosques were often described as "towers"—Javanese *tempels of toorens*, found, for example, in a text dating from 1686.[60] Another administrative building on the square was the prison,[61] already mentioned in the First Voyage. This habit of placing the prison on the public square would be maintained until colonial times and it is not uncommon even today to see an old prison on the edge of the *alun-alun*.

Finally, along the edge of the square, near the river and arranged under a shelter, were the king's boats, more ceremonial than war ships; however, there is no material source on this subject for the reign of Sultan Ageng.

---

[52] Tavernier, *Les six voyages*, 2: 439–40.

[53] Bogaert, *Historische Reizen*, p. 134.

[54] VOC 1440, f° 2440, 20.1.1688, AlgemeenRijksarchief, The Hague (ARA).

[55] Banten 14/3, 7.10.1789, Arsip Nasional, Jakarta (Ars.Nas.)

[56] *Dagh Register*, 27.7.1678.

[57] Cortemünde, *Dagbog*, p. 126.

[58] Schouten, *Voyage de Gautier Schouten*, 2: 302.

[59] E. Hesse, *Gold-Bergwerke in Sumatra, 1680–1683*. Reisebesdchreibungen von Deutschen Beamten und Kriegsleuten im Dienst der Nied. W- und O-Ind. Komp., vol. 10 (The Hague, 1931), p. 129.

[60] VOC 1409, f° 1418, 15.2.1686 (ARA).

[61] Cortemünde, *Dagbog*, p. 126.

The Market

Located between the mosque and the river, the market, known as Kapalembangan was according to the SB the primary market in Banten (SB, pupuh 26). However, it seems to have suffered from a lack of space in which to enlarge and answer to the needs of an increasing population and growing trade activities of the city. With the arrival of the Dutch in 1596, the principal market was located already outside the city walls, on the east side. The mosque's market was open every day at the end of the morning. In 1596, it seemed quite important and pepper was still sold there. In 1661, according to Schouten, only "essential items" were sold there.[62] In 1673, Cortemünde did not even mention it, citing only the large *passar* to the east and the *kitjill* of the Chinese section, to the west. It is impossible to know if it only lost its importance or if it completely disappeared. Hesse's mention of it in 1684[63] is not to be taken seriously because, as we have already noted, he largely took over Schouten's text.

The Residential Areas

Information on the rest of the city inside the walls is, of course, much less detailed. The first Dutch voyage gives an idea of its structure that is, however, quite clear:[64]

> Moreover the city is divided into several parts and for each one a gentleman is designated to guard it in times of war, of fire, or anything else and each one is walled and separated from the others and in each part hangs a great drum ... which is beaten ... when they see some fire or battle; the same for noon and dawn and late evening when the day is over.

Some seventy years later, the situation had hardly changed. In speaking of Javanese cities in general, Schouten wrote that they "were divided into several sections, of which each one was committed to the care of a notable or gentleman of standing who made inspections and then reported precisely what was happening there to the sovereign or to those designated by him. When there was something to fear or fire broke out somewhere, one beats the drums with a large mallet," and he added concerning Banten itself, "the city is divided into several sections where each one has a guard and they are closed with gates..."[65] Bogaert noted: "... the city is divided into sections which are closed each night with gates and are guarded against all bad things."[66] These closed and guarded compounds remind us, of course, of today's *kampung* with the *gardu* and *ronda*, words curiously borrowed from the West, and their decorated *gapura* which replaced the gates, still present, however, in the mind, as testified by the expression *masuk kampung*.

These areas are miniature copies of the city's structure. As all its inhabitants belonged to the king, all those of the *kampung* belonged to a dignitary whose palace was located there. This is a situation that has long survived in the principalities of Central Java, where some neighborhoods still carry the names of the prince. The dignitary's residence reflected the royal palace through its arrangement. It was surrounded by a wall which protected it from fire; one then entered into a guarded courtyard which was also called the *paseban*, where

---

[62] Schouten, *Voyage de Gautier Schouten*, 2: 304.

[63] Hesse, *Gold-Bergwerke*, p. 131.

[64] G.P. Rouffaer and J. W. Ijzerman, eds., *De eerste Schipvaart der Nederlanders naar Oost-Indie onder C. de Houtman* (1598: The Hague, 1915), p. 107 (Fr. Trans.: Premier livere de l'histoire de la Navigation aux Indes Orientales par les Hollandais et des Choses à eux advenues, p. 26).

[65] Schouten, *Voyage de Gautier Schouten*, 2: 328–29, 303.

[66] Bogaert, *Historische Reizen*, p. 133.

local affairs were taken care of and where the private oratory, the *langgar*, was located, that Pallu compared to "small barns all open from the front";[67] the house itself was made of carved wood and gold elements and was decorated with "tapestries and curtains of silk cloth or cotton material that was well painted."[68] These dignitaries had their own ulamas and guards, their musicians and dancers, in short, they were the kings of their neighborhoods. Their wealth and power depended on the population that belonged to them—the numbers varied from more than 2,000 to less than 200 persons. If they were the masters of their people, they were also responsible for them vis-à-vis the ones in power, as Schouten noted, from which originated the tradition that required each dignitary to appear at the royal *paseban* to render his accounts. At any moment, the government could depose a dignitary, regardless of his rank, and put another in his place.

This urban structure reflected quite well the social rule that organized the inner city: every dweller in this part of Banten had to belong to one of the dignitaries. Those who did not enter into this system were thrown outside the walls, as will be mentioned later, especially the foreigners. This ownership of the population greatly shocked the Westerners, for example like Pallu, who wrote in 1672:[69]

> The king of Bantam has total sovereignty over his subjects; they are all his slaves from the first to the last; he is the absolute master of their goods and their lives ... in one word, he has everything and they have nothing but board and provisions, like worthless slaves, all the rest of the fruits of their labors and industries are for the king.

The situation, which is not a topic for discussion here, was certainly more complex, and beside true slaves, bought or stolen, "free" inhabitants normally practiced a trade. It must be said, however, that the Bantenese had fewer rights than duties. And this situation contributed probably not a little to the enrichment of the foreign merchants. All the dwellings in this part of the city were built, as was usual in Southeast Asia, on piles of bamboo and covered with palm roofs, material that was highly inflammable. Thus Banten's history was but one long succession of fires. But it seems that at the end of the 17th century, a new building technique, between the traditional and that using durable material, was born. "Most of the houses were constructed with palm trunks or big bamboo, with walls of split canes whose interstices were jointed with clay or lime. They were covered with ... palms or red tiles."[70] Yet again in 1675, two-thirds of the city was consumed by fire.[71]

The importance of piles becomes evident when one realizes that during "most of the winter the river overflows over the city and one can only navigate the streets in boats."[72] The Westerners, with their Mediterranean concept of cities as an ensemble which is fundamentally artificial and from which all reminder of natural chaos must be chased, were completely disconcerted by Banten's appearance, or rather that part of the city where nature did not seem tamed: natural and often raw materials—palms, bamboos, trunks freshly felled for building houses, non-paved streets, almost total absence of monuments in stone or other durable material, houses and even the palace open to all winds, public baths in the river,

---

[67] AMEP 135, f° 239.

[68] F. Pyrard, *Voyage de Francois Pyrard, de Laval* (Paris, 1679), p. 100

[69] AMEP 135, f° 210.

[70] Bogaert, *Historische Reizen*, p. 133.

[71] *Dagh Register*, 6.1.1675.

[72] Pyrard, *Voyage de Francois Pyrard*, p. 100.

102 *Claude Guillot*

and, above all, the omnipresent vegetation with coconuts which grew in the middle of houses, used for food as well as for shade.

One does not find any other mention of commercial activities, besides the mosque's market or craft activities, except for the potters section to the southwest of the city.[73] Should this omission be treated as evidence of scorn on the part of the Westerners for the activities of the little people who did not concern them, or as an image of reality? Should it be the latter, it would mean imagining the inner city of Banten like another inner city, the Benteng of Yogyakarta, as it still can be seen today.

The Means of Communication

As was mentioned earlier, four large streets, not paved, intersected at right angles near the royal square, dividing the city into four parts. Inside these sections, irregular paths surrounded the houses themselves built without any order. "Due to their impracticality, the other passages could not be called 'streets.'"[74] In 1680, the ambassadors from Batavia, summoned to the palace, were led there through "small dark passageways," and they judged this crossing of the *kampungs* not quite in line with the dignity that was due them.[75] This almost total absence of streets was also explained by the fact that Banten was built in "a low and watery place,"[76] and that, like many other cities in Southeast Asia subject to monsoons, the most often used means of communication and the most dignified remained navigating a *perahu* on the rivers and little canals that crossed the city.[77] Thus, transport of goods and people as well as the official processions all used boats, inside the city itself as well as from the port to the city, from this capital city to the former one of Banten Girang, or even from Banten to Tirtayasa, a quite frequent trip in 1678. Banten gradually lost the "aquatic" nature that many other Indonesian cities, outside of Java, have retained. In fact, the build up of alluvial deposits gradually hindered navigation on these rivers which were already quite shallow during the dry season, while the irrigation works upstream contributed to this process by diverting water into the fields. From the beginning of the 18th century, the Sultans slowly abandoned their boats "equipped with a bright red tent, embroidered in gold and silver, covered with a parasol of white damask and decorated with three superposed gold crowns,"[78] and began using the carriages furnished by Batavia for their trips.[79] Diverting water for irrigation and alluviation was pursued, transforming the rivers and canals into swamps making it indeed difficult to picture the Banten of the 17th century as a Javanese Venice.

The Chinese City

Taken from Western sources and going back to the ethnic origin of the majority of its inhabitants, this designation masks the more fundamental aspect of the role played by this sector in the entire city. Located to the west of the inner city, it was separated from it by a wall to the west as well as by the river. Only one bridge, most likely a drawbridge made out

---

[73] Ijzerman, *Cornelis Buijsero*, XXIII.

[74] Bogaert, *Historische Reizen*, p. 133.

[75] *Dagh Register*, 10.7.1680.

[76] Pyrard, *Vogage de Francois Pyrard*, p. 100.

[77] Cortemünde, *Dagbog*, p. 124.

[78] Ibid., p. 96.

[79] de Bruijn, *Voyages de Corneille Le Bruijn*, 5: 59.

of freestone,[80] linked the two parts together. That is to say, the port at the mouth of the river seemed rejected by the royal city, recalling the situation of Bubat, distanced from the Majapahit capital. This sector only acquired its ethnic overtones fortuitously. As was mentioned earlier, all those who did not belong in the Bantenese social system were systematically thrown outside the walls. Already in 1596, the Dutch noted with surprise that the "Emperor of Demak," then in Banten, "to whom even the kings spoke with their hands joined," had his palace outside the inner city, "because he was not allowed to spend the night inside the city."[81] The same rule was applied in the 1670s to the crown prince of Jambi, moreover an ally of Banten, and to ambassadors from Mataram. The inhabitants of the inner city, on the contrary, could not settle outside the walls and had to return to their own neighborhood before nightfall.[82] Being located outside the walls, this neighborhood with its foreign population had a specificity: it made up the international trade center. Thus ships from far-off lands arrived here to trade; here also the local boats drew up alongside, bringing goods for export. Therefore those who took part in this trade, by force of circumstances, the foreigners, lived here. Among them, the Chinese made up the majority but Moors could also be found—Gujeratis and Bengalese among others—and many other ethnic groups. When the Portuguese arrived in the 16th century, they naturally settled in this section of the city. Finally, people from other European nations, who came here during the 17th century to take part in, and on a considerable scale, the great Asian trade, found themselves also quartered in this neighborhood.

Coming from the port, one entered the city by the mouth of the river which formed the harbor itself. The shallowness of the port, five feet at high tide,[83] permitted only little boats to operate the shuttle between the port and the city when the cargos of the big ships were loaded and unloaded. To facilitate its access, Sultan Ageng, during the dry season of 1661, had the river dredged and constructed two piers in the sea to fight against its silting up. The piers rested on large posts of *groenhout* and coral rocks that convicted drug users had to search for on the islands in the bay.[84] These piers are quite clearly depicted on the watercolor in the Bibliothèque Nationale of Paris which served as the original for the engravings that illustrated W. Schouten's book. From the sea coast and moving towards the south, following the long street that was called the Chinese street,[85] three separate sectors could be distinguished: the harbor administration, the European neighborhood, and finally the Chinese sector.

The Port Administration

The first sector began at the gate, the *boom* in Dutch texts, that was in fact made out of tree trunks, allowing access to the city by boat, and a detachment of soldiers to guard it were placed under the authority of an officer, *tumenggung,* who had two cannons at his disposal.[86] Nearby was the Customs Office, *pabean,* one of the rare ancient toponyms kept by contemporary Banten. It was an important administration because it controlled all importation and exportation of goods. The commodities forbidden for importation, like

---

[80] Cortemünde, *Dagbog,* p. 124.

[81] Rouffaer & Ijzerman, *De eerste Schipvaart,* p. 81.

[82] Scott, *The Voyage of Sir Henry Middleton,* p. 93.

[83] AMEP, Vachet, II, 404

[84] *Dagh Register,* 29.6. and 8. 1661.

[85] G/21/4, 27.10.1670 (IOR).

[86] *Dagh Register,* 4.3.1680, AMEP, Vachet, II, 405.

tobacco or opium, were placed in a warehouse "under bond," before being sent to other regions.[87] Duty for goods and other anchoring fees had to be paid here. For this, public weights, *dacing* (a word of Chinese origin) were used. This operation often raised protests from the Westerners who believed the scales to be rigged to their disadvantage.[88] It seemed that to facilitate unloading the enormous cargoes from their ships, the government accepted fixed fees, more or less advantageous, depending on the agreements reached separately with each European country.

A little further to the south, the shabandar administration was located. This building had been built by Kaytsu, the former shabandar, dead for four years; during his lifetime, as an economic advisor to the king, he played an eminent role in the development and prosperity of Banten from 1665 on. Since February 23, 1677, the function of shabandar was assumed by Kiayi Ngabèhi Cakradana. Economically speaking, it was the most important position in the city, as was noted by Guilben, head of the French lodge, because the shabandar was "as much master of the port as general head of trade."[89]

These three administrations, the Customs Office, the Public Weights, and the shabandar office, employed quite a number of clerks whose responsibilities were to keep the books, and all three had foreigners as head administrators; these were Chinese in 1678. Even if far from peculiar to Banten, the presence of foreigners at the head of such important administrations seems surprising. It corresponded, however, to a certain logic. In fact, the shabandar, besides being responsible for the port and trade, was also responsible for the foreign communities for whom he was the guarantor and whose representative he was to the government. It seemed that the head of Customs was, on the other hand, head of the Chinese community. Western sources sometimes designated him head of the Chinese, sometimes shabandar of the Chinese city,[90] which often led to confusion. One knows that in nearby Batavia, the Dutch had these same functions, under the titles of Chinese Captain and shabandar, the latter always being Dutch. Other places, other customs! Finally the presence of a Chinese in the position of Kepala Dacing was explained by the fact that he depended on the customs director, a Chinese himself, and that ethnic cohesion must certainly have played a role.

In fact, one can note that the entire administration of the port, as the geographical location indicated, was left to foreigners, particularly to Chinese, the most numerous and the best placed in the court of Sultan Ageng. The Sultan handed over to them the administration of by far the most important sources of revenue. The fact that these three responsibilities were leased out[91] indicated the total confidence the king granted the leaseholders, as well as the lack of interest that he showed for business details. The Bantenese sovereigns gave the impression of distancing themselves from trade tasks considered too low for a Javanese king, regardless of how necessary they were to the wealth and glory of the kingdom. The status of these administrators was not devoid of ambiguity because the function they could claim only because of their status as foreigner made them members of the Bantenese government, granting them related Javanese titles and names. It seemed indeed that the only condition imposed by the sovereign on their nomination was, irrespective of any religious

---

[87] G/21/6, 29.3.1672 (IOR).

[88] E/3/31, 29.12.1670 (IOR).

[89] AMEP, Vachet, II, 380

[90] P. Voorhoeve, F.H. Naerssen, Th. Pigeaud, *The Royal Library, Copenhagen: Catalogue of Indonesian Manuscripts* (Copenhagen, 1977), p. 162.

[91] G/21/4, 27.10.1670 (IOR).

belief, their conversion to Islam. In fact, in 1678 as before, all foreigners holding a position in the court were Muslims. The great majority of the Chinese seem to have retained the religion of their ancestors, as is discussed below.

The European Section

Next came the Western sector. Five European nations were officially present in Banten: the English, the Dutch, the French, the Danish, and the Portuguese.[92] Only the first four had a lodge. As for the Portuguese, they made up a half breed community difficult to discern. They had always been present in Banten, but for several years their numbers increased as trade activity with Macao increased, and two years earlier,[93] the arrival of "three ships filled with Portuguese from Jepara with their families and wishing to live in Banten," had been noted. These refugees had left that city, where there was a sizeable Portuguese community with its own church, to escape the war that was raging there. Without a contest, the English had the largest lodge, to the north of the section, and they continued expanding, during this booming period of the 1670s. In 1671, they built two new warehouses for pepper,[94] and in 1674, felt they had doubled the capacity of their warehouses during the last five years.[95] Taking advantage of the fire in 1675, they acquired approximately 4500 square meters of land that was adjacent to theirs.[96] Quite near the English lodge was the new Dutch one. The Dutch, having returned to Banten after signing the peace treaty with this kingdom in 1659, did not want to reclaim their former lodge, considering it too timeworn, and they located the new one a little further south. They took occupancy of the new lodge, built by the shabandar in 1663.[97] Admitted even by Batavia,[98] it was more for collecting political and economic information than for trade, strictly speaking. Finally, the last two lodges, the French and the Danish, were located near the former Dutch one and both were settled in 1671. They were built by the shabandar Kaytsu. The French lodge, which in 1678 had been forced into inactivity due to the war in Europe between the French and the Dutch, was built on a plot of land of approximately 1500 square meters.[99] As has been noted, all these lodges were constructed under the direction of the former Shabandar Kaytsu, and, therefore, it is not surprising that they were in brick and in the Chinese style, with the exception of the commons, built out of lighter material. As was remarked, the Bantenese political system required each country to have a representative to the government. The European countries did not escape this rule. The role of guarantor and representative of his community was held by the head of the lodge. But on several occasions, the Sultan tried to intervene and name the person of his choosing to the head of a Western community, as he had done for the Asian countries, the Moors and Chinese, accepting with difficulty the lack of a direct say in the constitution of the hierarchy imposed by the foreigners, usually by the heads of the trade companies.[100]

---

[92] *Dagh Register*, 27.8.1675.

[93] Ibid., 7.10.1676.

[94] Ibid., 28.6.1671.

[95] G/21/4, 4.12.1674 (IOR).

[96] G/21/4, 21.1.1675 (IOR).

[97] *Dagh Register*, July 1663.

[98] Ibid., 29.7.1659.

[99] G/21/4, 26.8.1671 (IOR); C2 193, f° 25 (AN).

[100] See for example, *Dagh Register*, 2.2.1659.

The Chinese Sector

Last, the Chinese street that still exists today, led to the Chinese sector. The number of Chinese, already considerable at the beginning of the century,[101] increased sizably during the last years, certainly for political reasons on the king's part. In 1670–1671, the king had a compound of "three lovely streets with twenty brick houses on each side as well as shops" built by the two Chinese heads Kaytsu and Cakradana,[102] which meant 120 houses to lodge the new arrivals coming from China as well as from Batavia.[103] Several years later, in 1676, with the war raging in Fujian as well as in Southern China, with the last manifestations of resistance coming from the legitimist Mings and the intervention from Formosa by Zheng Jing, the son of the well-known "Coxinga," with war on the north coast of Java, and with the chronic instability caused by the revolt of Trunojoyo, a real wave of Chinese immigrants, coming from China, from Amoy, as well as from East Java or Central Java, could be seen arriving in Banten.[104] Certainly more than a thousand Chinese were seen seeking asylum and working in Banten during the single year of 1676!

The aspect of this neighborhood, from its gate to the south, differed greatly from the inner city. Already in 1596, brick houses could be seen there, built according to the Chinese style found in the south from where the majority of the Chinese in Banten came. In 1659, "the majority of the houses on the Chinese street were in stone,"[105] meaning, made of durable material. Finally, the rate of durable construction was accelerated during the 1670s, certainly initiated by the sovereign, but above all by the two shabandars who wanted to fight against the fires that were all that much more feared in this neighborhood where all the merchandise was stocked.[106] Pallu, quite scornful of the general aspect of the city, noted in 1672 that one "began a few years ago to build several streets according to the fashion in China, that is to say straight, the houses all in a row and out of bricks but low and small and which have nothing of beauty to them."[107] This description could apply to any *pacinan* of a Javanese city of today. Straight streets, brick houses built on the ground and not on piles: a new style forced its way in, which during the next centuries would usurp the former one to the point that houses on piles would become rare in Java, even in the countryside.

In this part of the city, the status of the inhabitants was, conforming to the image of the urban landscape, very different from that which could be found in the inner city. Here, one paid a rent to the king for the land on which the houses were built,[108] because according to Javanese tradition, the land belonged to the state and "no one in the country had the right to own the land."[109] Foreigners, with a special system for Westerners, were subject to personal taxation,[110] while the Muslim foreigners, like their Javanese religious counterparts, were compelled to forced labor.[111] Indeed, people from all different countries were found here,

---

[101] Scott, *The Voyage of Sir Henry Middleton*, passim.

[102] E/3/31, 29.12.1671 (IOR).

[103] VOC 1389, f° 2935/6, 26.7.1683 (ARA).

[104] See *Dagh Register* 2.1.1676; 14.2.1676; 25.8.1676; 12.11.1676 for the different waves of immigrants.

[105] Ijzerman, *Cornelis Buijsero*, XXIII.

[106] G/21/6a, 20.12.1670 (IOR).

[107] AMEP, 135, 209.

[108] C2 193, f° 25 (AN) and *Dagh Register*, 14.6.1663.

[109] 0/21/4, 21.1.1675 (IOR).

[110] Banten 3/12, f° 33, 18.8.1731 (Ars.Nas.).

[111] E/3/31, f° 3467, August 1670 (IOR).

coming of their own free will or brought by boat as servants or slaves; they worked for the lodges or rich merchants. Apart from the lodges, living there also were the Europeans, mainly English but also Spaniards, Danish, French, and Portuguese, taking part in the flourishing private trade, and, more numerous still, those working for the king either in his trade flotilla or in other fields. These are not to be confused with the "renegades" who by virtue of their conversion to Islam, lived in the inner city, wearing Javanese clothing and in the employ of a dignitary or of the king.

Everything worked toward making this international trade center a very animated area. There was the Chinese market in the afternoons where probably, like today, the products most appreciated by foreigners were sold: pork for the non-Muslims, special vegetables, etc. There were, above all, shops where imported and other products could be bought. When the ships arrived from the coast of Coromandel, hundreds of small independent merchants installed stands in the Chinese street to sell their meager loads.[112] There worked the "dock hands," who filled the warehouses when pepper arrived from Sumatra or sugar from the southern plains, who loaded and unloaded the numerous *perahu*, assuring the shuttle between the ships and the port. It was there that the pepper was sifted, ground, and put into sacks; there the cases for packing sugar were still made; there ginger was candied and put into jars. Brickworks which made the bricks for houses and walls were found there, as well as lime ovens for making quick lime that was exported in sizeable quantities to Batavia in earthenware jars.

Like all ports, this one also had a section where one went for amusement. There were inviting cabarets where arak was drunk, distilled in Banten, and where chess, dice, or other games of chance were played,[113] and where, upon paying a kind of tax to the government, company could be enjoyed with women who were not too timid.[114] These delicate subjects wore a modest veil and Cortemünde was the only one to recount how sailors every evening left the port for merrymaking in the cabarets selling arak, and how, when they returned to the ships, "they had to be hoisted aboard like pigs" so drunk were they.[115] To be surprised by these excesses on the part of sailors who had spent long and difficult months at sea, one had to be a young Catholic priest like Gayme.[116] But there were more innocent pleasures in this sector where there were often *wayang* shows or theater, and where fireworks were held whose variety and splendor thrilled and astonished the Europeans.

A last word should be said about worship in this neighborhood. The Westerners had a small chapel or oratory inside their respective lodges and the companies usually put a chaplain at their disposal. No source mentioned a mosque in this part of the city. For the Chinese, we saw that the most important among them had converted to Islam. But their numbers must not be overestimated. The frequency of their appearances in sources was often relative to the importance and visibility of the positions they occupied. It was clearly evident to all these witnesses that the majority of the Chinese had retained the religion of their ancestors.

Curiously, there are only obscure references to the places where the Chinese worshipped even though the Banten of today largely owes its reputation to the *klenteng* that

---

[112] O/21/4, 27.10.1670 and E/3/37, 23.7.1676 (IOR).

[113] O/21/ II, 27.5.1635 (IOR).

[114] L'Estra, *Relation ou journal d'un voyage nouvellement fait aux Indes* (Paris, 1677), pp. 34–35.

[115] Cortemünde, *Dagbog*, pp. 101–102.

[116] AMEP, vol. 972, f° 172-3, 8.10.1672.

became Vihara Avalokitesvara. This *klenteng* is located in the present section of Pabean; it seems quite improbable that it could have existed in this sector in the 17th century without there being any mention of it. Lombard-Salmon in their study of the community and the Chinese epigraphy of Banten showed that the oldest stele of this temple goes back to 1754.[117] The first mention of this temple that could be found dated from 1747 and is found in a notarial act, where it is specified that a property was bordered on the west by the Chinese Temple.[118]

But what about the 17th century? The First Voyage mentioned a pagoda but Rouffaer-Ijzerman demonstrated that the engraving on which the text was manifestly dependent, had been taken from an illustration of a Hindu temple, found in Lonschoten.[119] One can recall Mandelslo, who confirmed that there were no temples or priests in Banten, or the inverse, with Leblanc, who recounted with as much conviction that the Chinese of Banten had a temple. But nothing is less sure than the descriptions of Banten written by these two travelers. That of Cortemünde is much more reliable; he devoted several pages to the description of the Chinese community of this city. After having spoken about altars, probably family ones, he added, "Moreover in Banten, they have magnificent temples, with images of devils, splendidly decorated but frightening, in gold and silver... They easily allowed the Christians to enter and look,"[120] which was different, as maintained earlier, from the Muslims who prohibited access to the great mosque. Therefore it is this one witness that confirms that the Chinese had several *klenteng* in Banten in 1673.

The Eastern Suburbs

A certain symmetry existed between this sector and the Chinese city: like the latter, it was separated from the inner city by a wall and a river; it had a port, called Karangantu, controlled by a customs office *(pabean)* and watched over by a group of guards, and was mainly populated with foreigners. But the similarities stopped here. It was not a question of a truly urbanized sector but a suburb extending along the coast and loosely regrouping all kinds of artisan or even "industrial" activities. Moving from west to east, the port, made up by the river, came first. Spanning it was a bridge that Cakradana had rebuilt out of stone a few years earlier. It led to the inner city[121]—let us note in passing that the Westerners, always very Eurocentric, judged this construction in durable material as "built like in Europe."[122] This bridge was built at the mouth of the same river. It could surely be opened up,[123] but it certainly formed an obstacle at the entrance of this river. One could imagine that the traffic in the port was quite limited and reserved for ships that brought their products to sell in the market and that, given the local character of this second trade center of Banten, only small boats could draw up alongside and were simply pulled up on the shore. The large market and the shops surrounding it made up the heart of this sector where retail trade was carried out. All the Western travelers described the richness and variety of this

---

[117] C and D Lombard-Salmon, "A propos de quelques stèles choinoises récemment retrouvées à Banten (Java-ouest)," *Archipel* 9 (1975): 100.

[118] Banten 14/6, f° 45. 19/1/1747 (Ars.Nas.).

[119] Rouffer & Ijzerman, *De eerst Schipvaart*, p. 125.

[120] Cortemünde, *Dagbog*, p. 124.

[121] *Dagh Register*, 24.6.1674

[122] AMEP, vol. 135, 209

[123] de Bruijn, *Voyages*, 5: 51.

market, which was held every day from dawn to morning, and insisted also on the number of nationalities that were found there. Its organization, described in extensive detail in the First Book and represented distinctly as well in the engraving that accompanied it, are so well known that it seems unnecessary to return to its description. It suffices to note that among the peoples of the Orient already cited, some of them were represented only by individuals while others formed true communities, particularly the Chinese and the peoples of India.

The image of 1596, with its bamboo stands, did not correspond to the situation of 1678. As early as 1659, the majority of the houses surrounding the large market were constructed in brick.[124] Cortemünde even let one believe that they formed the large rectangular streets.[125] This construction in durable material was also the work of the Chinese who built there a second *pacinan* but probably aimed at retail trading. The population seemed in any case much more mixed here than in the west sector; all the witnesses insisted on the presence of the "Moors," to such an extent that they sometimes called this market the "Moor bazaar."[126] But it was noted that the number of Chinese increased gradually. In 1706, De Bruijn described the *pasar* as filled with Chinese shops and remarked that even the captain or leader of the Chinese lived in this sector.[127] It seemed evident that the "Sino-ization" of this *pasar*, begun some time ago, was accelerated when Banten was taken by the Dutch in 1682 with its accompanying consequences: expulsion of the Moors and the Westerners, prohibition of all international traffic to Banten, and finally a Dutch monopoly in pepper. Once international trade was stopped, the Chinese who remained in the city had to revert back to retail trade and, logically, the Chinese sector to the west, after having suffered much during the war, also lost its reason for being there, and quickly disappeared. In 1683, there were only 138 Chinese left in the Chinese street.[128] In 1727, of the Chinese remaining in Banten, 667 lived to the east and only 128 in the Chinese street.[129]

More to the east, noted Schouten, was the fishermen's sector, "an infinite number of little houses and huts of poor people naturally coming from the countryside or from abroad and who furnished sailors and fishermen in quantities useful to the government."[130] This fishermen's sector extended along the beach and still existed in 1706.[131] The naval shipyards for Banten were also in this zone, where numerous traditional ships were built, from the junk to the pirogue,[132] vessels which Banten needed for all its maritime activities. Only the very large ships were constructed in the region of Rembang, known for its abundance in teak wood;[133] again it must be noted that due to the war in 1678, this was no longer possible. Finally, for maintenance and repair of their ships, Westerners used an island situated to the north of Bojonegara, to the northwest of the port and often called the English onrust.[134] The

---

[124] Ijzerman, *Cornelis Buijsero*, XXIII

[125] Cortemünde, *Dagbog*, p. 124.

[126] Banten 1/5, f° 75, 1727 (Ars. Nas.).

[127] De Bruijn, *Voyages*, 5: 51.

[128] VOC 1389, f° 2935-6, 26.7.1683 (ARA).

[129] Banten 1/5, f° 75 (Ars. Nas.).

[130] Schouten, *Voyage de Gautier Schouten*, 2: 304–305.

[131] De Bruijn, *Voyages*, 5: 51.

[132] Schouten, *Voyage de Gautier Schouten*, 2: 305, and, of course, Hesse, *Gold-Bergwerke*, p. 131, who copied him.

[133] For example, 0/21/4, 23.11.1669 (IOR).

[134] C2 22, f° 37, 25.1.1681 (AN).

final activity of this sector was represented by the saltworks,[135] about which unfortunately there is little information. One could believe that they were leased and that the fees were quite high. In fact, it is noted that the *soutpannen* made up part of the revenues of the crown prince, Pangeran Ratu, the son of Sultan Haji, who at the latter's death in 1687, ascended to the throne under the name of Abdul Fadhal Muhammad.[136] According to the information gathered there in 1987, these saltworks would have been in service until after Indonesian independence and belonged then to some Chinese of Serang. It could be imagined, given the proximity of the saltworks to the fishermen's sector, that they were also used for salting and drying fish.

As was mentioned earlier, the population of this sector was made up of foreigners. The tendency is to think of the countries situated the furthest away and the ones that were the most powerful economically. But peoples of the Archipelago also lived in this sector: the Malays of Sumatra and of the Peninsula, the Javanese of Mataram, and above all, for some years, the Bugis Makassarese and the Balinese. It is to be noted in passing that in this year of 1678, the last two groups had to be officially registered with the Bantenese authorities.[137] No source gave any information concerning their status, their rights, and their duties in this city and in the kingdom.

The Suburbs to the South

It could be questionable to use the word suburb to describe the countryside which extended approximately ten kilometers to the south of Banten, but history, feelings, and above all the economy made this area inseparable from the city. It was accessible from the river or by the road which ran more or less along it. The latter, started from the Chinese sector and ran through fertile and well-kept fields, going first of all to the *taman sari* and the animal reserve *(krapyak)*, then to Kenari where the tombs of ancestors closest to Sultan Ageng were found: his great-grandmother, Nyai Gedé (SB pupuh 44), his grandfather, Sultan Abulmafakhir, and his father, Sultan Abulmaäli, who died before he could ascend the throne. Like the king with his water palace, the Westerners also had their baths near the river, where they would come to cool off and amuse themselves and escape from the torrid and fetid atmosphere of the city and, in particular, from the Chinese sector, with its dense population and above all its brick houses, certainly fire resistant but also badly adapted to the humid heat that only flowing air could dissipate. The Europeans suffered more than the others from this climate and an Englishman noted: "He that escapes wihout disease from that stinking stew of the Chinese part of Bantam must be of a strong constitution of Body."[138]

Exactly one year before, in 1677, one of these parties held in the countryside among the Europeans of Banten ended in a drama which shook up the entire Western community of the city. The English from the lodge had invited their Danish and French colleagues to spend the afternoon at their baths, located three kilometers to the south of the city. Everybody, wives included, gaily took to the boats but on the return trip, at sunset, they fell into an ambush, prepared by Pangeran Kitradul, the hot-headed brother of the king, because of a personal dispute he had with an Englishman: two persons were killed and two others

---

[135] *Dagh Register*, 25.4.1678.

[136] VOC 1440, f° 2440, 20.1.1688 (ARA).

[137] *Dagh Register*, 20.2.1678.

[138] OCI 106, 20.6.1613 (IOR).

seriously injured.[139] However, the area was far from deserted. Houses could be seen along the river and this suburb furnished the city with fresh products.

Seven kilometers further, one arrived at Kelapadua. Here, food-producing farming gave place to raising products for export. This sizeable town was quite different from the others in that it was constructed out of bricks and the inhabitants were, for the majority at least, of Chinese origin.[140] Sugar cane had long been grown here and, of course, was processed here as well. During his visit, Cortemünde saw a sugar mill here that he described as "magnificent."[141] The same author alluded to another activity of this town: the distillation of arak. There were many distilleries of arak in Kelapadua, he noted. And furthermore, this activity was entirely in the hands of the Chinese. In 1671, a governmental decision was made that regulated this activity, which was practiced at the beginning of the 17th century almost everywhere and even in the Chinese sector.[142] One can guess its magnitude from the revenues that the government drew in the form of taxes: 1200 reales per year[143] that is the price of ten brick houses in the Chinese sector.[144] The English, who maintained close ties with the Chinese of Kelapadua for their purchases of sugar, owned a house there.

Serang was located quite near there; as its name indicated, because in Sudanese this word means paddy field, a center for rice production, developed by Abulmafakhir among others (SB, pupuh 46). Finally the former capital, Banten Girang, was reached. This court, deserted when the capital was transferred to the sea coast with the arrival of a new Muslim dynasty, had not been abandoned for all that. A palace still existed there; even in 1674, the king came here for his tournaments and secret councils.[145] In 1679, he had "a new court built to serve as a refuge for the queens . . . during times of war."[146] The same passage of the *Dagh Register*, indicated that a road linked Banten Girang to Tirtayasa, the new court of Sultan Ageng.

It seemed probable that these three centers: Banten Girang, Kelapadua, and Serang—the first two today having become simple suburbs of Serang—formed a compound corresponding to the former capital. Moreover, the presence of a Chinese community, well established in Kelapadua in 1678, reminds us that the Chinese frequented these places well before the arrival of Islam as proven by the numerous Chinese ceramic fragments from prior Ming dynasties, which were found in Banten Girang and in the surrounding area, and as testified by the popular tradition which attributed two tombs to two Chinese, Ki Jong and Agus Jo (see also SB pupuh 17), who converted to Islam and offered their services to Hasanudin. These two tombs, which can still be seen today, are located on a site which is believed to be where the palace of the last pagan king, Pucuk Umun, was located.

---

[139] E/3/38, 11.5.1677 (IOR).
[140] H 628, f° 187–194 (IOR).
[141] Cortemünde, *Dagbog*, p. 126.
[142] E/3/31, 30.1.1671 (IOR).
[143] Ibid.
[144] G/21/4, 21.1.1675 (IOR).
[145] *Dagh Register*, 23.1.1674.
[146] Ibid., 28.12.1679.

Banten, A Fortified City

The system of defense for the city is worthy of particular mention as it seemed dissuasive enough to prevent all foreign attack until 1682, when the Dutch took Banten. Yet they had the benefit of support coming from inside the city from a fraction of the population who viewed them favorably. These walls and the cannons that were installed on them, even if they sometimes provoked the irony of the Europeans, probably played a part in the prosperity of Banten which was, above all during the years between 1660 and 1680, a true harbor of peace—the peace so appreciated by merchants—in an Archipelago which never stopped changing by means of violence. Without attempting to develop a history of these fortifications, it suffices to mention that the SB (pupuh 22) attributed the credit for their construction to Maulana Yusup, who reigned between 1570 and 1580, according to Hoesein.[147] At the beginning of the 15th century, Ma Huan in the *Ying-yai Sheng-lan* affirmed that not one of the "four towns of Java" had surrounding walls.[148] The situation at the end of the 16th century was quite different. In the text of the first Dutch travel (ch. 20), almost all the ports of Java were described as enclosed by walls. The map of Banten in 1596 showed a brick surrounding wall built zig zag, as well as palisades. In the view of Banten published by Valentijn in which he detailed the conditions in the first half of the 17th century, one can still see the same zig zagging walls.

On the map of 1659, that is eight years after Sultan Ageng ascended to the throne, it can be noted that the western half of the wall along the sea had been rebuilt in coral rock, this time in a straight line with several bastions at the points.[149] This work had probably been done between 1653 and 1656.[150] Prior to 1673, the wall on the side to the sea appeared to have been entirely redone in this new style, as was shown in a sketch by Cortemünde[151] and the watercolor in the Bibliothèque Nationale in Paris. On the same map of 1659, the south wall, in brick, was no longer parallel to the north one but, along with its west part, formed a large hook toward the south, which caused the growing city to develop differently from the square plan, the ideal plan probably desired by the city founders.

Besides those that surrounded the city strictly speaking, ramparts along the sea could be found, as well as other works of fortification that protected, on the one hand, the Chinese sector, and the east suburbs on the other. Numerous European witnesses testified that two Chinese of Banten, the last two shabandars of Sultan Ageng, played a preponderant role in the construction or the reconstruction of these fortifications. This would confirm Scott's opinion that attributed the construction of the first fortifications to the Chinese.[152]

It would take a longer study to speak of the armament of this city whose strength struck every visitor; it is sufficient to note that throughout his reign, Sultan Ageng did not cease to acquire cannons of all kinds, muskets, and the indispensable powder from the Westerners, through purchases, gifts, or simply seizing them, lacking the means to have them manufactured in Banten. In this, he benefitted from the interested cooperation on the part of the European nations only too happy to find thus the means to counterbalance the disturbing Dutch power from Batavia.

---

[147] Hoesein Djajadiningrat, *Critische beschouwing van de Sadjarah Banten* (Haarlem, 1913), p. 163.

[148] W. Broeneveldt, *Historical Notes on Indonesia and Malaya compiled from Chinese Sources* (Jakarta, 1960), p. 45.

[149] Ijzerman, *Cornelis Buijsero*, XXII.

[150] *Dagh Register*, 2.6.1653 and 5.11.1656.

[151] Cortemünde, *Dagbog*, p. 123.

[152] Scott, *The Voyage of Sir Henry Middleton*, p. 169.

In Guise of a Conclusion

It would be desirable to end by giving the figures for the population in Banten. This is unfortunately quite difficult. The First Book compared Banten in 1596 to Amsterdam of the 16th century and Leblanc compared it to Rouen at the very beginning of the 17th century. Pallu estimated its population in 1672 as at least 100,000 souls.[153] Cortemünde, in the following year, evaluated the number of men in Banten at 200,000 able to go to war, while in 1677, an English source affirmed that one could recruit 10,000 men capable of carrying arms in the entire country.[154] The list of these estimates could be lengthened easily but in vain. The most reliable source, it seems, is a passage in the *Dagh Register* (16.1.1673) which indicated that during the census carried out in 1673, the men in the city capable of using a lance or musket were numbered at 55,000. If all men were counted, whatever their nationality, a total of approximately 150,000 inhabitants would be estimated, including women, children, and the elderly.

More uncertain would be the estimate of the number of foreigners and thus their percentage in the city. With this inability to calculate, one soon reaches limitations not encountered by historians of the Western world. The absence of quantitative data—a simple change in the number of the population for example—certainly accounts for much in the impression of a static society that Westerners believed had long existed in the Archipelago.

Whatever the case, it is undeniable that Banten represented in 1678, through its population and its wealth, the most important urban center of this Archipelago and certainly figured among the largest cities in the world of this era.

---

[153] AMEP, 135, 209

[154] Cortemünde, *Dagbog*, p. 122; E/3/38, 11.5.1677 (IOR).

ISLAM AND CHINESENESS*

Denys Lombard and Claudine Salmon

It is worth pausing for a moment to consider the relationships that were able to exist between the expansion of Islam in the East Indies and the simultaneous formation of "Chinese" communities. These two phenomena are usually presented in opposition to one another and it is pointless here to insist on the numerous conflicting accounts, past and present.[1] Nevertheless, properly considered, it quickly becomes apparent that this is a question of two parallel developments which had their origins in the urban environment, and which contributed to a large extent to the creation of "middle class" merchants, all driven by the same spirit of enterprise even though they were in lively competition with one another. Rather than insisting once more on the divergences which some would maintain are fundamental—going as far as to assert, against all the evidence, that the Chinese "could not imagine marrying outside their own nation," and that they remain unassimilable—we would like here to draw the reader's attention to a certain number of long-standing facts which allow a reversal of perspective.

Chinese Muslims and the Local Urban Mutation of the 14th–15th Centuries

No doubt the problem arose along with the first signs of the great urban transformation of the 15th century. The fundamental text is that of the Chinese (Muslim) Ma Huan, who accompanied the famous Admiral Zheng He on his fourth expedition in the South Seas (1413–1415), and reported at the time of their passage through East Java that the population was made up of natives, Muslims (*Huihui*), as well as Chinese (*Tangren*) many of whom were Muslims. A contemporary text, the *Xiyang fanguo zhi* [Records of the Foreign Countries in the Western Ocean] even goes as far as to say that "All of these Chinese were Muslims."[2]

---

* The French version of this article originally appeared in *Archipel* 30 (1985): 73–94.

[1] Note that in 1979 there appeared in Semarang (Central Java) an interesting little study by Amen Budiman, titled *Masyarakat Islam Tionghoa di Indonesia* [The Chinese Muslim Community of Indonesia] (Semarang: Tanjung Sari, 1979), 75 pp., in which the author makes an attempt to retrace the difficult history of the Muslim Chinese of Indonesia. Cf. our review in *Annales, Economies, Sociétés, Civilisations*, Paris, May–August 1980, pp. 859–61.

[2] Ma Huan, *Ying-yai Sheng-lan, The Overall Survey of the Ocean's Shores (1433)*, translated and edited by J. V. G. Mills (Cambridge: Cambridge University Press, Hakluyt Society, 1970), p. 93; *Xiyang fanguo zhi*, commentary editor: Xiang Da (Beijing: Zhonghua shuju, 1954), p. 8.

We know, moreover, from Chinese sources, that there was an important Muslim community and a mosque at Canton as far back as the 9th century, and that the Muslim merchants played a very important role in the coastal towns of China (Canton but also Quanzhou) in the 13th and 14th centuries.[3] One can easily understand that these communities had their contacts along the Champa coast as well as at the eastern ports of Java.

It is known that the late Javanese historian Slamet Muljana used these facts along with a few others to advance the theory that the Chinese were able to participate in the Islamization of Java,[4] and that his ill-considered work, which was published in 1968, was withdrawn from circulation in 1971, by order of the public prosecutor. Nevertheless, several facts of an archeological and textual order justify one in thinking that Prof. Slamet Muljana was not completely wrong. It is now commonplace to retrace the influences of a certain Chinese art in the first Islamized monuments of the Pasisir or Java's northern coastal area,[5] and the experts in *babad* (chronicles), the late Messrs. de Graaf and Pigeaud have clearly signaled, in their study on the first Muslim kingdoms in Java, the extent to which the presence of the Chinese is perceptible everywhere.[6] At Gresik (East Java), which Ma Huan presents to us in the 15th century as a small Chinese town, lived a certain Nyai Pinatih, of Chinese origin, born at Palembang (Sumatra) and converted to Islam, who received as a small child the future Raden Paku, the first Lord of Giri (East Java).[7] A little further south, at Surabaya, the *Pecat tanda*, that is "the head of the market" of Terung, was a Chinese used as an official by the administration of Mojopahit, who installed and protected the young Muslim who had come from Champa.[8] He was to become Raden Rachmat. At Demak (Central Java) not only the somewhat doubtful Chinese chronicle, referred to by Slamet Muljana, but also the *Hikayat Hasanudin* expressly stated that the founder of the first Javanese sultanate was a Chinese. Also at Japara (Central Java) it was a shipwrecked Chinese captain who married Ratu Kalinyamat and founded one of the most important harbor towns of the Pasisir. All of

---

[3] On these Muslim communities in southern China, see the study, fundamental for our purpose, of J. Kubarawa, "On P'u Shou-keng," *Memoirs of the Research Department of the Tôyô Bunko* [Tokyo] 2, 1 and 7, 1 (1928 and 1935). Pu Shougeng was an important Muslim merchant of Quanzhou who eased the way for the Mongol success. See also Chen Dasheng and Ludvik Kalus, *Corpus d'Inscriptions Arabes et Persanes en Chine. 1 Province du Fujian (Quan-zhou, Fu-zhou, Xia-men)* (Paris: Geutner, 1991), 443 pp.

[4] Slamet Muljana, *Runtuknja Keradjaan Hindu-Djawa dan Timbulnja Negara-negara Islam di Nusantara* [The Fall of the Hindu-Javanese Kingdom and the Rise of Islamic States in the Archipelago] (Jakarta: Bhratara, 1968), 272 pp. Note that before the appearance of Slamet Muljana's book, a controversial Javanese text, the *Serat Dermagandul*, no doubt written around 1878, in the Kediri region (East Java), positively considered the *wali* as Chinese comparing them derisively to white herons (*bangau*) of the paddy-fields whose hoopoe makes one thinks of a braid; cf. G.W.J. Drewes, "The Struggle between Javanism and Islam as illustrated by the *Serat Dermagandul*," BKI 122 (1966): 311, 364.

[5] See in particular Uka Tjandrasasmita, "Art de Mojopahit et art du Pasisir," *Archipel* 9 (1975): 93–98.

[6] H.J. de Graaf and Th. G. Th. Pigeaud, *De eerste Moslimse vorstendommen op Java, Studiën over de staatkundige geschiedenis van de 15de en 16de eeuw* [The First Muslim Kingdoms of Java, Studies in the Political History of the 15th and 16th Centuries], Verhandelingen van het Koninklijk Instituut voor Taal-, Land- en Volkenkunde (The Hague: Nijhoff, 1974), 318 pp.; see also from the same authors: *Chinese Muslims in Java in the 15th and 16th Centuries, The Malay Annals of Semarang and Cerbon*, edited by M. C. Ricklefs. Monash Papers on Southeast Asia, n° 12 (Clayton, Vic.: Monash University, 1984), 221 pp.

[7] According to the dynastic documents of the small state of Ryû Kyû, written in Chinese, it appears that Nyai Pinatih was no other than the elder daughter of Shi Jinqing, a Chinese native to Guangdong province, who from 1405 to 1421, ran the port of Palembang; cf. Tan Yeok Seong, "Chinese Elements in the Islamisation of South East Asia. A Study of the Strange Story of Njai Gede Pinatih, the Grand Lady of Gresik," in *Proceedings of the Second Biennial Conference of the International Association of Historians of Asia Oct. 6. 9. 1962*, held at Taiwan Provincial Museum, Taipei, Taiwan, pp. 399–408.

[8] A small state located in present Vietnam, which was gradually annexed by the Vietnamese.

this is confirmed by Tomé Pires who tells us that "The Javanese used to have affinity with the Chinese" and that the religion of Mohammed was widespread among the cosmopolitan population of the coast made up of Chinese, Arabs, Gujaratees, and Bengalees and other nationalities.[9]

Collaboration of the Chinese Muslim Merchants with the Social Order of the Sultanates

Whatever the origins may be, it is undeniable that Dutch and English sources have, from as far back as the beginning of the 17th century, provided us with plentiful information on Muslim dignitaries of Chinese origin employed in the principal towns of the Javanese Pasisir, and a little later, in some of the large ports of the outer islands. The research was never carried out systematically and here we shall only give a few examples gleaned at random from our readings. They allow us to seize upon a whole social group, sufficiently desirous of participating in local administration to be converted, take a vernacular title, and settle permanently in their host country. Most of these converts married native women, and it is obvious that in the following generation, the children sought to follow the model that had been set.

Without doubt, our best examples concern Banten (West Java), whose merchant society can be considered representative of that of the sultanates. From the end of the 16th century, the account of the first Dutch fleet[10] makes it clear that one must distinguish "natural Chinese," that is, those remaining loyal to their ancestral religion, from those "who have lived here for a long time, and who have adopted the Mohammedan faith." This evidence is confirmed a little later by Edmund Scott (1603–1605) who has a quite interesting passage on these two kinds of Chinese: "The Chyneses are very craftie people in trading, using all kind of cosoning and deceit which may possible be devised. They have no pride in them, nor will refuse any labour, except they turne Javans (as many of them doe when they have done a murther or some other villanie)."[11] John Jourdain, passing through Banten in 1614, also tells us that the Regent (the *Pangeran Protector*) had close to him two or three Chinese converted to Islam who were his principal advisers and assistants: "And therefore hee keepeth neere him two or three China slaves alias China torn coates beinge become Mahometans. These I say, are his cheife councell and doe direct all the buysiness under him."[12] Echoes of this can be found in a report of Cornelis Buysero, dated March 1617: "According to the Javanese themselves, he uses as his counsel nothing but greedy, false thieves: shaven Chinese."[13] A little later the *Dagh Register* (Daily Register kept in Batavia by the [Dutch] United East India Company or VOC) also speaks at various times of Chinese assuming high offices at the court of Banten, often pointing out that they were indeed Muslims. In November 1656, for

---

[9] *The Suma Oriental of Tomé Pires*, translated and edited by Armando Cortesao (London: The Hakluyt Society, 1944), second series, n° LXXXIX, vol. 1, pp. 179, 182.

[10] G. P. Rouffaer and J. W. Yzerman, *De Eerste Shipvaart der Nederlanders naar Oost-Indië onder C. de Houtman (1595–1597)* [The First Dutch Fleet to the East Indies under C. de Houtman (1595–1597)], vol. 1 (La Haye: Nijhoff, 1915), p. 124.

[11] Edmund Scott, *An Exact Discourse of the Subtilities, Fashishions (sic), Politics, Religion, and Ceremonies of the East Indians, as well Chyneses as Javans, there abyding dwelling together . . .* (London, 1606), re-ed. in Sir William Foster ed., *The Voyage of Sir Henry Middleton to the Moluccas, 1604–1606*) (London: The Hakluyt Society, 1943) second series, n° LXXXVIII, p. 174.

[12] W. Foster, *The Journal of John Jourdain, 1608–1617*, (London: The Hakluyt Society, 1905), p. 316.

[13] Cited in Léonard Blussé, "Western Impact on Chinese Communities in Western Java at the Beginning of the 17th Century," *Nampô Bunka* (Kyoto) 9 (1975): 33.

example, we are told of "a certain Chinese Captain and a certain Abdul Wakki, Syahbandar of Banten, both heads shaven for a long time, and Muslims, the first carrying the title of *Kyai*,[14] and enjoying a large fortune and great prestige, the other being one of our confirmed enemies." In 1682, the same year as the fall of Banten, we are told yet again of a certain Sincko, alias Abdul Mopit, who fled from Banten and took to Batavia news concerning Sultan Ageng and his castle at Tirtayasa (1st July).[15]

This model of a merchant-government official Muslim of Chinese origin is attested to throughout the 17th century in various parts of the Javanese Pasisir. In 1623 we are told of a certain Lim Lacco (d. 1645), a Chinese Muslim from Banten and adviser of the Pangeran who decided to side with the Dutch and settled in Batavia, where he was appointed Captain of his nation in 1636;[16] two years later we are told of a certain Inche Muda, the very son-in-law of the famous So Bing Kong (c. 1580–1644), who had settled at Kendal (between Pekalongan and Semarang) and traded in pepper with Jambi (South Sumatra).[17] There can be no question here of giving an exhaustive list of all these Chinese *syahbandar* or harbor masters. Let us again cite Kyai Aria Martanata, Captain of the Chinese of Cirebon from 1692 to 1697: "den geschoren Chinees Kiay Aria Martana, sijnde sabandaar en hooft van die van sijne natie tot Sirrebon. . . ."[18]

Other comparable examples are to be found in the same way in the various ports of the Archipelago. Here is what William Dampier tells us concerning a Chinese from Aceh, converted to Islam around 1689:

> While I was in Tonquin, a Chinese inhabiting here turn'd from his *Paganism* to *Mohametanism*, and being circumcised, he was thereupon carry'd in great state thro the city on an Elephant, with one crying before him, that he was turn'd *Believer*. This man was call'd the Captain of the *China Camp*; for as I was informed, he was placed there by countrymen as their chief Factor or Agent, to negociate their affairs with the people of the country. Whether he had dealt falsly, or was only envied by others, I know not: but his countrymen had so entangled him in law, that he had been ruined, if he had not made use of this way to disingage himself; and then his *Religion* protected him, and they could not meddle with him.[19]

At Makassar (Celebes), a local chronicle, still handwritten in Romanized Malay, alludes to a family descended from a Chinese Muslim from the end of the 17th century, and says of his origins:

> They were two brothers, originating from the land of the Huihui (that is Muslims come from China), the elder was called Panlaoetia, the younger Laitji, both of them had left their country after disappointments. They had boarded boats and migrated towards

---

[14] *Kyai*: appelation for a venerated scholar, teacher of Islam.

[15] Cf. C. and D. Lombard-Salmon, "A propos de quelques stèles chinoises récemment retrouvées à Banten, Java ouest" [About some Chinese stela recently found at Banten, West Java], *Archipel* 9 (1975): 109–11.

[16] Ibid., p. 109.

[17] B. Hoetink, "So Bing Kong, het eerste hoofd der Chineezen te Batavia (eene nalezing)" [So Bing Kong, The first Head of the Chinese at Batavia, a Supplement], *BKI* 79 (1923): 2.

[18] B. Hoetink, "Chineesche officieren te Batavia onder de Compagnie" [The Chinese Officers in Batavia under the Company], *BKI* 78 (1922): 101.

[19] William Dampier, *Voyages and Descriptions*, vol. II in three Parts: 1. A Supplement of the Voyage round the World, Describing the countreys of Tonquin, Achin, Malacca and their Products, Inhabitants, Manners, Trade, Policy (London: np, 1699), pp. 137–38.

Cirebon in Java. There Laitji married the daughter of the *tumenggung*[20] of Batang (to the east of Pekalongan), after which they shared their fortune and Panlaoetia asked his younger brother for permission to continue his voyage in the direction of the east as far as Makassar and up to the land of Sanrabone. There he stayed and sought to earn a living by all means possible.[21]

Beyond isolated examples, it is relatively easy to find a more consistent tendency, especially from the beginning of the 18th century, when our sources become a little more abundant. In almost every one of the principal towns there appeared at this time, a Peranakan (local born Chinese) community made up of converted Chinese. We shall not take up here the much cited eye-witness report of Wang Dahai (1791), who spoke of the Chinese *Selam* who had turned away from the teachings of the "old sages" and had been regrouped by the Dutch under separate Captains,[22] but will recall here a few more precise examples.

The first concerns the Chinese communities which from the beginning of the 18th century actively contributed to the exploitation of the tin mines at Bangka. Before the Dutch administration had recourse to the massive importation of Hakka coolies, these deposits were exploited by Chinese families converted to Islam. The report of Thomas Horsfield (1848) is clear on this point: "Several families, the names of the heads of which are recorded by the inhabitants of Minto (Muntok), formed the first stock of colonisation; the chief of these was the father-in-law of Raden Lumbu (i.d. Sultan Badaruddin); they were of Chinese descent, but their ancestors for several generations had embraced the Mahomedan religion ... the physiognomy of the present generation evidently indicates their Chinese derivation...." Horsfield also adds that it was a habit of the Sultans of Palembang to marry one of the daughters of these worthy people of Muntok: "The custom of marrying a daughter of one of the principal inhabitants of Minto has been kept as a religious duty by the the sovereign of Palembang; and it has been considered as treasonable for a subject from the capital to contract matrimony with any of the daughters of the descendants of the first migrants."[23] A little later, in 1854, J.F.B. Storm confirmed, for Palembang this time, the tendency of the Chinese to convert: "They distinguish themselves, like elsewhere, by their dress, their morals and their religion, but more than anywhere else in the Indies, they are attracted to local dress, and it has resulted in a large number of them becoming Muslims in the course of time; many of the Palembangese have, moreover, in the past, like today, married Chinese. Most of these Chinese women are of the Muslim religion."[24]

This collaboration of the Chinese in the social order of the sultanate of Palembang is found frequently in Java as well, where we have indisputable proof for the same era of their integration into the local society. Amongst the very many examples, we shall give here that of the Han family of Surabaya whose first ancestor in Java, Han Siong Kong (b. in China in 1673), died in Bojonegoro (to the southeast of Lasem) in 1744, and whose descendents we have been able to trace to the present day. It is interesting to observe how entire branches of this family have converted to Islam and have assimilated into the surrounding Javanese society, to the point of forgetting their origin. A genealogy, carefully kept since the 18th

---

[20] *Tumenggung*: title of high-ranking administrative officer.

[21] *Sedjarah Melajoe di Makassar* [History of the Malays in Makassar], manuscript kept at the Yayasan Sulawesi, Makassar, under the n° 139, pp. 29–30.

[22] Cf. Ong-Tae-Hae, *The Chinaman Abroad or A Desultory Account of the Malayan Archipelago, particularly of Java*, transl. by W.H. Medhurst (Shanghae: The Missions Press, 1849), p. 33.

[23] Thomas Horsfield M.D., "Report of the Island of Banka," *Journal of the Indian Archipelago, 1848*, p. 309.

[24] F. J. B. Storm, "De Stad Palembang" (The City of Palembang), *BKI*, 1856, p. 458.

century and currently retained by the Han family of Surabaya, has preserved the memory of certain members, converted in order to integrate into the ranks of the administration and those of the Javanese nobility. In the second generation, two sons of Han Siong Kong embraced Islam; one being appointed Adipati of Bangil (East Java) and the other Regent in Tegal (West Java). In the third generation, a son of a brother of the Captain of the Surabayan Chinese Han Bwee Kong (1727–1778) and in the fourth, two of the four sons of the Lieutenant of the Surabayan Chinese, Han Soe Sik (1767–1827), converted in turn. Whereas the memory of the two brothers of the Captain of Surabaya and of their descendants has been kept alive thanks to their high position within the Javanese society,[25] that of the rest of the converted Han is lost.

It so happens that one can rediscover in the European sources a trace of these ennobled Chinese. This is the case, it seems, for Kyai Dipati Suro Adinegoro, who is mentioned in the Mackenzie Collection reports as being Dipati of Bangil and nephew of the Captain of the Surabayan Chinese Han Bwee Kong. Daendels (Governor General of the Dutch Indies from 1808 to 1811) had found his manner of administering his district so exemplary, that he had summoned him to Semarang to confer a decoration upon him.[26] We know that on examining the *silsilah* or genealogies of numerous families of *bupati* or regents, some illustrious ancestor of Chinese origin can be easily recognized. Rothenbühler tells us that in 1798, with regard to Pekalongan, the grandfather of the Regent Raden Adipati Jayadiningrat, passed as having been "a Peranakan (or local born) Chinese who had embraced the Muslim religion," and he added, "This man having insinuated himself in favor with the Emperor Pakubuwono the first obtained this regentship from him."[27]

Running parallel to this assimilation on the highest level, there followed an integration on the most humble strata. At the beginning of the 19th century, before the Dutch took the political and economic situation of the Indies in hand, numerous towns had next to their Chinese kampung, a *kampung Peranakan* or local-born Chinese district, like Semarang, where Knops tells us in an 1814 manuscript report of their separate community and of their leader "titled exclusively Captain": "As the Parnakkangs have become Mohammedans or are by birth, they live more in the style of the country than in the Chinese way. Their job is generally fishing and the navy, hiring themselves out as sailors or skippers of entire vessels . . . they are whiter than the normal to be Javanese but not as white as the Chinese. They marry Javanese women; this results in mixed blood which become less so from generation to generation."[28]

---

[25] They even compiled their own genealogy which is kept in Sidoarjo, south of Surabaya. For more detail about the history of this family of long standing in Indonesia, see Claudine Salmon, "The Han Family of East Java— Entrepreneurship and Politics (18th–19th Centuries)," *Archipel* 41 (1991): 53–87 where a simplified genealogy of the family is to be found along with a list of the Muslim members of the Han family who were officials.

[26] India Office, London, *Mackenzie Collection*, Private 82 (n° 26, p. 268 sqq): "On the Present State and Management of the District of Bangel = Bangil, with an account of the origin and history of the celebrated Kiai Dipatty Sooro-Adi-Nogoro = Kyahi Dipati Sura Adinegara, Knight of the Order of Holland at present Tumunggung = Tumengung of Tuban = Toeban,"(India Office Library, London). Cf also Heather Sutherland, "Notes on Java's Regent families," *Indonesia* 16 (October 1973): 145, who in particular credits the conversions in the Han family to the first generation and not to the second; cf. also Salmon, "The Han Family of East Java," pp. 66ff.

[27] *Mackenzie Collection*, Private 7, p. 57 (English translation of the report of Rothenbühler on Pekalongan).

[28] *Mackenzie Collection*, Unbound translations, Class XIV, 32. A report of J. A. Middlekoop (*Mackenzie Collection*, Private 6, p. 211) mentions for the same period that the Peranakan Muslim community of Surabaya took to small business but was nevertheless in a state of great poverty. These communities gradually merged into the local Indonesian societies from the second half of the 19th century onwards. The fact is expressly reported concerning those of Makassar and Sumenep. Cf. The Siauw Giap, "Religion and Overseas Chinese Assimilation in Southeast

Cultural Contribution of Peranakan Muslims

Although our information is skimpy, we can try to retrace a few traits of this Peranakan Muslim "subculture." For this, we have at our disposal a few archeological and textual elements.

It is known that there existed in Java at the very least a few mosques traditionally attributed to Chinese Peranakan communities. One of the best known is the Mesjid Pacinan of Banten; its square-shaped minaret was restored by the archeological service in the mid-1970s.[29]

To tell the truth, we lack here a positive epigraph and are forced to remark that nothing in the decor is typically Chinese. This monument does not figure in the oldest plans and it can be supposed that the Peranakan slowly annexed the mosque, built by others (note that in another area of Banten, there exists a mosque with a similarly square-shaped tower whose history has nothing to do with the Chinese). We can also cite, at Jakarta, the mosque of Krukut, in the district of the same name (to the west of Molenvliet), which we know with certitude was founded in 1785, on the initiative of Tamien Dosol Seeng, Captain Commander of the Peranakan.[30] The mosque of Kebon Jeruk (not far from there, to the east of Molenvliet, in the actual Jl. Ayam Wuruk), seems to have served Chinese Muslims from the 18th century, as attested to by the famous tomb of Lady Cai, dated from 1792, which is close at hand, and which is most likely that of the founder.[31] It is interesting to note that when the mosque burned in 1937, it was the manager of a Chinese firm, Lauw Tjeng Yoe, who bore the cost of its restoration.[32] Note further that inside the so-called "Balinese" mosque (in Angke district) could be found until very recently a Muslim tombstone with a Chinese inscription.[33] In everything that has been previously mentioned, we have clear proof that at least certain believers were of Chinese origin, but there are many other mosques, in Java as

---

Asian countries," *Revue du Sud-est Asiatique* 2(1965): 73. However the development of collective ancestral temples and funeral associations in significant numbers after the mid-19th century, shows that some segments of the Chinese community tried very hard to stop the Islamization process, which apparently was still very strong in the 1850s and 1860s; cf. Claudine Salmon, "Conflicts of Customs in Surabaya: Around the Hokkien Kong Tik Soe (19th century)," forthcoming. Another line of research would be the participation of Chinese Muslims in the Indonesian anticolonial wars. To date we have found two pieces of information. The first concerns the alliance between Raden Prawiro and a Chinese Muslim of the name of Boengseng who launched an uprising in 1839 against the Dutch. We know little of this Chinese except that he spoke native and Arabic languages and that he concealed himself under an Arabic costume; cf. J. Steijn Parvé, "Landverhuur in de Vorstenlanden en javasche oorlog" [Landrenting in the Principalities and the Java War], *Tijdschrift voor Nederlandsch Indië* 2 (1850): 52–53. The second concerns Ibu Melati, a *dukun* of Chinese origin, who after her conversion to Islam, was adopted by a certain Hadji Getol of Kresek and who played a very important role in the preparation of the uprising which took place at Tangerang in 1924; cf. Sartono Kartodirdjo, *Protest Movements in Rural Java* (Singapore: Institute of Southeast Asian Studies/ Oxford University Press, 1973), pp. 50, 53–54.

[29] For a reproduction of the minaret, see *Archipel* 9 (1975), opposite p. 112.

[30] Cf. C. Salmon and D. Lombard, *Les Chinois de Jakarta, temples et vie collective/ The Chinese of Jakarta Temples and Communal Life*, Etudes insulindiennes-Archipel: 1 (Paris: Editions de la Maison des Sciences de l'Homme, 1980), p. 298.

[31] For a reproduction of Lady Cai's tomb, see De Haan, *Oud Batavia* [Ancient Batavia] (Batavia: Kolf,1922), Platen Album E.16.

[32] Cf. Phoa Kian Soe, "Islam Tionghoa di Jakarta" [Chinese Islam in Jakarta], *Sunday Courier* (Jakarta), May 6, 1953, pp. 10–11.

[33] For more details about this mosque see "A travers Jakarta (1), la mosquée balinaise" [Through Jakarta" (1), The Balinese Mosque], *Archipel* 3 (1972): 97–101; a reproduction of the tombstone inscription of "Lady Chen, née Wang" is to be found opposite p. 97.

122 Denys Lombard and Claudine Salmon

View of Japura, with detail of the
5-storey mosque (probably from
the 18th century); see n. 34.

elsewhere, where it is easy to recognize—be it in the architecture, the decor, or the furnishings—the hand of Chinese artisans; there is, however, no absolute proof that these artisans were themselves Muslims. Among the oldest mosques, one can mention that of Japara, whose five levels make one think of a pagoda, and the mosque of Hasan Suleiman, at Ambon in the Moluccas, whose ancient structure we know, thanks to a drawing by Valentijn, shows a circular door in the best style of the gardens of Suzhou.[34] Here we shall not

---

[34] Concerning the ancient mosque of Japura, destroyed at an undetermined date, see the articles of H.J. de Graaf: "De moskee van Djapara,"*Djawa* 16 (1936):160–62; "De oorsprong der javanese moskee," *Indonesië* 1(1947–48): 289–307 (English version: "The Origin of the Javanese Mosque," *Journal of Southeast Asian History* 4,1 [Singapore] (1963): 1–5. In the first article in *Djawa*, the author reproduces an illustration taken from the *Voyages* of Wouter Schouten (Amsterdam, 1676) representing well the five-storey mosque. We give here a more recent image (probably from the 18th century) of the same mosque which figures in a general view of the town of Japara, a watercolor kept at the Paris National Library under the classification: Port. 193, Div. 7P.1—As to the mosque built by Hasan Suleiman (in 1709), on the isle of Ambon and reproduced in the famous treatise of Valentijn, *Oud en*

treat the question of the many *mimbar*, whose decor, adorned with gilded wood, very often reveals the technique of the Cantonese cabinet makers.

Even more than in these hybrid mosques, one will find excellent proof of this cultural symbiosis in the development of the "Chinese *kramat*." The phenomenon makes it worth our pausing here because, strictly speaking, it is unknown in the Chinese tradition. The worship of the intercessors took place instead in the temples, and if a few real *kramat* are found in China itself, they appear in a Muslim context, like the one found in the northern town of Canton (the Wakkâs' holy tomb) or at the Lingshan or "Miracle Hill" tombs near Quanzhou. In Java and in several other towns of Insulinde one finds a very large number of sacred tombs attributed to people of Chinese origin considered converts, and likely to fulfill the hopes of those who invoke them. It should be noted that the Chinese Totok or newcomers, remaining loyal to the tradition of their ancestors, have always looked unfavorably upon these *kramat*, which they call *shengmu* and see as a sign of cultural integration (*ru fan*).[35] Most of these tombs are in an Islamic style, with a stele at the two extremities, but a few have kept the Chinese model in the form of a tumulus.

Although it is difficult to establish an exact chronology, there is every right to believe that these *kramat* are extremely old. Several must go back to the period of the first Islamization of the 15th and 16th centuries. Thus one can still see the tomb of Nyai Pinatih, at Gresik; that of the Chinese Captain who married Ratu Kalinyamat (and took the name of Pangeran Hadiri), at Mantingan, near Japara; that of Kyai Thelingsing, the master artisan who is assumed to have introduced a certain technique of wood carving, at Kudus; and also those of Mas Jong and Bagus Jong, at Banten Girang (they are believed to have participated in the Islamization of the Banten region and certain families, to this day, still claim descent from them).

In the same way, at these very personalized tombs, of which there can be no doubt they are historical monuments, there are a series of litoral or harbor *kramat* which mark special places where the culture of the newcomers merged into that of the autochthons. These Islamized sites are sometimes linked to the history of the famous Admiral Zheng He (1371–1433, better known by the name of Sam Po) or his followers. The best examples are those of the temple of Ancol[36] at Jakarta; and at the Gedung Batu at Semarang where one can see the "tomb" of one of the pilots (*juru mudi*) of Zheng He who would convert and enter into marriage with a woman of the area.[37] Again, one finds the example of a Muslim tomb associated with a Chinese temple on the isle of Kemarau, a little downstream from the town of Palembang (in the heart of the Musi River), and at the mouth of the River of Pekalongan (at

---

Nieuw Oost Indië, one can see its image in H. J. de Graaf, *De geschiedenis van Ambon en de Zuid-Molukken*, (Franeker: T. Wever, 1977), p. 106.

[35] One can find in the rules of the association created at Surabaya in 1864 by the Peranakan Chinese of Fujian, to regulate the question of marriages and funerals in the heart of their community, interesting texts warning members against the cults of Muslim tombs in which the Chinese took part, just as against the *selametan* or religious meal, another practice which became equally common in certain Peranakan circles; cf. G. Schlegel, *Chineesche begrafenis- en huwelijksonderneming (gevestigd te Soerabaya)* [Chinese Funeral and Marriages Association based in Surabaya], (Overgedrukt uit de *Bijdragen tot de Taal-, Land- en Volkenkunde van Nederlandsch-Indië*, 4e Volgr., DI VIII), tweede, verbeterde druk, 1885, where the original in Chinese is to be found, and the translation in Dutch (pp. 40–43); cf. also Salmon, "Conflicts of Customs in Surabaya: Around the Hokkien Kong Tik Soe (19th Century)," in press.

[36] Cf. Salmon and Lombard, *Les Chinois de Jakarta*, p. 86ff.

[37] Cf. I. W. Young, "Sam Po Tong, la grotte de Sam Po" [Sam Po Tong, The Sam Po Cave], *T'oung Pao*, IX, (1899), série 1, pp. 93–102.

the north of the town of the same name).³⁸ Let us note once more that from the 1730s, a Chinese traveler speaks of a *kramat* (*shengmu*) just at the mouth of the Ciliwung, where the Arab *kramat* of Luar Batang would later be built;³⁹ there likewise existed, to the north of Surabaya, near the sea, at the place named Moro Krembangan an analogous site which was "moved" when the airfield was developed. The new *klenteng* or temple built on this occasion (around 1930), in Jl. Demak, still shelters a large piece of wood, "having been part of Sam Po's boat," and several holy tombs which are of the same type as those of Ancol.

Finally there is a third group of holy tombs which largely correspond to the assimilation of the Chinese to the Javanese hierarchy which we have highlighted above for the 18th and 19th centuries. Let us cite, for example, the tomb of Kyai Joyolelono, who was *Bupati* or regent of Probolinggo (East Java) from 1746 to 1768; it can be found in the cemetery of Sentono in the village of Mangunharjo, near to this town. Kyai Joyolelono, who is still honored for his good administration, is none other than the son of Kyai Bun Jolodriyo alias Kim Bun, who was one of the companions of Untung Surapati, and even one of his principal advisers. This figure occurs several times in the text of the *babad* (chronicle) studied by Ann Kumar, who questions his historical character and asks whether he may be nothing more than "a literary invention," functioning as a sort of *spielman*—an initiator of the various stages in the drama."⁴⁰ Another example is that of Tumenggung Aria Wira Chulia (d. 1739 according to Chinese sources), alias Chen Sancai, who served Sultan Sepuh of Cirebon and whose tomb in Chinese style (repaired in 1765), is located in the city in a place named Sukalila.⁴¹ We shall here end the listing of the Chinese *kramat* which play a role that should not be underestimated in Javanese religion, and on which the local press is fond of publishing indulgent articles from time to time.⁴²

It can be equally useful to consider the literary contribution of these Chinese Muslims. To our present knowledge, the "corpus" of their work remains very modest, because from the time the authors assumed a "Javanese" or "Muslim" name, their Chinese origins can only be traced if they reveal it themselves in the introduction or in the course of the work. Even so, we are tackling the important question of knowing to what extent these Peranakan were able to participate in the spreading of literature itself. Let us remember that it is quite

---

³⁸ We have found no information concerning the story of the sacred tomb of Palembang. The one located beside the the river of Pekalongan, near to its mouth, is buried under a quite small, poor edifice, without any particular style. The tomb was still there in 1983 when the Indonesian Chinese of Pekalongan decided to repair it. Then the two *nisan* or gravestones were covered with cement so that now the interior of the small edifice offers a structure which is tiled and looks more like a traditional Chinese altar. On top of it have been placed two incense burners bearing the inscription *Shengmu gong* or "The Lord of the Holy Tomb" and dated 1849 and 1948 respectively. A modern painting representing the the holy tomb also hangs on the wall. When Wang Dahai (Ong-Tae-Hae) visited Pekalongan, at the end of the 18th century, this tomb already existed and was famous for the powers which were attributed to it; this author adds that the boatmen were always "burning incense" and depositing offerings; cf. Ong-Tae-Hae, *The Chinaman Abroad*, p. 12.

³⁹ C. Salmon, "Un Chinois à Java (1729–1736)" (A Chinese at Java, 1729–1736), *Bulletin de l'Ecole Française d'Extrême-Orient* 54 (1972): 293.

⁴⁰ The worship of the tomb of Kyai Joyolelono was indicated in R.M. Yunani Prawiranegara, "Altar Toapekong di rumah Kabupaten Probolinggo," *Surabaya Post*, February 1, 1982; cf. also Ann Kumar, *Surapati, Man and Legend, A Study of Three Babad Traditions* (Leiden: Brill, 1982), p. 340.

⁴¹ Cf. C. Salmon, "A propos de quelques tombes chinoises d'Indonésie des XVIIe et XVIIIe siècles" [About some Chinese tombs from the 17th and 18th centuries in Indonesia], *Archipel* 12 (1976): 213.

⁴² Such a small article as this appeared in *Liberal* (Surabaya), n° 156 (September 1956), p. 22 and is entitled: "'Baba baru', Makam Tionghoa untuk minta . . . kekajaan!" [A Chinese tomb at which to pray for wealth], which reports that the inhabitants of the Kuningan region (near Cirebon) are going to pray at the holy tomb of the first Chinese, Tjan Dji Tok, who came to settle there in the 17th century.

striking that the use of the *taman bacaan* or "reading rooms"—relatively attested to in China under the Tang dynasty—is to be found in the Archipelago, in two towns strongly influenced by the Chinese, Palembang and Jakarta. We also know of the famous copyist, Ching Sa'idullah Muhammad, who was very probably a Peranakan, and who transcribed a great number of manuscripts while employed at the secretarial office at Batavia in the second half of the 19th century.[43]

In particular we are concerned here with the few "theoretical" writings, confined often to *kebatinan* or Javanese mysticism, written by the converted Peranakan. The library of the municipality of Yogyakarta (Central Java) still preserves a curious little text in Javanese characters, printed at Surakarta in 1853, and attributed to a certain Tan Ing Soen. It is a *Serat Tasawoef* or "mystical treaty," which claims to teach, in 42 pages, a knowledge of the Islamic religion (*bab kawroeh agami Islam*).[44] One can equally cite the interesting *Sjair ilmoe sedjati dan Sjair nasehat* or "Poem about the True Knowledge and Poem of Admonition" re-edited in 1921 by Tan Khoen Swie at Kediri (East Java), and attributed to a certain Kyai Kiem Mas of Prajekan (near Panarukan, East Java). This Kyai Kiem Mas (1834–1896) was in fact a member of the great Han family, converted to Islam, of which we have spoken above. His great uncle was Han Bwee Kong, Captain of Surabaya, and his father, son of Han Swie Kong, had already converted, taking the name of Wirjo Adikoesomo. Kyai Kiem Mas, also called Tjekong Mas, or even Kyai Mas Asemgiri, settled at Prajekan, where he lived in retirement, teaching wisdom to a few disciples. After his death his tomb became a very well-known *kramat* throughout East Java, and is visited to the present day.[45] The *Sjair ilmoe sedjati* is composed of 120 stanzas[46] and the *Sjair nasehat* which follows, 105. Both are tinged with Islam, as certain verses of this genre go to prove

"Bahasa Arab ada membilang,
Noer Moehamad tjahjia goemilang."

But he also made allusion to Biblical principles:

"Tjerita Beibel aloes dan titi,
Moesti menoeroet dengan ingati...."[47]

---

[43] Cf. Claudine Salmon, *Literature in Malay by the Chinese of Indonesia, A Provisional Annotated Bibliography*, Etudes insulindiennes-Archipel 3 (Paris: Editions de la Maison des Sciences de l'Homme, 1981), p. 16.

[44] Tan Ing Soen, *Soerat Tasawoef, Njariosken pandita moemoelang dateng para siswanipoen bab kawroeh agami Islam, ingkang prajogi kanggé ing donja ngantos doemoegi gagajoehan ing ngakir pisan* (Surakarta: Tjahja, 1853), 42 pp.

[45] Cf. P.K.A. (Pouw Kioe An), "Keramat Tjekong Mas di Pradjekan," *Liberty* (Surabaya), n° 617, July 3, 1965, pp. 16, 25; "Makam K. Mas Prajekan dapat kunjungan ramai"[The tomb of K.M. in Prajekan has become a busy place], *Jawa Pos* (Surabaya), November 22, 1979. According to this article K. Mas Prajekan was also the founder of the *pesantren* or Koranic school of same name which is to be found just next to the tomb. The complex extends over 800 square meters. It is the descendants of K. Mas Prajekan who administer the foundation. Next to the tomb of Kyai Mas are to be found two others which are assumed to be those of his younger brother and the latter's wife. The site was refurbished at the end of the 1970s, and when we visited it in 1981 the three tombs were buried under a vast *pendopo* allowing dozens of people to partake in a communal meal or *selametan* together, around the tombs.

[46] According to the sayings of the descendants of Kyai Mas, the *syair* was written in Jawi (or Arabic) characters and kept until recently in the *pesantren* in manuscript form. The last borrower must not have returned it. No one in the *pesantren* seemed to know of the modern re-edition in Latin characters: Kiai Kiem Mas, *Sjair ilmoe sedjati dan Sjair nasehat* (2d ed., Kediri: Tan Khoen Swie, 1921), which is to be found conserved, as the only extent copy, at the Library of the Museum of Jakarta.

[47] "The Arab language states clearly,
The light of Muhammad is vivid....

Generally the thoughts of the author reflect a very Javanese syncretism. In fact the first of the *syair* gives an account of his quest with eight successive *guru* or masters, and the second warns against the evils of money which he calls *Si Ringgit*, and which turns one from the right path and belief in God. Belonging to the same genre is the small prose collection, entitled: *Poesaka jang amat kekal, jang dapet dipoenjai lebi dari saoemoer idoep*, or "A lasting heritage which may be owned even after death," published in Batavia in 1914 and attributed to a certain Kiai Hadji Koesta, of whom it is said: "that he was a Chinese ordinarily called Intjek 'M'Iah, but who then changed nationality" (*saorang Tionghoa totok, jang biasa diseboet I.M.I., kemoedian telah toekar laen bangsa*).[48]

However the most remarkable is without doubt the *Sair Tjioko dan Pitjoen* or "Poem on the Ghost Festival and Boat Races Festival," which Henri Chambert-Loir found in the depths of the manuscripts of the National Library in Jakarta, a copy of which he has generously shared with us. The manuscript is incomplete and anonymous, but the use of technical Hokkien terms (sometimes rendering comprehension difficult) proves that the author was of Chinese origin. In fact the poem is made up of three parts, each describing one of the great festivals of the community: the Festival of the Ghosts (The *Avalambana* of the Buddhists, usually called *Pesta rebutan* or *Tjioko* in Java),[49] that of the boat races, or *Pitjoen* (*Pecun*), to commemorate the death of the famous poet and loyal minister Qu Yuan (B.C. 332–295), and finally that of the Chinese New Year or *Capgome*. But instead of describing them in the manner of Tjiong Soen Liang, author of another *Pantoen Tjapgome* or "Poem on the New Year Festival" (published in Batavia in 1924), this author chooses to criticize at the same time the superstitious Chinese and the unscrupulous Muslims who do not hesitate to mix in the festivities. As converted, orthodox Peranakan, he laments seeing his fellow Muslims hurl themselves at the offerings exposed on the scaffolding and "snatch" them (*tjioko* literally "to scramble for the offerings made to the ghosts").

"Koempoel semoea Slam jang gila
Manelen loeda gojang kepala ...
Mangikoet gagares makanan Tjina,
Sajoer babi banjak disana ...
Kaloe ketemoe arak di mangkok,
Tidak oeroeng dia mandekok...."[50]

A little further on he regrets the promiscuity which is bringing Muslim women nearer to the young Chinese men by the banks of the River Angke, where the boat races took place:

"Prampoean Slam bedesek desekan,
Sama sengke Tjina Peranakan,
Itoe atoeran jang boekan boekan,

The Biblical story is written with care,
It must be followed and remembered."

[48] Cf. Salmon, *Literature in Malay by the Chinese of Indonesia*, p. 196.

[49] Cf. C. Lombard-Salmon, "Survivance d'un rite bouddique à Java: la cérémonie du *Pu-du*" [Survival of a Buddhist ritual in Java: The Pu-du festival], *BEFEO* 62 (1975): 457–86, and plates XXIII–XXIX.

[50] "Here they are reunited, these insane Muslims,
Swallowing their saliva and shaking their heads....
They, also gobble down Chinese food,
There are lots of vegetables and pork....
And if there is alcohol in a bowl,
They waste no time in lapping it...."

Di pingir kali dia pada makan ...
Tjina makan mengikoet badok,
Tjina mandi ikoet mengerobok,
Tjina tahon baroe mengikoet mabok...."[51]

The conclusion is that such a spectacle "breaks the faith that one has in one's heart" (*meroesaken ilmoe di dalem dada*).

After the *kejawen* or Javanism of the syncretic Kyai and the orthodoxy of puritan Peranakan, we have finally a third facet with the revolutionary hope of the author of the *Sair Serikat Islam* or "Poem on the Serikat Islam," published at Batavia by Kho Tjeng Bie in 1913. The author signs himself with the name of R. Pasisir which is evidently a pseudonym, but he claims to be writing at the request of the rich Toean Nio Tjiang Oen, drawing his inspiration from two Sino-Malay newspapers (*Sin Po* and *Pantjaran Warta*) and making repeated references to his Muslim faith (from the first verse: *Bismillah itoe permoelaan kalam* or "In the name of God, such is the beginning"). This text which manifestly addresses itself to a converted Peranakan public, curiously makes the apology of the Sarikat Islam which has just come into existence, praising all the diverse personalities who have participated in the first reunions, not only Haji Saman Hoedi,[52] but also Raden Goenawan, Tjokroaminoto, Hasan Ali Soerati, as well as the Arabs Said Mohamad Al Aijdroes, Said Abdoellah in Aloei Alatas, and the Chinese Khouw Kim An, Major of the Chinese in Batavia (appointed in 1910), and Nio Tjiang Oen. The tone is enthusiastic and open-minded and he only makes allusion to the regrettable incidents which cost a few lives at the beginning of the movement at Semarang and at Surabaya.

"Lagi di Kepoeteran bilangan Djawa,
Boemipoetra riboet dengan Tionghowa,
Beberapa banjak melinjapkan djiwa,
Nama Sarikat djadi ketjiwa."

It seems likely that at this time a certain group of Chinese Peranakan had aspired to associate themselves with this movement perceived as an awareness and a first step toward autonomy.

"Kaoem Islam empoenja bangsa
Berpoeloe tahon soeda merasa,
Segenap negeri kampoeng dan desa,
Seperti orang kena diseksa"[53]

---

[51] "The Muslim women gather,
All against the Sengke and the Peranakan,
What aberrant morals!
By the river banks, they all eat together....
The Chinese eat, the others gorge themselves,
The Chinese bathe, the others paddle,
The Chinese celebrate their New Year, and they get drunk...."

[52] These indications were drawn together with a note by M. Sartono Kartodirdjo in his *Protest Movements in Rural Java*, p. 154: "Before the founding of the *Sarekat Dagang Islam* the Kong Sing association including both Chinese and Javanese members, among whom was Haji Samanhudi himself; later on he founded his own association Rekso Rumekso. Hadji Samanhudi had been persuaded by Chinese to join their Kong Sing association because they were afraid of the founding of shops by Budi Utomo which could eliminate *toko*-owners."

[53] "And still at Keputran (district of Surabaya), in Java,

Hence their deep desire to minimize the first attacks formulated against the Chinese.

"Banjak kabar berita orang,
Waktoe keriboetan di kota Semarang,
Sarikat Islam katanja terang,
Bangsa Tionghoa hendak disarang

Perkataan demikian jang boekan boekan . . .
Diharap Toean-toean djangan dengarkan."[54]

Note that at the same time the interpreter of the Chinese, the journalist Sie Hian Ling (d. c. 1928) handed over to the Sarikat Islam his journal *Sinar Djawa*, which from then on took the name of *Sinar Hindia*..[55]

Re-Sinization and Dakwah

It was clear at this time, on the eve of the Second World War, that the old dream of assimilation, still nursed by some, was no longer as easy to realize as it had been previously. The general economic, social, political, and judicial conditions had changed considerably with the setting up of the Dutch Indies, the opening of large plantations, and the massive introduction of coolies. The steady arrival of Chinese wives contributed very strongly to the re-introduction of Chinese influences into the community whilst the emergence of Chinese nationalism from the Taiping, and especially with the revolutionary movement of Sun Yat sen, awoke sentiments toward the country of origin and slowed down tendencies to integrate. We know that from the second half of the 19th century onwards there was a small surge among the *klenteng* or Chinese temples, places of conviviality and symbols of otherness for those Chinese, henceforth called those from overseas (*huaqiao*). The new social statute promulgated in 1854 created the category of "Oriental Foreigners," which isolated the Chinese from the Europeans as well as from the mass of the natives.

However, even though all these new conditions tended to split the group of Chinese from the rest of the population, and to insist on their specificity, indeed on their peculiar ways, on their national pride, and on their reluctance to integrate culturally, one cannot deny that the old tendency to integrate persisted against all odds. It is possible to detect traces from the end of the 19th century and 20th century to the present day. This tendency was henceforth to be found supported by a calculated willingness to convert on the part of the natives themselves who, being less and less aware of the Chinese "danger," took the initiative in assimilation by the *dakwah* or Muslim proselytizing movement. One of the first

---

The natives fought with the Chinese,
Several have lost their lives,
And the Sarikat lost face.."

The Muslim nation
Has suffered for decades,
Throughout the country and in the heart of the villages,
It is as if one was being tortured. . . ."

[54] "Many have told
At the time of the events of Semarang,
That the Sarikat Islam had clearly said
That they were going to attack the Chinese,

All these mad words,
It is to be hoped that you do not listen to them".

[55] Cf. Salmon, *Literature in Malay by the Chinese of Indonesia*, p. 300.

witnesses we have goes back no doubt to Diponegoro[56] of whom we are told[57] that he promulgated an edict ordering the Chinese in certain districts to convert or face the death penalty. If this method appears a little strong, we have for the end of the 19th century, mentions of less harsh movements, organized by Javanese who were no less convinced. The administrators, generally very hostile to these transfers which called in question the social order they were trying to impose, signaled that they were opposed to the ventures of these visionaries. Citing only one example, they tell us of a certain Imam Doelkadir (*een Javaan*), who in 1876 converted a number of Chinese in the Semarang region, and who, in doing this, attracted the attention of the police. The sources add: "It is not without grounds that people who until now are registered as Chinese must be prevented from suddenly appearing in Javanese dress" (*zich op eenmaal in een Javaansch pakean kwamen vertoonen*).[58]

A very good example of the problems which this type of conversion could generate in the Chinese community in the process of turning back to Chinese ways is to be found in the novel published by Thio Tjien Boen in Solo in 1903 called *Tjerita Oey Se*, "The Story of Oey Se." The first part of the novel, which is of no interest here, tells of the way in which a young Chinese Totok of Pekalongan (Central Java) makes his fortune around the middle of the last century by wrongfully appropriating a box of paper money, whose value the Javanese who had found it did not realize. The second part tells us how the Totok, on becoming rich, takes to visiting the regent of the residency and how the latter falls in love with his daughter and marries her after she converts to Islam. The rich merchant who cannot bear the shame, has an empty tomb built in his garden, signifying the death of his daughter, and finishes by retiring to Batavia. The young convert, who takes the name of Fatimah, on the other hand, gets on very well with her Javanese husband and initiates a personal movement of *dakwah* in order to stimulate the conversion of the (poor) Chinese of her entourage.[59]

Toward the beginning of the 1930s there was a spate of various *dakwah* movements which at the same time took on political aspects. It must be noted that the seat of these

---

[56] Pangeran Diponegoro (1785–1855) was the eldest son of Sultan Hamengkubuwono III. He underwent a religious experience which convinced him that he was the divinely appointed future king of Java. In 1825 he initiated a rebellion which rapidly spread throughout Central and East Java. The religious community rallied to Diponegoro, among them Kyai Maja, who became the spiritual leader of the rebellion. Diponegoro was arrested by the Dutch in 1830 and exiled to Menado and then Makassar where he died. This rebellion, better known as the "Java War," was the last stand of the Javanese aristocratic elite.

[57] Cf. P.J.F. Louw, *De Java Oorlog van 1825* [The Java War of 1825], vol. 1 (Batavia: La Haye, 1894), Bijlage 58; see also The Siauw Giap, "Religion and Overseas Chinese Assimilation, p. 73 and Peter Carey, *Babad Diponegoro, An Account of the Outbreak of the Java War (1825–30)* (Kuala Lumpur, 1981), pp. 259–60, n. 106. Note that several Chinese also gathered spontaneously under Diponegoro. We may cite here Tjan Kong Sing, the great uncle of the well-known brothers Tjan Tjoe Som and Tjan Tjoe Siem; who took the name of Prawirasetja and married the sister of one of the spouses of Diponegoro (see Tjan Ing Bo, "Sedikit tentang Famili 'Tjan' dari Solo"[A note about the 'Tjan' family of Solo], *Liberal* 3, 89 (May 21, 1955): 5.

[58] Cf. the note of W. Hoezoo, in J.C. Neurdenburg, ed., "De Islam in Nederlandsch-Indië" [Islam in the Dutch Indies], *Mededeelingen van wege het Nederlandsch Zending-genootschap* 22 [Rotterdam] (1878): 387.

[59] This story is based on a news item apparently reported in the press; cf. Liem Thian Joe, *Riwajat Semarang* [History of Semarang], (Semarang: Ho Kim Joe, c. 1933), p. 129. The novel has an anonymous sequel titled *Tambahsia, soeatoe tjerita jang betoel soedah kedjadian di Betawi antara tahoen 1851–1856* [Tambahsia a true story which happened at Batavia between 1851 and 1856] (Semarang: n.p., 1906). It recounts the scandalous life of one of the brothers of Fatimah, named Tambahsia, who in the end is condemned to death by the law. To come back to the first story, it ends in the death of Fatimah, after the latter found her own tomb in the garden of the former house of her parents, and the author concludes that for months a voice was to be heard crying in the tomb. As she was neither Chinese nor Javanese, the earth would not accept her remains (*Orang bilang akan Fatimah itoe 'Tjina tanggoeng-Djawa woeroeng' maitnja tidak diterima oleh boemi*).

movements was to be found outside of Java. First, on Celebes, where a certain Ong Kie Ho, born in Toli-toli and founder of a Partai Islam, was deported to Java in 1932,[60] and in Medan (East Sumatra), where a certain Haji Yap A Siong (d. 1984), alias Haji Abdussomad, born in Canton at the end of the 19th century who arrived in Sumatra in the 1930s founded in 1936, with a few companions, the Persatuan Islam Tionghoa or the Muslim Chinese Union. In spite of the arrest of Ong Kie Ho, the movement continued in Makassar, where in 1933 or so the Partai Tionghoa Islam Indonesia (PITII or Indonesian Muslim Chinese Party) was founded, whose secretary was a certain Tjia Goan Liem. In 1934 the PITII initiated a "Malay school" which offered a religious course.[61] In September 1936 the PITII even launched an organ called *Wasilah* or "Connection" which was apparently short-lived.[62] On the eve of the second World War, the Medan group was hoping to make conversions in Java but without great success.[63]

After the war the movement continued: the Persatuan Islam Tionghoa (PIT) moved its seat from Medan to Jakarta in 1953, and took the name of Persatuan Islam Tionghoa Indonesia (PITI) whose name was changed to Pembina Imam Tauhid Islam or "Action for the faith and the unity of Islam" in 1972. One of the great figures of this new association was Haji Abdul Karim, alias Oey Tjeng Hien from Padang (1905–1988), who had become a good friend of Sukarno at the time the latter's exile in Bengkulen (South Sumatra). He became a banker after Independence.[64] As the old regime had had its converted Chinese regents, the new Republic also had a few high-ranking ministers as Peranakan Muslims, such as Lie Kiat Teng (1912–1953), born in Sukabumi and converted in 1946 under the name of Ali Mohammad, who was minister for health between 1953 and 1955; Tan Kim Liong, born in 1925 in Kalimantan, and converted under the name of Hassan Hadji Mohammad, who was minister of finance in 1964, or even Tengku Nurdin (Mao Tse Fang) who was *Bupati* in East Aceh.

In this long series, the very last movement is the BAKOM PKB or "The Communicating Body for Appreciation of National Unity," founded in December 1977 under the auspices of

---

[60] Cf. *Sin Tit Po* (Surabaya), May 20, 1932.

[61] Cf.*Berita Baroe*, June 5, 1934: "Maleische School PITII." According to the *Pembrita Makassar* of August 21, 1933, the religious course was given by Liem An Shui, alias Baba Moeh. Ma'soed (b. 1913), a third generation Peranakan from Makassar who had been trained in Arabic first at the Hadrami school in Surabaya and finally at Al Irsjad School in Jakarta.

[62] This magazine does not seem to have been kept in the public libraries.

[63] Haji Yap A Siong alias H. Abdussomad was one of the rare founder members of the Persatuan Islam Tionghoa still alive in the early 1980s. We met him in Jakarta in 1981, and he showed us several of the safe conduct letters (*surat jalan*) issued by the Dutch authorities at the time of the *dakwah* campaign that he and his companions led to Sumatra and Java. On September 24, 1938, for example, they left Sumatra after having made a tour of the large towns of this island, and arrived at Rankasbitung (West Java). They visited the main aglomerations (Cibadak, Bandung, Cimahi, Cirebon . . .) with the aim of founding branches there. In the weekly *Sin Po* of the October 13, 1938, p. 6, there is also to be found a photograph taken on the occasion of a meeting of Chinese Muslims held on the premises of the Kwong Siauw Hwe Koan. Among the representatives of the PITII were Liem Kie Chie (a Cantonese), then president, and a certain Mak Go and among the Indonesians Haji Agus Salim. *The Sin Tit Po* of February 9, 1939 equally echoes this round of propaganda in noting an incident which took place at the same time as the visit to Cirebon. It was then discovered that one of the founder members of Medan had already come the year before to collect funds in the name of Liem Kie Chie; but this unscrupulous messenger, a certain Gouw Hok Boen, alias Abdulrahman, had kept the money for himself. . . . He had been arrested but the incident could only harm the success of his companions on Java.

[64] See the very interesting account of his memories: H. Abdul Karim (Oey Tjeng Hien), *Mengabdi Agama, Nusa dan Bangsa, Sahabat Karib Bung Karno* [Devotion to the religion and to the fatherland (by) a close friend of Bung Karno] (Jakarta: Gunung Agung, 1982), 255 pp. and our review in *Archipel* 27, pp. 203–206.

the Ministry of Home Affairs, by Junus Jahja (Lauw Tjoan To).[65] This new body published a paper *Pembauran* "Uniting" (the first number dates from 1978) which misses no opportunity of pointing out that conversion facilitates integration. It must be mentioned, however, that the BAKOM not only reunites Muslims, and that several of its members are also Christians.

One may think that we have touched only lightly on the problem in indicating a few facts in passing, but we would consider ourselves satisfied if the reader agreed with us that this is a question of a long-term phenomenon to be placed in its historic context, and agreed as well to renounce the basic over-simplification which consists of dismissing all that is "Chinese" as foreign and insignificant. This dichotomy involves political developments which do not concern us here, but it has great consequences with regard to even the conception of the history of the Archipelago. It prevents the comprehension of the size of the merchant towns of the 16th and 17th centuries, which were based on cosmopolitism and on a combined and positive contribution of Islamic ideology and Chinese techniques; it also obscures the idea that in the 19th century the Europeans in ruining this "sacred union" have dealt a doubtlessly much harder blow to the local economies than by taking the *batigslot*.[66]

However one can see that this is a reversal of historical perspectives, and we are not so naïve as to believe that all historians are yet ready to accept it.

---

[65] See Drs H. Junus Jahja, penyunting, *Zaman harapan bagi keturunan Tionghoa, rekaman Dakwah Islamiyah 1979–1984* [Period of Hope for the descendants of Chinese, recording of the Muslim progaganda 1979–1984] (Jakarta: Yayasan Ukhuwah Islamiyah, 1984), 464 pp.; see also H. Junus Jahja, *Catatan Seorang WNI—Kenangan, Renungan and Harapan* [Notes of an Indonesian Citizen—reminiscences, meditations and hopes] (Jakarta: Yayasan Tunas Bangsa, 1988).

[66] *Batigslot*: balance credit, surpus of receipts emanating from the colony and taken back to Holland.

Religion, Tradition, and the Dynamics of Islamization in South Sulawesi[1]

Christian Pelras

The Bugis, Makassar, and Mandar peoples of South Sulawesi are known as having embraced Islam between 1605—when, according to local sources, the *datu'* of Luwu' La Patiware' Daéng Parabung, converted with all his family, adopting the Muslim name of Sultan Muhammad Waliu'l-Mudharuddin—and 1611, when the last pagan prince of Boné submitted to the Goanese troops.[2]

Ever since, Islam has been considered as a prime element of the cultures of these peoples, whom many in Indonesia take as being among the most "fanatik" Muslims in the Archipelago. And indeed, it cannot be by chance that South Sulawesi, together with Aceh and West Java, was during the fifteen years which followed the recognition of Indonesian independence, harried by a merciless civil war waged in the name of the Darul Islam.

However, an anthropologist staying for some time in the field cannot help being struck by the long-lived survival there of pre-Islamic elements—which would be called *tahyul* by many orthodox, especially non-Bugis, Muslims—such as: taking as truth the episodes of *La Galigo* which feature several godly couples living in heaven and in the underworld and populating the earth by sending their offspring and the latter's servants there as respective ancestors to the nobility and commoners;[3] venerating as *regalia* descended from heaven with the first rulers material objects such as spades, banners, ploughs, etc.; the existence in a few places of a class of transvestite pagan priests, called *bissu*, in charge of the cult of these *regalia* and of princely ceremonials;[4] the perpetuation of lively popular beliefs about place

---

[1] This article is based on a lecture given in October 1983 to the Indonesia Study Group, Australian National University, Canberra. I am grateful to the Department of History, Faculty of Arts, and Department of Southeast Asian Studies, Faculty of Asian Studies at the ANU for having kindly extended to me an invitation to visit there, for three months in the fall of 1983. The English text, which first appeared in *Archipel* 29 (1985): 107–35, has been revised by Josiane Massard and Stephen Headey to whom I express my best thanks.

[2] See J. Noorduyn, "De islamisering van Makassar," BKI 62 (1956): 247–66, and Mattulada, *Islam di Sulawesi Selatan* (Jakarta: LEKNAS/LIPI, 1976).

[3] For a short summary of *La Galigo*, see my article "Introduction à la littérature bugis," *Archipel* 10 (1975): 239–67.

[4] The most recent description of the *bissu* priests and their ritual is by Gilbert Hamonic, "'Les fausses femmes' du pays bugis (Célèbes-Sud)," *Objets et Mondes*, 17, 1 (1977): 39–46 and "*Mallawolo*, chants bugis pour la sacralisation des anciens princes de Célèbes-Sud," *Archipel* 19 (1980): 43–79.

spirits, guardian spirits, or evil spirits, to which offerings are brought; and a whole set of rituals including "rites de passage" (with aristocratic and popular variants) and house building, boat building, agricultural, and ancestor worship rituals.[5]

When confronting such contradictory evidence, one can raise several questions. One, of course, is to what extent do these apparently contradictory elements really coexist? And, if so, how is this possible in a society which claims to be genuinely Islamic, and what led to such a situation? Unavoidably, one will have to question the appropriateness of using here categories similar to those of *santri/abangan/priyayi* coined by Clifford Geertz for Java.[6]

But, to my eyes the main question should concern the validity for South Sulawesi of the concept of "Islamization" as it is commonly used. Indeed it seems to me that "Islamization" is too often taken as pointing to an event, or a series of events, all precisely dated, whereas one should understand it as a process, and a long one for that matter, including two important phases: first, the coming of Islam and its final official acceptance; and then, the long struggle, lasting often until now, for its complete implementation. In both phases, the same dynamics, made up of the opposition of constant contradictory forces, appear to be at work. And one has to identify these forces in order to understand better the vicissitudes of Islamization in that broader sense in South Sulawesi.

The Coming of Islam in South Sulawesi

As the quasi-official story runs, Islam was brought to South Sulawesi at the beginning of the 17th century by three *muballigh*, collectively known as Dato' Tallua in Makassarese or Dato' Tellué in Buginese (the Three Dato') and individually, after their burial places, as respectively Dato' ri Bandang (his name was Abdul Makmur, and nickname *khatib* Tunggal), Dato' ri Pattimang (Sulaiman, alias *khatib* Sulung), and Dato' ri Tiro (Abdul Jawad, alias *khatib* Bungsu). They are said to have come from Kota Tengah in the Minangkabau country of Sumatra, and the latter two must have been brothers.

According to local sources, they went first to Luwu', still the most prestigious kingdom in South Sulawesi and converted the Datu (ruler) La Patiware' Daéng Parabung, who on the 15 or 16 of Ramadhan 1013 AH (February 4 or 5, 1605) uttered the *syahadat* and took the name of Sultan Muhammad. They then proceeded to the twin state of Goa and Tallo' (known as Makassar by outsiders), which was at that time the most powerful in the peninsula. Due to their teaching, the "Old Prince" (Karaéng Matoaya) I Mallingkaang Daéng Manyonri' Karaéng Katangka, the ruler of Tallo' and prime minister of Goa, adhered to the new faith with several members of his family, and uttered the *syahadat* on Friday's eve, 9 of Jumadilawal (September 22, 1605), taking the new name of Sultan Abdullah. Then, under his influence, the young ruler of Goa, I Manga'rangi Daéng Manrabbia, who was his nephew and pupil, became a Muslim too. On Friday, 19 of Rajab 1016 (November 9, 1607), the first solemn public prayer was held at the newly built Tallo' mosque: the Makassar kingdom had officially become a Muslim state.

The next step of Sultan Abdullah was to invite the other South Sulawesi rulers to convert to Islam. On their refusal, he decided to resort to weapons and launched several successive campaigns known in Buginese as *musu' selleng* "the Islamic wars." In 1608, Sawitto, Bacukiki, Suppa', and Mandar on the west coast, Akkotengeng and Sakkoli' on the east coast submitted and were Islamized. In 1609, came the turn of Sidénréng and Soppéng; in

---

[5] See my article "Les éléments du rituel populaire bugis," *Ethnologica Helvetica*, 10 (in press).
[6] Clifford Geertz, *The Religion of Java* (Chicago-London: The University of Chicago Press, 1960).

1610, that of Wajo'; in 1611, with the final submission of Boné, all of South Sulawesi except for the Toraja mountains had accepted Islam.[7]

That story, combined with numerous local legends about the first arrival of the three Dato' and their marvellous deeds,[8] conveys the impression that the passage of the major part of South Sulawesi to Islam was very rapid indeed.

All those events are well known and the dates, about which previous authors had been disputing for a long time, have been established, in my opinion beyond any doubt, by J. Noorduyn. However, if, as he himself pointed out, one has to distinguish between conversion to Islam and the coming of Islam, it appears that that coming is not very well documented, except for a few data which one finds repeated everywhere: the bestowing, under the Goa ruler Tunipalangga (about 1546-1565) of a number of privileges to the Muslim community of Makassar, made up of traders from Champa, Patani, Pahang, Johor, and Minangkabau; the building of a mosque for that community in the Mangallékanna suburb of Makassar by his successor Tunijallo' (about 1565-1590[9]); or the visit paid to the latter around 1580 by Baabullah, Sultan of Ternate, who, according to a Moluccan tradition collected by Valentijn in his book *Oost Indië Oud en Nieuw*, was said to have brought him to Islam.[10]

It may be that the "golden legend" of the Three Dato', like that of the Nine Wali in Java, has shrouded many other events which would show that Islamization in South Sulawesi began with a long process of familiarization. However, I am convinced that a better scrutiny of written sources, including sources from other Indonesian areas, together with systematic collecting of local traditions, would lead us to a much more complicated picture than the one to be found in present textbooks, and beyond that, would help us understand which forces were at work in the Islamization of the area.

One point, already underlined by the three events reported about the reigns of Tunipalangga and Tunijallo' has to be made clear: the Makassar people, probably also the Bugis people, and their rulers, had known Islam for a long time when they decided to become Muslim themselves; when the first Portuguese known to have visited South Sulawesi arrived in 1542 in Siang (formerly a powerful state, and at that time still an important trading harbor), they were even told that the Muslim Malay traders from Patani, Pahang, and Ujung Tanah living there had been established in the country for about sixty years, i.e., since about 1480.[11] It is unlikely that Siang was the only harbor in South Sulawesi where Malay communities existed; there must have been others, which might be traced, *inter alia* through Malay sources.

For instance, one Sayyid Husein Jamadul Qubra is said in Kelantanese sources to have left Kelantan in 1448, and after a stay of four years in Java, to have gone to Wajo' where he

---

[7] Noorduyn, "De islamisering van Makassar."

[8] Mattulada, *Islam di Sulawesi Selatan,* pp. 9-11. See also in this volume the article by H. Chambert-Loir on "Dato' ri Bandang."

[9] G.J. Wolhoff and Abdurrahim, "Sedjarah Goa," *Bingkisan Sulawesi Selatan dan Tenggara,* A, 1 (Makassar, n.d. [1960?]), pp. 26-28.

[10] F. Valentijn, *Oud en Nieuw Oost-Indiën,* 8 vols. (Dordrecht, 1724-1726; new annotated edition by S. Keijzer, The Hague, 1858): 4, 140.

[11] H. Jacobs, "The First Locally Demonstrable Christianity in Celebes, 1544," *Studia* [Lisbon] 17 (1966): 295.

died in 1453.[12] The dates may be not completely reliable since at that time Wajo' was still an unimportant place, known under the name of Cinnottabi'. But at least, these are external data, which could be cross-checked with others, pointing to relations between the Muslim Malay Peninsula and South Celebes already in the middle of the 15th century. One should look for others in Malay sources in the Peninsula, Brunei, or other Bornean sultanates, and in Sumatra, as well as in Javanese and Ternatese sources; in short, in all places in the Archipelago where Islam was progressing in the second half of the 15th century.

The role of Muslim traders acting as *muballigh* is well known everywhere; we know also that Muslim traders were established at that time in South Sulawesi; no wonder if they acted in a similar way there too. The role of that region in the interinsular trade was then not yet very important, as compared to other places in the Archipelago,[13] but links existed with the most important trading centers in the area, including Ternate, north Javanese harbors, Banten, and Malaka.[14] People there, and especially the sailors or local traders in contact with foreigners from those centers, must have been well aware of the progression of Islam in those parts; whereas the rulers in the numerous South Sulawesi kingdoms then struggling among themselves in the wake of the decline of the formerly powerful Luwu', could not hear without interest the news about conversion to Islam in neighboring North and Southeast Sulawesi kingdoms such as Gorontalo (1525) and Buton (1542).[15]

By the middle of the 16th century, South Sulawesi was one of the very few important places in the interinsular trading network on which Islam had not yet taken hold. That kind of anomaly must have been keenly felt, by local Muslim settlers as well as by other Muslim communities in the Archipelago. As expected, it provoked projects or attempts, some of which can be cited here, whereas more might be found if systematic research were done on that question. For instance:

In 1548, when the Portuguese Manoel Pinto, on his way back to Malaka from South Sulawesi, called on the "main king of Java," probably the Sultan of Demak, the latter told him that he was contemplating the launching of a military expedition against that land in order to Islamize it.[16] That Sultan was killed in 1549, and this may be the reason why such an expedition never occurred.[17]

Probably around 1560, according to Acehnese sources, one Raja Abdul Jalil Putra, a son of Sultan Alauddin Riayat Syah al-Qahar of Johor (who reigned from 1537 to 1568) and a brother of Sultan Ali Riayat Syah of Aceh (who reigned from 1568 to 1575), is said to have

---

[12] Wan Muhammad Saghir, *Sejarah Ulama-ulama Islam Nusantara* (Kuala Lumpur: Kementerian Kebudayaan, Belia dan Sultan, forthcoming); cited by Abdul Rahman al-Ahmadi, "Sejarah hubungan Kelantan/Patani dengan Sulawesi Selatan." Paper for the Diplome d'Etudes Approfondies, Ecole des Hautes Etudes en Sciences Sociales (Paris, 1981), pp. 4–5.

[13] Ch. Pelras, "Célèbes-Sud avant l'islam, selon les premiers témoignages étrangers," *Archipel* 21 (1981): 163.

[14] Tomé Pires, *The "Suma Oriental" of Tomé Pires: An Account of the East, from the Red Sea to Japan, written in Malacca in 1512–1515*, translated and edited by Armando Cortesâo (London: Hakluyt Society, 1944), pp. 326–27.

[15] S. R. Nur, "Beberapa aspek hukum adat tatanegara kerajaan Gorontalo pada masa pemerintahan Eato," (Dissertation, Universiti Hasanuddin, Ujung Pandang, 1979), p. 20 and Zahari, *Sejarah dan adat Fiy Darul Butuni (Buton)*, vol. 1 (Jakarta, 1977), pp. 44 ff.

[16] Letter written by Manoel Pinto on the 7th of December 1548 to the Bishop of Goa in India, in Joseph Wicki, *Documenta Indica: Monumenta Societatis Jesu a patribus eus-dem Societatis edita*, vol. 11 (1550–1553) (Rome, 1950), pp. 422–23.

[17] Th. G. Th. Pigeaud and H. J. de Graaf, *Islamic States in Java, 1500–1700*, Verhandelingen KITLV (70), The Hague, 1976, p. 9.

traveled to South Sulawesi in company with a *muballigh* of Pidië (in the north of Sumatra). Those sources say that, due to their influence, a ruler of Boné was converted.[18]

Nothing of that kind is to be read in Bugis chronicles, but it might mean, either that the ruler was just made a sympathizer, or that the news concerned, not *the* ruler *of* Boné (the Arung Mponé), but just *a* ruler *in* Bone, i.e. the lord of a vassal lordship. Anyway, that raja Abdul Jalil married a Bugis wife, and one of their sons, Daéng Mansur, known in Aceh as Teungku di Bugéh, went back to Sumatra where he married the daughter of an ulama in Ribéë. Their daughter, Sitti Sani, was to become the wife of the great Sultan Iskandar Muda (1601–1636) and the ancestress of the so-called "Bugis dynasty" in Aceh.

In this connection, it may be interesting to note that in Bira, at the southeastern-most point of the peninsula, opposite Selayar island, people say that Islam was brought to the area by an Acehnese called Syeikh Ahmad who had come first to Sinjai, where he married the daughter of the Lord of Lamatti. From that union, two sons were born—one *went to Boné*; the other, known as Syeikh Abdul Rahman, came to Bira where he made many converts. His two sons, Abdul Jalil and Abdullah, carried his work on, but the most venerated figures there are Abdul Jalil's son, Abdul Basir Daéng Billa', and Abdullah's son, Abdul Haris *alias* Pua' Janggo'. Until now in Bira two groups claim to follow their respective teachings. The followers of Abdul Basir are said to have been more concerned with the "external" (*lahir*) aspects of religion, whereas those of Pua' Janggo' were mostly centered on "interiority" (*batin*) or mysticism. According to local tradition, the latter entered into competition with Dato' Tiro (Tiro is only a few kilometers from there), and of course Pua' Janggo' won. If the story is not anachronistic, and if the two masters were contemporaries indeed, it would mean that Pua' Janggo's great-grandfather might have come to South Sulawesi at about the middle of the 16th century.[19]

In 1564, according to Malay sources, one Syeikh Abdul Wahid bin Syarif Sulaiman al-Patani is said to have traveled from Patani to Buton, which had become Muslim not long before, to instruct poeple in the new faith.[20] He may have called at Makassar, which had had a long-standing relationship with that neighboring kingdom.

Around 1575, according to the Kutei chronicle, one of the future Dato' Tallua, Dato' ri Bandang, known there as Tuan di Bandang, had been in South Sulawesi with a companion called Tuan di Parangan, in order to propagate Islam. Their attempt having been unsuccessful, they came to Kutei, which they succeeded in bringing to their faith.[21]

In 1580, according to Valentijn, who based himself on Moluccan sources, Baabullah, Sultan of Ternate, whose influence extended as far as North, East, and Southeast Sulawesi, came to Makassar. His aim must have been to negotiate new frontiers between Goanese and Ternatese spheres of influence, but those sources say that he succeeded in converting the ruler of Goa, then I Manggorai Daéng Mamméta Karaéng Bontolangkasa', known after death as Tunijallo' (about 1565–1590).[22] No such conversion is recorded, however, in Makassar chronicles, which just say Baabullah recognized Goa influence on Selayar island.

---

[18] H.M. Zainuddin, *Tarich Atjeh*.

[19] Interview with M. Andi' Amiruddin Said Patunru', village head in 1984, and a descendant of the family of the *Karaéng* (local lords).

[20] Abdul Rahman al-Ahmadi, "Sejarah hubungan Kelantan/Patani," p. 4.

[21] C.A. Mees, *De kroniek van Koetei* (Santpoort, 1935), pp. 100 and 240. See also H. Chambert-Loir's article in this volume.

[22] F. Valentijn, *Oud en Nieuw Oost-Indiën*, vol. 4, p. 233.

Around 1591, according to the Wajo'chronicle, the "Old Prince" Karaéng Matoaya, then still young and not the ruler of Tallo' yet, but already the prime minister of Goa, visited the wise Arung Matoa La Mangkace' To Udama in order to conclude an alliance with Wajo'. And on that occasion, they had a discussion on how one should behave toward one's fellow men and toward God, which seems to reflect genuine religious preoccupations and may be a witness to the fact that both men had been influenced by foreign religious thinking and were in search of a new truth.[23]

In fact, around 1600, the Portuguese considered the Tallo' ruler as already won to Islam.[24] However, at the same time, according to the *Lontara' sukku'na Wajo'*, when the Malay community called the Three Dato' (again) to Makassar, they found it difficult to convert any of the Makassarese high nobility, upon which they chose to move to Luwu'.[25] According to oral Luwu' tradition, Islam was already known there: when Dato' Pattimang arrived in Bua (to the south of Palopo) he was welcomed by a nobleman called Tenriajéng, who was the first (local?) Muslim there, and that is why he is known also as I Assalang, from *asal*, origin. But he had kept his conversion secret, because nobody in the nobility could claim to have embraced Islam as long as the Luwu' ruler was not a Muslim himself, and that is why he was called also Tenripau, "Not-to-be-mentioned." A series of miraculous deeds convinced him that Khatib Sulaiman was really God's envoy, and he led him to the Datu in Pattimang (Malangkaé). After the latter's conversion, he became the Luwu' *kadhi* and that office remained in his family up to this century.

It may be in those first years of the 17th century that one Sayyid Jalaluddin al-'Aidid brought Islam to Cikoang, Laikang, and the Turatea area, south of Makassar. According to Cikoang sources, he was a son of Sayyid Muhammad Wahid, of Aceh, and Syarifah Halisyah. The latter's father, Sayyid 'Alawiyah Jalal ul-Alam was himself a son of one Sayyid Muhajirun al-Basrah. That "exile from Basrah" had fled Iraq at the beginning of the 16th century because of political troubles (maybe the wars between the Ottoman empire and the Persian kingdom which erupted in 1514). From Aceh, Sayyid Jalaluddin went to Banjarmasin, where by the end of the 16th century he was delivering a teaching heavily tinged with Shi'ite influence. There, he converted a Makassar nobleman from Binamu, exiled in Banjarmasin for murder, and married his daughter. He then went to Goa, where he met some sort of opposition from the ruler, so that he moved to Cikoang, where he converted the still pagan nobility and population.[26] His arrival there is still commemorated every year at the occasion of the Maulid festival.[27]

From all this scattered information, one can reach two kinds of conclusions. First, it seems that the propagators of Islam in South Sulawesi were linked to a Champa-Patani-Aceh-Minangkabau-Banjarmasin-Demak-Giri-Ternate network. We have seen that in 1548, Demak was willing to Islamize Makassar. Well, it may not be by chance that about the same

---

[23] J. Noorduyn, *Een achttiende-eeuwse kroniek van Wadjo': Buginese Historiography* (The Hague, 1955), pp. 259–61.

[24] M. Godinho de Eredia, "Report on the Golden Khersonese," trans. J.V. Mills, *JMBRAS* 7, 1 (1930): 245.

[25] The *Lontara' Sukku'na Wajo'* is a compilation made in Wajo' in the 18th century after the chronicles of the main South Sulawesi states. It was ordered from the *Ranreng Bettempola* (one of the three highest Wajo' officials), La Sangaji, by the Wajo' ruler (Arung Matoa), La Mappajung (± 1764–1767). The copy I have used was handwritten by the last Ranreng Bettempola (d. 1970) Andi' Makkaraka. I am very grateful to the owner of the copy, Prof. Andi' Zainal Abidin Farid, for procuring me photocopies of the relevant pages.

[26] A. Makarausu Amansjah, "Mazhab Sji'ah di Tjikoang," *Bingkisan Jajasan Sulawesi Selatan dan Tenggara* 3, 1–2 (1969): 28–30.

[27] See Gilbert Hamonic's article on the Cikoang Maulid in *Archipel* 29 (1985): 175–89.

time the head of the Muslim community there was called *nakhoda* Bonang, when one remembers that the first *imam* of Demak was Sunan Bonang, one of the Nine Wali of Java. He was a son of Sunan Ngampel, another Wali, whose disciple and adoptive son was Sunan Giri, a third Wali.[28] Now, in Giri, were trained Sultan Zainal Abidin, the first Muslim ruler of Ternate,[29] and much later, if one is to believe local tradition, Dato' ri Bandang.[30]

Makassar sources say that among the Muslim community were not only people from Patani, Trengganu, Pahang, and Johor, but also from Champa. Now, some traditions say that Raden Rahmat (Sunan Ngampel) was a nephew of the Cham princess[31] married to one of the last kings of Majapahit, whereas another one speaks of a daughter of the *putri Campa* called Raden Joko Krètèk, also styled Hadipati Makasar due to her marriage there.[32]

Banjarmasin also had links with Demak, which helped the kingdom of Nagara Daha, and introduced Islam there.[33] We have seen that it was also a kind of relay between Makassar and Aceh. And Aceh itself, which is mentioned several times as the starting point of *muballigh* who came to South Sulawesi,[34] exerted its influence on Minangkabau, where the three Dato' were to come from.

More research might help to enlighten links which, at the moment, are just conjectural, by looking for more evidence. The propagation of Islam in South Sulawesi would not appear to be a succession of isolated events any more, but can be seen as a part of an overall process.

But another remark seems to me more important: we have just seen that, prior to their official acceptance of Islam, the South Sulawesi people had been for more than 125 years exposed to regular contacts with Muslim traders and *muballigh*, familiarized with Islamic teachings, and had submitted to external pressures in favor of conversion, while managing to remain relatively unaffected by the new faith—although at some places there had been a number of Makassar and Bugis Muslims long before the official acceptance by the rulers. And then, within only seven years, everything changed. That fact has to be explained.

It is not enough to say, as did Noorduyn, that "conversion to Islam took so long because the deep changes it implied provoked strong resistance among a people keenly attached to its custom and proud of its own culture."[35] One has to understand how and why that resistance subsided. Did the people's attitude change, and how was that possible? Was Islam not seen as in conflict to their customs and culture any more? In brief, what happened which made those deep changes possible?

---

[28] H.J. de Graaf, *Geschiedenis van Indonesië* (The Hague, 1949), pp. 87–90; Pigeaud and de Graaf, *Islamic States in Java*, p. 7.

[29] Sartono Kartodirdjo, Marwati Djooned Poesponegoro, and Nugroho Notosusanto, *Sejarah Nasional Indonesia*, vol. 3 (Jakarta: Departemen Pendidikan dan Kebudayaan, 1975), p. 94.

[30] J. Noorduyn, *Een achttiende-eeuwse kroniek*.

[31] Pigeaud and de Graaf, *Islamic States in Java*, p. 5.

[32] A. Zainal Abidin, "Siapakah Radèn Djoko Krètèk?" *Bingkisan Jajasan Sulawesi Selatan dan Tenggara* 1, 21 (1968): 7–20.

[33] Sartono Kartodirdjo et al., *Sejarah Nasional Indonesia*, vol 3, p. 97.

[34] Ibid., p. 34. According to Drs. Abu Hamid, the Three Dato' themselves, although they were born in Minangkabau, had acquired their religious knowledge in an Acehnese *zawiyah*. And indeed, at that time, Aceh was an important center of religious studies, which was not the case for Minangkabau.

[35] Noorduyn, *Een achttiende-eeuwse kroniek*.

In order to answer, one has to try and discover more about the exact motives of that early resistance to Islam—the more so as we know that at the same time as South Sulawesi rulers resisted Islamization, some of them were showing signs of deep interest in Christianity.

There is a very well-known story, told by such people as Tavernier[36] and Gervaise,[37] about how, in his hesitation between both religions, "the king of Makassar" resorted to chance. At the same time, he asked for priests from Portuguese Malaka and for *ulama* from Aceh (Gervaise) or Mekkah (Tavernier), taking an oath that he would embrace the religion of the first who arrived. As the governor in Malaka neglected his duties as a Christian, the Muslims arrived first, and won. That story could well have developed from information given around 1630 by Barreto de Resende,[38] saying that the king had asked for a priest from Malaka to teach him the Christian faith, but that there was much delay, so that a "Moor" called "Lucar," having come first, succeeded in winning him to Islam. And indeed, around 1620, Karaéng Matoaya told Father Luis de Andrade that he had repeatedly asked for Catholic missionaries without any results, and that he had eventually become a Muslim at the instigation of the Sultan of Johor.[39]

Between Christianity and Islam

It is now a well-established fact that in 1544, two South Sulawesi rulers, those of Suppa' and Siang respectively, took the opportunity of the visit of a Portuguese trading ship to ask baptism from its captain, Antonio de Paiva, for them and a number of their followers. The following year, another expedition was sent to South Sulawesi, with a priest, Father Vicente Viegas, on board. The new rulers of Bacukiki' and Alitta and their retainers were baptized too. That same year, 1545, Father Viegas went to Tallo', where, according to a Portuguese source, he baptized the ruler. It must have been I Mappatangkangtana Daéng Padulung, known after his death as Tuménanga ri Makkoayang (about 1545–1577), a man who was to play an important role in Makassar history.[40]

After these auspicious beginnings, the relationship between Portuguese Malaka and South Sulawesi was, however, interrupted for fourteen years because of an unfortunate incident (a Portuguese officer had abducted a Suppa' princess). When regular relations were resumed, the baptized rulers of Suppa', Bacukiki, and Alitta were dead and their lands had lost their independance to the increasingly powerful Goa. What the attitude of Tuménanga ri Makkoayang—then the Makassar strongman—at the same time ruler of Tallo' and prime minister of Goa—was toward Christianity is not precisely known, but in several letters written by Portuguese he is still referred to as a Christian—although probably a nominal one. However, one repeatedly reads of local Christians asking in vain for priests to be sent to instruct them.[41] Strangely enough. for many years, no one volunteered for that mission.

---

[36] J.B. Tavernier, *Les six voyages de . . . en Turquie, en Perse et aux Indes . . .*, vol. 3 (Paris, 1679), pp. 443–44.

[37] N. Gervaise, *Description historique du royaume de Macaçar* (Paris, 1688), pp. 161–64.

[38] Barreto de Resende, "Account of Malacca," trans. G. Maxwell, *JSBRAS* 60 (1911): 4.

[39] C. Wessels, "De katholieke missie in Zuid-Celebes, 1525–1668," *Het Missiewerk*, 28, 1 (1949): 130.

[40] See my article "Les premières données occidentales concernant Cèlèbes-Sud," *BKI* 133, 2–3 (1977): 255. The *Lontara' Sukku'na Wajo'* acknowledges the conversion to the Christian religion (*agama keriseténg sarani* or *agama Yésuite*) of the rulers in Suppa', Bacukiki', and Siang, and the inclination of the Makassar people in Goa for that religion (p. 230).

[41] A. Basilio de Sá, *Documentação para a história das Missões do Padroada Português do Oriente; Insulindia* (Lisbon), vol. 2 (1550–1562), 1955, p. 348; vol. 3 (1563–1567), 1956, p. 103.

Even more strange, not much is known either from Portuguese or local sources about the four young princes sent in 1545, to the Jesuit college in Indian Goa. According to the *Lontara' sukku'na Wajo'*, two of them were of the Goa (Makassar) nobility, and Professor Andi Zainal Abidin Farid thinks that they were Tumapa'risi' kallonna's (dead about 1547) sons. We know also through Portuguese sources that in 1560 only one of them was still at the college.[42]

At least, at some time between 1580 and 1590, four Franciscans were sent to South Sulawesi.[43] It could have been the beginning of a prosperous mission, but their stay was short lived, for reasons which will be discussed later. No further attempt was made to Christianize those people although, from that time on, many Portuguese settled in Makassar, where they constituted an important community, which at times numbered about 500 residents.[44] Eventually, two other Franciscans did come, but this was in 1610, when the "Islamic wars" were nearly over, and they could just take care of the Portuguese and mestizo Christians.

Still, strangely again, although they had become devout Muslims, the Makassar rulers continued to show more than benevolence toward Christians and, especially, the Catholic faith.

For instance, in 1614, Sultan Ala'uddin wrote to Manila to invite the Franciscans there to establish a house in Makassar.[45] Again, in 1621, a Spanish report tells us that "the king has sent to the Governor of Ternate to seek clerica," and that two Jesuits and two Dominicans had been there recently from the Philippines.[46] At one time, there were in Makassar three churches and 3,000 Christians, including local ones, some of them even related to Makassar princely families: Francisco Mendes, the secretary of Sultan Hasanuddin for Portuguese affairs, was probably a son of Sultan Malikussaid by a Portuguese wife.[47]

Moreover, reports written by successive clerical visitors to Makassar, such as Father Luis de Andrade in 1625,[48] Sebastian Manrique in 1643,[49] Jacques Maracci in 1651,[50] Alexandre de Rhodes in 1653,[51] Domingo de Navarrete in 1657,[52] Joseph Tissanier in 1663,[53] all show that Karaéng Matoaya, his son Karaéng Pattingalloang, and his grandson Karaéng Karunrung always manifested an outward sympathy to Catholicism. Karaéng Pattingalloang had

---

[42] J. Wicki, *Documenta Indica*, vol. 4, (1557–1561), 1956, p. 838. The *Lontara' Sukku'na Wajo'* just says that these two Christian princes came back to Goa, and that they were responsible for the calling of Portuguese priests.

[43] P. de Trindade, *Conquista espiritual do Oriente* (Lisbon, 1967), vol. 3, p. 492–93.

[44] B. Schrieke, *Indonesian Sociological Studies*, 2 vols. (The Hague and Bandung, 1955): 1, 69.

[45] A. Reid, "A Great Seventeenth Century Indonesian Family: Matoaya and Pattingalloang of Makasar," *Masyarakat Indonesia* 3,1(1981).

[46] H. de los Rios Coronel, *Memorial y relacion parc Su Magestad del procurador General de las Filipinas*, (Madrid, 1621), in Blair and Robertson, *The Philippine Islands (1493–1898)* (Cleveland [Ohio], 1903), vol. 19, pp. 262–89.

[47] C.R. Boxer, *Francisco Vieira de Figueiredo: A Portuguese Merchant-Adventurer in Southeast Asia, 1624–1667*, Verhandelingen KITLV (52) (The Hague, 1967), p. 17.

[48] Wessels, "De katholieke missie."

[49] S. Manrique, *Travels of Fray Sebastiën Manrique, 1629–1643*, trans. C. Eckford Luard (Oxford, 1927), vol. 2, pp. 79–81.

[50] J. Maracci, *Relation de ce qui s'est passé dans les Indes orientales . . .* (Paris, 1651), pp. 75–77.

[51] A. de Rhodes, *Divers voyages du Père Alexandre de Rhodes en la Chine et d'autres royaumes de l'Orient* (Paris, 1653), p. 279.

[52] D. Navarrete, *The Travels and Controversies of Friar Domingo Navarrete, 1618–1686* ed. J.S. Cummins (Cambridge, 1962), pp. 114–16.

[53] J. Tissanier, *Relation du voyage depuis la France jusqu'au royaume de Tunquin* (Paris, 1663).

a deep knowledge of the works of contemporary Catholic theologians and even used to participate in church services or processions.

Thus one is left with more questions: if the South Sulawesi people had resisted so long before accepting Islam because it implied "deep cultural changes," why is it that they were so much attracted by Christianity, conversion to which implied no less deep cultural changes? But also, why were their reiterated demands for priests so inadequately answered by the Portuguese? Why was the Franciscan mission so short lived? And what happened, finally, which changed everything almost instantly, in such a way that South Sulawesi, still almost completely pagan in 1605 and sympathetic towards Catholicism, had turned completely Muslim in 1611?

My working hypothesis is that, when first acquainted with Islam, South Sulawesi rulers found in its teachings certain aspects which they feared would jeopardize social order and threaten their power; so that, although it was clearly in their interest in terms of both foreign policy and trade to adhere to the same religion as their main partners in the Archipelago, they delayed their conversion for more than a century. Now, in their eyes, Christianity, and especially Catholicism, was different in that respect, and would have made a very convenient state religion. Their religious sympathy was on a par with their sympathy for the Portuguese as their favorite Western trading partners, and later as their best allies against Dutch enterprises.

In fact, their sympathy for Catholicism may have rested on some misunderstandings, and this is probably what caused the Franciscans to interrupt their mission. Not hindered by Christian competition any more, Islam now had full scope for winning the contest. The main role of the Three Dato' must have been to contrive a way of solving the apparent incompatibility between Islam and traditional order. That obstacle put aside, conversion could take place in a very short time.

According to that working hypothesis, the main point of incompatibility was the myth of the divine descent of the nobility through the *manurung*, white blooded people descended from heaven, which all local dynasties (be they Makassar, Bugis. Mandar, or Toraja) claim as their founders. That myth was narrowly linked to theological views in which a unique *Deus otiosus* (in Bugis: Déwata Séuwaé) had generated a primordial, divine couple, who in turn, had begotten a number of gods—*dewata*— from whom the *manurung* originated. Ordinary mankind descended only from the latters' servants and slaves. From the beginning, political roles were thus distributed. Clearly, such a myth could not be shaken without putting traditional social order in danger. If the first, mostly Malay, Muslim settlers, when preaching their faith, insisted on *tauhid,* stressing the uniqueness of God and the fact that He was not begotten and does not beget;[54] and if, being traders, not noblemen, they claimed, as Islam teaches, that all men, being all Adam's offspring, are equal—then one can understand the reluctance shown by local rulers toward that religion. It is enough to know how strong the belief in *manurung* and in the heavenly origin of the nobility still is in present day South Sulawesi, after nearly four centuries of acceptance of Islam, and how much traditional social and political structures depended on it, to guess what opposition Muslim propaganda may have met at first.

Conversely, after the establishment of the Portuguese in Malaka, people could have gathered information about Catholic teachings, perhaps through polemic arguments forwarded by the Muslims themselves, which may have appeared as contrasting strongly with

---

[54] See *Surat al-tawhid* of the Qur'an, and particularly CXII, 3.

Islamic *tauhid*, such as, for instance, the dogma of the Trinity, calling Christ the "son of God," and the Virgin Mary the "Mother of God," the worship of saints, etc. This could have given the South Sulawesi rulers the impression that, by adhering to such a religion, they would be able to maintain their political myths and keep at least part of their original creeds. Moreover, the Portuguese would become their allies.

In that respect, it is significant that, during the visit that Karaéng Matoaya paid again to the old Arung Matoa Wajo' ToUdama in 1607, shortly before the latter's death, and although the Karaéng was already converted to Islam, the questions he asked of him were "Is God one or many? Can God have a father and a mother? Can He beget children?"[55]

In 1544 the questions the rulers of Suppa' and Siang asked Antonio de Paiva before accepting baptism, concerned *inter alia* the worshipping of saints, and especially of St. James, the patron saint of Iberian countries, whom South Sulawesi peoples may have compared with the semi-divine founders and protectors of their local kingdoms. Other questions then debated were about the reasons for hostility between Portuguese and Muslims, and of course about God, creator of everything; about Christ, the Son of God, and how after His ascension to Heaven, He had sent His Apostles to bring forth His word to all men; and about God's commandments. All these points must have been raised in answer to precise preoccupations of the two rulers, who then debated them again with their families and retainers.[56] What is clear is that, despite fierce opposition from Muslim settlers, and strong objections from the *bissu* clergy, they decided to become Christian.

However, the *bissu* were to remain a ticklish point in case of change to any religion, be it Christianity or Islam. Their incompatibility with the latter was evident for a number of reasons, and not only because of their transvestism. The main reason was rather that they were priests and that they specialized in elaborate rites, centered on offerings to spiritual beings, whereas Islam knows no clergy, and has simple rites, centered on prayer, which is directed toward the Only God.

With Christianity, differences were less conspicuous. The Portuguese had correctly identified them as the rulers' priests (os *podres destes reis*);[57] conversely, South Sulawesi people may have identified Catholic priests with a kind of *bissu*, since they too conducted intricate ceremonies with offerings (at Mass) and processions, where, as the *bissu*, they acted as intermediaries between heaven and Man; and as the *bissu*, they wore different garments from other men's and had no commerce with women.

Particularly interesting in that respect is that the reason given by the four Franciscans for not having carried on their mission in Makassar in the 1580s is that "they were assumed to be homosexuals and thus became the object of unwelcome attention."[58] That confusion cannot have been produced just by the fact that "they were clean-shaven and did not carry krisses," since most Makassar men depilated their (scarce) beards and not all of them wore krisses. In any case, it was easy for the Franciscans to grow beards and have a weapon on them. My impression is that they soon discovered that those measures were not enough, and that, considered as Portuguese *bissu*, they were assumed, not only to indulge in the "hateful sin," but also to play the same role as they did as the specialists in princely rituals and as guaranteeing the semi-divine status of the nobility. It must have very soon been

---

[55] Noorduyn, *Een achttiende eeuwse kroniek*, p. 263.

[56] Jacobs, "The First Locally Demonstrable Christianity in Celebes," p. 295.

[57] Ibid., p. 301.

[58] de Trindade, *Conquista espiritual do Oriente*.

obvious to them that much of the sympathy professed by South Sulawesi rulers toward Christianity had rested on deep misunderstandings of the Catholic faith, and equally obvious to the rulers that no compromise could permit them to maintain their *bissu* along with the Catholic clergy, and that Catholic dogma was no more reconcilable with the *manurung* myth than Islam.

Acceptance of Islam

At that point, Christianity and Islam could be considered, from a religious point of view, in a similar situation. But from an economic and strategic point of view, Islam was in a better posture, since most of the trading partners of the South Sulawesi people were Muslims, and already a number of Muslim communities, including foreign traders and probably also local converts, were established in several parts of the land. Moreover there were Muslim pressures in favor of conversion, whereas the Catholics, on the contrary, did not seem to be willing to respond to overtures. So, already around 1600, the Portuguese believed that Christianity had lost the religious competition, and considered Karaéng Matoaya already a Muslim, although he had not yet taken any decisive step.

The importance given by local tradition to the Three Dato' leads me to think that *they* were the ones who found out how to overcome the hesitations of Karaéng Matoaya and his fellow rulers—probably at the initiative of one of them, namely Dato' ri Pattimang.

We have seen already that, probably around 1576, Dato' ri Bandang had tried to propagate Islam in Makassar, to no avail. At the beginning of the 16th century, he came back with two more companions, known later as Dato' ri Pattimang and Dato' ri Tiro. There, they again met (the probably usual) difficulties. At that point, they decided to go to Luwu', for, "if power was in Goa, excellence was in Luwii'" (*ri Luwu'alebbirenna, ri Goa awatanna*).[59]

If my hypothesis is correct, that move was not intended only to convert the Luwu' ruler because of his remaining prestige but, more essentially, because Luwu, as the cradle of South Sulawesi nobility, and the central place in the myth of origin, was felt as the key strategic point, the conquest of which would open the whole of South Sulawesi to Islam.[60] For there, according to *La Galigo*, Batara Guru, the eldest son of the main god of Heaven, was believed to have set foot on earth, until then still unpopulated, to create the first human kingdom; there his first born infant had died and changed itself into rice; there, his grandson Sawérigading, the cultural hero of the Bugis, considered by some as the ancestor of all *manurung* in South Sulawesi, had lived his childlhood, and there he had come back at the end of his earthly life before being swallowed up by the waters of the gulf and becoming the new ruler in the Underworld; there, also had the *bisu* rites been celebrated for the first time on earth.

According to local traditions, Dato' Pattimang, who was to spend, from then on, most of his life in Luwu', centered his teaching on *tauhid*, not in the usual Muslim way but by using Bugis beliefs about the One God (Dewata Séuwaé) and about Sawérigading. No text, to my knowledge, permits us to know what his teachings were exactly, but I suspect that many stories found in *lontora'* (manuscripts) concerning the Creation, giving Adam and Eve as the parents of the former Bugis gods, or showing Sawérigading as a kind of prophet *avant la*

---

[59] Mattulada, *Islam di Sulawesi Selatan*, p. 20. According to the Lontara' *Sukku'na Wajo'* (p. 240) they took that decision after consultation with the local Malay community.

[60] The answer of the Malays had been "*Malebbi'-é Datu-é ri Luwu', nasaba' ku maneng-i poléang-poléangenna arung-é*" = "the most exalted is the king of Luwu', because it is from there that all the (local) lords have their origin."

lettre who, before his descent to the Underworld, announced the coming of Islam, etc., may at least represent some of their off-shoots.[61] The only place where Dato' ri Pattimang traveled once in Luwu' was Wajo';[62] this is probably not by chance, since after Luwu', most of the *La Galigo* episodes are located there. Until now, it has remained the place where the hierarchical system is the strongest and where the *La Galigo* is most widely known.

From Luwu', Dato' ri Pattimang's younger brother, known as Dato' ri Tiro, went to the *konjo*-speaking area near Bira, which was, in some respects, for the Makassar people much the same as Luwu' was to the Bugis people. There, until now, the *patuntung* community, and especially the Amma Toa ("Old Father"), the spiritual leader in Kajang, bear witness of an ancient system of beliefs strongly marked by mysticism.[63] No wonder that Dato' ri Tiro chose to center his teachings on *tasawuf*. According to Mattulada, he might have been influenced by the (somewhat heretical) thought of Hamzah Fansuri. Research on the spot might provide more insights on his doctrine.[64]

As for the third Dato', Dato' ri Bandang, he left Luwu' for Goa/Tallo' and he was the one who succeeded in converting Karaéng Matoaya. One cannot help being struck by the rapidity of his conversion, since he uttered the *syahadat* only eight months after the Datu of Luwu'. One legendary story relates that when Dato' ri Bandang landed, Karaéng Matoaya went to meet him and greeted him with the Muslim salutation *Assalamu alaikum warrahmatullahi wabarakatu*, and that he pronounced the *syahadat* on that same day.[65] It is generally understood by the people as a miraculous event, since they assume that Karaéng Matoaya knew nothing of Islam before. Of course, he was probably well instructed in that religion, and one can interpret the story as showing that he was awaiting the Dato', ready for conversion insofar as prior obstacles would have been removed. And that was what the three Dato' had just done in Luwu'.[66]

---

[61] Such texts are exemplified in G. Hamonic, "Pour une é'tude comparée des cosmogonies de Célèbes-Sud. A propos d'un manuscrit inédit sur l'origine des dieux bugis," *Archipel* 25 (1983): 35–62, and Ch. Pelras, "Le panthéon des anciens bugis vu à travers les textes de La Galigo," ibid., pp. 63–96.

[62] Mattulada, *Islam di Sulawesi Selatan*, p. 42. On hierarchy in Wajo', see my article "Hiérarchie et pouvoir traditionnels en pays Wadjo'," *Archipel* 1 (1971): 161–91 and *Archipel* 2 (1971): 197–223.

[63] Mattulada, *Islam di Sulawesi Selatan*, p. 30; on Kajang and the Amma Toa, see K.M.A. Usop, *Pasang ri Kajang : kajian sistim nilai di "Benteng Hitam" Amma Toa"* (Ujung Pandang: PLPIIS, 1978). According to the Lontara' *Sukku'na Wajo'*, "Katté' Bungsu maélo' palebbang-i mappaguruang-i paddisseng ngeng tasaupu' (hakiki), nasaba' naseng-i magampang ttama ri akkalenna tau-é nalolongeng ana'guru.... Na péné maraja-na assisalanna, naléppangna Katté' Bungsu ri Kajang ri wanua ri Tiro, na ku-na nappaguru, mébbu' to-ni masigi' ri wiring salo '-é, na-ko to-na maté nariaseng-na Dato' ri Tiro" "Khatib Bungsu wanted to preach Islam through the teaching of mystical knowledge, which he thought easier to accept to those who had become his disciples.... And as their disagreement was increasing more and more, he stopped in Kajang, in the village of Tiro, and there he delivered his teaching, and he built also a mosque near the river. And there also he died, so that he was called the Dato' from Tiro" (p. 241).

[64] According to Drs. Abu Hamid, Dato' Tiro's teachings can be found in a manuscript which is still kept in Bira.

[65] Mattulada, *Islam di Sulawesi Selatan*, p. 11. Other versions are that summarized by Henry Chambert-Loir in this same issue and that of the *Lontara' Sukku 'na Wajo'* which runs as follows: after having established himself in Kaluku Bodoa, Abdul Makmur had the habit of visiting regularly Karaéng Matoaya in Tallo's fort (*bénténg*), looking for a way to win him to Islam. One night, Karaéng Matoaya dreamt that he met the Prophet at the gate of the fort, and that the latter spat in his mouth, thus giving him religious knowledge; whatever question would be asked him by Dato' Bandang, he would know the answer. In the morning, Karaéng Matoaya went to the place he had seen in his sleep, and there he discovered the Prophet's footprint printed in a stone. Convinced of the truth of his dream, he went to Dato' Bandang's palace, and expressed to him his will to become a Muslim (p. 241).

[66] Noorduyn, "De islamisering van Makassar." The story is also told in the *Lontara' Sukku'na Wajo'*.

However, not everybody was ready for conversion. Enough has survived in local traditions to assume that there was some fierce opposition from two categories of persons. Among them must have been a number of *bissu*, since some of them were forced into exile in Kaili. The others were part of the nobility, among whom one of Karaéng Matoaya's sons, who tried to take up arms against his father, whereas a brother of the ruler of Goa, by name I Mangnginyarrang Daéng Makkiyo Karaéng Kanjilo Tumamaliang ri Timoro', resorted to "humiliation."[67] We learn the nature of the humiliation from Tavernier's and Gervaise's accounts: when the first royal mosque was built (probably that in Kaluku Bodoa) and on the eve of the first Friday public prayer, that prince introduced pigs into the building, slaughtered them, and smeared the walls and the pulpit with their blood,[68] thus derisively desacralizing it, probably by the very rites used in pagan South Sulawesi to consecrate a newly built house!

That incident (if it is true) and other acts of opposition may have been the cause of the twenty-six months' delay between the date of the official conversion of the Tallo' ruler and the first public prayer of the people of Tallo' and Goa in the rebuilt royal mosque. It was during that time, not long before that momentous event, that Karaéng Matoaya paid his last visit to ToUdama in Wajo', to ask him questions about God, an indication that, even then, there must still have been much debate in Makassar. But after November 9, 1678 the page was definitively turned.

The Long Struggle for Islamization

Local traditions say that Dato' ri Bandang had first concentrated his efforts on building the *sara'* (*sy'ariat*) putting the main stress on the religious obligation of the "five pillars," on the correct celebration of rites such as circumcisions, marriages, and funerals according to Islamic rules, and the development of religious teaching. As for prohibitions, those concerning the consuming of pork and adultery were among the most strongly enforced. Other forbidden actions, such as consuming alchohol and opium, lending money with interest, gambling, and even bringing offerings to sacred places or worshipping the regalia, although getting lip-condemnation, do not seem to have been very energetically fought at the beginning.

Around 1630, the organizational aspects of the *syariat* began to be implemented in all of the South Sulawesi kingdoms, and it appears that the nobility, now that it had chosen to side with Islam, endeavored to monopolize all the important positions.

At the beginning, there was only one mosque in each kngdom or petty kingdom. All offices, such as *imam, khatib, bilal, kadhi*, were handed over to people of high nobility. Those people, called *paréwa sara'* (the instruments of the *syariat*) in Bugis and in Makassar as well, were put on an equal footing with the former customary officials (*paréwa ade'*), and were equally members of the ruler's council. The *syariat* itself became incorporated in the body oi customs called *pangaderreng* in Bugis and *pangadakkang* in Makassar.[69] For instance, Islamic funerals completely replaced traditional funerals, although some elements of the former rituals were maintained in the funerals of the highest nobility; the reading of the Qur'an and of the *kitab Barazanji* on Friday's eve or on the occasion of domestic rites tended to replace, but never to put completely aside, the reading of the *La Galigo* epic. In other cases, Islamic

---

[67] Information received from Prof. Andi' Zainal Abidin.

[68] Tavernier, *Les six voyages*, p. 444, and Gervaise, *Description historique*, pp. 164–66.

[69] About all that process, see Mattulada, *Islam di Sulawesi Selatan*.

practices were combined with traditional ones; for instance, the Islamic ceremony of *hakikah* performed for newly born children was combined with the traditional ceremonies of putting the child in his cradle for the first time (*mappénré' ri tojang*) and of the purification of the young mother (*makkuwaé lawi'*); and the traditional tooth-filing ceremony was often combined with Islamic circumcision, which, besides, replaced traditional subincision but preserved elements of the former ceremony. Sometimes, again, an Islamic part was just added to an otherwise almost completely traditional ceremony, as for instance in weddings, where the Islamic *akad nikah* was just introduced in the sequence of rites without much modification of the rest.

Such a mixture of heteregoneous elements may not be just a mark of the propensity of South Sulawesi people, like other Indonesian people, toward spontaneous syncretism. It may be, on the contrary, the result of a conscious policy of the first propagators of Islam, not much different from that adopted in pagan Europe by the first Christian missionaries: given the impossibility that the people, and especially the nobility, would abandon immediately those elements of the former tradition which they considered essential to their culture, and maybe for fear of losing the contest to the Portuguese Christians, the Dato' may have chosen to come to terms with those elements, probably hoping that religious teaching and *daqwah* would in the long run bring them into disuse. To them, conversion must have been the main goal to achieve first; then real Islamization would be able to begin.

Conversely, the nobility, conscious of their inability to oppose any longer the rise of Islam in South Sulawesi, at least among the most progressive and economically well-to-do people, and anxious to maintain and even improve their position in society, had tried to combine the advantages of both systems, by monopolizing Islamic offices on the one hand, and on the other hand by maintaining those elements of the former system on which their political power had rested. Most of them must have seen that equilibrium as ideal, and have been hoping to carry on the *status quo* for ever. But, with such a contentious situation at the start, the equilibrium could not be maintalned for long, and sooner or later the opposing forces were to bring forth the dynamics of evolution.

Through Tensions Toward Evolution

The description given in 1688 by Nicolas Gervaise of Makassar of religious life shows that in less than three generations after official conversion, Islam had already become an essential part of South Sulawesi culture.

Particularly noteworthy in his description is the important role played by religious masters called by him *aguy*, i.e. *haji*, who seem to have been hierarchically dependent on higher masters called by him *Touan* (*Tuanta* is actually a term used by the Makassarese toward renowned *ulama*). His mention that that title was awarded in Mekkah by high authorities seems to indicate some acknowledgement of the teaching role performed by the *syaikh* of some mystic order, the more so as the places where those *Touan* were teaching their (male and female) *santari* (students) look in Gervaise's description, not just like present-day *pesantren*, but much more like some kind oI *zawiya* (monastery).[70]

As a matter of fact, it is well known that, already in the second half of the 17th century, mystic orders had made their way into South Sulawesi. One of the key actors in that penetration was the celebrated Syeikh Yusuf, known by the Makassarese as *Tuanta Salamaka* (Our

---

[70] Gervaise, *Description historique*, pp. 82 and 194–201.

Gracious Master). Probably a (lower?) relative of the princely Goa family,[71] he had left Makassar for Mekkah in 1645, at the age of 19. He is said to have stopped on his way in Aceh to follow the teaching of Nuruddin ar-Raniri, and then in Yemen, where he studied with two other mystic masters. After some time spent in Mekkah with another two other Sufi masters, he went to Damascus where he became initiated in the Khalwatiyah order and therefore received his title of Taju'l-Khalwati.[72] Makassar tradition says that on his return from the Holy Land, around 1678, Syeikh Yusuf was much shocked by the state of *syariat* in South Sulawesi, and tried to purify religion there from pagan remnants and improper behavior. Those attempts, so the story runs, were strongly opposed by the nobility who were not prepared to have an end put to gambling, palm-wine drinking, opium smoking or bringing offerings to sacred places or objects. One must be careful to recognize that those are not just examples of un-Islamic behavior, but that through them more was at stake. Gambling had not only been a favorite pastime of the nobility since time immemorial (cockfights are a prominent feature in the *La Galigo* epos); it had, and still has among the Toraja, a ritual significance, being usually held on the occasion of communal festivals, such as harvest festivals, and at princely weddings; it was also a source of income for the rulers, as was the opium trade. Opium smoking and palm-wine drinking were not just addictions, but were indulged in by warriors before going to fight. Bringing offerings was not only a superstitious habit, but was thought of as the means to insure prosperity for the community, and in the case of *arajang*, or sacred places commemorating the ancestors of local dynasties, established the link between present-day rulers and their semi-divine forebears. In short, the nobility, by refusing changes on those particular points, showed that they were still holding tightly to the compromise put into being when Islam had become the state religion. Clearly, they were not prepared yet to accept an evolution which would endanger social order as they understood it. As a consequence, Syeikh Yusuf, who could not accept that compromise, left Makassar and settled in Banten where, as is well known, he married one of the Sultan's daughters. Later, he took an active part in the resistance to the Dutch, was caught by them, and was exiled, first to Ceylon and then to South Africa where he died in 1699.

All South Sulawesi nobility was not unanimous in supporting the above compromise; a few were in favor of a more Islamic way of life. That is well exemplified by the case of La Maddaremmeng, Sultan of Boné from 1631 to 1644, who had decided to apply the *syariat* literally, forbidding all superstitious practices, discarding the *bissu*, and liberating the slaves. Those measures had stirred up huge discontent in his kingdom and provoked an uprising led by the ruler's own mother, who sought protection and support in the Goa court. The result had been a war between Boné and Goa which in 1644 made the ruler prisoner and established direct rule on Boné. Those events were to have far-reaching consequences on the destiny of South Sulawesi, since it was in order to liberate Boné from Goanese oppression that the famous Arung Palakka allied himself with the Dutch, contributing to the fall of Makassar into their hands and to their establishment there as a colonial power after the Bonagaya treaty (1667).

The future Syeikh Yusuf had left South Sulawesi just at the end of the Goa-Boné war, at a time when the supporters of an Islam "adapted" to local conditions were triumphing; he

---

[71] There are conflicting stories about his birth. Some say he was the son of a Shyeikh Khaidir from Binamu; some see in this Khaidir an incarnation of Nabi Khidir. And a tradition kept in some aristocratic families which claim descent from him says he was in fact born of a secret marriage of Sultan Malikussaid (and thus Sultan Hasanuddin's half brother) and that Syeikh Khaidir was only his adoptive father.

[72] Mattulada, *Islam di Sulawesi Selatan*, pp. 37–38. More will be known about Syeikh Yusuf after publication of Abu Hamid's dissertation on him, including the translation of five of his books.

had come back and gone again when he had seen the same prevailing attitudes. However, the seeds of a more radical Islam had been sown, and were beginning to grow. Syeikh Yusuf himself contributed to its development by his teachings and written works, which were disseminated by one of his sons and three disciples, the most famous among whom was the Bugis (from Rappang) Abdul Basir Adlarir al-Rafani, known locally as Tuan Rappang.

Their main efforts appear to have been directed against what seemed to be the main stumbling-block, that is to say, the nobility. It was among them primarily that Yusuf's disciples chose to implant the Khalwatiyah mystic order, and, it appears, not without success. It may have seemed to them another means, more congruent with true Islam, to assert their preeminence in society.

Such had been Syeikh Yusuf's indirect influence that after his death in South Africa, Sultan Abdul Jalil of Goa insisted on having his mortal remains brought back to Makassar, which was granted by the Dutch in 1705. His grave in Lakiung is now one of the most visited places of pilgrimage in South Sulawesi.

In the long struggle for Islamization, a new phase had thus been initiated, where the South Sulawesi nobility, or at least part of it, played a new role: it can best be seen in such literary works (probably written in the 18th century) as the "Book of Budi Istirahat Indra Bustanil Arifin," a book of Islamic Malayo-Indo-Persian inspiration, very akin to, if not literally adapted from, the *Mahkota segala raja* or *Taju's-Salatin*, written in 1603 in Aceh by Syeikh Bukhari of Johor. That text, and others, might be seen as attempts to replace the pagan bases on which aristocratic power had rested until then (and especially the myth of the heavenly descent of the rulers) by an Islamic based ideology, where the rulers appeared as the representatives and instruments of Allah on earth. That ideology, new to South Sulawesi, was not new in the Malay world; indeed, the medieval Islamic, Persian-influenced idea of a kingdom centered on a ruler considered as the "Shadow of God" had been the basis of, among others, those Malay sultanates which South Sulawesi aristocrats had been connected with for years.[73]

We must keep in mind that South Sulawesi, marked as it was by deeply rooted traditions, was nevertheless not isolated in its island world, but was also part of an intricate network of commercial, political, and intellectual relationships with other Muslim kingdoms all over the Archipelago, and that it had connections as well with other Asian countries, including Muslim countries in India and the Middle East, where some of its young men went to study, and where some *ulama* came from. So the movement of ideas in the rest of the Muslim world was not unknown, and eventually had its echoes here too.

For instance, in the first quarter of the 19th century not very long after the end (1818) of the first Wahabite "empire," an Arung Hatoa (ruler) of Wajo' called La Memmang ToAppamadeng (ruled between about 1821-1825) tried to enforce, under the influence of an *ulama* known as Syeikh Madina, a Wahabite-inspired kind of Islam in his kingdom: superstitious habits were fought, sacred places were destroyed, attempts were made to apply Islamic law literally (lapidation for adulterers, cutting off of hands for thieves, etc.) and to introduce Islamic customs (wearing of veils by women).[74] Those attempts were short lived, but showed that, among the South Sulawesi nobility, a more radical form of Islam was making its way, little by little. Wajo' is, by the way, among other kingdoms in South Sulawesi, one where, paradoxically, the *La Galigo* lore has been the most cultivated, the preeminence of nobility

---

[73] A.C. Milner, "Islam and Malay Kingship," *Journal of the Royal Asiatic Society*, 1 (1981): 46–70.

[74] Mattulada, *Islam di Sulawesi Selatan*, pp. 50–51.

has been the most asserted, and, at the same time, a kind of political democracy has existed for centuries, the role of merchants has been the most important, and the progress of Islamic reformism has been the most rapid.

In fact, what the word of a ruler could not obtain, i.e. the implementation of an Islam cleansed of its South Sulawesi impurities, was to be achieved by commoners, little by little. And it is their emergence as protagonists of Islamization which marks the next phase of its history.

Much is still to be done to document it precisely. Local manuscript sources mostly originate from aristocratic circles; and Dutch archives may not be very rich in information on topics which were not central to their interests in the 19th century; but one might find more relevant data after the extension of their sway to all of Sulawesi in 1906.

The advancement of two markedly different Islamic movements can be taken as examples of a deepening Islamization among commoners.

One is the Khalwatiyah, not the branch brought in by Syeikh Yusuf's disciples, but another one called Sammaniyah, founded in Medina by a Syeikh Muhammad bin Abdul Karim as-Samman. It was then introduced in the 18th century from Arabia to Palembang by his disciple Abdussamad al-Palembani and brought to Sulawesi in the middle of the 19th century by a Syeikh Abdullah al-Muniz.[75] There were among its first members a number of high aristocrats (two of the first adherents became later, respectively prime minister (until 1854) and ruler, from 1860 to 1871, of Boné (under the name of Sultan Ahmad); but that branch also developed very quickly among the commoners; and even if there have always been some noble people among its members, their position there is no different from that of other, ordinary members. The loss of their preeminence in that domain has also been marked by the near disappearance as a separate branch of Syeikh Yusuf's Khalwatiyah.[76]

The expansion of the new order has continued until now. In 1976, according to the Bureau of Religious Affairs in Ujung Pandang, 150,000 members were registered throughout the province, as compared to less than 10,000 in the Naqsybandiyah and less than 5,000 in the Qadiriyah, which are otherwise the strongest mystic orders elsewhere in Indonesia.[77]

In South Sulawesi, those orders bear witness to the development of a mysticism set on purely Islamic bases, as contrasted with a syncretist mysticism including many elements taken from the pre-Islamic local religious system, which may be much more diffused in the province, but remains unorganized, and is probably doomed to gradual weakening and eventual oblivion.

The second important movement corresponds to the emergence of a new, egalitarian brand of Islam—of course more in conformity with primitive Islamic teaching, according to which there should be in Islam no differences between ranks, races, or genders— expressed by the establishment of "reformist" organizations which at the same time advocated a return to the purity of the doctrine as it was preached by the Prophet and an open mindedness toward the challenges of modern life. It is probably not by mere chance that most of

---

[75] Abu Hamid's forthcoming dissertation, pp. 32–33.

[76] According to Drs Abu Hamid, there are at the moment in Maros two Khalwatiyah *khalifah,* one for each branch—the Khalwatiyah Yusuf and the Khalwatiyah Samman—who ignore each other. But the followers of the Khalwatiyah Yusuf are now very few. Maros became a center of Islamic, mostly mystical studies, from the time when the ruler of Boné La Maddaremmeng, a *sufi* himself, was exiled there after his defeat.

[77] Mattulada, *Islam di Sulawesi Selatan,* p. 115.

their promoters were not from the nobility, but commoners, mainly traders. The pioneer here was one Haji Abdullah bin Abdurrahman, from Maros. After having spent ten years in Mekkah, in 1917 he came back to Makassar, where he founded a *madrasah* in which the teaching was decidedly reformist. A conflict soon burst out between him and the *kali* (Kadhi) of Goa with regard to the correct way of performing the Friday public prayer (should regular *lohor* prayer be performed after Friday prayer or not), which he eventually won. In 1923, he founded an organization called As-Sirath al-Mustaqim, which, three years later, at the initiative of an Arab batik trader from Surabaya called Mansur al-Yamani, united with the national reformist movement Muhammadiyah (founded in 1912).[78]

The South Sulawesi branch of that organization grew rapidly, despite the declared opposition from many in the nobility, especially in the ruling families of Boné and Goa. However the local aristocracy did not present a unified front any more: among them, an important minority was already open to new ideas. That was especially true of Wajo', with the democratic trends of its traditional government, the role of its inhabitants, including the ruling elite, in trade overseas, and the entry there, already mentioned, of Wahabite ideas in the 19th century. It was in Wajo' that the first local branch of the Muhammadiyah outside of Makassar was opened in 1928, due to the active approval and help of one of the most eminent Bugis princesses, Andi' Ninnong, then in charge of the office of Ranreng Tuwa. In Wajo' also were held, in 1928 the first, and in 1941 the sixteenth South Sulawesi regional conference of the movement, which at the latter meeting could already boast of 7,000 members, 30,000 sympathizers, and 5,000 pupils, a fifth of which were in Wajo' alone.[79]

Indeed, one of the main efforts of the movement was directed toward the development of schools alongside *madrasah* and *pesantren* organized according to modern conditions.

Confronted with those developments, which were felt by more traditional circles as a menace against the social and religious *status quo*, some local *ulama*, encouraged by a part of the ruling aristocracy, created also teaching institutions following the same model of modernity, but still professing the established doctrine of the *syafi'i* school, which has been the legal school followed in South Sulawesi since the introduction of Islam. One of the most important of those institutions was the Madrasatu'l-Arabiyah Islamiyah, founded in 1932 in Wajo' by Haji As'ad (locally known as Haji Sade'), and renamed As'adiyah after the death of its founder, a Mekkah born and trained *ulama* of Bugis descent. That institution now boasts more than 7,000 pupils.[80]

After the Second World War, several similar institutions were founded by Haji As'ad's disciples, the most prominent being the Daru'l-Daqwah wal Irsjad, founded by Haji Abdurrahman Ambo' Dalle', which has now around 1,200 schools all over South Sulawesi, as well as in Kalimantan and Sumatra, among the Bugis diaspora there.

Although the teaching given in those institutions is plainly orthodox and not reformist, their action has had the same consequences on local socio-religious structures as that of the Muhammadiyah, by strongly lessening the religious role of the ruling aristocracy and undermining the pre-Islamic bases on which its power was established. Through both Muhammadiyah and non-Muhammadiyah teaching institutions, a new elite was shaped, of which only a minority came from the nobility, and many more from urban or wealthy rural

---

[78] Ibid., pp. 55–56 and Abu Hamid's dissertation, pp. 54–55.

[79] H.S.D. Moentoe, *Langkah dan oesaha kami tentang peringatan Conferentie Moehammadijah Daerah Selebes Selatan ke-XVI di Sengkang* (Makassar: Labbakang, 1941).

[80] Mattulada, *Islam di Sulawesi Selatan*, pp. 62–64.

commoners. That elite is constituting a significant proportion of the civil servants, teachers, entrepreneurs, and, of course, Islamic clerics (*imam, khatib*, teachers of religion, etc.) at work now, so that the influence of purified (be it reformist or orthodox) Islamic teaching is much more important than could be guessed from the given figures.

The same might be said of the Muhammadiyah, whose registered membership did not exceed 50,000 in 1975 (for a population of about 6 million);[81] but their sympathizers are much more numerous and their influence is still stronger, due to the number of pupils in their schools, and to the key positions of many of their members at all levels of administration, teaching, and business.

The last fight for survival of the socio-religious order brought into being at the beginning of Islamization in South Sulawesi lasted from about 1945 to 1965.

At the outset of the Indonesian independence struggle, a clearcut cleavage could be seen between a large section of the nobility, leaning on a number of traditionnal *ulama*, still clutching to and defending the old system, on the one hand; and on the other hand, the partisans of a new religious and social order, many of whose leaders were former pupils of the Muhammadiyah schools or former members of the Muhammadiyah Hizbu'l-Wathan Boy Scout Association. Although both were in favor, mostly, of Indonesian independence, the former did not conceal their preference for the East Indonesia State (Negara Indonesia Timur), brought into being under Dutch influence in order to counterbalance the Nationalists and Unitarists of the Republik Indonesia. They probably saw there a chance to perpetuate or even revive their former status at the top of society, now that the old myths and rites on which it had formerly rested were dying, with political power on all South Sulawesi concentrated in the hands of a Conference of Rulers called Hadat Tinggi. Most of the officials of the *syari'at (paréwa sara')* were on their side. On the opposite side, independence fighters *(pejoang)* were not only struggling against the Dutch and for the establishment of a unitary Indonesian Republic; they also wanted to suppress what they branded as the "feudal" aspects of traditional society.

In the aftermath of the *Revolusi*, the disillusioned former partisans continued their fight as rebels *(gerombolan)*, not only against the policy of the Central Government and what they considered as the denial of their rights, but also, still, against those "feudal" remnants, which they linked, not without good reason, with the perpetuation of superstitions, the continuation of *bissu* ceremonies, the visits to sacred places, etc.

It may be that, at the beginning, the rebellion had been caused by many other reasons; but the choice of the banner of Darul Islam by Kahar Muzakkar shows that his troops were really conscious of fighting a new *musu'selleng* for the completion of Islamization in South Sulawesi.[82]

The Religious Situation in South Sulawesi: A Product of History

This rapid survey of the history of Islamization in South Sulawesi is, I think, enough to enable the reader to understand how so many pre-Islamic and non-Islamic elements have managed to survive in the culture of the Bugis and Makassarese, two peoples who at the same time used to affirm their Islamic character. Indeed, the co-existence of such contradictory elements is not only to be found in one and the same culture, but even, often, in one

---

[81] Ibid., p. 115.

[82] The best work on that period and on the Darul Islam movement in South Sulawesi is Barbara Harvey's dissertation, "Tradition, Islam and Rebellion: South Sulawesi 1950–1965" (Cornell University, 1974).

and the same individual, such that the dichotomy of people into clear-cut groups, according to the model set up by Geertz for the Javanese of Mojokuto, and which some would like to use all over Muslim Indonesia, seems here inappropriate. One cannot group the Bugis or the Makassarese in really distinct *santri* or *abangan* categories, nor even see in their religious attitude a *santri*, an *abangan*, or a *priyayi* variant. Rather, one could distinguish a number of variables, which are not always linked to each other, such as: acceptance, partial acceptance, or refusal of Islam; the degrees of adherence to Bugis or Makassar pre-Islamic tradition (with its *bissu* and popular variants); the adherence to a Muslim tradition, be it the plain *syafi'i* tradition or that of a particular *tarékat*, or the support of reformist ideas, and the degree of Islamic religious practice and observance of *syari'at*.

Islamization can thus be seen from an external point of view as a process acting on all of these variables, to achieve a full acceptance of Islam; a complete rejection of those Bugis or Makassar traditions which are not consistent with it; and a full observance of the *syari'at*. Further, from a reformist point of view, Islamization would also include those Muslim traditions which are not, to their eyes, in accordance with the pure, original, Islam, and are thus *bid'ah* (heresy). However, other Muslims would deny that.

On one end of the Islamization axis, one would thus find the less Islamized people, such as the members of the Tolotang community, and namely those called Tolotang Sammang—a Bugis community living mostly in and around Amparita in the Sidénréng *kabupatén*—who have refused Islam altogether and follow "Sawérigading's tradition." On the other end of that same axis, however, one could find different kinds of people, who would all be styled *santri* in Geertz's terms: religious masters in Islamic schools, *ulama* of the *syafi'i* tradition, leaders of different *tarékat*, activists of the Muhammadiyah movement. Thus they do not form a homogeneous group, some people in that category even viewing the others as imperfect Muslims.

In between, the interplay of the above-mentioned variables would allow us to distinguish many different groups, which cannot be set on a continouous line. There are, for instance:

A few groups of Bugis and Makassar Christians, who have rejected both Islam and local religious traditions (a tiny minority indeed);

Other Tolotang, called Tolotang Bénténg who, having much in common with the other Tolotang, have however accepted part of the Muslim *syari'at*, and integrated some Muslim teachings in their tradition, so that they are sometimes called Tolotang Islam, although their adherence to pre-Islamic Bugis tradition is still strong;

The *bissu*, who, as priests of the former Bugis faith and practitioners of non-Islamic rites should logically be considered among the less Islamized people in South Sulawesi; however, most of them also acknowledge Islam as their religion, and some of them even went on the pilgrimage to Mekkah, so that there are now Haji *bissu*!

Conversely, many people who are zealous practitioners of Islam, who do their five prayers a day, are assiduous at the Friday congregation, fast scrupulously during Ramadhan, and manifest a real piety, at the same time participate in pre-Islamic rituals and believe in the reality of the *déwata*, as well as in the historicity of the myths. Besides, the coexistence of those heterogeneous traditions can take different forms. Some people could be called syncretists, insofar as elements of different traditions are, in their minds, integrated into one single system; others manifest a kind of split-personality, keeping two different and completely distinct systems, referring to one or the other according to circumstances. Others, again, while adhering completely to orthodox Muslim ideas, at times behave in a way or follow practices foreign to Islamic tradition. And one could find other different examples.

All those contradictions, which look strange at first sight, are much easier to understand when referred to the historical process of Islamization in South Sulawesi. They manifest the interplay of two competing systems, one of which, Islam, used at the beginning elements of the other in order to be accepted, thus opening the path for a long-lasting struggle, the last phases of which we are now witnessing.

COLLECTIVE MEMORY AND NOMADISM: ETHNO-HISTORICAL INVESTIGATIONS IN BORNEO*

Bernard Sellato

Foreword: *By the time this appears in print, it will have been ten years since this paper, one of my first, was written. To a certain extent, it now sounds clumsy. Some of the ideas put forth in it have since been much developed in subsequent publications. I feel now that a translation calls for some editing of the original text. Therefore, I have both introduced some slight changes into the text and recombined the original notes with added editorial notes. Table 1, which suffered from typos, was rectified.* Jakarta, November 1990.

An 18-month (1979–1981) study among central Borneo ethnic groups was partly aimed at reconstructing these groups' histories, over a 20,000 sq. km. region and as far back in time as possible. Some of these groups were nomadic hunter-gatherers in a more or less remote period of their history, but all are now practicing some degree of swidden rice agriculture. Different types of subsistence economy co-exist, however, with the dominant feature that they all resort to both cultivated paddy and wild sago, in varying proportions. Besides allowing for ethno-historical reconstructions, this investigation uncovered a clear connection between an ethnic group's collective memory and its social structure and, ultimately, its way of life, which ranges from complete nomadism to sedentary rice agriculture.[1]

---

* Translated by the author from: "Mémoire collective et nomadisme (Enquête ethno-historique à Bornéo)," *Archipel* 27 (1984): 85–108.

[1] See Bernard Sellato, "Les nomades forestiers de Bornéo et la sédentarisation: essai d'histoire économique et sociale" (PhD dissertation, Paris, EHESS, 1986), pp. 54–56. I now consider that the connection is really of a different kind: it is ideology, determining both way of life and social organization, that conditions both the need for, and the practice of, maintaining and preserving historical tradition, thus the capacity for collective memory. In the case of the nomads, ethnic identity is supported by an ideological identity, which expresses itself in a way of life (see Sellato, *Nomades et sédentarisation à Bornéo—Histoire économique et sociale* (Paris: Editions de l'EHESS [Etudes Insulindiennes/Archipel no. 9], 1989), pp. 248–50; and idem., "The Punan Question and the Reconstruction of Borneo's Culture History," in *Change and Development in Borneo*, ed. V. H. Sutlive, Jr., forthcoming). Note that throughout this paper, the term "nomadism" refers particularly to "tropical rainforest nomadism" while "sedentary agriculture," in contrast, stands for what is currently called "semi-nomadic swidden cultivation."

Oral tradition plays a foremost part in the functioning of these societies. It touches on every aspect of daily life, regulates the individual's behavior under every circumstance, allowing for a very low degree of autonomy within the group, whose identity, coherence, survival, and expansion it guarantees. Historical tradition, upon which this study is based, is not conceived of as distinct from the other segments of oral tradition.

The Historical Data In Bornean Oral Tradition

Its Sources

Where do we find historical data? First, by asking the elders: this is the simplest and chief source of information. It is also the most prone to alterations, as will be described later. Contrary to folktales, which almost never yield historical data positioned in time and space, the epics are valuable sources, as it is well-known that their being sung is a very positive feature for their preservation (mnemonics based on rhythm, verse length, rhyme), and some are obviously very old. One often observes elders looking to an epic for a historical fact when their memory fails them: "The epic goes like this . . ."

A difficulty is that the language of the epics is replete with archaic terms, loanwords, and metaphors, making it somewhat esoteric. In socially stratified societies, only in the aristocratic families were the keys to this language transmitted from one generation to the next, and today only elderly aristocrats still master, although not always totally, this grand and beautiful poetic tongue. Sections of the epics have now become (definitively?) inaccessible to us, and the singers no longer know anything of the story they tell except for what the epic itself says, if even they can still comprehend it. Historical data are sometimes found in narrative tales, most often with distinctive mythical traits—like some allusion to an ancient settlement, a landmark near which the group lived in forgotten times—that the narrator recites without knowing anything of the historical episode they refer to.

The Constituent Elements of Historical Data

An event of the past can be roughly defined by the knowledge we have, through a given *text*,[2] of a certain number of elements: the plot of the story, its *scenario*; the main characters it puts into action and their names; its localization in space and time; its setting and the causal relationship between units of action; some minor elements concerning secondary characters or details of the action; finally, an assessment of the historical objectivity of the narrative. The minimal account we can have of an event is an outline of its scenario: "Someone did this." Past events can only be partially captured, as accounts rarely submit their "complete" form, that is, all the elements above, to the investigator.

Besides, whatever historical information a text might contain can be found disconnected from its historical context, because the *historical narrative* has been diluted in a later, superimposed literary formulation and has been transmuted into a legend or a myth. Then, the investigator faces the task of reconstituting in the best possible way—by cross-checking with other texts—the event referred to, its plot, its protagonists and their deeds, and its position in space and time.

---

[2] Throughout this paper, I call "text" any recorded or transcribed document, originating from an informal interview or representing a piece of formal or informal oral literature.

The Forms of the Historical Data

A piece of information with historical value, that is, referring to an event of the past, has been recorded in the group's collective memory. The form in which it was immediately recorded is that of a *historical narrative*. If it survived, this narrative might have evolved through time into a *historical-legendary narrative*, a kind of saga or chanson de geste in which, progressively, the original elements were altered and supernatural elements introduced. In a later stage, the narrative might have acquired a mythical dimension, where an intermingling of the human and supernatural worlds was consummated. I am not referring here to a myth, strictly speaking, but to a narrative with mythical traits, or *mythical narrative*.

How do the historical data appear to the investigator in these crudely categorized forms of texts? A historical narrative refers to a relatively recent event that the informant has learned about first-hand, for example, an expedition in which his grandfather participated.[3] The scenario of such a narrative is rich in details; names of characters, even secondary ones, are remembered; the space and time setting of the action is precisely determined; the deeds and their causes and consequences are indicated; style is realistic; and eventual stylistic additions by the informant do not much alter the reliability of the account.

The historical event to which the legend refers is already ancient, and several generations of narrators have kneaded the original narrative, embroidering on it, emphasizing certain sections, shading off others sometimes till they totally fade away, adding in supernatural and magical elements. Historical objectivity disappears, ascription of deeds to characters becomes chancy, certain sections are totally implausible. Place and time assignation, however, remains generally possible, and the outline of the scenario can be reconstructed through an interpretation of intertextual and other elements.

What remains, in the mythical narrative, of the historical data after innumerable manipulations? What we know of the historical event we suspect shows through the myth is most often restricted to the basic plot, and yet we have to transcribe it after having stripped it of its mythical attributes. We then find that we most likely face a real historical event, but that it has been disjointed from its context and is now drifting in time. Its geographic location is often hazy, some "region of origin" of the group, not always the true one.[4] Sometimes, because of an outstanding landmark referred to in the narrative, the location is very precisely ascribed, but nothing allows a determination of the time, as the narrative clearly refers to a period beyond the oldest historical memories. The characters are often unknown, sometimes they are archetypal ones and, though their names might have reached us, their ethnic affiliation may remain uncertain. These characters are often alluded to as being "spirits" or, sometimes, mythical animals.[5]

Then, historical data can be found at every stage in the evolution of the account of a historical event, as it can persist, though in a minimal form, through time and through the adulteration of the original narrative. At the stage of the mythical narrative, it might represent only a particle of history suspended in time, no longer connected to anything known, and all we can say is that it is very ancient.

---

[3] This also includes narratives of events which the informant himself witnessed or took part in, usually called "personal history" or "personal narrative."

[4] More, perhaps, than other constituent elements of narratives, the "region of origin" is the focus of idealized, or rather ideologized, constructions and manipulations (on the Busang and Kayan, see Sellato, "Les nomades forestiers de Bornéo," pp. 301–307, 417).

[5] See Bernard Sellato, "Le mythe du Tigre au centre de Bornéo," *ASEMI* 14, 1–2 (1983).

The Ethno-Historical Reconstruction

The main step in ethno-historical reconstruction is to determine, from pieces of historical information originating in many different texts and sources, the relative chronology of events, and to arrange them in a sequence. Sometimes the informant spontaneously provides such a sequence, positioning the event under scrutiny in chronological relation to other events. Most often, however, this has to be done by the investigator, who confronts various sets of data bearing a chronological value (genealogies, sequence of settlements) and validates a relative chronology of salient historical events for a given community or ethnic group. Historical interaction of two communities (wars, alliances) allows, through the cross-checking of their respective chronologies, for a more reliable time frame.

Absolute chronological approximations can be secured through a computing of genealogies and, sometimes, settlement shifts, insofar as precise data on the reasons of these shifts[6] is available. Absolute datings are also provided by certain events of regional reach, that are documented in written sources, such as the Krakatau volcanic explosion, the Sarawak Iban wars, or the colonial interferences.

The investigator also attempts to reconstruct the event's scenario, its causes and consequences, and its major phases, by cross-checking several mutually illuminating texts. It is important, in order to ponder the subjectivity of the opinion the members of a given community have of an episode of their own history, to investigate also among the neighboring communities that were that community's protagonists in that episode. A fair knowledge of all these groups' customs allows the investigator to deduct, by comparison of two prejudiced accounts, the event's most plausible scenario.

More generally, a critical comparative analysis of the various versions offered by informants concerning the same event is necessary, and the investigator can establish his own version, the *objectively* most plausible of all. Indeed, by the end of his work, the investigator has at his disposal more data on that event than any individual informant.[7] To the reductionist approach, taking as historical tradition the *minimal version* generally agreed upon by the whole set of informants, I am tempted to oppose a maximalist approach: Historical tradition would be represented by *the most plausible broadest, "maximal" version*, such as the investigator has established it, taking into account the data he has at his disposal, plus his insider's intuitive knowledge of the customs and mode of rationalization of the ethnic groups he studies, which allows him to deconstruct alterations of the narrative using *a contrario* the same specific local patterns that determined the alterations.

This does not mean that this "maximal" version is to be seen as definitively validated, and the use of the conditional is recommended. However, it should be recognized that the "maximal" version likely is the closest representation we can get of the real historical event. Contrary to the minimal version, it allows for fertile speculations.[8]

---

[6] It should be first established whether a given settlement referred to in a narrative was a long-term hardwood longhouse or a light temporary settlement. The latter usually lasts three to ten years, whereas the former would last two or three decades. Besides the periodical need to move the village closer to fresh swidden land, other common causes for settlement shift are practical ones (wars or epidemics) or supernatural (curses or omens).

[7] Indeed, through inspection of other communities' oral tradition and whatever written sources are available, he often has more data at his disposal than the sum of all the community's knowledgeable individuals.

[8] Contrary to the minimal version—a mere skeleton of successive facts with little juncture—the maximal version gives flesh and blood to the account and also provides a better understanding of the causal relationships between the facts. In short, it *makes more sense,* it gives sense to history (see a discussion in Sellato, "Les nomades forestiers de Bornéo," pp. 29–56).

Ethno-Historical Analysis of Texts

We have described three formal categories of texts in which historical data can be found. This data can either be apprehended directly, or needs to be observed through a screen and processed, or again cannot be used at all.

Three Texts

Here below are three texts, such as they were told by the elders, rendered in translation with as little change as was possible. Between brackets, I provided comments that I deemed necessary to the general understanding of the texts. For names of rivers and settlements, the reader is referred to maps in other publications.[9]

The first text is an Aoheng historical narrative, describing an attack by the Iban of Sarawak against the Long-Apari subgroup of the Aoheng (or Penihing) of the Upper Mahakam River around 1915. The second text is a sort of saga, a blend of history and legend, told by the Hovorit subgroup of the Hovongan (or Punan Bungan) of the Upper Kapuas River to account for a destructive expedition by the Taman against them around 1835. The third text, displaying clear mythical traits, provides an account by the Upper Kasau subgroup of the Seputan (Upper Mahakam) of their initiation to the major purification ritual; the historical event alluded to is ascribed to a period before or around 1750.

Text 1 : The Iban Expedition to Noha Maci'

After the Great Iban War [1885] against the peoples of the Upper Mahakam, our community lived scattered for several years. Then, we gathered again at Long Okap, far downstream from our village of Long Apaé [burnt to the ground by the Iban, like all other Aoheng villages]. We lived there a long time. Part of us went back upstream to settle at Monyu'i, not far from Long Apaé. There we caught some Iban who had come to steal [to collect] resins on our territory and we took their heads. For fear of reprisals, we moved again downstream, somewhat scattered, staying one year at Long Kasau, one year at Nango Marï, then three years at Noha Boan Ori.

We were not welcomed by the other Aoheng, who were making us responsible for having triggered the Great Iban War [they certainly were right] and feared that these new heads we had just taken would cause another massive Iban expedition. Bang Lawing, the chief of the Kayan of Long Belu'u, and Lijiu Li' [probably the grand-son of Lijiu Li' the Great, the "Dayak Napoléon"], the chief of the Busang of Long Pahangai, wanted to prevent us from going back to our traditional territory, near the Sarawak border [the Kayan and Busang were the largest regional groups and the Aoheng's *de facto* suzerains, in charge of regional politics and security]. They forced us to settle at Noha Silat, a short way downstream from the confluence of the Kasau (or Kacü) River.

There we remained a long time. But our king, Tingang Kuhi, was not happy to have to take orders. He had to yield, though, since he deemed it necessary to ensure the Kayan's and Busang's protection. After several years, however, he moved upstream with a part of our community, settling at Penyevahan, while the rest of us, under old Mira', chose to remain at Noha Silat.

---

[9] See Bernard Sellato, "The Upper Mahakam Area," *Borneo Research Bulletin* 12,2 (1980): 40–46; idem, "Les nomades forestiers de Bornéo"; idem, *Nomades et sédentarisation à Bornéo*.

At that time, a group of warriors from Long Cihan [the Cihan subgroup of the Aoheng, some distance downstream] went to Litu [the Barito River headwaters] and took four heads. When they returned, the [Dutch] administration learnt about their deed and caught them, but one of them, Savang Turi', escaped to Penyevahan. The Dutch wanted to prevent us from taking heads and to take our children away to school [the first missionary school opened at Laham, far downstream, in 1915]. We were afraid of school. Tingang Kuhi was taken to the military outstation of Long Belu'u for having hidden Savang Turi', but he ran away and walked upstream along the Mahakam to Long Cihan. From there he was taken by canoe up to Noha Silat, and walked again to Penyevahan.

He was very upset with the [political] situation on the Upper Mahakam and, following his wife Dirung's advice [she was the daughter of the chief of the Huvung subgroup of the Aoheng], he decided to take his people across to Sarawak. First, he moved his settlement to Noha Maci', near the sources of the Mahakam [the starting point of the track across the mountains], then he went himself with a few men to Sarawak to request the [Brooke] Raja's permission to settle there. At the start of the track toward Sarawak, he met with a party of Iban building canoes. They pretended they were going to the upper Meraseh River [on Busang territory] to collect resins. Actually, they were preparing to attack the Aoheng but Tingang, unaware of the fact, went on on his way toward Sarawak.

Shortly afterwards, these Iban sent a messenger to Noha Maci', summoning the Aoheng leaders to their camp. Savang Kulau and a party of Aoheng warriors went up the Mahakam and bumped into the Iban on their way down. All of Savang Kulau's party, eight men, were killed. Among them, Nyangun, Lasah, brave warriors. The Iban casualties amounted to a canoe crew, three men. The Iban went on down the river to Noha Maci' which they attacked en masse, killing many people, including Tingang's wife, Dirung, three of his children, and two slaves. Then they returned home, leaving some of their men on the battlefield, including their chief Akeng, killed by Moring.

The Aoheng survivors fled to join their kin in Noha Silat. As for Tingang Kuhi, he remained a long time in Sarawak, where he learnt about the slaughter of his people, then he went to Pontianak and up the Kapuas River, crossed the [Müller Range] mountains via the Bungan and Huvung Rivers, and reached Noha Silat. There he remained many years, before finally [when the Pax Neerlandica was achieved] moving all his people back again to their traditional territory, settling at Long Apari [1935; they are still there today].

Text 2 : The Tüari War

Lavang Daru' [Lavang the Long, the Tall] and Lavang Carï are two brothers, chiefs of the village of Diang Bovo' [*diang*, limestone peg or cliff]. Their younger sister, whose name I forgot, has just died and her funeral is being prepared. Lavang Daru' leaves for downstream, carrying a large jar [the funerary jar in which the deceased's bones will be gathered after the body has been left to weather; meanwhile, a fresh human head must be secured; the jar is then stored in a cave]. He moors at a Tüarï [the name the Hovongan use to refer to the Taman and Maloh] village and tries the jar on the head of a chief's daughter [an aristocratic head is more highly valued], but the child's head is too big. So he goes, from one Tüarï village to the next, trying his jar on the heads of all chiefs' daughters. Nobody dares oppose him, as he is very tall and very strong. Finally, in an Embalo village [the Taman or Maloh of the Embaloh River], he finds a chief's daughter whose head fits exactly the mouth of his jar. He cuts it and returns to Diang Bovo'. Now the deceased's dried bones are ready. They are placed in the jar, and the girl's head becomes its stopper.

All the Tüari of the Kapuas basin now get together to kill Lavang Daru'. They go up the river and gather on the flat of Data Halo' [the cassava flat], at the foot of Diang Bovo' buttress. Lavang Daru' comes down to offer rice to the assailants and says: "Tomorrow we shall fight; today you shall build huts, eat, and rest." The next day, Lavang Daru' comes down in full war attire, attacks the Tüari and kills them all. He spares some, however, whom he urges to come back with a larger army of stronger warriors. The Tüari survivors are halted on their way back home by the neighboring Hovongan people of chief Tesoing Loing [the one who can fly] who, by order of Lavang Daru', cut a hand off one, an ear off another, and punctured an eye of a third.

Shortly afterwards the Tüari return, more numerous, to attack Diang Bovo', but suffer the same defeat. Lavang Daru' again spares three men, whom he entrusts with the following message: "I wish to die now, since my little sister is dead; if you want to kill me, you ought to forge war swords one fathom long, because I am very tall; only then will you be able to kill me." To his younger brother Lavang Cari he says: "I want to die but you, you must live for our progeny."

The Tüari forge fathom-long war swords, one for each warrior, and return again to Data Halo', thousands of them. Lavang Daru' first kills his wife and his children, to the last. Then he comes down to fight. He kills half of the Tüari, but then his two feet are chopped off, he goes on fighting, but then his two knees are chopped off, he is still fighting, but then his two thighs are chopped off, and he still fights. Finally, his right arm is chopped off, and he collapses. Only one third of the assailants remain alive. Lavang Cari has time to chop his brother's head off and take it to a safe place [to give it a funeral], so that the Tüari do not have it.

The Tüari go back home, without taking the chance to attack the other Hovongan village, because chief Tesoing Loing and his fellow Bang Kahavong [the one who splits (his enemy) in two] are even stronger than Lavang Daru' was. The latter and all his family were laid to rest by his brother in caves at Diang Lavang Daru' [Lavang Daru's caves], near Data Halo'. The Tüari never came again.

Text 3 : The Gong of Long Nekerahé

The first ones of our group [the Upper Kasau subgroup of the Seputan] who were real human beings were Otü Tarin and Otü Koeng [a woman and a man]. They are called *otü* [spirits] because they were born of spirits, but they were human beings. Their forebears were Tingang Takin Bala [a male spirit] and Uhing Tuban Baja' [a female spirit]. These were brother and sister and, at the same time, husband and wife. After their union was consummated, Uhing fell ill and could not recover, her face was livid [the regular symptoms after the transgression of a taboo]. All sorts of four-legged animals were sacrificed, in vain.

One night, an old man of the village had a dream in which a tiger, coming from Orong Hïvan [literally, the lower region of Iban country], appeared to him and told him: "Uhing won't get well again if you do not shift your village." Upon waking up, the old man spread the news, and the people started dismantling the village. The tiger appeared again to the old man, saying: "The chief's house should be built first." Then, the villagers went to the confluence of the Nekerahé River [an upper tributary of the Kasau] and dug a hole in the ground for the principal pile of the chief's house. At a depth of about a half fathom, they found a gong and, after they dug it up, they found two pigs [the domestic pig, as opposed to the wild boar]. It was the first time humans had ever seen this animal. The pigs were raised with much care. Then a little blood, taken from one of the pigs' ears, was used to anoint Uhing. She progressively recovered.

Then the tiger appeared again and said: "See what I have taught you; from now on, you shall be able to make your life better." It was at this time that our people first carried out the great ritual of *mengosang*, with the blood from one of these pigs' offspring that was sacrificed to purify the whole village. This ritual of *mengosang*, we still carry out nowadays, in the same way, should circumstances require it [after an epidemics, a serious breach of taboo, or several poor crops in a row].

Analysis of the Elements of the Texts

Text 1 : A Historical Narrative

The event itself is precisely positioned in its historical context and the text provides a number of details on the protagonists, their names, their kinship relations, and the action's successive settings and successive phases, even minor ones (like Tingang's return). The text shows a concern for objectivity: It recognizes that the Aoheng suffered a major setback, that their provocations were the cause for the Iban expedition, that the Aoheng were under a protectorate imposed by the larger ethnic groups of the Upper Mahakam. Therefore it is a historical text in the full sense of the word, objective and without self-flattery.

Text 2 : How to Transform a Defeat into a Victory

Besides the loss of certain names (Lavang's sister, the Tüarï chiefs), this text displays complacent alterations to the original historical narrative, which became "the Saga of Lavang Daru'." A number of transpositions and interpretations occurred that we can try to deconstruct and interpret in the opposite way. For instance, Lavang's ostentatious and provocative quest for a head certainly stands for a less-than-glorious ambush against an isolated child (and maybe not a chief's daughter). In the triplicated episode of the Tüarï expedition, the first two failed attempts only serve to introduce in the narrative the undeniable final victory of the Tüarï, a very numerous ethnic group. The hero's desire to die and his murdering his whole family only serve to conceal another historical fact that could not be evaded, that Lavang and his family were killed by the Tüarï, who came specially for him. The Hovongan found some consolation in the fact that Lavang's head could be made away with by his brother. The Tüarï did not dare attack the other village, because "Tesoing Loing is even stronger." This avoidance probably conceals the other Hovongan subgroup's escape to the forest or to caves and their abandonment of their village.

The whole episode can then be reconstructed as follows: For the funeral of his sister, the hero went to "steal" a head (this corresponds to a local expression, meaning to ambush an isolated individual, preferably a woman or child, and run away with the head), and a Tüarï expedition (maybe just a small party was enough) wiped out the Hovorit subgroup of the Hovongan, in spite of the hero's bravery. The end of the narrative is particularly revealing: The Tüarï, the text concludes, "never came again," which implies to the audience: "They've learned the lesson we taught them." The lesson, really, is that the Hovongan have refrained ever since from ambushing the Tüarï to take their heads (they subsequently took heads among the neighboring Mandai group).

Text 3 : Two Great Mythical Themes

Two important myths of the Seputan and Aoheng are found here. The myth of the original incest is not specifically a Seputan theme, nor even a Dayak one. Incest, conceived of as a compulsory practice when it concerns either the first human couple or, as is probably the case here, the only two aristocratic (spirit) individuals, entails disease, typically a slow decline.[10] This can be cured only through the performance of the major purification ritual which, somehow, evacuates the incest and allows the real human beings to be descended from the spirits.

In Aoheng myths, the initiating or "civilizing" hero is always the tiger or a character by the name of Tiger,[11] coming from elsewhere (commonly downstream). He acquaints the "still stupid" humans with the rites (*adet*) and introduces new cultural elements and techniques. Here he is responsible for the discovery of the domestic pig and the ritual practiced with its blood.

What historical data do we find? The couple are really spirits, precursors of mankind. Their genealogy is hazy and cannot be linked to chiefly genealogies, known from around 1800, but they are considered the forebears of the whole Seputan subgroup. Except for them, no personal name is recalled in the narrative, not even the old man's. The episode is situated at Long Nekerahé, for this is the oldest settlement (around 1800) of which the Seputan have a remembrance. We know, however, that these Seputan lived earlier on the Busang River (a tributary of the Barito). This initiation to the major ritual must really have occurred before the period of their residence at Long Nekerahé.

We can, then, consider this text as a myth. Its geographic localization is chancy, the characters of the mythical forebears cannot be connected to the genealogies, and the dating is impossible. There is precious little in this text that might be of any use in a historical reconstruction.[12]

Erosion of a Text's Historical Contents

The study of the three texts above shows that the historical contents of a historical narrative erode progressively through time. The episode referred to in the first text dates back to 1915; in the second, to about 1835; and in the third, to around 1750. Observation bearing on dozens of such texts leads us to recognize that the various constituent elements of a text show a differential resistance to erosion. These elements were enumerated earlier, in decreasing order of resistance. It is the minimal plot of action that resists best, even through alterations (embellishments, confusion with episodes of other periods, inversions).

When reconstructing history by confronting data from all available sources, the investigator searches through a network of clues and hints for the most plausible scenario. As he sails up the stream of time, however, texts become less frequent, their content of historical data lower, the data itself more blurred, and he ends up being unable, for lack of data, to propose a coherent and reasonably plausible scenario. Here and there a toponym, a more or less mythical character's name, or a very ancient particle of action subsist, but they cannot be connected to each other. I use the term *extreme time depth* for the collective memory of a given community, the approximate date beyond which any attempt to reconstruct history is

---

[10] A general term for this affliction all over Borneo is *busung* (see R. Blust, "Linguistic Evidence for Some Early Austronesian Taboos," *American Anthropologist* 83[1981]: 285–319).

[11] As elsewhere in Southeast Asia, the tiger is linked with the taboos. In Borneo the Tiger is the avenger of transgressions, the agent of punishment, but he is at the same time the mystical healer of man's suffering (see Sellato, "Le mythe du Tigre").

[12] However, the very fact that the Seputan at some point acquired the domestic pig and became acquainted with the ritual is relevant to the reconstruction of cultural interactions and Seputan cultural history. Besides, the names of the spirit-forebears probably refer to real Seputan leaders of forgotten times.

doomed to failure. This date is then the limit for the articulated collective memory of the whole of the community. Of course, this memory is disseminated amongst the various informants of the community. We will see that this time depth differs from one ethnic group to the other, and how it differs.

From History to Myth

Historical and mythical elements are intimately intermingled in oral tradition. Mythical stories may carry some historical information. Where do we find, between historical narrative and myth, this dividing line we have called the extreme time depth?

Text number 3 is barren of historical information to be used for reconstructions; that is, it cannot be linked to Seputan history such as can be seized through genealogies. Nevertheless, this purification ritual has really been transmitted to the Seputan by another ethnic group (or one of its members). A minimal plot of action subsists. Some cultural hero was transformed into the Tiger. Here, he appears in a dream, whereas in Aoheng texts he is made of flesh in the shape of either tiger or man, always named Tiger, and he eats food raw. The groups of Borneo distinguish well between tiger and panther, and describe the former correctly although they have never seen one. Collective memory has probably preserved the remembrance of real encounters with tigers in very ancient times, and maybe not in Borneo.[13]

The transformation of a historical character into an animal through a historical narrative's evolution into a mythical story is a common thing, and it is further stimulated by the use of names of animals as common personal names. An Aoheng myth of West Kalimantan features a Seluang, a stranger coming from downstream the Kapuas River, who waged war on two brothers. In the course of the war, he eventually transformed himself and his whole army into small fish, the *seluang* fish,[14] but the brothers' grandfather, a magician, caught them all in his blowpipe and blew them away into the sky. It can be assumed that, one day, some chief by the name of Seluang came to wage war on some proto-Aoheng group, but no conclusion can be reached regarding this war's outcome. The East Kalimantan Aoheng, who do not (or no longer) know this myth, keep on mentioning the "war of the *seluang* fish" and wondering how those tiny fish might well have attacked men.

A similar transposition is found in the "war of the ants" that the Aoheng relate as follows: "A high river flood followed by a sudden subsidence had left huge quantities of dead fish on firm ground, and ants (*nyevérang*) invaded the area to eat the fish. They eventually assailed the Amüé [an ancient subgroup of the Aoheng], who abandoned their village and took refuge with the Acüé [another subgroup]. To obtain shelter and protection, they had to enter into vassalage." According to reconstructions based on settlement sequences, this episode dates back to slightly before 1800. The whole story could have been taken literally had it not been for the Dutch traveler Nieuwenhuis' mention of an ancient tribe called Neberang that had lived in this area.[15]

---

[13] See Lord Medway, *Mammals of Borneo*. Royal Asiatic Society (Malaysian Branch) Monograph no. 7 (1977), p. 139. Note that all Borneo languages distinguish lexically between tiger and panther, although there are no tigers in Borneo.

[14] The small *seluang* fish may be *Chola oxygastroides* (Cyprinidaeae).

[15] A. W. Nieuwenhuis, *Quer Durch Borneo*, 2 vols. (Leiden: Brill, 1904–1907): 1, 277; See also Sellato, *Les nomades forestiers*, pp. 295–301, 309–11, 416–18.

Then, it might well be that those Ne-berang attacked the Amüé, forcing them to request protection from the Acüé. The homophony of the two names and the temptation for the Amüé to erase the memory of a terrible episode of their history leads me to believe that a whole scenario was elaborated by the Amüé around the word *nyevérang* ("ant") to explain their escape and the loss of their sovereignty. As in Text number 2, the investigator thinks he has a grasp on the real historical event, but doubts remain cast on his hypothesis because no other text is available to validate it, since the Aoheng themselves do not know (any more) who the Ne-berang were.

This story of the "war of the ants," which could be called historico-mythical, is an extreme case: it provides a real historical fact—the Amüé took refuge with their neighbors and became their vassals—which has been confirmed by other texts. But, as for the reason for this retreat—a war of the ants or a war of the Ne-berang—a decision cannot reasonably be reached between the tradition's version and the investigator's. In this particular example, we probably stand exactly at the extreme time depth of the Aoheng's articulate collective memory.

Social Structure and Way of Life

Before I attempt a parallel between way of life and collective memory, I will contemplate four ethnic groups as references and describe briefly their social-economic features, at least those seeming relevant to the scope of this study: an outline of the history of their way of life, some population figures, their economic features, and their social organization. The extreme time depth of coherent historical reconstruction will be provided, with some comments relevant to each group's specific features.

Three of these groups, studied in 1979–1981, are tiny, little-known ethnic entities, whose main feature is the partial reliance of their economy on several species of wild sago, mainly *Eugeissona utilis* (*nango*). The fourth group, introduced for comparison purposes, is a large one, having been practicing swidden rice farming for at least some 250 years.

The Bukat

The Bukat[16] maintained their traditional, almost totally nomadic way of life until around 1925–1930. Their economy, based on wild sago, collecting, hunting and fishing, implied frequent traveling. The migration unit, the band, was the extended family or a group of two or three related families. It seems that, for subsistence reasons, group size was limited to around 30 individuals. Originating, they say, from the Upper Mendalam River (West Kalimantan), the Bukat bands nevertheless dispersed on long-ranging, more or less circular migrations through the headwaters of the Baleh (Sarawak) and the Mahakam (East Kalimantan). Territorial notions are in fact rather vague. Most Bukat bands lived in areas upstream from settled farming groups, trading with them and, eventually, helping them with agricultural tasks and establishing, in some cases, a temporary symbiotic system. Their notions of identity also seem hazy. Two facts must be stressed: the extreme spatial mobility of each economic unit (the band) and a leaning toward band fissioning and fusing in the course of migrations.

---

[16] See a more elaborate reconstruction of the history of the Bukat in Sellato, *Nomades et sédentarisation*, pp. 35–108.

Around 1925, after a transitory period near the Aoheng of East Kalimantan, the Bukat built their first autonomous village. A similar process took place around 1930 for the Bukat of West Kalimantan. They do cultivate some rice nowadays, but they are said to be poor farmers, since they disappear regularly into the forest, abandoning their fields. They remain nomads at heart, do not much like the taste of rice, preferring that of sago, and they possibly spend as much as six months a year in the forest in small, scattered groups.

The leader was traditionally chosen for his/her qualities of wisdom and experience and was the one best able to take the band along the sago-clump and fruit grove itineraries, also taking advantage of wild boar herds' migrations and of the ripening of wild fruit. Nowadays, in their hamlets of little more than 100 souls, they display an egalitarian social organization, although it might be that, in some communities, the function of the leader has tended to become more hereditary under other ethnic groups' influence.

A reconstruction of Bukat history is easy for the period since their sedentarization. It is more difficult for the period 1880 to 1920 because of the high number of tiny bands, some of which have since disappeared as separate entities. For the period prior to 1880, the historical data provided by Bukat oral tradition alone have become insufficient.[17]

The Hovongan (or Punan Bungan)

The Hovongan disavow the ethnonym Punan and state that they have always practiced agriculture. Indeed, their secondary forest extends over vast tracts of their territory.[18] They live in three small hamlets[19] of some 100 people each, but stress that once they were much more numerous. They display little social differentiation, with no aristocratic category, and their genealogies show a half-hereditary, half-elective type of leadership that subsisted until the Dutch administration intervened (early 20th century), introducing ranks and titles which have since become hereditary.

Although all Hovongan practice some agriculture, they spend an average of four months a year in the forest (between the firing of the fields and the sowing, and between the weeding and the harvest), living off wild sago, hunting, and fishing, scattered in family groupings similar to the Bukat bands. During these periods in the forest they always remain within their traditional territory—the Bungan River basin and the left tributaries of the uppermost Kapuas—and, often, within less than three days' walk from the village. Their mobility outside their territory is low, but their segmental mobility (extended families) within it is high. This territorial sedentarity contributes to making their feelings of ethnic identity stronger than the Bukat's. The whole middle Bungan river area (the heart of the Hovongan country) displays plenty of historical sites (sites of old settlements, caves, boul-

---

[17] However, using also a few written sources and the oral tradition of neighboring settled groups, some sense can be made of this poor data obtained from the Bukat's own oral tradition, allowing the investigator to propose a reasonably reliable historical reconstruction extending well back into the first half of the 19th century (ibid., pp. 39–47).

[18] A. W. Nieuwenhuis (*In Centraal Borneo*, 2 vols. [Leiden: Brill, 1900], p. 189), visiting the Hovongan in the 1890s, noted that they were subsisting on a combination of cultivated rice and tubers and of wild sago. This was still true in 1980. I suggested that the Hovongan first got acquainted with farming in the second half of the 18th century ("Les nomades forestiers," pp. 299–300, 416) and with rice several decades later (ibid., pp. 319, 326; *Nomades et sédentarisation*, pp. 222, 253), but have remained, to this day, uninterested in making rice their staple food. Indeed, they are now earning much of their living from the gold they pan in their streams.

[19] There are now (1990) five hamlets, as two of the original three have each split in two, the outgoing sections moving downstream to the mouth of their respective tributaries.

ders, and other landmarks) and the rooting of the oral tradition in the landscape strengthens the collective memory.

The history of the Hovongan can be reconstructed from their own tradition with not much difficulty up to about 1800. Names of leaders and settlements from that period remain coherently connected. For the Hovongan, as for the Seputan of East Kalimantan, the term Punan still applied to them by outsiders should be reconsidered.[20]

The Aoheng (or Penihing)

The Aoheng form a homogeneous ethnic group of about 2,000 people and their biggest village has some 600.[21] For the Long-Apari subgroup, the most numerous and the most Aoheng of all five subgroups, history can be summarized in two periods. The pre-agricultural period saw a half dozen small, rival groups scattered on the tributaries of the uppermost Mahakam and living, the Aoheng say, in caves or on top of rocky spurs. They stress that they have always lived there, and it seems that they were hunter-gatherers with a relatively fixed settlement pattern (hamlet or cave). This situation deserves a special study, as it does not seem viable, except for very small groups similar in size to the Bukat band, on territories wide enough for their subsistence. Around 1800–1820, the Aoheng were "civilized"; that is, settled and controlled, if not really subjugated, by the downstream Busang and Kayan groups which taught them rice agriculture and lent them their social stratification and some of their religion. In these three fields the Aoheng, even today, show less rigidity and diligence than their mentors, and partially resort to wild sago for one or two months at the end of the farming cycle.

From the times prior to 1800, we still have a few names and plots, but nothing really articulate enough to allow for a coherent reconstruction. For the second, agricultural period, history is recalled with precision through sung epics, genealogies, and the wars and alliances of boisterous dynasties.

The Bahau, Busang, and Kayan

This important ethnic complex consists of the Bahau of the Middle Mahakam, and the Busang, Uma' Suling, Long-Gelat, and Kayan of the Upper Mahakam.[22] These groups have arrived there in successive waves since the mid-18th century, as their tradition has it, from the northern plateaus of Apo Kayan where they were already practicing swidden agriculture. The Kayan have been thoroughly studied in Sarawak, where they are also present, and also in West Kalimantan.[23] We have only to stress here that these societies are rigidly stratified in named classes and that leadership is strictly hereditary.

---

[20] These groups belong to the same linguistic grouping (see S.A. Wurm & S. Hattori, eds., *Language Atlas of the Pacific Area: Part II: Japan Area, Philippines and Taiwan, Mainland and Insular Southeast Asia* [Canberra: The Australian Academy of the Humanities/Tokyo: The Japan Academy, 1983]). New data led me to reconsider an earlier statement concerning the date of sedentarization of the Seputan and to push it back to the very early 19th century at the latest for the Upper Kasau subgroup of the Seputan.

[21] The Aoheng number now about 2,500. The distribution and population figures of the villages have been much altered, since the Aoheng have recently been subject to government-sponsored *Resetelmen* (Resettlement).

[22] On history of in-migration to the Upper Mahakam area, see a brief outline in my 1980 paper and a more substantial description in my dissertation ("Les nomades forestiers," pp. 301–307, 316–20, 417).

[23] On the Kayan, see J. Rousseau, "The Social Organization of the Baluy Kayan" (Ph.D. dissertation, Cambridge University, 1974), idem., "Kayan Stratification," *Man* 14 (1979): 215–36; idem., *Central Borneo—Ethnic Identity and*

In their oral tradition, genealogies extend over about one dozen generations, and precise detail has been preserved of the migrations from Apo Kayan. Their oral literature is rich in historical epics seemingly referring to events as ancient as the first half of the 18th century.

Collective Memory

Collective memory is an abstract concept, and the ways it proceeds, are not easy to analyze.[24] We have seen above several processes of alteration of the historical narrative. How are, in Borneo, oral tradition—and particularly historical tradition—preserved and transmitted? Relevant socio-economic factors will be reviewed. Then, the question of Bornean peoples' notion of time will be considered.

Preservation and Transmission of the Historical Tradition

Individual factors first intervene. Who is the narrator? There are good narrators, and others who do not have the necessary qualities: some do not have a good memory; others do not socialize enough; others again do not have a good voice or a musical ear. A good narrator, such as it has been described to me by a dedicated listener, has lived in the house or in the surroundings of a famous deceased narrator, has felt like listening many times to the same story and learning it, is fortunate in having a good memory, and has a good and strong voice which is a plus for sung epics. As Jacques Dournes[25] describes it, in mainland Southeast Asia: "A narrator recites, at night; in the audience, a youngster listens, dozes off at times, but the words keep on being recorded in him to the point that, after several auditions, he can reproduce himself the original text."

Familial and neighborhood factors are also relevant. Oral transmission, more often than not, occurs within the family, from grandfather to grandchildren, concerning some forebear or other, and their deeds. Epics, more appreciated and thus gathering a larger audience, reach the singer's wider surroundings.

The social factors are certainly the most important. It has been observed that in groups with a strong social stratification, it is the aristocratic class that is the recipient and guardian of the historical tradition and of the oral tradition in general. There are several reasons for this. One is that tradition is often ritual, and the important ritual functions are ascribed to members of the nobility. Furthermore, for a given ethnic group, history is equated with the history of the reigning family or dynasty. As Ida Nicolaisen[26] notes: "Historical and mythical traditions . . . [are] closely connected to the ruling aristocrats." Then, transmission will preferably take place in these genealogical lines. It should also be stressed that, thanks to the corvée system, the high nobility families live in a relative idleness that allows them to devote much of their time to the arts and letters.

In highly structured societies (states or societies with incipient state formation), like the kingdoms of western Africa, the rulers devolve responsibility for preservation and transmission of the historical tradition to a special category of professional narrators (the *griots*),

---

Social Life in a Stratified Society (Oxford: Clarendon Press, 1990); on their oral literature, see S. Long Lii' and A. J. Ding Ngo, *Syair Lawe', Bagian Pendahuluan* (Yogyakarta: Gaja Mada University Press, 1984).

[24] See M. Halbwachs, *Les cadres sociaux de la mémoire* (1925: Paris/The Hague: Mouton, 1976).

[25] *Forêt, Femme, Folie* (Paris: Aubier-Montaigne, 1978), p. 196.

[26] "Form and Function of Punan Bah Ethno-historical Tradition," *Sarawak Museum Journal* 24, 45 (1976): 65.

whose function is equivalent to that of the official chroniclers at the kings' courts in literate societies.

Finally, modern factors in the current way of life of the ethnic groups under scrutiny must be taken into account. These are detrimental to the preservation of the corpus of oral tradition and, clearly, the young people are no longer motivated to learn it. Although they like to listen to an epic once in a while, they are not always able any more to grasp the esoteric, metaphoric tongue. The use of the tape-recorder might well trigger renewed interest in oral literature. Few people, however, are interested in their group's or village's history, as a heroic or grand past is not any more an emotionally relevant element for most of today's populations, living in the present and facing its daily challenges. History is of little concern to the bulk of the people, mainly because it is not really their history but rather that of their princes, who cling desperately to history to try and maintain their privileges. With social structures largely shattered by the modern world, people tend to look for individual solutions for the future (emigration, trade activities) at the expense of the village's future.

Socio-economic Factors

Collective Memory and Population

The number of individuals forming the community—village or ethnic group—is the most immediately relevant factor in the process of memorization and transmission of oral tradition. The more numerous the community, the more likely it is that individuals with qualities appropriate to a narrator are found. What probability is there of finding a good narrator in a band of thirty people? What opportunity would such a narrator, if any, have to find a gifted novice?

On the other hand, although it cannot be assumed that a small community has no history, it can be postulated that its history is less rich in salient episodes—wars, great expeditions, alliances—than that of a large ethnic group. The latter, besides providing a wide pool of good narrators and a guarantee for successors, offers abundant historical material, since its leaders strived for glory and fame.

Collective Memory and Social Structure

We said that in groups with a strong social stratification, a relative idleness allowed the nobility to keep oral tradition alive. In these groups, there is no differentiation into professional categories, and the narrators are amateurs (thus distinct from the *griots*), who practice their art in their leisure time (or in specific ritual contexts). It is then enough that such leisure time exists.

In these societies, keeping the oral tradition alive is compulsory. As Nicolaisen[27] puts it: "The myth of origin and ethnohistorical tradition are of vital importance for maintenance of identity." The bond of a people to their reigning dynasty, and thus their feeling of ethnic identity, resides in the pride they have in the glorious episodes of their past; that is, the history of their royalty. The princes of the past needed, for their own sake, to maintain this pride, even if they had to induce alterations in the narratives in order, for example, to turn a trouncing into a victory. The nobility of today need badly to keep oral tradition alive and to resort to their forefathers' glory to maintain their hold on their commoners who, in the last decades, have strived to emancipate themselves from their social bond, refusing ritual

---

[27] Ibid., p. 90.

corvées, questioning their leaders' decisions, and simply emigrating. The commoners of the past, working full time to ensure their subsistence, not to mention corvées imposed by the nobility, were not much concerned with learning and transmitting the tradition, restricting themselves to suffering under it. The commoners of today are just not interested in it.

In a small nomadic community, the picture is different. All individuals are equally busy full time with economic activities that are primordial to the group's survival. A *griot* would be an economically unproductive person, something acceptable for a disabled elder but not for a young person, the potential recipient of the oral tradition from the elderly one. Such a community simply could not afford (and indeed, would refuse) to feed idlers.

Notions of Time

Here again is a delicate point. As seen above, the coherent collective memory of a large sedentary group covers at least ten generations (reaching 25 in some documented cases), whereas that of a small nomadic community hardly extends over one century, and sometimes little over a half-century. For example, the Punan Busang cannot remember their history prior to 1900–1920,[28] and the Punan Lusong seem not to recall anything of times prior to 1870.[29] This has been confirmed by several other studies on the Punan (or Penan) groups of Sarawak.[30]

This is certainly due *pro parte* to the factors mentioned above. But we can go further. "The Punans appear to have very little in the way of traditions, and they do not usually have heroes, . . . , or in any way keep alive the past."[31] The same author notes elsewhere:[32] "A Pennan has no sense of time and very little sense of numbers." To say that the nomads have no sense of time is certainly somewhat excessive. It is true, however, that Borneo does not have clear-cut seasons, with the monsoons hardly perceptible. True also that the ripening of wild fruit is erratic, like the wild boars' migrations. Possible time markers along the year for the Punan are the episodic contacts they have with the farming peoples, but these markers are hardly relevant to nomads to whom the agricultural cycle is meaningless.

When recent events are concerned (say, between five years and one generation ago), the Punan are no less competent than the farmers. When I returned among the Busang and Aoheng farmers in 1979, no one was able to recall with precision what year my earlier visit was (1975). If they had taken the pains to compute their successive swiddens, they would have come up with an accurate answer. It is not a new idea to say that the Dayak are not very interested in computing time.

It is in the notion of historic time, the time that is measured in the number of generations, that nomads and farmers differ. This notion exists only when it is supported by a historical tradition which in turn exists only if the society needs it to maintain itself as it stands, to maintain its stratification and its identity. We can then posit the following causal sequence: Existence of a social stratification → need to maintain it → need for a historical tradition → need for a notion of historic time. As it appears that, in Borneo, the correlation

---

[28] D. B. Ellis, "A Study of the Punan Busang," *Sarawak Museum Journal* 20, 40–41 (1972): 237.

[29] Jayl Langub, "Distribution of Penan and Punan in the Belaga District," *Borneo Research Bulletin* 7, 2 (1975): 46; I.A.N. Urquhart, "Some Notes on Jungle Penans in Kapit District," *Sarawak Museum Journal* 5 (1951): 498.

[30] See references in Sellato, *Nomades et sédentarisation*, p. 249.

[31] Urquhart, "Some Notes," p. 497.

[32] I. A. N. Urquhart, "Nomadic Punans and Pennans," in *The Peoples of Sarawak*, ed. T. Harrisson (Kuching: Sarawak Museum, 1959), p. 79

between nomadic hunting-gathering societies and the absence of social stratification (see Note 1) is established for most known cases, it seems consistent that these societies lack a notion of historic time.

So these nomads do remember their recent past leaders but do not care to preserve the memory of a reputed leader in order to maintain or legitimize a social stratification they do not have. Why would they need to learn long genealogies? They have no titles, no functions, even no lands of which they could claim ownership. If "(T)he aristocratic genealogy serves as measurement of time,"[33] we can just as well state that this measurement of time is, within historical tradition, a tool for the aristocrats to maintain their society as it stands, and maintain themselves where their genealogies have placed them. A society of nomadic hunter-gatherers, having traditionally no nobility, does not feel the need to preserve a historical tradition.

Ethnic Identity

A notion of ethnic identity rests on other notions people have of their linguistic, racial, cultural, or territorial affiliation or ascription. Local use of ethnic or other categories or typologies and the problem of ethnonyms tend to blur the picture. The Busang consider themselves ethnically distinct from their Mahakam Kayan neighbors and identify with the Kayan of Apo Kayan, Sarawak, or West Kalimantan, since they speak the true Kayan language originating in Apo Kayan, although they are probably not true ethnic Kayan. Conversely the Mahakam Kayan, although they are true ethnic Kayan from Apo Kayan, speak a language derived from that of their numerous Ot Danum slaves. The Cihan (Tiong Ohang) subgroup of the Aoheng see themselves as primarily Aoheng, because they are ethnically and linguistically Aoheng, but they are also proud to consider themselves Kayan, because their leaders are descended from Kayan nobility and their customs have been Kayanized. The Seputan are proud of practicing the sophisticated *adat* of the Busang and despise the Hovongan, who are really their close ethnic and linguistic kin.

The feeling of ethnic identity likely rests on a varying consideration of these linguistic, geographic, and cultural factors. How is it among the nomads? They move around a lot, often migrating over long distances, and their territorial notions are hazy. Besides, they speak several languages fluently, their own being subject to heavy linguistic influences from neighboring farmers, and they do not seem to have much of a feeling of linguistic identity. Their customs and taboos have been found generally to be either poorly elaborated or borrowed (most often from the large neighboring agricultural groups). This is a common feature among Borneo's hunting-gathering groups. These cultural borrowings do not preclude the existence of another, underlying cultural layer, which is their own but is not easily detectable.[34]

Commonly, hunting-gathering groups have no autonym, and when they do have one, it often is of the "we, human beings" type,[35] which refers more to a rainforest zoological taxonomy than to an ethnic feeling. The nomads of Borneo generally comply to this rule. They have, however, numerous exonyms, referring to river or mountain names and changing in the course of their migrations and according to the various agricultural groups with whom

---

[33] Nicolaisen, "Form and Function," p. 65.

[34] This comment was from A. Testart (1980 personal communication; see also idem, "Pour une typologie des chasseurs—cueilleurs," *Anthropologie et Sociétés* 5, 2 (1981): 177–221. I have developed this idea further for Borneo in *Nomades et sédentarisation* (pp. 251–55) and particularly in a forthcoming paper.

[35] Testart, personal communication.

they are in contact. In such contacts, the nomad defines himself as "Punan," followed by a toponym, in order to position himself in the farmers' typology. He makes no effort to impose his autonym, if any, and does not care about the names applied to him. The name Bukat itself (autonym: BukØt) comes from the ancient name of the Mendalam River (Upper Kapuas basin) and now applies only to communities remaining in this area and those having left recently.

These nomadic groups, we have said, split, move, and change names. Each band goes through its respective history, in various regions, and undergoes influences from various farming groups. In a Borneo which offers "a picture of populations continually *becoming* something else,"[36] each band progressively becomes something other than its cousin band. How, then, can several small bands, having culturally and linguistically evolved along different lines and residing far away from one another, have a feeling of common ethnic identity? How, in a band of thirty persons, can a feeling of ethnicity exist, which might rather be called a familial feeling? Without a strong historical tradition, giving each of these bands the pride of a famous common forebear, a name, or an original territory, ethnic identity seems unable to develop (see Note 1).

Collective Memory and Way of Life

Finally, it appears that it is the way of life that conditions the more or less extensive capacity for collective memory. If we dig further into this, we might say that the way of life determines the need for collective memory and conditions the ability to fulfill this need, and the result is the capacity for collective memory in a given community, which can be measured by its extreme time depth.

Among the groups considered in the course of this study, two polar extremes can be described briefly. The small nomadic band, because of its limited population and, mostly, of its egalitarianism—two inferences from its type of economy—does not need to preserve its historical tradition over long periods. Conversely, a large settled group produces narrators from an idle aristocratic class which inherited a rich oral tradition that it needs to keep alive in order to maintain the group's social structure and identity. To the practice of swidden agriculture and the sedentary habitat is attached a vast set of rites—farming rites, of course, but also purification and funerary rites—that also provide matters for oral tradition and that the nomads appear to ignore.

Between these two poles, the Aoheng and Hovongan constitute mixed types, in two different ways. The Aoheng form a mixed type in a time frame: a period where they lived scattered, probably as hunter-gatherers, is followed by a period of sedentary agricultural economy. It is the same sequence as for the Bukat and Punan, but the transition of the two periods occurred much earlier—around 1820, instead of 1925 for the Bukat and 1960–1970 for the Sarawak Punan. From the second period, we still have a historical tradition as rich as that of the Kayan and Busang, the marginal resort to wild sago having apparently little bearing. From the first period, very little remains.

The Hovongan form a mixed type in a space frame: they have lived and still live a double life. Their need for wild sago leads them to spend an important part of the year as small isolated family groups, with an economy very similar to that of the Bukat before 1925 and to that of some Sarawak Punan to this day. This is particularly interesting. The Hovongan live in two distinct environments, the village and the forest, and in two distinct

---

[36] T. Babcock, "Indigenous Ethnicity in Sarawak," *Sarawak Museum Journal* 22, 43 (1974): 196.

socio-economic contexts, one of the sedentary type—involving a village life, a need for social structure and ethnic identity, problems of influence, leadership, inheritance, and collective decisions and rites, and therefore a need for oral tradition—and the other of the nomadic type, canceling these very same needs. As a result of this double life, as we saw, social organization is hazy and ethnic identity is weak. Here the recourse to wild sago is a factor inhibiting village life, thus limiting the capacity for collective memory, which is similar to that of the Aoheng but inferior to that of the large sedentary groups.

In the studies on the Punan, there is an exception, that of the Punan Aput, whose historical tradition goes back in time to the period when the Kayan were still in Apo Kayan;[37] that is, the second half of the 18th century. Several authors have raised the hypothesis that the nomadic groups of Borneo had been agriculturalists in the past and came to hunting-gathering through a devolutionary process.[38] A study of the extreme time depth, carried out along with one on social organization, might prove helpful in discriminating amongst nomadic groups.

From the above, it appears that we can reasonably, in the context of Borneo, establish the following implications. The existence of social stratification implies the need to maintain it, thus the need for a historical tradition. Practically, the recourse to the historical tradition contributes to maintaining the stratification, which requires the preservation of the historical tradition; thus the greater time depth of collective memory. Conversely, a nomadic hunting-gathering economy with the band as the economic unit determines the absence of social stratification. Then there is no need for a historical tradition nor for a maintenance of the collective memory, hence a shallower time depth. Secondarily, the absence of a historical tradition seems linked to a hazy notion of ethnic identity and to the absence of a notion of historic time.

Table 1 summarizes the major factors of social structure, economy, and way of life for the four ethnic groups under study, and signals without nuance their positive (+) or negative (–) influence on these groups' capacity for collective memory and the resulting extreme time depth.

---

[37] Tuton Kaboy, "The Punan Aput," *Sarawak Museum Journal* 22, 43 (1974): 287.

[38] E.g., Martinoir (cited in J. Rousseau, "Ethnic Identity and Social Relations in Central Borneo," in *Pluralism in Malaysia, Myth and Reality*, ed. J. A. Nagata [Leiden: Brill, 1975]: 37); C. L. Hoffman, "The 'Wild Punan' of Borneo: A Matter of Economics," in *The Real and Imagined Role of Culture in Development: Case Studies from Indonesia*, ed. Michael Dove (Honolulu: University of Hawaii Press, 1988); S. Seitz, "Die Penan in Sarawak und Brunei: Ihre Kultur-historische Einordnung und Gegenwärtige SItuation," *Paideuma* 27 (1981): 275–311. I have dealt at length with this question of *devolution* of farming groups into nomadic groups in several publications ("The Nomads of Borneo: Hoffman and 'Devolution'," *Borneo Research Bulletin* 20, 2 [1988]: 106–20; *Nomades et sédentarisation*, pp. 153–55, 257–62; and "The Punan Question"), and concluded that there was no serious evidence to support the devolutionist theory. In any case, I stressed the total irrelevance of a polar opposition, often found in the literature, between hunting-gathering and paddy-farming economies, and the existence of a continuum of stable mixed subsistence economic systems relying on a combination of wild sago, cultivated tubers, and cultivated rice (*Nomades et sédentarisation*, pp. 216–31).

Table 1. Factors Influencing Collective Memory

Group		Bukat	Hovongan		Aoheng	Busang
Social Factors	Leadership	elected (−)	mixed type		before 1820: ? aft. 1820: heredit.(+)	hereditary (+)
	Social structure	egalitarian	vague (−)		after 1820 (+) rather rigid	very rigid (+)
Economic Factors	Economic unit	nomadic unit 30 persons (−)	village 100 p.	forest 30 p.	village (+) 200–600 pers.	village (+) 200–1,000 p.
	Need for wild sago	bef. 1925: 12 mo (−) today: 6 mo?	8 mo (+)	4 mo (−)	bef. 1820 ?: 12 mo (−) today: 1 mo (+)	nil (+)
Way of Life (Economic Mobility)	Notion of territory	very weak (−)	strong (+)		strong (+)	strong (+)
	Mobility out of territory	strong (−)	weak (+)		weak (+)	very weak (+)
	Mobility in territory	strong (+)	strong (+)		weak (+)	very weak (−?)
Collective Memory	Extreme time depth	1870–1875 nomadic 1870–1925 / settled aft. 1925	1800		1800 nomadic 1800–20 / settled aft. 1820	before 1750
	Known Generations	5 or 6	9		8	11 or 12

THE SECOND LIFE OF BUNG KARNO
ANALYSIS OF THE MYTH (1978–1981)[*]

Pierre Labrousse

"Saya hendak mengepal dunia, ayah"

Sukarno

The assessment of the personality and of the historic role of Sukarno constitutes the theme of an already considerable amount of literature, diverse and sometimes controversial. From the end of the 1920s in the Dutch East Indies his sharp awareness of the colonial system, his political struggle, his exile followed by his sudden rise on the international scene, as well as the rapidity of his decline, alone present the grandeur and excess to feed the popular myths which arose from around 1928.

After March 1966, we are aware of Sukarno's withdrawal from the political scene, of his house arrest under the pretext of an investigation to determine his role in the events of September 30, 1965, of his rather hasty—although declared "national"—funeral, and finally of his passage into purgatorial silence by the official erasing of his historical role—particularly in relation to the birth of the Pancasila—and by the embargo on the republishing of his political writings.

The year 1978, with the announcement of the construction of a funerary complex in Blitar dedicated to the Father of the People (*Bapak Rakyat*), to the Proclaimer of Independence, to the first President of the Republic of Indonesia,[1] marks the end of this period and the officially controlled liberation of Sukarno's memory. Along with pre-election reasons, we can suppose that mystical motives were also at play: commemoration of the first *windu* of his death (eight-year cycle), as well as personal ones: asking forgiveness to Bung Karno (*minta maaf*).

The re-establishment of the memory immediately sparked a surge of commemorative items: articles, popular books sold on the sidewalk, posters, stickers . . . which quickly

---

[*] This article was presented at the Third European Colloquium of Malay and Indonesian Studies, in Naples (June 2–4, 1981). The French version appeared in *Archipel* 25 (1983): 187–214.

[1] See Chronology, p. 177.

forced the government to take authoritarian measures of containment, denouncing the commercialization of the affair.

It is through our best efforts to bring together books published upon this occasion[2]—which are not, strictly speaking, oriented toward a mass audience (reading being a privilege in itself)—as well as newspaper articles—coming for the most part from the Yayasan Idayu, which holds in its possession a remarkable body of documentation[3]—that we have constituted the corpus of our work.

In comparison with the Sukarnian legend, such as it exists in an oral tradition difficult to delimit, it is evident that these texts, liable to various forms of censorship,[4] find themselves at odds with what one might hear in private. Writing does not possess the freedom of oral expression, and the information available today—privileged due to its lack of political (and financial!) risks—concerns Sukarno's birth, his childhood, and the period of independence. After 1957, political references are not officially authorized, so that only family anecdotes, marriages, and his international actions with regard to the Third World persist.

With the above limitations, does the corpus still allow an analysis of the complexity of popular representations of Bung Karno? Certainly it does. First of all from the point of view of diversity—images of the man (his culture, women, suffering, and death)—and then from a perspective more difficult to analyze, that would be the correspondence between certain types of images and certain social groups. Finally, along with the permanence of a particularly Javanese vision of the sovereign, we have determined two other poles toward which the memory of Sukarno still seems attracted—Islam and the New Order. And still beyond this—but in a very fragmentary way in our corpus—we find the claiming of the Sukarnian model by two less homogeneous groups, namely, certain factions of the opposition, and the young people who no longer maintain toward this Father they never knew, the inhibitions of their elders.

To be complete, this study should also have focused on the authors and editors, in order to verify the rumors concerning the intention of these publications: former PNI circles, new opposition, family clan, or simply sensible merchants. To tell the truth, we had neither the time nor the conviction to be able to come up with facts sufficiently established to appear in a publication such as this. Nevertheless, this dimension of the subject does not escape us, but allows only difficult-to-verify intuitions.

1. Supernatural Powers

The idea of political power resulting from the convergence of a personal predestination with supernatural powers can doubtlessly be linked to certain Javanese beliefs, and is still largely shared by the lower strata of Indonesian society. Nor is it surprising that the Javanese, and Java in general, play a particularly active role in the elaboration of the myth. In this vision of power, no rupture of continuity exists between royal and presidential office, nor between mythical ancestry and family descent, and it would be equally easy to find traces of this phenomenon in the current regime as in the Sukarnian legend. The glory of

---

[2] See Bibliography, below, pp. 195-96.

[3] The Yayasan Idayu, which we deeply thank for the welcome we received, collects press clippings as well as iconography relating to Sukarno. It has published a complete bibliography: *Bung Karno, Sebuah bibliografi* (Jakarta: Yayasan Idayu, 1979).

[4] Such as, for example, *Wasiat Bung Karno*, edited by Gunung Agung in 1978.

Chronology of Bung Karno's Revival

June 21, 1970	Death of Engineer Sukarno. National funeral as the Proclaimer of Independence. He is buried in Blitar near his mother. Extinguishment of the judicial action concerning his role during the events of 1965.
January 24, 1978	Before members of the PDI celebrating its fifth anniversary in Solo, Minister of Information Ali Murtopo announces that "Pak Harto, both personally and in his capacity as President of the Republic, has decided to renovate Bung Karno's tomb."
March 4, 1978	Pilgrimage to Blitar by Ali Murtopo and members of a seminar of the East Java PDI. The main principles of the renovation are announced: tomb, oratory chapel, and inscriptions: "Penyambung lidah rakyat, Pemimpin Bangsa Indonesia, Proklamator Republik Indonesia" (Spokesman of the people, Leader of the Indonesian Nation, Proclaimer of the Republic of Indonesia).
May 1978	Family and national squabbles over the site of the tomb. Various proposals regarding the site: close to his mother in Blitar; in a rustic site of the Priangan where he conceived of Marhaenism; in the Monumen Nasional (Monas) in Jakarta. Banning of the book *Wasiat Bung Karno* "Bung Karno's Legacy," edited by Masa Agung. Performance in Yogya by the Kelompok Kampungan of *Putra Sang Fajar* "Son of the Dawn," depicting the life of Bung Karno.
June 1, 1978	June First can be commemorated again as the anniversary of the Pancasila.
June 1, 1978	Preliminary ceremonies at the tomb renovation in Blitar.
June 21, 1978	Inauguration of the funerary complex in Blitar.
August 20, 1979	Exposition of a part of the Bung Karno Collection (paintings and other works of art) at the Taman Ismail Marzurki (15 days; 147,713 visitors).
March 14, 1980	Death of Bung Hatta.
April 4, 1980	Performance of *Putra Sang Fajar* in Jakarta.
May 14, 1980	Death of Fatmawati.
June 21, 1980	Commemoration in Jakarta and in Blitar of the tenth anniversary of Bung Karno's death, of the 100 days since Bung Hatta's death, and of the 40 days since Fatmawati's death.
June 23–27, 1980	Exposition on the theme: Bung Karno dan Asia Afrika "Bung Karno and Asia-Africa" in Semarang (131,500 spectators for the films; 40,835 for the photographic exposition). The exposition was to continue on, with other themes, to Den Pasar and Menado.
August 17, 1980	Inauguration of statues of Bung Karno and Bung Hatta as Proclaimers of Independence in Pegangsaan Timur, by President Suharto.
Sept. 14, 1980	Swara Maharddhika, large-scale performance by Guruh Sukarnoputra.
Sept. 15, 1980	Article by Rosihan Anwar in *Kompas* on the Sukamiskin letters, raising doubts about Sukarno. Arguments in the press.
June 1, 1981	Non-authorized commemoration with Rachmawati at the Gedung Kebangkitan Nasional.
June 15, 1981	In the year following June 1, 1980, 1,458,057 visitors went to meditate at Bung Karno's grave in Blitar.

178 Pierre Labrousse

Bung Karno is thus explainable only by divine interventions on several levels, of which we will later collect premonitory signs—"In Java, there is a prophesy that one day will come a fighting cock crowing in the East, a rooster of mixed blood, born of a hen from Bali and a rooster from Java"[5]—but also by the possession of weapons and other magical objects (*ajimat*, *pusaka*), and by esoteric sciences (*ilmu*), the most superior of which will here be scientific (*ilmiah*), since Sukarno was an engineer.

Photograph of the Javanese-style edifice (with a three-tiered roof symbolizing birth, life and death) which shelters Sukarno's tomb at Blitar.

The Mystery of Origins

On the testimony of even his own mother,[6] the birth of the child was marked by supernatural signs—by the appearance of a comet (*bintang kemukus*) in the East, a "sign of changes in the life of humanity," and by a violent eruption of Mount Kelut, which caused widespread damage.

These extraordinary signs, along with Sukarno's unusual destiny, invalidate somehow the status of the son of Ida Nyoman Rai and Raden Soekemi Sosrodihardjo, following the idea that "great men are brought into the world only through a lineage of great men, since one's character and soul are determined by one's ancestors.... It is impossible that a head of State is not of royal descent."[7] The only exception to this rule, according to the writer cited, would be Ken Arok, an adventurer born of the people, yet if one looks more closely, he may have descended from Brahma....

---

[5] Andjar Any, *Bung Karno siapa yang punya?* (Solo: Badan Penerbit Sasongko Solo, 1978), p. 42.

[6] I.N. Soebagijo, *Idayu Nyoman Rai, Sukarno anakku* (Jakarta: Antar Kota, 1978), pp. 36–37.

[7] Andjar Any, *Menyingkap tabir Bung Karno* (Semarang: Aneka, 1978), p. 6.

Several hypotheses are therefore put forth. Sukarno is either:

—A son of Paku Buwono X, the proof being that all of the names of this monarch's children began with Kus- (Sukarno's first given name was Kusno, changed because he was ill and because he found its overtones unpleasant—*kakus* "toilet," *tikus* "rat").

—A son of Sarinah, the family maid, later immortalized by Sukarno as a symbolic woman of the people. The father would have been a Dutchman working on a Jember plantation, whose son inherited his open and audacious character. Raden Soekemi would thus have agreed to pass the child off as his own son.

—A descendant of Sunan Kalijogo, since Sukarno claimed this filiation in one of his speeches.

—A descendant of the kings of Pajajaran, owing to his affinities with Sunda (Marhaen, Ibu Inggit . . .), his aptitude for learning the Sundanese language, and his choice of Priangan as his final dwelling place.

It is an interesting fact that ancestral ties both natural (Paku Buwono X) and spiritual (Sunan Kalijogo) are found on the same plane. The invention of ancestors serves, of course, not only to legitimate power, but also to designate moral and political models serving as reference.

The Gift of Prophesy (*peramal kelas satu*)

As early as his first speeches, particularly in *Indonesia Menggugat*, Sukarno proclaims his faith in the liberation of Indonesia and announces upcoming major conflicts in the Pacific.[8] The proclamation of independence in 1945, the realization of these national ideals that he had expressed at a moment where the majority of the inhabitants of the Dutch East Indies had not the slightest idea of such a possibility, confirm the prophetic nature of his words and project him into a long line of predictions, Joyoboyo's in particular.

This reinterpretation of Sukarno's persona seems to merge with the rumors which apparently circulated throughout Java around 1930, but of which one also finds echoes in the Surabaya press in 1928, on the imminent arrival of a King of Justice (Ratu Adil Herucokro). The newspaper *Sin Po* (January 13, 1930) spoke of a *Kyai* from Kudus selling talismans (*ajimat*) and announcing major changes, while the journal *Darmokondo* (January 8, 1930) calculated, from an interpretation of a *tembang* from Ronggowarsito, that that year would see extraordinary upheavals.[9] Would this event be Sukarno's trial, and the Ratu Adil Herucokro or Imam Mahdi, Sukarno himself?

Furthermore, Sukarno also compared himself to the character of the *wayang*, Kroksono (who becomes Prabu Baladewa), abandoning his asceticism to Argoso in order to descend the mountain and bring a magical weapon destined to reunite clashing factions. Then he is kept in the background and finally reappears. The relationship to the theme of the Bharatayuda—as opposed to a New Order which would be more Ramayana-esque[10]—constitutes a popular belief regarding the Sukarnian period, since the president's fate is in keeping with

---

[8] For example in the article "Indonesianisme dan Pan-Asiatism," in *Suluh Indonesia Muda*, 1928, reprinted in *Dibawah Bendera Revolusi*, 1963, pp. 73–77.

[9] Andjar Any, *Bung Karno siapa yang punya?* p. 94.

[10] See G.J. Resink's address at the Tenth Congress of Asian Historians, Yogyakarta, 1974.

Baladewa's, in short, "satu nujuman yang cespleng sekali" (an absolutely effective prediction), as one author writes.[11]

But these Sukarnian prophesies have, in comparison with Joyoboyo or Rongowarsito, a further and higher dimension. They are the "result of neither nocturnal meditations, nor astrological calculations, nor consultations of a crystal ball."[12] They are, for the first time, founded upon scientific analysis and the reading of books, modern predictions. Here again, Sukarno, at the same time prophet and prophesy of the Ratu Adil, marks the era with his innovative genius.

The Thaumaturgic President (*ajimat, pusaka*)

To the characteristics we have touched upon above—royal lineage, prophesies of the *pujangga*—popular belief adds a multitude of traits which fall within the realm of the magical powers of *dukun* or *pawang*, and of which we can only give here the examples which seem to us the most significant:

—In Bali, the people attribute to Sukarno power over rain, symbol of fertility. His visits were indeed regularly accompanied by storms and beneficial rains.

—As a child, his grandfather made him lick the wounds of the sick, which healed. The remarkable power of his tongue was "like a meteoric iron that chased away illnesses. It can even drive back the Dutch."[13]

—He had the eyes of the mythical cat Candramawa. This is confirmed by the American ambassador, Howard P. Jones, in his memoirs *The Possible Dream*, where he mentions Sukarno's magnetic gaze.

—He was capable of improvising patronymics for the infants who were often presented to him.

—The discovery of the Pancasila also attests to his status as one chosen by God.

All sorts of parallel speculations have developed concerning protective objects which guarantee his power and legitimate his superiority. These rumors are all the more fertile in the collective imagination since the possession of such objects is, by tradition, discreet, and often secret. Sukarno would thus have possessed:

—A fragment of *besi kuning* (magic iron) obtained in East Java and coming from a magical weapon of Menakjinggo, which, as the story goes, was broken into pieces and fell into the possession of several elected officials.

—Aji Lembu Sekilau, name of a magical iron which protected Gajah Mada and rendered him invulnerable.

—A *pusaka* kris from his Balinese great-grandmother who had dipped it in the blood of Dutchmen.

—The military cane that he always held in his hand was made from *pucang* wood[14] from Kalak, near Pacitan. This wood has the distinctive characteristic, when reflected in water, of

---

[11] Andjar Any, *Menyingkap tabir Bung Karno*, p. 37.

[12] Ibid.

[13] Ibid., p. 42.

[14] A species of tree.

taking on the form of a swimming snake. What is more, this stick contained a little kris inside it.

These objects refer to famous personages both real and legendary, each associated with various forms of power: Menakjinggo is linked to the idea of a violent conquest of power, Gajah Mada is the symbol of unification, and the Balinese kris refers to the resistance against colonialism.

It must be noted that after Sukarno's death, the rumors were revived by the mysterious disappearance of all these objects and by the problem of the legacy. Although Sukarno had few personal possessions, and his collection of paintings could be considered presidential and therefore belonging to the State, the fate of his library and of the wardrobe where he kept at least his kris and his stick, which everybody would have been able to see, has not been officially clarified. The coffin in which he was placed during the three hours following his death, before it was changed for a model more befitting his rank, is piously conserved by the official morticians (*paling hitam*), for a future museum, despite numerous purchase offers. The same mystery enshrouds the several canvasses painted in Flores, which are priceless. Some of them belong to the collection of Adam Malik, but as for the others, it seems that the owners prefer to remain anonymous. The books of his son Guntur (*Bung Karno dan Kesenangannya*)—who was only able to save his father's *peci*, pen, razor, and cologne (Shalimar de Guerlain!)—continue to sustain, more mundanely, this cult of objects.

2. The Great Lover (*pecinta agung*)

"Pecinta agung, pecinta keindahan, pecinta kesenian, pecinta persatuan, pecinta wanita."[15]

The extent of the literature devoted to this dimension of Sukarno's personality is what most strikes the Western observer, for it quite evidently goes beyond simple anecdote in order to portray the vital syncretic vigor that was the very personality of Sukarno, and which seemed to want at times to encompass all creation. Love, the essential component of his persona, often gives the impression of knowing no limits; and it must be emphasized that women were only one aspect of this. It is the sign of conquest, of success, and it also bears the mark of creative genius and therefore of God. But it would not have incited such a mass movement had it not been placed under the heading of conviviality. The Indonesian people are, after all, associated with the panache of his career, and were drawn into this vast psychodrama where elected officials—friends, artists, women, and common people who have but one name (Sarinem, Samiun, Marhaen . . .)—are pulled out of anonymity and exposed, through the president's desires, to public admiration.

The Women

That Sukarno appeared to get carried away by the ease of his success with women, due as much to his fascinating personality as to his position as president, is a rather well-known fact. But the indulgence and admiration which come up in the analyzed works suggest, first of all, that his behavior is hardly perceived as different from that which is authorized by the tradition of the Sultan or the Susuhunan. Secondly, these women are seductive, and espe-

---

[15] "The great lover, lover of beauty, lover of the arts, lover of women," or rather, The Great Lover, according to Hartini, in Andy Any, *Bung Karno siapa yang punya?* p. 237.

cially appear in public as reinforcing the presidential aura, through complex signs that we can attempt to suggest here:

—These women contribute to the geographic and national dimension of the hero: with Utari, Tjokroaminoto's daughter, in the very specific urban context of Surabaya; with the Sundanese Inggit Garnasih; with Fatmawati from Bengkulu; with Haryati and Hartini from Java; the young Menado women Yurike Sanger and Kartini Manoppo; and finally with Ratna Dewi Sri, who represents the outside world. They are thus points in the national space, a space unified through the person of Sukarno.

—These same alliances are read in an historical perspective. Utari symbolized the nuptials between the revolutionary movement in all her youth and purity, with the seizing of Indonesian consciousness at Surabaya. Inggit is the companion of difficult moments, of prison, of exile in Endeh and Bengkulu. Fatmawati is the result of the relations between Sukarno and the Muslim circles of Bengkulu; she is the Mother as well, with an image of moral uprightness when she falls back on her family life at the time of her husband's escapades. The others appear caught in the whirlwind of younger and younger women who punctuate the accelerated personalization of the regime, until its loss. Lastly, with regard to Ratna Dewi Sri, one recalls the Putri Campa or Putri Cina,[16] by which the rulers of long ago reinforced their alliances with the North,

—Obviously, these women also endow the image of the president with the dimension of virility, of fertility (*rejeki*), of generous seed, as well as with the analogy of the Javanese *banteng* of the PNI.

Art and Beauty

The privileged relationship that Sukarno had with art is perpetuated today by his collections, of which the most famous is that of Indonesian paintings. The first partial expositions (see the Chronology above) enjoyed a considerable public success. Artists and writers—like Sitor Situmorang, who wrote the preface to the catalogue *Bung Karno dan Seni* "Bung Karno and Art"[17]—can recall memories of the grand presidential tradition, when they were invited to speak about their arts' contribution to national expression, and when their paintings decorated the walls of the palaces in Jakarta and Bogor.

Sukarno's personality also appears entangled with the vast renovation movement which aroused the Affandis, Sudjojono, Hendra Gunawan, and Henk Ngantung as interpreters of Indonesia's deep realities and aspirations. Authors of the period stress, along with the president's passion for art (*keranjingan*), the public and social aspect of the collection: "Buying and collecting paintings, works of art, is not, after all, the same thing as hoarding gold or diamonds."[18] The motivation of the president's choice of canvasses was not based upon any aesthetic quality or upon overly personal tastes, but rather upon the works' aptitude in expressing an authentically national tradition, which thereby associated artists to the country's construction.

Sukarno's passion for social art is further evoked with respect to all monumental forms: "Architecture, urban planning, the environment, and the organization of space are various

---

[16] "Daughter, princess of Champa, of China"—we found this allusion twice.

[17] Edited by the Yayasan Bung Karno on the occasion of the presentation of the collections, Jakarta, 1979.

[18] Ibid., p. 27.

The Family

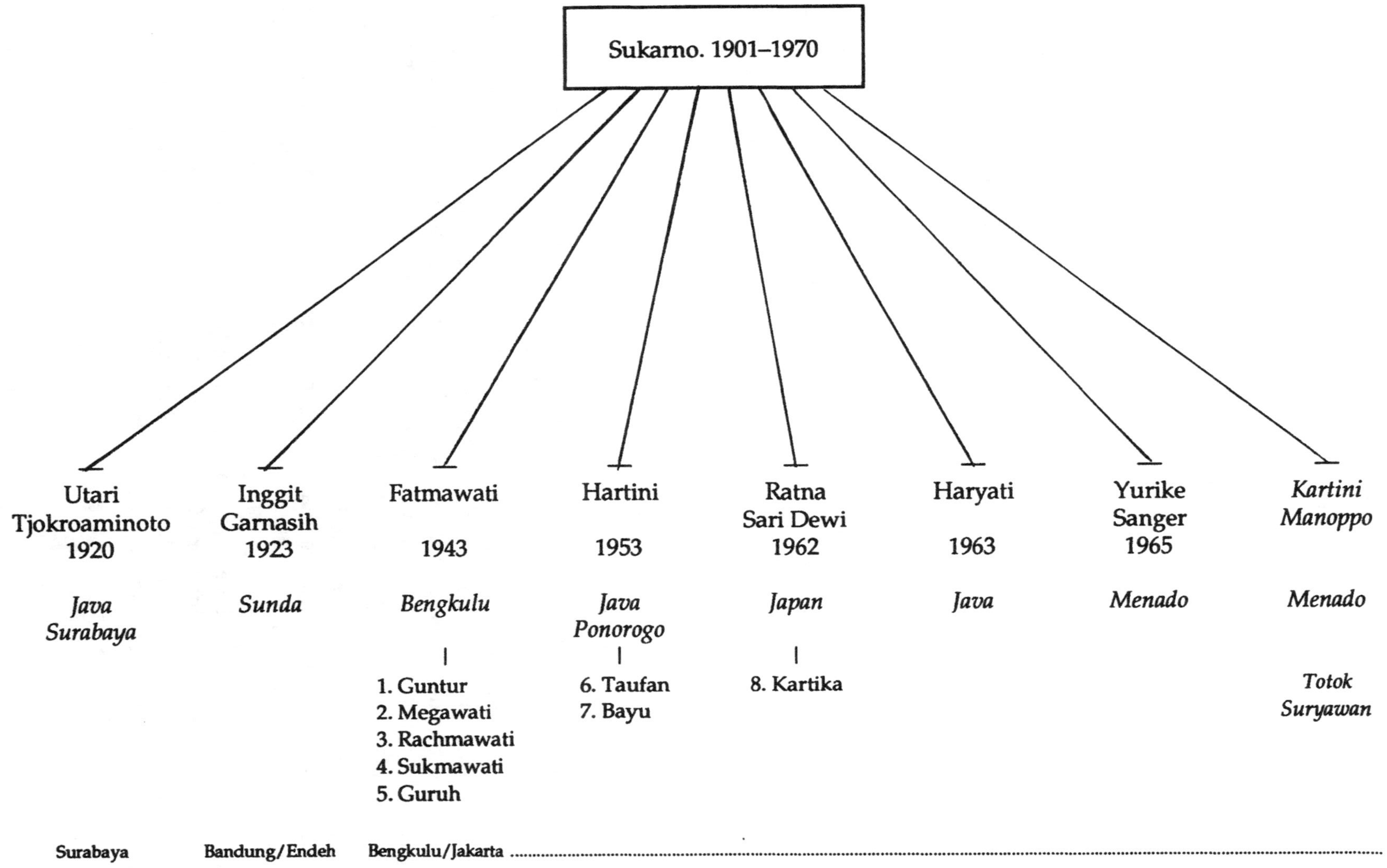

Utari Tjokroaminoto 1920	Inggit Garnasih 1923	Fatmawati 1943	Hartini 1953	Ratna Sari Dewi 1962	Haryati 1963	Yurike Sanger 1965	Kartini Manoppo
Java Surabaya	*Sunda*	*Bengkulu*	*Java Ponorogo*	*Japan*	*Java*	*Menado*	*Menado*
		—	—	—			—
		1. Guntur	6. Taufan	8. Kartika			Totok Suryawan
		2. Megawati	7. Bayu				
		3. Rachmawati					
		4. Sukmawati					
		5. Guruh					

All married to Sukarno, 1901–1970.

Surabaya   Bandung/Endeh   Bengkulu/Jakarta

aspects of the prolongation of Indonesian tradition in Bung Karno."[19] Insofar as these preoccupations strive toward harmony between human construction and the natural environment, they recall—through a mixture of reason, emotion, and romanticism—certain traits of Javanese mysticism. Foreign observers, Sitor continues,[20] make a misinterpretation when they see the Sukarnian attitude based upon the mysticism of the *wayang*, since it leads there only by way of certain analogies.

Whatever the case may be, in 1979, Indonesians—particularly those from Jakarta—realized that all of their surroundings bore the mark of Sukarno. His annotations on the sketches of the statue of the Liberation of Irian Barat, or of the Tugu Selamat Datang (Statue of Welcome), prove his direct intervention. The National Monument (Monas, symbol of the city), the beltway highway (described in the 1960s as a "folly of grandeur"), the perspective from Kebayoran to Thamrin, the Hotel Indonesia, the Wisma Nusantara, the Sarinah department store (quite a name!), Senayan, Ancol, and the Great Mosque Istiqlal—in short, the entire present-day organization of the capital's space which corresponds to the central idea of "going to the sea" (*melaut*)—reflects the will of the "Architect of Indonesia." For a decade, Indonesians believed they had forgotten Bung Karno, when in reality he never ceased being there, in the scenery of their everyday lives.

Love of Life

Lastly, we have found recurring the idea of the love of life, love of peace, and horror of spilled blood—all of which suggest that the political turmoils had faded from memory, and which impose today the image of a Sukarno forever seeking unity and convergence through raising debates. Beneath the surface lie the events of 1965–1966, and one is led to believe—according to these authors—that they are the opposite extreme of what Sukarno had always wished, and consequently outside his responsibility.

Several anecdotes are cited to support this thesis:

—The pardon of the AURI pilot who machine-gunned the palace.

—The pardon of most of the dissidents engaged in the PRRI.

—Sukarno respected life and never did any hunting. He prevented the destruction of birds' nests—and even anthills!—in the Jakarta palace.

One of the most interesting themes one finds is that of the president's non-violence. It will be recalled that marhaenism is founded upon peace, harmony, and autonomy, as opposed to other doctrines doubtless considered as more aggressive. Sukarno had high ideals for his country, and the path he proposed for the future was a collective progress, without exploitation of one class by another.

The recurrence of this theme merits sketching out an explanation. The first fact, vaguely expressed, seems to be a refusal to imagine Sukarno's implication in the troubles of 1965, entirely rejected as the responsibility of the Communists. The period before 1965 appears in contrast as particularly peaceful and idealistic, while in fact it was often characterized by sporadic verbal violence. These images appear strongly conditioned by certain types of reactions to the economic situation of the time, which is perhaps now considered as socially more conflictive than before, due to the widening gaps in standards of living. The virtues which we attribute to Sukarno are precisely those which are not found in today's regime,

---

[19] Ibid., p. 25.
[20] Ibid.

Advertisement for Guruh Sukarno Putra's film (above), *Untukmu Indonesiaku* "For you, my Indonesia," with Guruh. Text upper left: "Hey, you young Indonesians, come see this film. One of the rare films that will make you proud!" Bottom line text: "In this film, you will be carried away by the eternal nostalgia of Bung Karno and Fatmawati in the company of the major international star Marlon Brando" (the meeting with Marlon Brando comes from a film on Sukarno's visit, at the time of his passing through Hollywood).

and their idealization may just as well constitute an unconscious escape route, a veiled critique of present injustices.

3. The Tragedy of Sukarno

Parallel to the exaltation of the hero and to the image of success, another portion of this popular literature plays upon the register of pity (*kasihan*), of misfortune—first on the level of compassion, when it concerns the pains and hardships of Sukarno's parents in the raising of their son, with the image of the poor family, thrifty and virtuous, making sacrifices in order to ensure their son's academic and social success. Then, on a second level, we find the image of misery and solitude with the Sukamiskin prison, the exile to Endeh and Bengkulu. Lastly, we encounter the tragic horror and irony of fate which has it that, as B.M. Diah writes, "He died under a free government of the Republic of Indonesia, for the independence of which he had fought with all his might."[21] Behind the image of the brilliant young man, of the engineer's success, of the president bestowed with titles, honors, and decorations as "Great Leader of the Revolution," remain quite alive the edifying clichés of the poor schoolboy, studying by candlelight at Tjokroaminoto's house, of the prisoner, of the exile, and finally of the man with dulled senses, in sandals and an undershirt, who ended his life under house arrest, alone and cut off from "this people whom he had loved so much."

---

[21] Syamsu Hadi, ed., *Tragedi Bung Karno* (Jakarta: Pustaka Simponi, 1978), p. 105.

A Life Full of Privations (*hidup serba kekurangan*)

The anecdotes covering Sukarno's youth are innumerable. For the most part they are taken from his mother's and sister's memoirs,[22] then amplified and reinterpreted under titles like: *Miskin di waktu kecil melarat di masa muda* "Poor in his childhood, needy in his youth";[23] *Segunung penderitaan di masa kecil* "A mountain of suffering in his childhood";[24] *Sengsaranya selangit* "Infinite suffering."[25]

It is known that, even if his parents endured doing without upon several occasions to ensure their son's future, Sukarno's youth—although very close to the people—was rather far from the poverty described in order to move the reader to pity. It was composed, rather, of thrift (Raden Sukarno was the director of a school and had bought a coconut grove, after which Sukarno's studies at THS in Bandung were paid for by Poegoeh) and especially of a sensible orientation (HBS, Tjokroaminoto), and lastly, of a great deal of individual energy. One must wonder, then, what the development of all of these childhood episodes signifies; for example those we have chosen from a comic book called *Bung Karno Putra Sang Fajar* "Bung Karno, Son of the Dawn":[26]

—The illnesses, malaria, and dysentery, which pushed him into changing his name from Kusno to Sukarno.

—A childhood of misfortune and suffering, like Abraham Lincoln's.

—Work consisting of pounding rice each morning in order to save one cent for his parents.

—He does not have the money to buy firecrackers on the day of Lebaran.

—His father is angry with him when he knocks down birds' nests.

—He is beaten by his father when he abandons watching over drying rice to play in the rice fields.

—His first love-affair with a young Dutch girl.

—The windowless room without electricity at Tjokroaminoto's house.

In the book's introduction, Guntur writes: "Children must know how the leaders of days past lived, how they exhausted their strength and their time to attain Indonesia's independence in order to understand the real meaning of the Message of the People's Suffering."

Two aspects dominate this version of Sukarno's childhood. First, the idea of necessary suffering, of poverty on the level of the people's, with which most readers identified. Then the idea that from this suffering develops, over a historic duration, a climb toward a better future, that of Amanat Penderitaan Rakyat. These true anecdotes have the function of appealing to the common reader right where he is, at the humblest rank of society, and making him follow the hero along the path of individual energy which could be his own, toward the heights. In relation to the theses of divine predestination mentioned earlier, this interpretation of the merits of personal effort refers to a notion of Man that is, if not more

---

[22] See Bibliography below.

[23] S. Saiful Rahim, *Bung Karno masa muda* (Jakarta: Antar Kota, 1978), p. 32.

[24] Erka, *Bung Karno, Kepada Bangsaku* (Semarang: Aneka, 1978), p. 128.

[25] Andjar Any, *Bung Karno siapa yang punya?* p. 129.

[26] M. Ali S., *Bung Karno putra sang fajar* (Jakarta, 1979), with an introduction by Guntur Soekarno.

secularized, at least more individual and modernistic. But what is the impact of this moral in the Indonesian society of today?

The Solitary Death

Today, the context of Sukarno's death is still enveloped in mist (*kabut*), on account of his retreat from the political scene and the rarity of last testimonies, which are seldom found outside his close family. It is also full of shadowy areas, unanswered questions, and ambiguities. Was the president directly implicated in the 1965 coup? Was there any collusion with the PKI? Certain articles recall that no proof or clear answers have been given,[27] and that the investigation built up around his involvement appeared to be intended more to keep it in the background than to shed real light upon the subject. With time, political and economic critiques have faded away. Some representatives of the 1966 generation admit the whole truth. A part of Bung Karno thus emerges in the collective memory of Indonesians under the heading of suffering (*dia banyak menderita*), of the victim (*korban*), and of solitude. A parallel with Napoleon is even drawn (the French are admired for having brought his ashes back with great pomp from St. Helene and placed them in Les Invalides, for having built the Pantheon, and for knowing how to honor great men). And one could, concerning Bung Karno, apply the very terms of Chateaubriand: "His renown is for us brought about by his misfortune; his glory benefited from his unhappiness."

The confused situation in which Sukarno died "accused but not condemned," causes the Indonesians of today to question themselves with a bad conscience, with deep-seated doubt, and a guilt complex. "All of this is our fault as a nation, if one goes by the axiom according to which a nation only gets the leaders it deserves."[28] Moreover, "when 99% of cultivated Indonesians only thought of living comfortably under the colonial period, he spent all of his time struggling against colonialism," the same author adds, while Nasution declares: "Bung Karno was already in prison for Indonesia's independence before I had any idea about the fight for Independence."[29] To this are added doubts concerning the quality of medical care given to him at the end of his life. The physical suffering he endured makes his destiny appear like a calvary with mystical resonances, a martyr.

Another path for freeing oneself of this nuisance of a death consists of aestheticizing it through the fable of the creator devoured by his creation: "He attained his ideals only to be devoured by them afterwards."[30] It is true that everything in the Sukarnian lifestyle recalls the image of the fire, and of a flamboyant life ending in sacrifice. He once said of himself, "I feel like a firebrand among hundreds and thousands of others in an immense blazing furnace. I have given a little to this fire, but I have been devoured by it."

We have also found through analyzing the spirit of popular compassion, certain traits of the suffering of heroes in Indonesian novels, which originally develop upon the feeling of social leveling, with the contrast here between past power and a morally miserable end, in the expiation of a man who was great due to his superhuman qualities, but who dies of his human failings. But we especially find tragedy in the image of the final solitude of an individual definitively cut off from his own and from his people. A solitary end all the more poignant since all of Bung Karno's life had only had meaning through the contact and the

---

[27] This is one of the main themes of B.M. Diah's article in *Tragedi Bung Karno*.
[28] Ibid., p. 115.
[29] *Sonata* 112 (August 1978): 10.
[30] This theme is quoted as a chapter heading and on the back cover of the book, *Tragedi Bung Karno*.

expression of this Indonesian people (*penyambung lidah rakyat*), which nobody contests as being the grand passion of his existence.

4. The New Man (*manusia baru*)

The return of the concept of *manusia baru*—"new man"—with respect to the leader of the Orde Lama may seem rather paradoxical. However, at this end of the 1970s, which are terminating in a certain moroseness, intellectual circles are making their disenchantment known, and the students—who did not live through the last moments of the Sukarnian regime—are asking themselves questions. To ontological questions as well as dialectical questions, one realizes that all the answers already exist in Sukarno: on foreign imperialism, on national solidarity, and on the conception of power (*kepemimpinan*) in Indonesia. These answers contrast more and more with those supplied by the current regime, and therefore appear as a possible alternative. At the level of discourse as well as action, the Sukarnian model thus finds itself once again available for various attempts at recuperation.

The Builder (*tukang membangun*)

We have already touched upon the realization of Sukarnian omnipresence in the decisions concerning urban planning in Jakarta.[31] But in fact, all the touching scenes of the traditional family life of his childhood—reading in his father's school library; the invitation to Tjokroaminoto's house; the diploma in engineering from the THS in Bandung; the participation in an architect's office with Roosseno—also bring out the image of the studious will, of the zeal toward work, in short, of the *pribumi* effort and aptitude for enterprise (*berdikari*). On the one hand, there is of course the political agitator, but on the other is the determination with which he tackles his studies, an ambition for knowledge which one could opportunely recall today for the students of the ITB.

In a book already old yet still available, Solichin Salam,[32] a well-known and prolific writer, published a list of the books from Sukarno's library, a list of his 224 written works and itemized speeches, as well as of his 26 honorary doctorates, the last being from Universitas Muhammadiyah of Jakarta in Science and the Unity of God. The inflationary aspect of this rain of titles (to which must be added over twenty decorations) has faded today, and the panegyrists only retain from it the mark of an immense knowledge.

This knowledge was certainly the result of a great will, but particularly stressed is the pursuit of assimilation, the Indonesianization of foreign elements. Essentially tactical, it demonstrates that Sukarno assimilated this knowledge only to better defend himself against foreign aggression, and to succeed in battling it with his own weapons, by finding and facing foreign challenges, a purely Indonesian response. This superiority complex—found in reflections such as "You have nuclear weapons, but we have Art" for the benefit of the Americans, or for the benefit of the Soviets, telling them that their revolution is of minor consequence compared to the Indonesian Revolution[33]—evidently allows the youth of the 1978 generation to remain dreamers.

---

[31] See p. 184.

[32] Solichin Salam, *Bung Karno Putera Fadjar*.

[33] Cited again by Diah, in *Tragedi Bung Karno*.

OPINION POLL
of the visitors at the exposition *Bung Karno dan Seni*
Jakarta. August 1979. (550 responses).

Excerpts from the 14 questions:

10. You came to this exposition because:

a.	Bung Karno is the first President of the Republic	15%
b.	You feel nostalgic about him (*rindu*)	11%
c.	His collections are beautiful	8%
d.	By curiosity (*sekedar penasaran*)	2%
e.	You want to understand who Bung Karno really was	56%
f.	For want of anything better to do	1%
g.	You like him	15%
h.	Other reasons	15%

14. What are your impressions?

a.	Admiration (*kagum*)	39%
b.	Enthusiasm (*bersemangat*)	16%
c.	Sadness (*sedih*)	3%
d.	Happiness (*gembira*)	5%
e.	Emotion (*terharu*)	18%
f.	Pride (*bangga*)	40%
g.	Mundane impression (*biasa-biasa saja*)	2%
h.	Discontent (*tidak senang*)	0%
i.	Others	9%

This concept of the new man, therefore, allows greater importance to be given to the president as engineer, accentuating his education by individual effort and the Sukarnian participation in the construction of the country, thus erasing the aspects of his political action currently judged undesirable. Nor is it surprising that Frans Seda could remark in the visitors' book at the Bung Karno exposition: *"Juga dia telah membangun"* (He, too, has built).

Islam on the Move

If the relations between Sukarno and the Muslim parties were often conflict-ridden, and if some aspects of his personal nature—like his taste for festivals, or his participation in certain mystical ceremonies (in Kalibata, for example)—were suspected of being tinged with paganism or a return to Hindu tradition,[34] it nonetheless remains that among the multiplicity of facets of his persona, many of them are still susceptible to drawing enthusiastic support from the upholders of an innovatory Islam.

In fact, Sukarno never missed the opportunity to proclaim—among his many alliances—his tie to Islam. And it is in this perspective that his exile in Endeh and Bengkulu lends itself to being interpreted as part of the fight for a renovation of Islam. Today one would call it "secularization" (*sekularisasi*). Over this period, he kept up a regular correspondence with T.H. Hassan—a professor from Bandung—on Islamic problems, deplored the ignorance and conservatism of the *kyai* of Endeh, and had numerous debates with people from the Mohammadiyah of Bengkulu. The authors we have studied do not neglect to recall Sukarno's various declarations against the *taklid*, seen as "narrow-mindedness, blind and short-sighted belief," and on the idea of a dynamic Islam, often taken in substance from Ataturk: "Islam

---

[34] An accusation made partiucularly in the Constituent Assembly debates. See *Pantjasila, Trente années de débats politiques en Indonésie* (Paris, 1981), p. 130.

does not drive people to sit around all day, to dream in mosques, to say one's beads over and over again. Islam is a fight (*Islam adalah perjuangan*)."[35]

One book, *Bung Karno, Milik Rakyat Indonesia*, by someone named Bung Mawi,[36] presents itself as a Penilaian Ummat Islam terhadap Pribadi Bung Karno "Judgment of the Muslims on the Personality of Bung Karno," and constitutes a sort of apologia of Bung Karno's superiority, thanks to divine intervention. This book's emphasis organizes itself around the following themes:

—Bung Karno believed in the unicity of God (*jiwa ketuhanan yang Maha Esa*), unicity here confused with Islam, with the Nation, and with the Pancasila. Unlike some universities rather embarrassed by their conferral of honorary doctorates before 1965, Bung Mawi does not renounce that of Doktor Ilmu Tauhid.[37]

—The elevation of Sukarnian ideals to attain independence for the country.

—The never-ending struggle (*tidak menegal lelah*) for fighting not only against colonialism and imperialism, but especially against feudalism.

—His audacious (*berani*) attitude which consisted of designating his enemies outright, to bring them down certainly, but also to confer their existence on them by naming them. This courage conflicts, of course, with the latent mistrust with which the Muslim opposition is surrounded today.

—Bung Karno had a moral doctrine which, through struggling, gave life a new meaning and oriented time toward a better future, without bending to "any man or any myth, because Islam forbids it."[38] All of these remarks hinge upon the following idea: God had given Sukarno superior qualities, but also human weaknesses. Thus, in the supernatural and divine nature of the Sukarnian revolutionary dynamic, as in his fall from power due to all-too-human weakness, Muslims find the familiar apologetic terrain of their religion. Sukarno's destiny, therefore, constitutes a magnificent parable of divine greatness and power. To the last man, Indonesia's Muslims have the greatness to respond, like Hamka, with forgiveness: "I am bound to the promise of Allah which says that, even if the amount of sins is infinite, provided that one asks forgiveness, he will be forgiven by Him."[39] The Muslims devote themselves to taking over as the holder of universal ideals.

5. The Images of Power (*kepemimpinan*)

It is also appropriate to wonder as to the basis of, in the years studied herein, the repeated evocation of the characteristics of authority (*sifat-sifat kepemimpinan*). Neither the disenchantment of Indonesian society, nor governmental action for the training of veritable corporate chiefs—which have provoked the appearance on the market of all sorts of evaluation tests and methods for achieving success—suffice to explain the return to the Sukarnian

---

[35] this extract of a 1936 letter is reprinted in Soewarto, *Kejayaan dan saat-saat akhir Bung Karno* (Jakarta: Gunung Jati, 1978), p. 71.

[36] Jakarta: Rose Group, 1978. Bung Mawi still claims to be *Putra Petani, Pencinta Tanah Air*.

[37] This was the last honorary doctorate degree given to Sukarno "dalam falsafat Ilmu Tauhid," by the Universitas Muhammadiyah, August 3, 1965, in Jakarta.

[38] Bung Mawi, *Bung Karno milik rakyat Indonesia*, p. 48.

[39] "Kenang-kenangan Buya Hamka. Pernah jadi teman, pernah jadi lawan Bung Karno," in *Sonata* 110 (July 1978): 69. It basically concerns an article published in *Pedoman*, July 25, 1970.

model. Apart from these contingencies, we should also stress the permanence of a more particularly Javanese questioning (and for good reason!) on the morality of power and the qualities suitable for a leader of the people (*pemimpin rakyat*).

The Relationship with History

Sukarno's ancestry places him in a great anticolonialist historical tradition. Through his mother, he receives the heritage of the Balinese resistance and the Perang Puputan. Through his father's line, he is the guardian of the soul of the Javanese resistance embodied in Nyi Ageng Serang, a woman who fought beside Diponegoro.[40]

In this perspective, Sukarno—who did not need to remake his own genealogy—finds himself at the confluence of the ancient histories of Bali and Java, a place predestined for a new historic destiny; and it is exactly this which seems to legitimize him in the popular tradition which, unlike ours, does not distinguish between myth and history.

The Relationship with the People

The manner in which Sukarno calls out directly to the masses—haranguing them, making them participate directly in the psychodramas of his grand ideological geneses—remains for all Indonesians who knew him, a vibrant memory of which all the works testify: "The people would have continued to acclaim Bung Karno if he had asked them to eat stones rather than receive the aid of the United States."[41] This feeling of being associated with action, of being called to witness, certainly represents the essential change in the practice of power in Java in the time of Sukarno. And the temptation is strong to mention here the very fashionable notion of the "spectacle State," as if every State was not precisely a spectacle whose layout and changes can only be revealing.

This privileged relationship with the people has a particular dimension as well, for it is marked by generosity, conviviality, and love. The gift he made in the appearance of his person to the people (*dia banyak memberikan kepada kami*), the love of the homeland (*cinta pada tanah air*), the idea of sacrifice (*pengorbanan*) that Nasution himself willingly recognizes, gives to the already semi-legendary personage an exceptionally human and close connotation. His inventiveness in ideological matters is constantly raised, at least within the authorized limits: nationalism, active neutrality, Marhaenism, and especially Pancasila, which has demonstrated its quality, since it has stood the test of time, since it is more than ever the "source of all sources" (*sumber dari segala sumber*). Although the rehabilitation of his ideas does not go beyond 1950, with the principal speeches of August 17—from *Sekali merdeka tetap merdeka* "Once free, always free"(1946), to *Dari Sabang sampai Merauke* "From Sabang to Merauke"(1950)—this genius of ideas (*pintar menyusun gagasan*) is more than ever living in the memories, as well as in certain themes, which still stir people into action.

Lastly we must classify under this same aspect the titles such as *Keluarga Sukarno tidak ada yang kaya* "Nobody in Sukarno's family is rich" or "Sukarno never gave any important post to a family member," or the supposedly forthcoming memoirs of Manggil, who reports that the president had dreamed of buying himself a house, but did not have enough money.[42] All of these anecdotes, passed on, transformed, add to the familiarity that Sukarno

---

[40] See Mashoed Haka, *Dunia Nyi Ageng Serang, Wanita pejuang bangsa* (Jakarta, 1976).

[41] *Tragedi Bung Karno*, p. 112.

[42] Announced in *Sinar Harapan*, March 29, 1981, p.1.

Genealogy of Sukarno

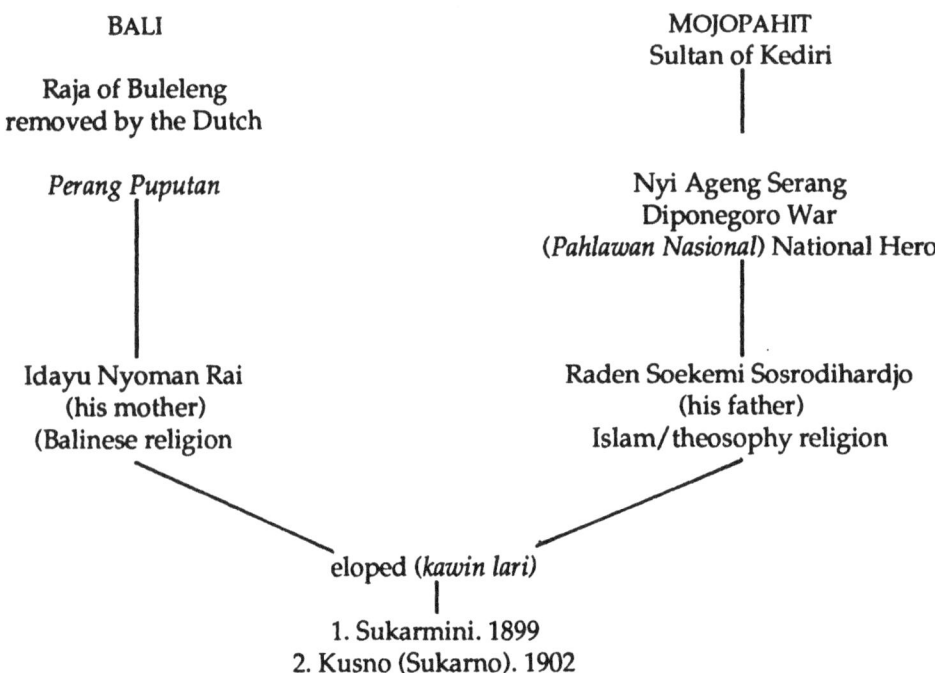

NB. The descent of Sukarno's father from Nyi Ageng Serang is clearly indirect.

inspired in the Indonesian people, and for which the absence of the money barrier is retrospectively considered particularly sensitive.

The Regard of the Outside World

The photos so often reproduced of his meeting with the Pope, with Kennedy, with Sihanouk—not forgetting his wax image at Madame Tussaud's, between Gandhi, de Gaulle, and Castro, which has since, however, been removed—also maintain the legend of the leader of the Third World, for this international recognition has an essential function. Indeed, to exist, to be Indonesian and independent, naturally amounts to being recognized as such in the eyes of the world. It is the duplication of the regard of the other which confirms, through the person of Sukarno, the very existence of Indonesia, which, thanks to him, is considered, named, and recognized as such (*bangsa bernama*).

By the same token, articles like "Bung Karno di mata para penulis Barat,"[43] contribute to the reflection, through the existence of the president, of the image of an Indonesia finally raised to a level of dignity and speaking on equal terms with the world's great ones.

Among the works which recall this emergence as it was symbolized by Sukarno, one book, *Perjalanan Bung Karno. Mengenal sejarah dan tanah airnya adalah suatu kewajiban bagi setiap orang* [The journey of Bung Karno. To know his homeland and its history is a supreme

---

[43] In *Matahari* 1,6 (August 16, 1978): 10–14.

The Second Life of Bung Karno 193

Examples of books cited. Cf. Bibliography.

duty of each person], is one of the most unexpected in today's context, since it concerns itself with Sukarno's visit to the USSR in 1956. This book, distributed and edited by the Yasasan Multatuli of Bogor, relates the foundations of a "pure friendship" (*persahabatan yang murni*) between the Indonesian and Soviet peoples. It also brings up the significance of this return of the figure of Bung Karno. Indeed, to untangle that which arises from popular spontaneity, from commercialization, and from political intentions requires delicate research, whereupon the affair of the Sukamiskin letters could also serve as a subject for reflection.

The Sukamiskin Letters

The commander's statue had hardly been put back on its pedestal when a new blow struck him, with the revelation of the Sukamiskin letters. Let us briefly recall the facts: in his book *Road to Exile, The Indonesian Nationalist Movement 1927–1934*, John Ingleson refers to four letters written by Sukarno while he was imprisoned at Sukamiskin, to ask pardon from the public prosecutor and to swear never again to involve himself in politics. Several researchers had already learned of these archival letters, but hardly reported on them insofar as they were non-authenticated copies, and added nothing determining to Indonesia's history. But the fact had not been brought in front of Indonesian public opinion before an article by Rosihan Anwar appeared in *Kompas*.[44]

It is not for us to judge here the historical value of these letters, but rather to analyze the effects of this attack on Sukarno's image. For the reactions are extremely vivid: "I was stunned," writes H. Mahbub Dhunaidi, "if a tiger had entered my room, I would have let it be, like a cat."[45] "I was stunned, too," writes M. Roem, while Adam Malik preached moderation: "It no longer serves any purpose to put into question problems concerning Sukarno, because he is no longer here."[46]

For many readers, it appears more probable that the letters were a fake, made at the time by the Dutch police; and Rosihan Anwar, likened to Ingleson, is accused by Sitor Situmorang of replaying the colonialist game of fifty years earlier, and of being "a mediocre individual, incapable of understanding his own nation's history."[47]

Supposing that Rosihan Anwar had actually sought to downplay Sukarno's role, indeed even to discredit him as "easily bending his knees," it is interesting to note that the result is a general nationalist outcry wherein Indonesians instinctively tighten ranks as if facing a colonialist subversion (also meriting analysis would be the Indonesian reactions of pride and irritation over the foreign appropriation of Bung Karno's persona): "They (foreigners) are fascinated by Sukarno because they consider him as something exotic, while they feel more at ease with Bung Hatta."[48] Between the insidious destruction of the myth that Rosihan Anwar indulges in, insisting upon the divergences between Sukarno and Hatta, and the nationalist reflex to come to his defense, the staff historians Ong Hok Kham and Taufik Abdullah try to dismiss as too intellectual for the public, the distinction between the private man and public figure. But the proof is there, that doubtlessly for a long time, the Indonesian nation has largely identified itself with Sukarno.

---

[44] Rosihan Anwar, "Perbedaan analisa politik antara Sukarno dan Hatta," in *Kompas*, September 15, 1980.

[45] *Kompas*, October 7, 1980.

[46] Ibid., January 25, 1981; for M. Roem and Adam Malik see *Tempo*, February 28, 1981.

[47] *Merdeka*, February 19, 1981.

[48] *Majalah Zaman* 2, 23 (March 1–7, 1981).

* * * *

Although the period we have just analyzed is extremely brief in the eyes of history, it gives the idea of the multiplicity and complexity of the Bung Karno phenomenon, a polymorphous model wherein anyone can identify himself in some way. Moreover, the importance of his role in recent national history makes for his becoming a core around which certain social confrontations crystallize for the appropriation of the symbol: *Bung Karno siapa yang punya?* "Who possesses Bung Karno?" He was already the sovereign, the Muslim, the nationalist, the builder; he is appealed to as much for unity as for division. Today's students, who see in him the image of the unknown Father, recall his ghost in books like *Wawancara imaginer dengan Bung Karno* "Imaginary Interview with Bung Karno."[49] Others set out to revive the political message to give more consistency to the opposition. As the reader will have understood, this reactivation of the engineer or of President Sukarno subtly implies a negative value judgment on his successor, an intention which does not escape a public familiar with the interpretation of allusive processes. Bung Karno's installation into the national perspective, then, is both necessary—for one party like the other—but delicate in the art of salvaging pieces of the historical figure without bringing back to life the old demons from Indonesian history. But wherever the pedestal upon which Bung Karno will finally be installed, it is hardly rash to think that no political establishment will be able to do without him, or without the Pancasila. A simple matter of dialectics.

Annotated Bibliography

The most recent bibliography of Sukarno's writings (1,079 titles) and of writings on Sukarno (71 titles) can be found in:

Bung Karno, Sebuah bibliographi, Jakarta, Yayasan Idayu, 1979, 84p. Reedited in 1981, 130p.

Books:

Andjar Any, Menyingkap tabir Bung Karno, Aneka, Semarang, 1978, 168 p. Mostly anecdotes.

Andjar Any, Bung Karno siapa yang punya?, Badan Penerbit Sasongko Solo, Solo, 1978, 256 p. Multitude of anecdotes.

Bung Karno kenang-kenangan kepergiannya, s.l., s.d., 40 p. On the funerals.

Bung Karno dan Seni, Jakarta, 1979, 68 p. It concerns the catalogue of an exposition of a part of the Bung Karno collection at the TIM. Sitor Situmorang's article.

Bung Karno antara mithos dan demithologiasi (dari surat Sukamiskin), Yogya, Pusat Pelayanan Informasi, LP3Y, 1981, 50 p. Reprinted articles relative to the controversy surrounding the Sukamiskin letters.

Perjalanan Bung Karno, s.l., Yayasan Multatuli Bogor, 1978, 112 p. Photos and text on Sukarno's trip to the Soviet Union in 1956.

Bung Mawi, Bung Karno milik rakyat Indonesia, Rose Group, Jakarta, 1978, 52 p. A Muslim's point of view?

Erka, Bung Karno, Kepada bangsaku, Aneka, Semarang, 1978, 202 p. Anecdotes.

Erka, Bung Karno, Perginya seorang kekasih, suamiku, kebanggaanku, Aneka, Semarang, 1978, 218 p. On Sukarno's wives.

Fatmawati, Catatan kecil Bung Karno, I., Dela Rohita, Jakarta, 1978, 218 p. Abundant and original iconography on the Bengkulu period, with the initial collaboration of Sitor Situmorang.

Guntur Soekarno, Bung Karno, bapakku, kawanku, guruku, Dela Rahita, Jakarta, 1978, 270 p. Numerous anecdotes on Bung Karno's family life by his oldest son.

---

[49] This book by Christianto was banned in 1978.

Guntur Soekarno, Triwikrama generasi muda, Dela Rohita, Jakarta, 1979, 166 p. Collection of articles (1973–78) to reawaken hope in Indonesian youth with the example of national combat.

Guntur Soekarno, Bung Karno dan kesayangannya, Karya Unipress, Jakarta, 1981. 218 p. New anecdotes.

Swara Maharddhika, Jan. 1979. Show program for Guruh Sukarno Putra.

Husmi Lain, Mengenang proklamator RI, Soekarno-Hatta, Kreasi Jaya Utama, Jakarta, 1980, 152 p. After M. Hatta's death, yet another account of the proclamation of independence.

Ramadhan KH, Kuantar ke gerbang. Kisah cinta Ibu Inggit dengan Bung Karno, Sinar Harapan, 1981, 466 p. Account of the successes of Bung Karno's romantic (and Sundanese) years from the confidences of Ibu Inggit, faithful and courageous companion of the difficult years.

S. Saiful Rahim, Bung Karno masa muda, seperti dituturkan oleh Ibu Wardoyo, kakak kandung Bung Karno kepada wartawan: S. Saiful Rahim, Antar Kota, Jakarta, 1978, 34 p. Memories of Bung Karno's older sister, still living.

Soebagijo I.N., Idayu Nyoman Rai, Sukarno anakku, Antar Kota, Jakarta, 1978, 80 p., first edition 1949. Memories of Sukarno's mother often repeated afterwards.

Soewarto, Kejayaan dan saat-saat akhir Bung Karno, Gunung Jati, Jakarta, 1978, 272 p. Indonesian translation of World Star magazine, edited in Jakarta.

Solichin Salam, Bung Karno dan kehidupan berpikir dalam Islam, Widjaya, Jakarta, 1964, 134 p. Old book brought back out of storage.

Solichin Salam, Bung Karno putera fadjar, Jakarta, Gunung Agung, Jakarta, 300 p., reedited in 1981. Interesting book, which Gunung Agung had inopportunely printed in 1966.

Solichin Salam, Bung Karno di mati bangsa Indonesia, Dela Rohita, Jakarta, 1980, 116 p. Accounts of contemporaries.

Solichin Salam, Bung Karno dalam kenangan, Pusaka, Jakarta, 1981, 274 p. The golden book with the memories of all the great names of Indonesia.

F.A. Suprijatna, Bung Karno milik rakyat semua, Dela Rohita, s.d., 112 p. Reprinting of various articles and passages from books already cited.

Suripto, Bung Karno. Hari-hari terakhirnya, Grip, Surabaya, s.d., 62 p. The death and the funerals.

S. Suyountoro, Sukarno-Hatta-Soeharto menggembleng bangsanya, Bina Ilmu, Surabaya, 1980, 140 p. Why wasn't the foundation of this book cited: the Pancasila?

Syamsu Hadi, Tragedi Bung Karno, perjalanan terakhir seorang proklamator, Pustaka Simponi, Jakarta, 1978, 160 p. Reedition of articles, particularly by B.M. Diah, which appeared around 1970.

Muhammad Tito, Kumpulan kata-kata pilihan Bung Karno, Blitar?, 1980, 40 p. The little red-and-white book.

Kenangan lama, koleksi pidato-pidato Bung Karno, 45–50, s.l., s.d., 184 p. From August, 1945 to Dari Sabang sampai Merauke.

80 Tahun Bung Karno, edited by Aristides Katoppo, Sinar Harapan, Jakarta, 1981, 342 p. With 25 articles by Indonesian personalities from Sayuti Melik, Mochtar Lubis, Nugroho Notosusanto to Buyung Nasution . . . published after the editing of our article. Very interesting for the reflection upon the lessons of the Sukarnian experience (democacy, law, humanism . . .) as an alternative to the current political situation.

Illustrated for Children:

M. Ali S., Bung Karno putra sang fajar, Jakarta, 1979.

Newspapers:

We utilized the documentation of Yayasan Idayu, that is to say around 100 articles published in the press from 1978 to September 1981.

THE NEW ORDER AND ISLAM,
OR THE IMBROGLIO OF FAITH AND POLITICS*

François Raillon

1. Islam and Power: From Accommodation to Insurrection

At 10.00 sharp, on that Monday August 20, 1984, John Naro, general chairman of the PPP United Development Party, requested president Soeharto, vice-president Umar Wirahadikusuma and their respective spouses to take their seats at the grand stand. Some 2,500 guests filled the Senayan meeting hall in Jakarta. Above the tribune, a large panel read: "The first PPP convention supports *Pancasila*." [1]

The national anthem, Indonesia Raya, was heard, and Mirwan Batubara, famous for his recent victory in the Kuala Lumpur Koran reading contest *(Musabaqah Tilawatil Koran)*, chanted a few verses from the Book, urging the faithful to be united. Then Naro appeared.

Wearing a dark gray suit and a black *kopiah*, he was visibly in excellent form on that morning and full of self-confidence. He improvised a fluent speech that aroused cheers and laughter from the audience. Then with Soeharto's assent, he introduced the head of state to the participants, using laudatory terms: "The president is a true Muslim and a genuine *pancasila-ist*. In 1965, he saved our *Pancasila* State from chaos.... And *Ibu* Tien [Mrs Soeharto] will not disagree if I say that he is a good family man and the most handsome president in the world."[2]

---

* The French version of this article appeared in *Archipel* 30 (1985): 229–61.

[1] *Pancasila*: The Five State Principles formulated by Sukarno on June 1, 1945 are worded, under the New Order, as follows: 1. Belief in the one and only God, 2. Just and civilized humanity, 3. Unity of Indonesia, 4. Democracy wisely led by deliberations of the representatives, and 5. Social justice for the whole Indonesian people.

[2] Quote from *Tempo* magazine, August 25, 1984: "Ketua baru dari Ancol" [The new Chairman from Ancol]. Most current data used in this paper is drawn from *Tempo* weekly. Set up in 1971, Indonesia's top political magazine, *Tempo* is an invaluable source on the New Order and Islam. The core of its editorial board is made of members of the 1966 Generation, who took an active part in the beginnings of general Soeharto's regime. *Tempo* has been an objective mirror of the New Order's development. Under Goenawan Mohammad's leadership, *Tempo* pays sustained attention to Islamic problems. *Tempo* was banned from April 12 to June 11, 1982, for its too intensive

This official and seemingly relaxed ceremony opened the convention of PPP (Partai Persatuan Pembangunan), the party that since 1973 has associated the various streams of Indonesia's political Islam, although its own name (United Development) bears no reference to Islam and fits well with New Order priorities. Harmony was prevalent, and allegiance was being paid by Muslim politicians to military and secular powers as well as to the Five State Principles, including the first one—Belief in the one and only God, which recognizes Indonesia's monotheist religions. However, and this is the source for various problems, no special place is given to Islam, which is professed by the majority of the population.

If the symbols of this scene are to be taken for granted, it looked as though everything was smooth between the New Order and Islam, while Muslim politicians seemed to get along well with the military and developmentalist regime born in the aftermath of the aborted September 30, 1965 coup attributed to the Communists. Such a facade of unanimity was presumably only one aspect, however real, of the relationship between the State and Muslims. In the country of shadow theater plays, while face value is often equivalent to reality, what is behind the screen of official ceremonies obviously cannot be ignored. A displayed consensus may not hide the diversity and complexity of political Islam in Indonesia's New Order.

The events that occurred in Tanjung Priok some three weeks after the PPP convention were not precisely the other side of the picture and were probably not even an expression of the political game that goes on backstage: There may not have been any direct causal link between the performance of a tamed political Islam on August 20, 1984 and Islam-influenced riots on September 12, 1984. But it can be assumed that there was a general correlation between the containment of Islam as a social political force, and the violent though limited explosion of mass and fundamentalist Islamic feelings. The contrast between a well-oiled convention and the people's furor was manifest.

The affair[3] started with a minor incident. On Friday September 7, 1984 in the evening, sergeant Hermanu, a *Babinsa (Bintara Pembina Desa*, non-commissioned officer in charge of village surveillance—a low-level New Order official), was on duty in the South Koja district in Tanjung Priok when he discovered three posters on the wall of the Assa'adah mosque. Women were urged to dress in line with Islamic decency, and wear the *jilbab* (or *kerudung*, Islamic head scarf). The sergeant took off his shoes, went into the mosque, and politely asked a few youths at prayer to remove the posters. They declined to do so. Coming back on the following day (September 8), he soaked a sheet of newspaper in the mosque gutter and dripped its black juice on the objectionable writings.

Then mass mobilization began. Inhabitants of the neighborhood gathered and rumors of desecration started to circulate: the sergeant was said to have come into the mosque without taking off his shoes. In another version, the military man had defiled the mosque with gutter water. Finally (and more serious): sergeant Hermanu was said to be Christian (he actually is a Muslim).

On September 10, with some of his friends, Achmad Sani, a leader of the Assa'adah mosque went to sergeant Hermanu to demand, to no avail, that he apologize. Asked about

---

coverage of incidents during the election campaign and its breaking of the "consensus" between the government and the press.

[3] This story is retold from *Tempo's* report, September 22, 1984, "Huru-hara di Tanjung Priok" [Riots in Tanjung Priok]. According to another version of the starting point of the affair, writings posted on the mosque wall would have been insults against the head of state and his entourage. Beyond facts, attention here is mainly focused on mentalities and popular behavior as revealed by the situation.

his religion, Hermanu declared himself a Muslim, but was sufficiently unwary so as to mispronounce Allah's name (instead, the word *alah* was heard, which is an utterance for impatience). "Therefore he certainly is not a Muslim," stated an eye witness. A mob that had gathered and was about to hit him was prevented from doing so by Achmad Sani. As people then tried to destroy the sergeant's motorbike, the police arrived. Achmad Sani and three of his friends were arrested.

The four arrests completed the mobilization process in the neighborhood, and encouraged an informal young leader in Tanjung Priok, Amir Biki, to step in. A former 1966 New Order activist, and a former member of the anti-Sukarno student regiment Laskar Arief Rahman Hakim,[4] he was a devout Muslim, born in Gorontalo (North Celebes) in 1948. A businessman, he headed PT Irajaya, a small subcontractor to Pertamina. As such, he was typical of the thousands of small Muslim entrepreneurs gravitating around Indonesia's oil company, then a major knot of military bureaucratic power in the New Order, who were having trouble competing with the Chinese in international tenders. *Haji* Amir Biki derived his status as a local leader from his economic role, his piety, his past as a 1966 activist, but also from his endeavors to unite and propagate Islam *(dakwah)*. He used to organize speakers to give Koranic lectures which had an anti-government tone. He was regarded as able to avoid inter-racial or inter-ethnic strife, and was sometimes asked for help in freeing lecturers or preachers *(mubalig)* who had been arrested.[5] That is why, on September 11, Amir Biki attempted to have the four Muslims released, but in vain.

What happened during the night of the 11th is not well documented, but it can be assumed that a lot of organizational work took place via the Islamic network, with results apparent on the following day. On September 12, a speaking stand was erected in Sindang street, while dozens of loud speakers were set up in neighboring streets. Leaflets were disseminated by Pemuda Islam Sindang (the Sindang Muslim youths) inviting local teenagers to a Koranic recitation, and to listen to lectures delivered by religious teachers *(ustad)*.

The evening program was opened at eight by Amir Biki who got on the tribune. Brandishing a dagger *(badik)*, the bearded *haji* started a vehement but rather mixed up diatribe against expeditious expropriations due to land speculation, against birth control, and the bill on Mass Organizations *(RUU Ormas)* that was about to oblige all organizations, including religious ones, to insert *Pancasila* into their articles of association. He was in fact attacking the government. He asked the audience to wait for his instructions and demanded the release of the four arrested Muslims. A deadline was set for the demand: at 23.00, their release should take place, or else he would call for demonstrations, which might get out of hand and turn into a bloodbath *(banjir darah)*. Actually, Amir Biki phoned the officials twice, to repeat his demands. Other speakers delivered equally harsh speeches and made statements later branded by the government as "racialist," not to say anti- Chinese.

At 23.00 the detainees had not been released, and Amir Biki launched his men, allegedly as many as 1,500. He formed two columns preceded by the green standard of Islam, with most of their members armed with *celurit* (Madurese scythe-shaped knives). The rioters—should we say the insurgents?—were soon stopped by the police. Some shots were heard, Amir Biki fell; he never stood up again. His entourage believe he died as a martyr *(syahid)*.

---

[4] This para-military regiment was one of the spearheads of the 1966 student movement. On that period, see my *Les étudiants indonésiens et l'Ordre Nouveau,* (1984), 352 p. In 1978 with former 1966 activists, Amir Biki took part in setting up of a study group, Fosko 66 (Forum Studi dan Komunikasi), gathering evicted New Order generals such as general Dharsono, and Muslims. The group's activities were "frozen" in 1979 by the authorities.

[5] Biographical data drawn from "Malam terakhir buat Amir" [Amir's last night], *Tempo*, September 22, 1984.

While retreating, the rioters set houses and cars afire. As they were about to burn down the Tanjung chemist's shop, it was said that the owner, albeit a Chinese, was a Muslim. However his shop eventually burned down because it caught fire from the next shop. Eight Chinese bodies were found afterwards in the remains. The police managed to restore order, and the following day Indonesia's three political parties—including PPP—made statements unanimously condemning the Tanjung Priok events.

What is the connection between this outburst of Muslim popular violence on the night of September 12, 1984 and the well-oiled convention of the official Muslim party three weeks before? In both cases, although under different forms and with opposite results, social political Islam entered a bipolar relationship with the same dominant partner, the New Order government. Both events must be seen in their context, which means not only recent developments but also a longer-term perspective—at least since the beginning of the New Order in 1966. A brief overview of the ups and downs in the relation between Soeharto's government and Islam for 20 odd years is thus a way to explore how the system works.

2. Face to Face: Armed *Priai* and Unarmed *Kiai*

There may be some difficulty in associating two basically different entities, one, the New Order, being political, whereas the other, Islam, is religious. While they respectively belong to a different realm, they combine and confront each other in a common field, which is somewhere between morals and politics. Besides, both quarrel over the same constituency, Indonesia, and the same clientele, Indonesian civil society. Most of the population (85 percent) is allegedly Muslim, and the country is regarded as an Islamic land; the New Order claims to be a political, social, economic, and cultural system applying to the society as a whole, which it means to transform, renovate, and modernize. Islam is a world view derived from a conception of the hereafter, and therefore is an ideology that envisions a social organization and a type of political order applicable to the whole *ummat* [community]. Religion is not separate from politics: Islam is holistic. It addresses all Muslims, including those who are not Muslim yet, and it regulates all ways of life: not only does it articulate the relation between Man and God, but also among men themselves.

The New Order, the province of which is the whole society, interferes with material and spiritual matters: it hopes to mould these two dimensions according to an ideology, *Pancasila*, that has been increasingly interpreted as an all-encompassing creed. It is the New Order's aim to grid and control the Indonesian space more and more closely. As a value system, it means to endow each individual with specific standards and forms of behavior, a State morality supportive of development—and of the political establishment.

Since they compete with each other, politics and religion may be associated and contrasted. Their totalizing and holistic aspects make them potentially antagonistic. Beyond the social political swamp of the silent majority—nominal Muslims and lukewarm New Order supporters—more convinced and vocal elites form the New Order's and Islam's harder cores; they are the game leaders, and they may conflict with each other. These elites can be labeled, in a short-cut, as armed *priai* and unarmed *kiai*.[6]

---

[6] *Priai*: Javanese upper class officials with aristocratic overtones, sometimes related to a *keraton* (palace) family. *Kiai*: Javanese title for *ulama* (Islamic scholars). By symbolically applying these Javanese terms to competing Indonesian elites, emphasis is put on the cultural and geopolitical localization of power in Java.

To be sure, each competing elite pays at least lip service to its rival's ideology or religion: the Javanese military are often Muslims, while *ulama* may have supported—many of them actually do support—general Soeharto's regime. But eventually both elites are clearly definable, distinct, and opposed in many aspects. With no excessive oversimplifying, it is convenient to view contemporary Indonesia as a bipolar system whereby *priai* New Order leaders confront Islamic *kiai*.

Both terms refer to two precolonial Javanese traditions, that of the heirs to Hindu-Javanese culture, and that of Muslim *santri*, the *pesantren* Islamic school students. The *priai* aristocrats, turned into Westernized civil servants by the Dutch, became in large numbers the leaders of modern secular parties, mainly Sukarno's Nationalist Party, and to a lesser extent of the Indonesian Communist Party. Since independence, Javanese *priai* have dominated the civil service and the armed forces. Thus, they have had long practice in power, which has been reinforced and completed under the New Order: through the Dual Function, the *priai* Army has taken over a *"priai*-zed" civil service.

Quite different is the *ulama's* inheritance, which is made of an ambiguous relationship with political power. While they felt entitled to replace the *priai*, either as power holders or at least as its inspirers, *kiai* were prevented from doing so by the Dutch colonial system. This is probably one of the reasons for their ambivalent feelings and frustration toward (secular) government. While the Islamization process was well on its way and about to generate Islamic forms of state, it was thwarted by the Europeans. The only alternative left to Muslims was to collaborate passively with the colonial government or revolt against it. Both attitudes were successively or simultaneously adopted.

The Islamic awakening early this century,[7] the reformist movement that gave birth to Muhammadiyah in 1912, and the resistance of Muslim entrepreneurs against Chinese economic dominance led to the emergence of modern political Islam, with the adoption of modern ways of struggle through new types of organizations. A movement also set up in 1912, Sarekat Islam, catalyzed the process, and led a successful mass mobilization drive; however it was soon deprived of its troops and supremacy by secular forces, the Communists and the nationalists. Counter-reformist groups reacted in 1926 by setting up the "Renaissance of the *Ulama*" (Nahdatul Ulama) movement.

From the late 1930s to the Japanese occupation, Islam was seemingly able to unite again. However, despite its low and cooperative profile during the Physical Revolution (1945-1949) and in the early 1950s, it was again undermined by its secular competitors. Compromised in regional rebellions, Masyumi was banned in 1960 by Sukarno and the military; other shades of political Islam were tamed, and survived through the Nahdatul Ulama and two residual parties (Perti and PSII) used as a security by Sukarno in the syncretic coalition he had conceived under the acronym *Nasakom* (Nationalism, Religion, and Communism).

For a while, the advent of the New Order was seen as a historical chance for political Islam. In the context of anti-Communist suppression (late 1965), an alliance was struck between Javanese *santri* and *ulama* landowners on one side, and the military on the other as they were willing to fight "the moral and economic decline" *(kelunturan akhlak dan ekonomi)* caused by the Sukarno years. Muslim business people from Java's north coast and the Outer

---

[7] Many a comparison could be made between the first Islamic revival and the current Muslim renewal in Indonesia. This theme is partly dealt with in my "Les musulmans Indonésiens," *Hérodote*, n° 35 (1984), "Géopolitique des Islams." Also see Harry J. Benda, "Southeast Asian Islam in the Twentieth Century," in *The Cambridge History of Islam*, vol 1, ed. P.M. Hold (1970), pp. 182–207.

Islands thought that the rehabilitation and reform program launched by the military would be beneficial to them. The more so as general Soeharto took more than one and a half years (October 1965-February 1967) to evict Sukarno, and was therefore in need of allies and legitimacy. He was prepared to accommodate political Islam, and he even let it be believed that Masyumi might be rehabilitated—which eventually was done in 1968, but at the cost of a change in name (the new party was called Partai Muslimin Indonesia or PMI) and of many concessions that would jeopardize its credibility.

Muslims were soon disappointed as they did not obtain what they expected. In the economic field, the military opted (but did they really have a choice?) for an exogenous type of development, based on a massive injection of foreign capital and technology, which impaired small-scale Muslim enterprise. Even before the 1968/69 economic upturn, Muslim business people had already become victims to the ruthless anti-inflation and monetary adjustment policies implemented by the technocrats. At a later stage they collided with the Chinese favored by the military, and even more with multinational, mainly Japanese, corporations.

As the country opened to the West, religious leaders and disturbed believers were discontented with foreign cultural penetration which they deemed to be too secular and materialistic. In 1973 for the first time, Islamic feelings came into the open in a well-organized way, when the marriage bill was discussed in parliament. The new bill modernized woman's legal status in a way seen as inappropriate to the Koranic tradition. Under pressure from the *ulama*, the government had to step back and redraft the bill.

Disappointment was even more bitter at the political level. As early as 1966, the military's preferred allies were the Christians (over-represented in the higher ranks of the civil service and actively promoting their own religions), and reformist and modernist students of the Association of Muslim Students (Himpunan Mahasiswa Islam) whose leaders adhered to a more technocratic than Islamic ideology. Soon, Islam and traditional political parties were depicted as obstacles to Indonesia's development and modernization, and many official efforts were directed against them. During the first general election under the New Order in 1971, the government-backed organization Golkar won 62.8 percent of the votes, by mustering support among secular voters (including former pro-Sukarno nationalists). Political Islam had been undermined, as the four Islamic parties together only got 27.1 percent of the votes, compared to 43 percent in the 1955 general election.

In January 1973, Islamic parties ceased to exist as such and lost their identity: Nahdatul Ulama (NU), Partai Muslimin Indonesia (PMI), Perti, and PSII were merged into the Unity Development Party (PPP), whose appellation no longer contained anything Islamic. The new party was kept under the close scrutiny of the military who interfered with it until it took on the expected form and could be allowed, eleven years later, to hold its first national convention, as described above.

However, to mitigate the new Islamic aggressiveness shown in the marriage bill affair, and to face the renewed student protest that led to the Jakarta 1974 riots, the government had to appease Islamic opinion: its ideologists started to describe the New Order as a defender of the True Faith. In 1975 the government set up the Indonesian Council of *Ulama* (Majelis Ulama Indonesia), while during the 1977 election campaign, Golkar recruited many *haji*: all of this was meant to improve its relationship with *kiai*, whose only weapon was their oratory but who were not deemed to be harmless.

At this stage, the basic and symbolic dichotomy of armed *priai* facing unarmed *kiai* needs to be somewhat refined. As a matter of course, neither of these two power elites is monolithic. Islamic elites are not limited to *ulama* and *pesantren* masters. Mention has already been made of early 20th century Islamic reformism and of its modern heirs, some of whom have joined the New Order. Beside tradition-minded *kiai* who are generally members of the Nahdatul Ulama, reformist Muslims make up a large part of Indonesian Islam. The reformist stream was once embodied in the former Masyumi party (although its base may have been more conservative than thought), then in its successor the Partai Muslimin Indonesia, and recently in the PPP faction led by John Naro. Moreover the large modernist Muhammadiyah organization is still very much alive and active in social work and education. Also witnessing to the vigor of the reformist stream were the debates held in the early 1970s on Islam and politics, on the relation between religion and the secular world, and the polemics launched by Nurcholis Madjid.[8] But after a short period of prominence in the early New Order period, most proponents of Islamic modernism have joined the regime, and their moderation toward the government has made them hardly visible. On the contrary, *kiai* and Nahdatul Ulama, as is shown below, seem to channel part of the Islamic malaise.

Similarly, the New Order hard core is not only made up of military *priai*. One reason for this is that the army itself has a composite origin and recruitment, and includes non-Javanese (Bataks for instance) or Javanese commoners, even though the dominant model is that of *priai*. Another reason is that by the late 1960s, when "West winds" were blowing over the Archipelago, Javanese-ness was not entirely agreeable. Some of the foremost allies of the New Order would even go so far as to be frankly hostile to Javanese culture: intellectuals, students, technocrats, urban modernist bourgeoisie, pro-Western elements from the Outer Islands would regard Javanism as an obstacle to modernization, just like traditional Islam. But after 1973/74, as the regime detected possible threats coming from the Muslim side, Western influence was more filtered, and the notion of national identity was revived. However, for the military, national specificity was dependent on the culture that historically dominated all the others, namely Javanese culture.

The "Majapahit" reflex—originating in the Javanese imperial tradition that peaked in the 14th century—would play again. Propagation of *priai* ideology as conveyed by the army, and also by the civil service was emphasized, with the blessings of the Javanese head of state. Since then, the Javanization of Indonesia and the *"priai*-zation" of government have been felt in modes and expressions of power. Such neo-traditional tendencies expressed by Javanese leaders are the counterpart for the rise of fundamentalism among Muslims: in fact, the whole society has been pervaded by a movement of relative backlash and return to "safer" values (either Javanese or Islamic). Brought about or interpreted by *priai* and *kiai* elites, this regressive tendency is a reaction to the disturbing impact of modernization and to the upheavals caused by economic growth.

Among the clearer signs of the Javanization of power, is the irresistible expansion of *Pancasila*, the State philosophy.

3. *Pancasila* vs the Jakarta Charter: State Management of Islam

An old dispute over the form of the State brings secularists into opposition with supporters of theocracy. On June 1, 1945, Sukarno presumed he could persuade everyone to endorse the Five Principles of the State. In typical Javanese style, he made a syncretic

---

[8] On this theme, see Muhammad Kamal Hassan, *Muslim Intellectual Responses to "New Order" Modernization in Indonesia* (Kuala Lumpur, 1982), 250 p.

attempt to associate nationalism and belief in the one and only God, social justice, Indonesian democracy, and humanism.

However, Muslims were not satisfied with this vague wording and demanded that the future constitution make it compulsory for believers to apply Koranic law, namely *shari'at*. Such an obligation as defined in a document called the Jakarta Charter would have given the Republican State a more Islamic form of government, without transforming it into a full-fledged Islamic theocracy. But Republican legislators were not ready to accept this amendment, and the Muslim parties provisionally compromised in order to give the appearance of a united front to the outside world.[9] However this setback to the Muslim cause was the source of a long-standing resentment that eventually led to a rebellion against the Republican government, with the aim of setting up an Islamic State (Darul Islam, 1949-1960).

In 1967, after Sukarno's downfall, the new juncture seemed favorable for Islamic quarters to exert pressure on the New Order and obtain the enforcement of the Jakarta Charter. As the military had promised fully to apply the 1945 Constitution and *Pancasila*, Muslims contended that *shari'at* should be enforced by the government upon believers, in line with the July 5, 1959 Decree that reenacted the first constitution of the Republic of Indonesia. In fact, they misunderstood general Soeharto's intentions. Once he was firmly established as the head of state in March 1968, he discarded a few "New Order radicals" and other would-be or real rivals among the military, and continued to build a secular, Javanese-shaded state. He evolved *Pancasila* into a shield to be used against radical Islam and the political consequences of the faith revival. In 1978 the understanding of the first principle (belief in God) was extended to include mystical beliefs of the Javanese type *(kebathinan,* since 1973 officially called *kepercayaan* to conform with the first *sila)* beside monotheist religions. In March, the draft Outlines of State Policy (GBHN) that put religions *(agama)* and mysticism on a par were submitted to the People's Assembly (MPR) for approval. However, for the first time in the New Order's history, consensus in the Assembly was broken and unanimity could not be reached: The Nahdatul Ulama component of the PPP was so adamantly against the text that *voting* had to be held. Nevertheless the text was adopted.

Despite this breach of *priai* etiquette, from 1980 onwards, president Soeharto started a "*pancasila*-ization" process of public life in Indonesia, going ever further in the search for the cosmic harmony that is ideal in Javanese aristocratic culture. The first targets were civil servants who were requested to improve their knowledge of *Pancasila* by taking compulsory *Pancasila* classes based on the "Guide for Living and Practicing *Pancasila*" (*Pedoman Penghayatan dan Pengamalan Pancasila* or P-4). Then all political forces, all social organizations, were firmly invited to explicitly and exclusively adhere to *Pancasila*: the Five Principles must be inserted into their articles of association as a sole principle (*asas tunggal*). Was the government trying to get a philosophical guarantee of loyalty to the president as the ultimate repository of *Pancasila*? Such a guarantee would seem more apparent than real, even if it bore some weight because of the strength of symbols. Was it intended to undermine the impact of religious forces, i.e. Islam, by enforcing allegiance to the *Pancasila* State? Probably so, and such was the interpretation of political Muslim forces that strongly opposed this attempt at ideological locking up. Eventually, the ultimate aim lay in the basic drive of the New Order to "de-Islamize" even more the PPP, and complete the process by which it was

---

[9] The Jakarta Charter never became the preamble of the 1945 Constitution. When Indonesia's independence was recognized by the Dutch in 1949, another constitution was enforced. On July 5, 1959, Soekarno reenacted the 1945 Constitution with the support of the military. He made a formal concession to Muslims by stipulating that the spirit—but only the spirit—of the Jakarta Charter *inspired* the 1945 Constitution, which had no legal effect.

deprived of its Islamic identity. Through protracted political engineering (Nahdatul Ulama under-representation), PPP was eventually made to adopt *Pancasila* as its sole principle, at its August 1984 convention. For secular and Javanese forces, adherence was never a problem—Golkar as the government party and PDI, the heir to the nationalist and Christian parties, saw *Pancasila* as a protection against feared Islamic encroachments.

Thus, the Jakarta Charter, let alone the Islamic State, seem to be a long way off. Islam does not inspire government in the least, while the *Pancasila* foundations of the State have been consolidated. But the State does not ignore religious practice, especially Islam; on the contrary it is a modern *penata agama*, it "regulates"—rules?—religion. Three recent examples illustrate how the New Order manages Islam.

The first one relates to the pilgrimage *(haj)*, which is controlled by the government, mainly through the Department of Religious Affairs. An old fiefdom of Nahdatul Ulama, the Department was purged of its politician elements by minister Mukti Ali in 1971, and by general Alamsyah Ratuprawiranegara in 1978. In March 1983, when the 4th Development Cabinet was formed, a cosmetic concession was made to Muslim opinion: a *kiai's* son, Munawir Sjadzali, was appointed as Minister of Religious Affairs. But this former career diplomat and dedicated technocrat in fact continued the New Order policies, which sometimes seemed inspired by Snouck Hurgronje, the colonial Islamologist (1857-1936): as in older times, politics would officially be separated from religion, the former being hindered while the latter would be encouraged. In order to promote "religious" Islam, the Department controls a large part of Islamic schools, from *madrasah* (Koranic schools) to IAIN (Islamic universities). Together with other official bodies, it supervises the propagation of the faith *(dakwah)* and Friday sermons. It filters foreign aid donated to Muslims from the Middle East, and more important still, it takes care of the organization of the pilgrimage to Mecca.

In the early New Order period, it had been envisaged that the administration of the *haj* would be liberalized, as it had just been assigned to the Department of Religious Affairs by Sukarno. At least so reformist Muslims hoped.[10] But the bureau which since then has become the general directorate for Islamic mass guidance and *haj* affairs *(Ditjen bimas islam dan urusan haji)* preferred to keep its *haj* monopoly and continued to organize the pilgrimage. The more so as Islamic unrest in the Middle East was worrying the Indonesian government. The system is cumbersome (for instance during the pilgrimage season, Indonesian passports are not valid for Saudi Arabia) and too expensive for most Indonesians who still have a low buying power: the fee per pilgrim *(Ongkos naik haji)* is above costs, since it costs Rp. 3 million in Indonesia against Rp. 2 million in Malaysia (1984). This is why "unofficial pilgrims" *(haji gelap)* are still numerous (24,000) compared to 50,000 official *haji* in 1983.[11]

Whether official or not, *haji* represent economically strong Islam. A cheaper and more popular way to assert one's faith is to wear a *jilbab* (women's Islamic head dress) that Islamists intend to impose on women—at least on their own spouses. To counter this fundamentalist attitude, the *Pancasila* State, through the Department of Culture and Education, did not fail to exert its administrative control, and endeavored to regulate a practice deemed to be backward. Its unfortunate efforts aroused general protest from Islamic opinion, which

---

[10] See Deliar Noer, *Administration of Islam in Indonesia* (Ithaca: Cornell Modern Indonesia Project, 1978), 82 p., especially chapter 4: "Administration of the *haj*."

[11] Most of these 24,000 clandestine *haji* were Muslims who did the small pilgrimage *(umroh)* and stayed until the *haj* season. A new regulation (Keppres n° 63/1983) aims to control *umroh* pilgrims. See "Umroh ditata, Haji kena [Pilgrimage overhaul hits pilgrims]," *Tempo*, January 21, 1984.

reverberated as far as Tanjung Priok with its pro-*jilbab* wall writings. In March 1982, the director general for primary and secondary education *(Dirjen pendidikan dasar dan menengah)* made it mandatory for government school children of both sexes to wear a "secular" uniform, which meant a ban on *jilbab*. Until recently, female students from Islamist families would still go to school wearing a veil, which usually results in their being sent back home *(dirumahkan)*.[12] The problem was provisionally settled through various compromises, although in the process Daoed Joesoef, the then minister of Culture and Education, lost his portfolio.

The third example showing how the *Pancasila* State regulates Islam, or rather, uses it for its own purposes, relates to a quasi official body that is coordinating the uneasy relationship between the government and the *ulama*. This body, the Indonesian Council of *Ulama* (Majelis Ulama Indonesia, MUI) banks on the influence of cooperative *kiai* to improve the government's impact on the *ummat*. Set up in 1975, the MUI originally derived some clout from the prestige of its first chairman, the reformist Hamka,[13] but it was soon perceived as a government tool. For example, out of four recommendations issued by the Council during its March 1984 national meeting, three undoubtedly reflected government priorities while only the last one gave satisfaction to the *ulama* as can be seen from the following:

1. *Vigilance regarding shi'ism*. Sunni Indonesians were invited to be careful about the Iranian Islamic model, while the Iranian embassy in Jakarta was accused of being a propaganda channel for shi'ism in Indonesia.

2. *Use of inherited land in Java*. The Council recommended that inherited agricultural lands not be divided, but rather, one of the following solutions be chosen: use such land in a cooperative, have it bought by a rich heir, or sell it back to a neighboring landowner. Otherwise, have a Muslim from the same village buy the land to transform it into paddy fields, with a poor-tax levied on it to be allocated to impoverished neighbors (those who could not afford to buy the land in the first place). It was suggested that landless heirs, duly compensated for giving up their landed heritage, "transmigrate" to the Outer Islands.

3. *Haj*: the pilgrimage is a duty to be fulfilled only once, and only by those who can afford it. Rather than making the pilgrimage for a second or third time—which is a costly habit among Indonesian *haji*—it would be better to give to a charity.

4. *Ahmadiyah*: the Council requested cancelation of a 1953 ruling issued by the minister of Justice as it gave official recognition to Jamaat Ahmadiyah Indonesia, a brotherhood deemed to be heretic by the MUI because the Ahmadis regard their founder, Ghulam Ahmad, as a prophet.[14]

Despite efforts directed at them, the *Pancasila* State rather failed to attract the *ulama* who make up the main focus of potential and real opposition to the New Order, as an alternate

---

[12] "Tahun ini, batas kerudung [This year is the limit for wearing a veil]," *Tempo*, August 11, 1984.

[13] See Nasir Tamara, ed., *Hamka di mata hati umat* [Hamka seen by his Muslim friends]," (Jakarta: Sinar Harapan, 1983), 437 p. Since Hamka's death, MUI has been chaired by K.H. Syukri Ghozali and by K.H. E.Z. Muttaquien. Similar bodies exist for other religions recognized by the State: MAWI (Catholicism), DGI (Protestantism), Parisadha Hindu Dharma (Hindu-Balinese religion), etc.

[14] "Satu fatwa, empat rekomendasi [One religious edict and four recommendations]," *Tempo*, March 17, 1984. The *fatwa* dealt with adoption, a problem that recently disturbed Muslim opinion, following a number of cases whereby Indonesian children were adopted by Christian European nationals. According to MUI, adoption is a good deed *(amal saleh)*, provided the religious status of the child is not modified and his blood links with his parents are recognized.

elite with a rival legitimacy. *Ulama* are in touch with Islamism which is watched by the authorities, and the religious leaders could direct and channel it, if not ignite it. They could take advantage of the current return to the roots of Islam, since more than ever they assert their title of "heirs to the Prophet" *(warasatul anbiya)*.

4. The "*Ulama* Renaissance"

One of the most visible signs of the awakening of *kiai* is the recent evolution of their political movement, Nahdatul Ulama (NU). Despite its merger with PPP, this former party with an auspicious name (rebirth of *ulama*) still works as a social religious organization, and for the last few years has been experiencing a restlessness that may herald a new start for the *ulama*.

Despite almost 60 years of existence and a major role in contemporary Indonesian Islam, NU has not attracted the attention it deserves.[15] As a counter-reformist organization, it has been mostly presented to the outside world by its opponents. The image given was that of a reactionary, archaic *(kolot)* movement, led by Javanese *ulama* whose Islamic credentials were somewhat doubtful and tinted with syncretism. *Kiai* are often—though wrongly—perceived as the promoters of a "blind," sometimes superstitious faith because they support the principle of obedience *(taqlid)* to one of the four Sunni schools of law *(mazhab)* against the idea of freer interpretation *(ijtihad)* of the Koran and *hadith*. However, counter reforms are often reformations of reforms and rarely consist of a mere return to the *status quo ante*: Nahdatul Ulama was at first meant to resist Western-influenced modernism as conveyed by the Indonesian supporters of Djamal Uddin Al Afghani (1839-1897) and Muhammad Abduh (1849-1905). In the process of opposing the Muhammadiyah type of modernism, NU somewhat reformed itself by eradicating a few heterodox and syncretic aspects of Javanese Islam. So that rather than traditionalist or reactionary, NU should better be termed orthodox.

However, after becoming a party under the Republic of Indonesia, NU's close and continuous relationship with government and its knack for political U-turns—it thrived through the three regimes of independent Indonesia—gave it a reputation for opportunism that was not undeserved and that its enemies did not fail to amplify and propagate. Among the latter, the foremost was the reformist Masyumi.

The two parties have had a long history of conflicts induced by the cleavage between Java, a traditional NU stronghold, and the Outer Islands, the Masyumi's major constituency. Philosophical differences and territorial oppositions first materialized when NU seceded from Masyumi in 1952[16] and started its own career as a political party. Relations kept worsening, and their political fortunes constantly drew them apart, until Masyumi was banned following the PRRI rebellion (1958-1960), while NU continued its collaboration with president Sukarno and survived without major problems the 1965-1967 change of government.

NU did even more than support the new regime at its inception: its Ansor youths took a very active part in the anti-Communist suppression by the end of 1965. In the first years of

---

[15] However Allan Samson gives valuable information on NU in "Conceptions of Politics, Power, and Ideology in Contemporary Indonesian Islam," in *Political Power and Communication in Indonesia*, ed. Karl D. Jackson and Lucian Pye (Berkeley: University of California Press, 1978), pp. 198–226. He insists that Western scholars only know NU through the unfavorable views of reformist Muslims. So far NU has failed to correct this negative image, and it still has little communication with non-Muslims.

[16] Set up in 1943 at the instigation of the Japanese, Masyumi brought together Muhammadiyah and NU, that is two basically opposed components. In 1945, Masyumi became a political party.

the New Order, NU was the only significant civilian force and was needed by the military—the Communist party had just been eliminated, the Nationalist party had been demoted, Masyumi was still banned, while Golkar had not yet been revived. NU's leader, Idham Chalid, was again made a minister. After a while, rather than a useful ally, NU soon became a nuisance, as a Muslim, non-*Pancasila* party. Perceived as backward and anti-modern, it also represented the old regime with which it had had a lasting relationship. Its *ulama* were not so malleable as they had a capacity to mobilize Java's rural masses, which could not be forcefully opposed by the *priai* unless they were ready to trigger violent conflicts. On top of that, one of NU's leaders, Z.E. Subchan, was increasingly vocal in his criticisms against the New Order.

To offset NU's influence, the New Order allowed the establishment of a rival party, Partai Muslimin Indonesia (known as Parmusi or PMI), as an heir to Masyumi. PMI was easily manageable, since its foundation (in 1968) and leadership had been approved by the government. PMI was modernist, in line with the developmental ideology of the New Order, and most of its members were hostile to NU. Furthermore, the existence of PMI fulfilled the demands of a part of the Islamic community.

Despite new competition from PMI, NU was able to gain 18.6 percent of the votes at the 1971 general election (while PMI only got 5.3 percent). The 1973 merger of the Islamic parties was a means to check NU's advance by associating it with its main rival that was closely supervised by the military. Another means was to exploit the dual aspect of NU, which had long helped it weather political changes, but could also become a weakness.

NU is divided into two bodies, the council of *syuriyah* chaired by the *Rais Aam* and consisting of *ulama* who exert a remote control over its political executive, the *tanfidziyah*. The politicians (the *tanfidziyah* members) are in charge of routine affairs and can be part of the government or the civil service when needed. Such a division of labor is very efficient since it enabled NU to join spiritual prestige and political clout. Nahdatul Ulama could give the image of a party promoting religion and morality, while being part of the power establishment and participating in political games. Compromises and opportunism could be ascribed to politicians, so that the party's moral reputation could be kept unimpaired. In the 1970s, NU was still the institutional association of religion and politics, a formidable formula when it worked; as long as the *ulama* and their politicians could maintain their solidarity, NU remained strong. On the contrary, any dissension between its two basic components would weaken it deeply.

As the hard core of anti-government protest inside PPP was NU, while inside NU the identity hard core was the *ulama* group, the military tried to keep the latter in check by exerting pressure on NU's politicians, by nature more amenable. This strategy was adopted in the aftermath of the 1977 general election, when Golkar's performance had not been as good as in 1971 (60 percent instead of 62 percent), while PPP had achieved some progress, which was worrying for the government. To further weaken the NU component inside PPP, PMI's undue supremacy had to be amplified, and this was done with John Naro's help.

John Naro was already well known for the controversial role he played at the time the military first tried to mold PMI according to their wishes. A former attorney and member of KASI—the nominally Islamic Action Front of Intellectuals (1967)[17]—Naro had sat in the

---

[17] Kesatuan Aksi Sarjana Indonesia, an active supporter of the New Order, was established in 1966, following the KAMI Student Front pattern. On John Naro, see his biography in *Apa dan Siapa, sejumlah orang Indonesia* (Indonesia's *Who's who*), (Jakarta: Grafiti, 1984), 1170 pages, p. 550.

Gotong Royong Parliament from 1968 to 1971 with the pro-government Karya Pembangunan group that was to evolve into Golkar later on. While still holding this position, he was promoted to PMI's board and became its general chairman for a few months, following an internal "coup." Provisionally expelled from PMI, he was nevertheless appointed as one of PPP's chairmen, when the new party was formed in 1973.

So as a close associate of the military, in 1978 Naro was promoted to the position of PPP's general chairman. He soon started to reduce NU's role in PPP by picking a majority of PMI members as candidates for the 1982 general election. NU then threatened to leave PPP if it did not get more candidates from its own ranks. In January 1982, the young Abdurrahman Wahid, grandson of NU's founder, even suggested that NU not only leave PPP but focus and limit its activities to nonpolitical affairs, as had been the case before World War II. Naro was not impressed, and delivered the list of PPP candidates unchanged (i.e. heavily dominated by PMI people) to the chairman of the election committee, Amirmachmud, the then home minister.

In the May 4, 1982 general election, PPP recorded a setback with only 27.8 percent of the votes (compared to 29.4 percent in 1977), despite an aggressive campaign climaxing in the Jakarta March 18, 1982 riots.[18] Most of its elected MPs were members of the PMI faction.

Two days before the election (May 2, 1982), dissension between NU politicians and *ulama* had become apparent: Four well-known and venerable *kiai* [19] went to Idham Chalid, and asked him to resign. After 26 years as NU's leader, Idham Chalid was the archetypical NU politician who prospered under the old order as the new one. The *ulama* pointed out his age and his fragile health, but actually they were blaming the tremendous concessions made to John Naro, which had cost NU dearly, while he had had the means as the *"Presiden"* of PPP (not to be confused with *Ketua umum*, general chairman) to better defend NU's stance. Idham Chalid first agreed to offer his resignation but took back this agreement on May 14, 1982, when NU's apparatus (politicians, maneuvered by the military?) refused to approve his resignation, on the grounds it was not compatible with the articles of association.

From this incident on, the breach between politicians and *ulama* was almost beyond repair and paralyzed NU until the August 1984 PPP convention, when there was a total debacle. John Naro was able to consolidate his hold over PPP and have it adhere to *Pancasila*.

All through the preceding months, the quarrel had developed between Idham Chalid's *Cipete group*, named from a Jakarta district where NU has its headquarters, and the *ulama* the *Situbondo group*, from the name of a large East Java *pesantren*. Ironically, and out of political finesse, the government had not authorized NU to hold its 27th national convention until its two factions reconciled:[20] the idea was to maintain the image of the government as working for the unification of Islam, even though it was taking advantage of its divisions. Thanks to Abdurrahman Wahid, reconciliation took place in September 1984, following the PPP convention,[21] and NU was eventually allowed to have its own convention

---

[18] Leo Suryadinata, *Political Parties in the 1982 General Election in Indonesia* (1982), 81 p.

[19] K.H. As'ad Syamsul Arifin, K.H. Machrus Ali, K.H. Ali Ma'sum (*Rais Aam* since 1981), and K.H. Masykur. See Idham Chalid's biography in *Apa dan Siapa*, p. 141.

[20] *Tempo*, February 18, 1984, "Rujuk dulu, baru Muktamar [Reconcile first and then have a convention]."

[21] *Tempo*, September 8, 1984, used a significant title: "Rujuk setelah terbantai [Reconciliation after a massacre]." The massacre was that suffered by NU and especially the *ulama* group at the August 1984 PPP convention where they had very few representatives.

by the end of 1984. On that occasion, *Pancasila* was officially adopted by NU as its sole principle.

However, the weakening of NU politicians inside PPP and NU's internal discord had an unexpected effect, that is, the new assertiveness of NU *ulama*, as formulated during their National Conference *(Musyawarah Nasional)* held in Situbondo from the December 18 to 21, 1983.[22] The meeting took place at the large East Java *pondok pesantren*, under the guidance of the venerable As'ad Syamsul Arifin, 86, a *kiai* said to be a descendent of Sunan Ampel, one of the nine apostles of Islam in Java. Besides, *Kiai* As'ad is related to a number of *pesantren* masters throughout East Java and Madura. Right in the middle of the quarrel dividing NU ranks, the *ulama* group was gathering to reassert its authority over the movement, but also to define a new line that was to herald their renaissance and reflect the revival of Islamic faith.

The place for the meeting, a *pesantren*, was quite significant, since for the first time in 43 years the *ulama's* National Conference convened in the precincts of a Koranic boarding school. This was a symbol, a return to the initial tradition of those educational settlements that played a large role in propagating Islam, and not so long ago still showed a reserve, if not declared hostility, toward the government. And the 500 *ulama* gathered in Situbondo actually stated their intent to quit the field of conventional party politics to come back to 1926 sources: NU had to go back to the line of struggle *(khittah)* it was pursuing when it was founded, and again become a basically social religious organization, where the *ulama* of the *syuriyah* (deliberative council) would hold power over the *tanfidziyah* (executive), that is, over the NU politicians. NU was to go through a new period of glory *(kejayaan)* and a new awakening of the *"ulama"* by means of political activity held at the bottom level rather than only at the top of society.

The conclusions of the conference were clear: power inside NU belongs to the *kiai* as founders, leaders, and guides of the *nahdliyyin* (NU members). It must rest with a "government of *kiai*" or inspired by them. *Ulama* also decided that members of the NU leadership would not be allowed to hold leading positions in any political party (read PPP).

The more aggressive attitude of the *ulama* must not be seen as seditious—they even went so far as to accept *Pancasila* as their sole principle.[23] It rather reflected a new self-confidence and a reaction against government interference, as well as a genuine desire for "regeneration." Would-be *kiai* Abdurrahman Wahid, who played an intensive role in Situbondo, and later in reconciling the two NU factions, is a symbol of the tentative new mood. He was a very strong candidate for one of the higher positions in NU at the convention planned for December 1984. "Able to dialog" *(sanggup berdialog)* with New Order leaders, which matters a great deal because NU must remain able to "talk" to power holders, Abdurrahman Wahid is a young intellectual born in Jombang 44 years ago, who studied at Al-Azhar University in Cairo. A direct heir to NU tradition but with a democratic reputation, he is the grandson of K.H. Hasyim Asjari, a founder of NU, while his father, A. Wahid Hasyim, was a minister of religious affairs; if he was to take over the leadership of NU, then the "family tradition" of the movement would be secured. As required by custom, Abdurrahman Wahid leads a *pesantren;* but contrary to tradition, he set it up in town, in the capital

---

[22] *Tempo*, December 24, 1983, "Dari Asembagus, mencari kejayaan kembali [Starting from Asembagus, in search of a new glory]," and "Kalau NU ingin berjaya [If NU wants to be successful]."

[23] *Tempo*, December 31, 1983, "Munas NU: Asas tunggal akhirnya halal [NU conference: The Sole Principle is eventually rightful]."

city,[24] and not off the beaten track like in the past. This is an indication of the will shared by a number of *ulama* to get closer to urban *ummat*. The world and the *ummat* require them to do so anyway, and Wahid's attitude is a way to address a demand which, if unfulfilled, would seek and find its own original, syncretic—uncontrollable—ways and means.

5. Pop Islam

So far, not much has been said about the community of believers in its ordinary dimension. One major protagonist in the drama involving the New Order and Islam has hardly been discussed, or only between the lines, almost as a mere setting. Rather than as an actor, the *ummat* was mentioned more as a stake in the dispute between *priai* and *kiai*, as an object of their self-seeking solicitude. The common people were seen to arise during the Tanjung Priok affair, with inescapable violence, but unclear direction. Who are they? As Indonesian perceptions tend to contrast elites *(pemimpin)* and the mass of those who do not lead anything (the people), they can be best identified as the "Muslim people," *rakyat muslimin*. Beyond elite games and politics, the *wong cilik* (small people) are the main locus for the Islamic revival; the Muslim rank and file who crowd mosques but will never become *haji* deserve specific attention. These usually silent Muslims should be considered *per se*, as a rather autonomous lot, and not necessarily as the respective clienteles of conventional elites. It must be admitted, however, that little is known about them.

General elections do not give much information since they only indicate the variation of clienteles and patronage. What are the reasons for, and the variation of, faith intensity? Observers are usually taken by surprise at the recurring outbursts of religious fervor. What is the meaning of increased recourse to Islam, what does it reflect? Social economic frustrations can be easily assumed, as well as the impact of cultural uneasiness induced by the permeation of external values; conversely, the religious fraternity appeals to and comforts people by providing new solidarity networks. Surveys and studies are still rare on this point.[25] The only obvious fact is that mosques are packed, that around them (especially minor ones) a system of parallel socialization develops in competition with that provided by the New Order government. A network based on mosque leaders and infrastructures is at work.

Many mosque complexes include facilities supporting not only religious activity, but also cultural promotion and daily politics: clinics, dormitories, canteens, shops, printing workshops, libraries, sports equipment, etc. These *pesantren*-like complexes are used by young people on the occasion of Koran reading or of lectures given by famous preachers *(mubalig)*. What is being said there? As public statements, Friday sermons are closely scrutinized by government officials.[26]

---

[24] See A. Wahid's biography in *Apa dan Siapa...*, p. 1108.

[25] Such surveys, when available, are not entirely satisfactory as their sampling may be too limited. See Joseph B. Tamney, "Functional Religiosity and Modernization in Indonesia," *Sociological Analysis, A Journal in the Sociology of Religion* 44, 1 (Spring 1980): 55–65.

[26] The government sees to it that mosques are organized. In 1972, based on official suggestions, an Indonesian Council of Mosques was set up *(Dewan Masjid Indonesia)*, which federates mosque associations. Its task is to coordinate activities, to propagate the Koran, to train *khatib* (preachers), to organize seminars on mosque architecture, resilience, etc., and to convey government views. The council can make proposals: it suggested the establishment of the *Majelis Ulama Indonesia* (1975) and played a role in the debate on the marriage bill (1973).

A possible way to assess small people's Islam would be to consider visible examples that can help identify an Islamic "little tradition." This indirect approach is helpful in understanding mentalities, and two cases can be briefly reported here, that of the Islamic pop singer, Rhoma Irama, and the phenomenon of the "scientific Koran."

Rhoma Irama (the name by itself is a syncretic feat: *Raden* [a Javanese nobility title] *Haji* Oma, Irama [rhythm]) has succeeded in achieving a synthesis between popular Islam and Rock 'n roll music: The "knight of faith propagation" (*satria dakwah*), the "king from below" (*raja dari bawah*)[27] expresses popular Islam through heavy-rhythm songs (*dangdut*). A superstar credited with over 15 million young fans (*penggemar*), he is used to starting his concerts with a few verses from the Koran, and in his songs he blends romance and pleas for social justice, ballads, and Islamic precepts. A social phenomenon, Rhoma Irama followed an initiatory career that became a legend through movies. His beginnings are worth recording. Born in 1946 in Tasikmalaya from a noble Sundanese family, he decided after finishing high school to go to the Tebuireng *pesantren* in Jombang, East Java (the cradle of Nahdatul Ulama) in order to improve his religious knowledge. He ran away from home with his younger brother, but for lack of money he stopped in Solo, the heartland of Central Java. To survive, he became a street singer (*pengamen*), but he was soon helped out of destitution by a tattooed man (that is, according to a stereotype, an outlaw). Shortly before the 1965 coup, he came to Jakarta and started his musical career.

Today, Rhoma Irama leads the life of a pious Muslim. His children study the Koran (*mengaji*), he learns Arabic from a private religious teacher (*ustad*), and his home replicates the atmosphere of a *pesantren*. He gives very generous alms, holds an open table, and pays as much *zakat* as taxes to the government. His musicians, the Soneta Group, are required to be good Muslims, and Islam is increasingly present in his music: his band, *The Sound of Islam*, is about to be given a new name, "*Haji Sembilan*"[The Nine Pilgrims] as a reminder of the *Wali Songo*, the Nine Apostles who, says Rhoma Irama, Islamized Java by use of *wayang* and *gamelan*.

Such a good Muslim, with more supporters than any Indonesian party has members, necessarily has been involved in politics. Since 1971, he has supported Muslim parties. In 1977 and even more so in 1982, he campaigned for the PPP. At a huge political meeting in March 1982 where he presented his show, incidents burst out among the audience, causing several casualties. However, after the August 1984 convention, Rhoma Irama withdrew his support from the PPP, which he defined as a "transvestite" (*banci*), and gave an assessment of political Islam that would not have been disapproved of by an *ulama*: PPP did not reflect Islam's aspirations any longer, and was only a place for power bickering. For an Islamic party to accept *Pancasila* as a sole principle was a loss of identity. It was a mistake to sacrifice religion and forget that priority is given to Allah and His message. Rhoma Irama predicted that PPP would get into serious trouble at the 1987 elections; until then, he saw an "apathy" among Muslims and "frustrations" that would brutally burst out since they had no channel (*saluran*) left to express their aspirations.[28] Some three weeks after Rhoma's statements, the Tanjung Priok events strangely echoed his analysis. The "Muslim beat" singer is not permitted to go on the air at TVRI, the State television station. Besides, the

---

[27] "Satria dakwah, raja dari bawah," is the fine title of the article devoted to Rhoma Irama by *Tempo*, June 30, 1984, which is extensively used in the following lines.

[28] Comments made by Rhoma Irama and reported by *Tempo*, August 25, 1984 in "Ini partai, bukannya komplotan [This is a party, not a conspiracy]."

Indonesian Council of *Ulama* (MUI) issued a ruling *(fatwa)* banning *(mengharamkan)* the singing of Koranic verses to swinging tunes.

The second phenomenon reflecting effervescence in grassroots Islam and confusion in people's minds is somehow related to the first one as it uses the same means of communication, i.e. magnetic tape cassettes. This media is closely checked by the government, as it was widely used by Imam Khomeini, when he lived in Neauphle le Château before returning to Iran. However the Indonesian cassettes have no political content, but, rather, a didactic or apologetic tenor, including "religious lessons" *(kuliah agama)* giving a "scientific" interpretation of the Koran. Sold by the tens of thousands through an underground network, these cassettes were banned and seized by the government in March 1984 upon request of the Indonesian Council of *Ulama* (MUI). The religious teachings that were so propagated aimed to reassure believers disturbed by modern scientific progress. Far from contesting the Koran, such was the implicit argument, Western science only supports it.

According to a lesson entitled "Divine Unity and logics" *(Tauhid dan logika)*, the prophet Adam was created by God from a meteor, and became himself an asteroid, which enabled him to move to the earth with his companion. "By divine grace, he was saved from the effect of friction during his travel as he was protected by air molecules, so that he could breathe while flying throughout space." The rationalization technique used here consists of relating all supernatural aspects to outer space. In "Ka'bah and planet earth magnetism" *(Ka'bah dan magnet bumi)*, we are told how the earth poles shifted by 68 degrees following a comet attack against the solar system, which upset the axis of all planets; before this incident, the north pole was located right at the Ka'bah (the central shrine of Islam) in Mecca, and the south pole in the Tuamotu islands (!) in the Pacific ocean, etc.[29]

The author of this creative thinking is Naswar Syamsu, an obscure, retired policeman, originally from West Sumatra. Trained in a Dutch school, he studied astronomy *(ilmu falak)* from a Bukittinggi Sheikh. During a retreat into the jungle with the PRRI guerillas, Nazwar Syamsu had forebodings and received the revelation of his mission, which was to defend the true faith against the encroachments of science. Until his death (1983), he conceived and propagated heterodox views that were meant to strengthen fundamentalism: to those who read the Koran by the letter, they would bring scientific certainty as to the perfect truth of the Book.

Despite its relative success, such an attempt, if it was uncommon, would have limited significance. However a whole corpus of similar literature has been recently developing; it is abundant, but its influence is unknown although it is probably rather wide, and its authors are as diverse as for instance a professor of Islamic Law at Universitas Indonesia or a former Tebuireng (Jombang) *santri*. The former tried to measure the distance between the earth and the throne of Allah *(Arasy)*, which according to the Koran was traveled by angels made of light in one thousand years (32:5); the distance would then be one thousand light-years, a modern and scientific measurement unit implied by the Koran. In an almanac entitled "The Solar System according to the Divine System" *(Tata surya menurut sistim Ilahiyah)*, the Tebuireng *santri* proved that the number of days in a week should be six in conformity with the time needed to create the earth according to the Koran, and that Saturday is an unnecessary day, an interpolation due to "Jewish influence." Because of the seven-day week, thousands (only?) of Fridays were "lost," as well as Friday sermons.

---

[29] *Tempo*, March 24, 1984, "Sebermula adalah meteor [In the beginning was a meteor]."

While some are trying to make the Koran "scientific" or compatible with the teachings of modern science, others want to stick to it strictly. Since mid-1983, various fundamentalist Koranic study groups have claimed to reject any text other than the Book. The reason for this is simple: Allah is supernatural *(gaib)* and the Messenger is dead. The only source is the Koran that contains Allah's and His Messenger's words. The so-called *hadith* are only legends transmitted from mouth to ear. This doctrine, supposedly originating in Klaten (Central Java), was most popular among the working class. The "Sunnah-rejecting" *(Inkarus-sunnah)* movement was banned by the Ministry of Religious Affairs.[30]

These symptoms are mere illustrations of the revival of popular faith which spontaneously evolves toward syncretic or fundamentalist forms. The government continuously strives to control unbridled syncretism for fear of its political consequences; by doing so, it also gives the official *ulama* and defenders of the Islamic faith some satisfaction. On the whole, persecuting instinctive and often naive expressions of popular faith, combined with *pancasila*-ization of the State and political containment lay the grounds for Islamic radicalism. While the government claims to prevent and fight violence, the impression is that it provokes it through an excess of precautions, let alone security psychosis. The government arouses what it fears, unwillingly but also perhaps deliberately, for Islamic unrest may serve the New Order by legitimizing its existence when security is endangered.

6. The Mirage of the Islamic Revolution

Violent Islamic protest thrives on fertile ground when the community is bewildered. However, determined proponents of violence are a very small minority that seeks under certain circumstances to mobilize its environment, by exploiting social economic discrepancies and obstacles to political Islam, as well as inter-ethnic or racial strife.

Islamic activists are often young people, who organize around worship places in popular urban districts. Unemployment may induce some of them to take part in violent actions. As they have forced leisure time, they can more easily engage in underground militancy through the network of small mosques. Radicals aim to suppress the *Pancasila* State by force and replace it with an Islamic State, the shape of which is not clearly defined. As they cannot convince all Muslims to accept total Islamization of public life, they are ready to resort to armed struggle, namely terrorism.

Beyond harassment by the New Order, activists are stimulated by foreign models offered by various Islamic countries with a political regime approximating theocracy, including Iran and its Islamic revolution. However, their effect is not easy to prove, even if the government tried to explain Islamic terrorism as a consequence of the dissemination of Khomeini's ideas in Indonesia. The easy argument of a plot fomented from abroad or more simply of an international underground conspiracy is often put forward to account for internal, locally based phenomena. In fact, the authorities carefully—though not always efficiently—control links between the *ummat* and the Middle East like the pilgrimage, or information on the Iranian revolution, which was tightly filtered in the Indonesian press in 1979 and 1980.

While external models may influence Islamic radicals to some extent, the major factor seems to be the local history of armed struggle to establish an Islamic state, as it developed

---

[30] Ibid., "Ingkar Sunnah atau ingkar apa [To reject Sunnah—traditional sayings of the Prophet—, or reject what else?]."

from 1945, parallel and in opposition to the republican movement. The Darul Islam uprising was active in West Java, Aceh, and South Celebes until its main leader, Kartosuwirjo was arrested in 1960. Under the New Order, Muslim radicals have continued the same struggle, some even being its direct heirs as was the case with two of Kartosuwirjo's sons. Both of them were on trial in 1982 for having set up an underground movement named "New Style Indonesian Islamic State," active from 1970 to 1977. According to the government, the movement included a secret army led by guerrilla officers under a Commander-in-chief *(Panglima)* and an *Imam*. As a defense plea, Kartosuwirjo's sons claimed to have acted on behalf of Bakin, the intelligence agency, by recruiting former Islamic rebels to help the government fight Communists. In the official version, it was admitted that after their amnesty in 1962 some former members of the Darul Islam movement had indeed been rehabilitated by the *Pancasila* Republic, but that they had taken advantage of it to reconstitute a banned organization.[31]

Kartosuwirjo's posterity in the New Order is wide. The "Father of the Proclamation of the Indonesian Islamic State" *(Bapak Proklamasi Negara Islam Indonesia)*, as he was named by a fundamentalist magazine,[32] still inspires a lot of his former followers who proselytize among the younger generation. For instance, a terrorist group led by Timzar Zubil claimed to revive Darul Islam through a series of bombings perpetrated in Medan in 1976. The targets were symbolic: bombs were thrown at an expensive hotel, a night-club, a methodist church, and a movie theater. The group was arrested.

From 1978 to 1981, a "Holy War Command" *(Komando Jihad)* murdered several people and attacked various targets, until its leader, a former Darul Islam member, Wardiman, was killed in a police raid.

More serious seemed to be the case of the Imron Group that claimed to be the military arm of a Council of the Indonesian Islamic Revolution *(Dewan Revolusi Islam Indonesia)*, with alleged but not proven links with Iran. After a spectacular attack on a police post in Bandung, the group hijacked a Garuda plane to Bangkok. However the five hijackers were killed and the plane recovered by special forces sent over from Indonesia. Imron was arrested and executed.[33]

On the whole, Islamic terrorism in the 1970s and the early 1980s remained rather marginal, since it could never trigger mass mobilization, let alone a revolution. But it was endemic, as new groups repeatedly emerged, always pursuing the establishment of an Islamic State, unified or separate as in Aceh *(Aceh Merdeka)*, or in Celebes *(Republik Federasi Sulawesi*, with former followers of Kahar Muzakkar, a local Kartosuwirjo ally).

Should the Tanjung Priok events be regarded as part of these various attempts? The answer is ambivalent, as the Jakarta harbor riots, despite their fundamentalist tone, did not aim to set up an Islamic State. But there clearly was a feeling of hostility against secular authority perceived as encroaching daily on Islam and supporting the Chinese. And the binding factor, the emotional catalyst, was indeed Islam.

---

[31] *Tempo*, December 24, 1983, "Mengadili para pewaris [Judging (Kartosuwirjo's) heirs]."

[32] This semi underground magazine, *Al Ikhwan* [Brothers] was recently banned. Published by the Coordinating Body of Mosque Youth *(Badan Kordinasi Pemuda Masjid* or BKPM—!), *Al Ikhwan* printed as many as 20,000 copies and was distributed all over Indonesia. Its last issue (March 1984) contained a panegyric of Al Banna, the founder of the Muslim Brotherhood, and an article entitled "Pancasila, berhala menghalang Islam [Pancasila, the idol that hinders Islam]." See *Tempo*, May 26, 1984, "Persaudaraan lewat bulletin [Fraternity through a bulletin]."

[33] On the chronology of Islamic terrorism in Indonesia, see *Tempo*, October 13, 1984, "Dari granat di Cikini sampai bom di BCA [From the Cikini grenades to the BCA bombs]."

The apparent difference with 1970s Islamic violence was that in 1984 Islamic radicals seemed to have gained a small measure of popular support. Islamic terrorism seemed to better adjust to Muslim demands and sensitivity. Shortly after the Tanjung Priok riots, on October 4, 1984 a bank was bombed in Jakarta. The target was carefully chosen—Bank Central Asia (BCA), owned by a Chinese, the richest of them all, Liem Sioe Liong, a close associate of the New Order top leader. This was undoubtedly efficient symbolism, and quite appealing to Muslim public opinion. Besides, the link between the BCA attack and the Tanjung Priok riots may have been rather direct, as asserted by some sources,[34] since the main actors in both events, namely Amir Biki and Rachmat Basoeki, were friends and members of the same Ka'bah Youth Movement *(Gerakan Pemuda Ka'bah)*. Set up shortly before the 1982 elections and meant to mobilize votes for PPP, this organization strongly denied involvement in the events. To "avenge" the death of his friend Amir Biki, Rachmat Basoeki was alleged to have organized the BCA bombings. Previously he had been involved in the March 20, 1978 bombing of the People's Assembly building, together with the Islamic Revolutionary Struggle group *(Perjuangan Revolusioner Islam)*. As already mentioned, the Assembly was then about to approve a text putting Javanese *kebathinan* mysticism on a par with monotheistic faiths, to the great discontent of Muslims.

7. Conclusion?

Confusion, ambiguousness, and manipulation have continuously characterized the relationship between the New Order and Islam. It is a relation difficult to clarify, even over a period of some 20 years. Despite their antagonism, the two orders share common goals, as both strive to gain more faith and more power. The line between secular and spiritual realms is not easy to draw, assuming it can be done, especially as these two fields are equally coveted by two competing forces with a propensity toward absolutism for one, and absoluteness for the other.

Despite an early alliance, the New Order and Islam soon split. The anti-Communist compact could not survive the dramatic suppression of the common enemy. Common interests that seemed to bind the military and Muslim entrepreneurs or landowners in the mid-1960s eventually diverged: Muslims were soon overrun by foreign capital called in by the government and undermined by the emerging middle class that is still one of the regime's main pillars.[35]

More important, the primary opposition between social cultural attitudes sharpened over time: the *priai* side of the officers increasingly collided with *kiai* modes of perception. There was not only a confrontation of two cultures, but also of two rival leaderships, i.e. Javanese military bureaucrats and spiritual Muslim leaders.

While these conventional elites were vying over the allegiance of the faithful called on to take sides and choose between *Pancasila* or the True Faith, or both of them, popular masses confused by social differentiation and cultural modernization were being seduced by fundamentalism, a refuge valued as early as the 1970s. The new *ulama* are monitoring this trend which can give them new clout provided they adjust to it and leave the malignancy of conventional politics.

---

[34] *Tempo*, November 3, 1984, "Mereka dengan bom di tangan [Those with a bomb in hand]."

[35] On the middle class, see my "Les classes moyennes en Indonésie, opacités culturelles et réalités économiques," *Tiers Monde* 26, 101 (January–March 1985): 207–18.

Fundamentalism also brought back into motion former outcasts in Republican history, i.e. proponents of a stern Islamic State; they have emerged again, and found followers among the younger generation. Can they, will they, forge an alliance with the *ulama*?

Most probably the future could belong to the new middle class generated by rapid economic growth under the New Order. Are these groups really pro-*pancasila*, or are they likely to surrender to the wave of Islamic revival that also affects some of their members?

Meanwhile, power holders are watchful. In the aftermath of the September and October incidents, they were full of consideration for the *ummat*. Generals visited villages where they were seen wearing a *kupiah* and a sarong, the dressing insignia of popular Islam. They would go to mosques, pray, preach, and display great piety. They made trips to *pesantren* to reassure people and call for moderation. General Try Sutrisno, commander of the Jakarta military region (KODAM) and a former *santri*, was often seen in Koran reading sessions. The military meant to reconcile with Islam (*bersilaturahmi*), and to reduce misgivings. "No *kiai* has been arrested," they said. *Pancasila* was not Islam's enemy.[36]

As on similar past occasions, they tried to appease the *ulama* and the *ummat*. So far, they have always succeeded in doing so, at least until they resume their containment policy, then taking the risk of another Islamic implosion.

November 1984.

Seven years later (*post scriptum*)

The imbroglio goes on. In 1990, the first Association of Muslim Intellectuals ever in Indonesia was set up. It was quite a feat since, except for Abdurrahman Wahid who has become the chairman of the NU *tanfidziyah*, every shade of Islam was represented in the new organization, from fundamentalist to extreme modernist. Initiative came from below, but the organization sought approval from the Palace. Without second thoughts, president Soeharto gave his blessings to such a unified intellectuals' association, as he had been looking for Islamic support for the last few years. The new association was established with B.J. Habibie, the modernizing technologist, as its chairman. A few months later, president Soeharto made the pilgrimage to Mecca (June 1991).

In one of the latest improvements to the New Order, the Islamic dimension was being restored. Islam is part of Indonesia, the head of state is every citizen's president; he himself is a good Muslim, besides being a convinced Javanese (he has not abandoned his Javaneseness, see *Wejangan Pak Harto*). Politics and heaven have to integrate all available dimensions to provide the best security. A new syncretic alliance between *santri*-ized (Islamized) *priai* and *priai*-ed *kiai* was being designed, in the context of the forthcoming general (1992) and presidential (1993) elections. Toward the presidential succession and the possible end of the New Order, the tendency was like a replay of the beginning: a self-confident and lonely Javanese general approaching the *ummat*, in search of a new political ally to face potential rivals, and to gain an ultimate legitimacy. Having acquired a new maturity and in search of a new dignity, political Islam seemed to be ready to play the game. The circle was coming to a close.

July 1991.

---

[36] *Tempo*, October 27, 1984, "Mencoba melawan Yuwaswisu [Trying to fight anxiety]."

SOUTHEAST ASIA PROGRAM PUBLICATIONS

Cornell University

East Hill Plaza

Ithaca, New York 14850

Studies on Southeast Asia

Number 1 *The Symbolism of the Stupa,* Adrian Snodgrass. 1985. Reprinted with index, 1988. 2nd printing, 1991. 469 pp. ISBN 0-87727-700-1. $20.00.

Number 4 *In the Center of Authority: The Malay Merong Mahawangsa,* Hendrik M. J. Maier. 1988. 210 pp. ISBN 0-87727-703-6. $14.00.

Number 5 *Southeast Asian Ephemeris: Solar and Planetary Positions, A.D. 638–2000,* J. C. Eade. 1989. 175 pp. ISBN 0-87727-704-4. $15.00.

Number 6 *Trends in Khmer Art,* Jean Boisselier. Ed. Natasha Eilenberg. Trans. Natasha Eilenberg and Melvin Elliott. 1989. 124 pp., 24 plates. ISBN 0-87727-705-2. $15.00.

Number 7 *A Malay Frontier: Unity and Duality in a Sumatran Kingdom,* Jane Drakard. 1990. 215 pp. ISBN 0-87727-706-0. $15.00.

Number 8 *The Politics of Colonial Exploitation: Java, the Dutch, and the Cultivation System,* Cornelis Fasseur. Ed. R. E. Elson. Trans. R. E. Elson and Ary Kraal. 1992. 266 pp. ISBN 0-87727-707-9. $18.00.

Number 9 *Southeast Asian Capitalists,* ed. Ruth McVey. 1992. 220 pp. ISBN 0-87727-708-7. $16.00.

Number 10 *Tai Ahoms and the Stars: Three Ritual Texts to Ward Off Danger,* trans. and ed. B. J. Terwiel and Ranoo Wichasin. 1992. 170 pp. ISBN 0-87727-709-5. $16.00.

Number 11 *Money, Markets, and Trade in Early Southeast Asia: The Development of Indigenous Monetary Systems to AD 1400,* Robert S. Wicks. 1992. 354 pp., 78 tables, illus., maps. ISBN 0-87727-710-9. $20.00.

Number 12 *Fields from the Sea: Chinese Junk Trade with Siam during the Late Eighteenth and Early Nineteenth Centuries,* Jennifer Cushman. 1993. 214 pp. ISBN 0-87727-711-7. $16.00.

Number 13 *Fair Land Sarawak: Some Recollections of an Expatriate Officer,* Alastair Morrison. 1993. 196 pp. ISBN 0-87727-712-5. $16.00.

Number 14 *Sjahrir: Politics and Exile in Indonesia,* Rudolph Mrázek. 1994. 536 pp. ISBN 0-87727-713-3. $20.00.

Number 15 *Selective Judicial Compentence: The Cirebon-Priangan Legal Administration, 1680–1792,* Mason C. Hoadley. 1994. 185 pp. ISBN 0-87727-714-1. $16.00.

SEAP Series

Number 2 *The Dobama Movement in Burma (1930–1938),* Khin Yi. 1988. 160 pp. ISBN 0-87727-118-6. $9.00.

Number 3 *Postwar Vietnam: Dilemmas in Socialist Development,* ed. Christine White and David Marr. 1988. 2nd printing, 1993. 260 pp. ISBN 0-87727-120-8. $12.00.

Number 5 *Japanese Relations with Vietnam: 1951–1987,* Masaya Shiraishi. 1990. 174 pp. ISBN 0-87727-122-4. $12.00.

Number 6 *The Rise and Fall of the Communist Party of Burma (CPB),* Bertil Lintner. 1990. 124 pp. 26 plates, 14 maps. ISBN 0-87727-123-2. $10.00.

Number 7 *Intellectual Property and US Relations with Indonesia, Malaysia, Singapore, and Thailand,* Elisabeth Uphoff. 1991. 67 pp. ISBN 0-87727-124-0. $8.00.

Number 8 *From PKI to the Comintern, 1924–1941: The Apprenticeship of the Malayan Communist Party,* Cheah Boon Kheng. 1992. 147 pp. ISBN 0-87727-125-9. $12.00.

Number 9 *A Secret Past,* Dokmaisot. Trans. Ted Strehlow. 1992. 72 pp. ISBN 0-87727-126-7. $10.00.

Number 10 *Studies on Vietnamese Language and Literature: A Preliminary Bibliography,* Nguyen Dinh Tham. 1992. 227 pp. ISBN 0-87727-127-5. $15.00.

Number 11 *The Political Legacy of Aung San,* ed. Josef Silverstein. 1972, rev. ed. 1993. 169 pp. ISBN 0-87727-128-3. $14.00.

Number 12 *The Voice of Young Burma,* Aye Kyaw. 1993. 98 pp. ISBN 0-87727-129-1. $10.00.

Number 13 *The American War in Vietnam*, ed. Jayne Werner & David Hunt. 1993. 132 pp. ISBN 0-87727-131-3. $13.00.

Number 14 *Being Kammu: My Village, My Life*, ed. Damrong Tayanin. 1994. 138 pp. ISBN 0-87727-130-5. $14.00.

Translation Series

Volume 1 *Reading Southeast Asia*, ed. Takashi Shiraishi. 1990. 188 pp. ISBN 0-87727-400-2. $12.00.

Volume 2 *Indochina in the 1940s and 1950s.* ed. Takashi Shiraishi & Motoo Furuta. 1992. 196 pp. ISBN 0-87727-401-0. $14.00.

Volume 3 *The Japanese in Colonial Southeast Asia*, ed. Saya Shiraishi & Takashi Shiraishi. 1993. 172 pp. ISBN 0-87727-402-9. $14.00

* * *

In the Mirror, Literature and Politics in Siam in the American Era, ed. and trans. Benedict R. Anderson and Ruchira Mendiones. 1985. 2nd printing, 1991. 303 pp. Paperback. ISBN 974-210-380-1. $12.00.

Data Papers
In Print

Number 18 *Conceptions of State and Kingship in Southeast Asia*, Robert Heine-Geldern. 1956. 8th printing, 1993. 23 pp. ISBN 0-87727-018-X. $3.50.

Number 75 *White Hmong-English Dictionary*, comp. Ernest E. Heimbach. Linguistics Ser. 4. 1969. 6th printing, 1993. 523 pp. ISBN 0-87727-075-9. $16.00.

Number 92 *Feasting and Social Oscillation: A Working Paper on Religion and Society in Upland Southeast Asia*, A. Thomas Kirsch. 1973. 4th printing, 1990. 67 pp. ISBN 0-87727-092-9. $5.00.

Number 102 *No Other Road to Take, Memoir of Mrs. Nguyen Thi Dinh*, trans. Mai Elliott. 1976. 5th printing, 1993. 77 pp. ISBN 0-87727-102-X. $8.00.

Number 115 *The Maniyadanabon of Shin Sandalinka*, translated L. E. Bahshawe, 1981. 132 pp. ISBN 0-87727-115-1. $7.00.

Number 116 *Communicative Codes in Central Java*, John U. Wolff and Soepomo Poedjosoedarmo. 1982. 188 pp. ISBN 0-87727-116-X. $7.50.

Indonesia

Indonesia, a semiannual journal, devoted to Indonesia's culture, history, and social and political problems. The following issues are still available:

> No. 17, April 1974, No. 20, October 1975, $4.50 each
> No. 21, April 1976, No. 22, October 1976, No. 23, April 1977, $5.00 each
> No. 32, October 1981, $6.50 each; No. 37, April 1984, $7.50 each
> No. 41, April 1986, No. 42, October 1986, $7.50 each, $14.00 both
> No. 43, April 1987, No. 44, October 1987, $8.50 each, $16.00 both
> No. 45, April 1988, No. 46, October 1988, $8.50 each, $16.00 both
> No. 47, April 1989, No. 48, October 1989, $8.50 each, $16.00 both
> No. 49, April 1990, No. 50, October 1990, $9.50 each, $18.00 both
> No. 51, April 1991, No. 52, October 1991, $9.50 each, $18.00 both
> No. 53. April 1992, No. 54, October 1992, $9.50 each, $18.00 both.
> No. 55, April 1993, No. 56, October 1993, $10.50 each, $20.00 both.
> No. 57, April 1994, No. 58, October 1994, $10.50 each, $20.00 both.

Special Issue of *Indonesia* (1991):

The Role of the Indonesian Chinese in Shaping Modern Indonesian Life $10

* * *

Accessions List of the John M. Echols Collection on Southeast Asia, ed. John H. Badgley. Compiled monthly. Annual subscription $20.00.

STUDY AND TEACHING MATERIALS

Obtain from Southeast Asia Program Publications
Cornell University, East Hill Plaza, Ithaca, New York 14850

Thai

A.U.A. Language Center Thai Course, J. Marvin Brown.

Book 1, 1974, 1991. 267 pp. ISBN 0-87727-506-8. $12.00
Book 2, 1974, 1992. 288 pp. ISBN 0-87727-507-6. $12.00
Book 3, 1974, 1992. 247 pp. ISBN 0-87727-508-4. $12.00
Small Talk (dialog A), 1974, 1986. 204 pp. ISBN 0-87727-510-6. $9.00
Thai Reading, 1979, 1986. 164 pp. ISBN 0-87727-511-4. $9.00
Thai Writing (workbook), 1979, 1986. 99 pp. ISBN 0-87727-512-2. $9.00

Indonesian

Beginning Indonesian through Self-Instruction, John U. Wolff, Dédé Oetomo, and Daniel Fietkiewicz. Third revised edition, 1992. 1,057 pp. 3 volume set. ISBN 0-87727-519-X. $34.00.

Indonesian Readings, John U. Wolff. 1978. 4th printing, 1992. 480 pp. ISBN 0-87727-517-3. $16.00.

Indonesian Conversations, John U. Wolff. 1978. 3rd printing, 1991. 297 pp. ISBN 0-87727-516-5. $14.00.

Formal Indonesian, John U. Wolff. 1980. 2nd rev. ed., 1986. 446 pp. ISBN 0-87727-515-7. $16.00.

Vietnamese

Intermediate Spoken Vietnamese, Franklin Huffman and Tran Trong Hai. 1980. 2nd printing, 1991. 401 pp. ISBN 0-87727-500-9. $12.00.

Khmer

Cambodian System of Writing and Beginning Reader, Franklin E. Huffman. Originally published by Yale University Press, 1970. Reissued by Cornell Southeast Asia Program, 1987, 1992. 365 pp. ISBN 0-300-01314-0. $14.00.

Modern Spoken Cambodian, Franklin E. Huffman, assist. Charan Promchan and Chhom-Rak Thong Lambert. Originally published by Yale University Press, 1970. Reissued by Cornell Southeast Asia Program, 1984, 1987, 1991. 451 pp. ISBN 0-300-01316-7. $16.00.

Intermediate Cambodian Reader, ed. Franklin E. Huffman, assist. Im Proum. Originally published by Yale University Press, 1972. Reissued by Cornell Southeast Asia Program, 1988. 499 pp. ISBN 0-300-01552-0. $16.00.

Cambodian Literary Reader and Glossary, Franklin E. Huffman and Im Proum. Originally issued by Yale University Press, 1977. Reprinted with permission by Cornell Southeast Asia Program, 1988. 494 pp. ISBN 0-300-02069-4. $16.00.

Tagalog

Pilipino through Self-Instruction, John U. Wolff with Ma. Theresa C. Centano and Der-Hwa U. Rau. 1991. Series, 1,490 pp. 4 vols. ISBN 0-87727-524-6. $50.00/set.
Vol. 1, 362 pp. ISBN 0-87727-525-4. $15.00; Vol. 2, 384 pp. ISBN 0-87727-526-2. $15.00;
Vol. 3, 436 pp. ISBN 0-87727-527-0. $15.00; Vol. 4, 308 pp. ISBN 0-87727-528-9. $15.00.
Vol. 4 contains the answer key, glossary, and index for all four volumes.

Cebuano

Beginning Cebuano, John U. Wolff. 1966. Yale Linguistic Series, 9. 1,233 pp. 2 vol. set. $35.00.

A Dictionary of Cebuano Visayan, Vols. 1 and 2, John U. Wolff. 1972. 1,200 pp. $10.00 **as is (weak spines).**

Language Tapes

Cassette tapes are available from The Language Laboratory, Tape Sales, Room G11, Noyes Lodge, Cornell University, Ithaca, NY 14853-4701. Tel: (607) 255-8793, Fax (607) 255-6882, for the following books:

A.U.A. Language Center Thai Course *Beginning Indonesian through Self-Instruction*

Indonesian Conversations *Modern Spoken Cambodian* *Beginning Pilipino through Self-Instruction*

CORNELL UNIVERSITY
MODERN INDONESIA PROJECT PUBLICATIONS

640 Stewart Avenue
Ithaca, New York 14850

In Print

Number 6 *The Indonesian Elections of 1955*, Herbert Feith. 1957. 2d printing, 1971. 91 pp. ISBN 0-87763-020-8. $3.50.

Number 7 *The Soviet View of the Indonesian Revolution*, Ruth T. McVey. 1957. 3d printing, 1969. 90 pp. ISBN 0-87763-018-6. $2.50.

Number 25 *The Communist Uprisings of 1926–1927 in Indonesia: Key Documents*, ed. and intro. Harry J. Benda and Ruth T. McVey. 1960. 2d printing, 1969. 177 pp. ISBN 0-87763-024-0. $5.50.

Number 37 *Mythology and the Tolerance of the Javanese*, Benedict R. Anderson. 1965. 6th printing, 1988. 77 pp. ISBN 0-87763-023-2. $6.00.

Number 43 *State and Statecraft in Old Java: A Study of the Later Mataram Period, 16th to 19th Century*, Soemarsaid Moertono. 1968. Rev. ed., 1981. 180 pp. ISBN 0-87763-017-8. $9.00.

Number 48 *Nationalism, Islam and Marxism*, Soekarno. Intro. by Ruth T. McVey. 1970. 2d printing, 1984. 62 pp. ISBN 0-87763-012-7. $4.00.

Number 49 *The Foundation of the Partai Muslimin Indonesia*, K. E. Ward. 1970. 75 pp. ISBN 0-87763-011-9. $3.00.

Number 50 *Schools and Politics: The Kaum Muda Movement in West Sumatra (1927–1933)*, Taufik Abdullah. 1971. 257 pp. ISBN 0-87763-010-0. $6.00.

Number 51 *The Putera Reports: Problems in Indonesian-Javanese War-Time Cooperation*, Mohammad Hatta. Trans. and intro. William H. Frederick. 1971. 114 pp. ISBN 0-87763-009-7. $4.00.

Number 52 *A Preliminary Analysis of the October 1, 1965, Coup in Indonesia* (Prepared in January 1966), Benedict R. Anderson, Ruth T. McVey, assist. Frederick P. Bunnell. 1971. 174 pp. ISBN 0-87763-008-9. $9.00.

Number 55 *Report from Banaran: The Story of the Experiences of a Soldier during the War of Independence*, Maj. Gen. T. B. Simatupang. 1972. 186 pp. ISBN 0-87763-005-4. $6.50.

Number 56 *Golkar and the Indonesian Elections of 1971*, Masashi Nishihara. 1972. 56 pp. ISBN 0-87763-044-6. $3.50.

Number 57 *Permesta: Half a Rebellion*, Barbara S. Harvey. 1977. 174 pp. ISBN 0-87763-033-8. $5.00.

Number 58 *Administration of Islam in Indonesia*, Deliar Noer. 1978. 82 pp. ISBN 0-87763-002-X. $4.50.

Number 59 *Breaking the Chains of Oppression of the Indonesian People: Defense Statement at His Trial on Charges of Insulting the Head of State, Bandung, June 7–10, 1979*, Heri Akhmadi. 1981. 201 pp. ISBN 0-87763-001-1. $8.75.

Number 60 *The Minangkabau Response to Dutch Colonial Rule in the Nineteenth Century*, Elizabeth E. Graves. 1981. 157 pp. ISBN 0-87763-000-3. $7.50.

Number 61 *Sickle and Crescent: The Communist Revolt of 1926 in Banten*, Michael C. Williams. 1982. 81 pp. ISBN 0-87763-027-5. $6.00.

Number 62 *Interpreting Indonesian Politics: Thirteen Contributions to the Debate, 1964–1981*. Ed. Benedict Anderson and Audrey Kahin, intro. Daniel S. Lev. 1982. 3rd printing 1991. 172 pp. ISBN 0-87763-028-3. $9.00.

Number 64 *Suharto and His Generals: Indonesia's Military Politics, 1975–1983*, David Jenkins. 1984. 3rd printing 1987. 300 pp. ISBN 0-87763-027-5. $12.50.

Number 65 *The Kenpeitai in Java and Sumatra*. Trans. from the Japanese by Barbara G. Shimer and Guy Hobbs, intro. Theodore Friend. 1986. 80 pp. ISBN 0-87763-031-3. $8.00.

Number 66 *Prisoners at Kota Cane*, Leon Salim. Trans. Audrey Kahin. 1986. 112 pp. ISBN 0-87763-032-1. $9.00.

Number 67 *Indonesia Free: A Biography of Mohammad Hatta*, Mavis Rose. 1987. 252 pp. ISBN 0-87763-033-X. $10.50.

Number 68 *Intellectuals and Nationalism in Indonesia: A Study of the Following Recruited by Sutan Sjahrir in Occupation Jakarta*, J. D. Legge. 1988. 159 pp. ISBN 0-87763-034-8. $8.00. Monograph.

Number 69 *The Road to Madiun: The Indonesian Communist Uprising of 1948*, Elizabeth Ann Swift. 1989. 120 pp. ISBN 0-87763-035-6. $9.00.

Number 70 *East Kalimantan: The Decline of a Commercial Aristocracy*, Burhan Magenda. 1991. 120 pp. ISBN 0-87763-036-4. $11.00.

Number 71 *A Japanese Memoir of Sumatra, 1945–1946: Love and Hatred in the Liberation War*, Takao Fusayama. 1993. 150 pp. ISBN 0-87763-037-2. $12.00.

Number 72 *Popular Indonesian Literature of the Qur'an*, Howard M. Federspiel. 1994. 170 pp. ISBN 0-87763-038-0. $14.00.

Number 73 *"White Book" on the 1992 General Election in Indonesia*, Trans. Dwight King. 1994. 72 pp. ISBN 0-87763-039-9. $10.00.

www.ingramcontent.com/pod-product-compliance
Lightning Source LLC
Chambersburg PA
CBHW080635230426
43663CB00016B/2873